THE QUOTABLE Abigail Adams

Editorial Assistants

Yvonne Greenwood
Jeanne Wray

THE QUOTABLE Abigail Adams

EDITED BY
John P. Kaminski

THE BELKNAP PRESS OF HARVARD UNIVERSITY PRESS

Cambridge, Massachusetts, and London, England

2009

Library of Congress Cataloging-in-Publication Data
Adams, Abigail, 1744–1818.
The quotable Abigail Adams / edited by John P. Kaminski.
p.   cm.
Includes bibliographical references and index.
ISBN 978-0-674-03532-4 (cloth : alk. paper)
1. Adams, Abigail, 1744–1818—Quotations.
2. Adams, Abigail, 1744–1818—Political and social views.
3. Adams, Abigail, 1744–1818—Philosophy.
4. Presidents' spouses—United States—Quotations.
I. Kaminski, John P.   II. Title.
E322.1.A38A25 2009
973.4'4092—dc22 [B] 2009011300

For

Jan L. Miller and Linda DeLeon

and

The Law Related Education Program

of the Texas Bar Association

Contents

Preface   xi

Introduction   xix

The Quotable Abigail Adams

Advice   I

America   5

The Arts   14

Cities, Countries, and Other Places   17

Communications   33

Death   44

Dreams, Imagination, Memories   56

Duty, Honor, Citizenship   59

Economics   72

Education   82

Family and Home   86

Food and Drink   109

Foreign Affairs   110

Freedom, Liberty, and Equality   115

Friends and Enemies   117

Contents

Government   119

Health, Medicine, and Exercise   137

History   144

Human Nature   147

Human Relations   153

Language, Grammar, and Penmanship   208

Life's Blessings   211

Life's Difficulties   215

Life's Uncertainties   237

Love   241

The Military   244

Morality   247

The Natural World   255

Pain and Pleasure   266

Peace   267

People   269

Politics   289

Religion   293

Travel and Transportation   318

Vices   322

Virtues   332

War   348

Women   356

Alternate Spellings Commonly Used
by Abigail Adams   373

Chronology   375

Bibliography   381

Acknowledgments   383

Index   385

⁓ Preface

Abigail Adams's literary legacy would have surprised her. She was embarrassed by her lack of formal education and was aware of shortcomings in spelling, grammar, and handwriting that led her to refer to her writings as "incorrect and unpolished."[1] On at least four occasions she asked her husband to destroy her letters, once suggesting that he light his cigars with them. To a friend she confided that she would "make a bond fire" of her letters rather than "they should some hundred years hence be thought of consequence enough to publish."[2]

Abigail wrote more than 2,100 letters. She greatly admired poets, pamphleteers, newspaper essayists, historians, and playwrights, but she felt incapable of producing works like theirs herself. She wondered why "Apollo and the Muses could not have indulged me with a poetical Genious. I have always been a votary to her charms, but never could ascend Parnassus myself."[3] If only she could "borrow the powers and faculties" of her friend Mercy Otis Warren, she could use them "with advantage to myself and delight to others." Nonetheless Abigail would not allow her "incorrect and unpolished" skills to deter her from corresponding with her family and friends.[4]

Abigail valued letters highly, even if they contained "nothing but an account of the Health" of loved ones.[5] As a young woman she wrote to her fiancé about how much she appreciated his letters: "I do not estimate everything according to the price the world set upon it, but according to the value of it is of to me, thus that which was cheapest to you I look upon as highly valuable."[6] A decade later, she delighted in informing her husband, then serving in Congress in Philadelphia, how their four little children "run upon the sight of a Letter [from their father]—like chickens for a crum, when the Hen clucks."[7] She confided to him that when she received his letters her heart was "as light as a feather" and her spirits danced. Letters from him were "like cold water to a thirsty Soul"; like "a feast to me."[8] When she received letters, Abigail felt an urgency to respond: "My Heart overflows, and longs to give utterance to my pen."[9] Whenever she heard of a safe conveyance for letters, especially a ship readying to cross the Atlantic, she seized on the opportunity to write.

Almost all of Abigail's letters were written on one sheet of paper folded once to produce four pages. The completed letter was then folded and tucked in such a way that the fourth page became a cover upon which was written the recipient's name and address. The folded letter was then sealed with a spot of wax.

Abigail nearly always filled the first three pages of her letters. "My pen will always run greater lengths than I am aware of when I address those who are particularly dear to me and to whom I can write with unreserve."[10] But even to those closest to her she sometimes exercised self-restraint. To her son she wrote, "Upon some subjects I think much more than I write."[11] Short letters disappointed her because they "always give one pain as well as pleasure since a few lines only from such a distance looks as if the Friend we wrote to possessd but a small share of our attention and regard."[12] On several occasions she complained to John that his letters were not "half long enough."[13] She most enjoyed letters that he wrote on Sundays, because he seemed to have "a greater command" of his time on that day.[14]

To a great extent the nature and number of Abigail's letters were dictated by circumstances. When at home while her four children were young, she wrote primarily to her husband, who, as an up-and-coming provincial attorney, rode the judicial circuit throughout Massachusetts and Maine for almost half the year. During these early years, Abigail seldom wrote to her family members because they were nearby and often visited one another. Her correspondence with John increased when he served in Congress in Philadelphia. When her husband and ten-year-old son sailed for Europe in 1778, she wrote to them whenever a nearby American ship prepared to put to sea despite the constant danger from the British navy. On several occasions a packet of her letters was thrown overboard to prevent their falling into the enemy's possession. When, after the war, Abigail joined her husband and son in Europe, she had eighteen regular correspondents. Her sisters, Mary Cranch and Elizabeth Shaw, received frequent dispatches. Her younger boys, Charles and Thomas, residing with their aunt and uncle Shaw, also received letters from their mother, as did John Quincy Adams after he returned to Massachusetts to pursue his education. Abigail also wrote frequently to her uncle, Cotton Tufts, who administered the Adamses' business affairs when they were away. She also delighted in writing to her nieces, nephews, and dear friends. When the Adamses returned to Massachusetts in June 1788, Abigail's correspondence with family and friends near Braintree lessened, but she wrote often to her children, especially Nabby, her daughter, who, after marrying William Stephens Smith in London in 1786, returned to America and settled in East Chester, New York. After John left Braintree to become vice president in 1789 and then president in 1797, Abigail's correspondence with him blossomed again whenever she stayed home, as she often did.

When Abigail joined John in New York City, Philadelphia, or Washington, D.C., her correspondence with him naturally ceased while the family correspondence burgeoned. But whether at home in Quincy or in the nation's capital, she still awakened early and spent "almost every morning in writing" letters.[15] When John lost his bid for a second term as president, the Adamses retired to Quincy. No longer separated, they never wrote another letter to each other. Now Abigail regularly wrote to her two surviving sons (Charles died in 1800) as they served on diplomatic missions in Europe, to John Quincy's wife Louisa Catherine, to her daughter who now resided in upstate New York, to her two sisters, to numerous nieces and grandchildren, and to a handful of close friends. Only when she was confined to her bed with disabling rheumatism or life-threatening fevers, often for weeks at a time, did her correspondence cease.

Writing multiple letters to family and friends when she was away was a daunting task. Because the recipients usually shared the letters with each other, Abigail could not duplicate the contents of any one letter. Each letter contained fresh information. In one letter she would describe the theater, in others the opera, card parties where ladies gambled into the early hours of the morning, or the Handel music festival in London that made her "shudder [with delight] from the beginning to the end of the performance."[16] She frequently bewailed her difficulties with servants or the harsh weather, described the beauties of the garden and landscapes, or condemned the sedition of partisan politics.

While at home she always wrote about the health of family and friends. Between a quarter and a third of her letters mentioned the death of the young, the maturing, or the elderly—"the Infant Bud, the blooming Youth, and the Mature in Life have fallen around me."[17] She regularly advised those who suffered the loss of a close friend or relative to mourn as Jesus himself had done at the tomb of Lazarus. But, after a respectable amount of time, grief had to give way to a submission to the will of Almighty God, whose "ways are just and right, however hidden in mazes and perplexed to us short sighted mortals."[18] She wrote of domestic matters—the farm, servants, field hands, the weather, and financial matters—and politics at the state, national, and international levels. When writing to children—whether her own, her nieces and nephews, or her grandchildren—she regularly admonished them to develop a proper morality. To a greater degree than any other correspondent of the era (even including Jefferson and John Adams), Abigail regularly followed her admonitions with a reinforcing quotation. About half of these came from the Bible (mainly Psalms, Proverbs, Ecclesiastes, and the Book of Matthew); the remainder drew on such literary giants as Shakespeare and particularly Alexander Pope, especially his *Essay on Man*. She acknowledged that Thomas Paine had written in "Common Sense" of the "use of quotations [by] those who are destitute of Ideas of their own,"[19] but felt comfortable reinforcing her own often pithy admonitions with appropriate quotations.

It was through her voluminous correspondence that Abigail sustained herself when so often separated from her family and friends. During their first twenty years of marriage, Abigail and John were apart more than half of the time. Household matters, the education of the children, and family business affairs fell to her. Early in the Revolution, she wrote to John, "I know not How I should support an absence already tedious, and many times attended with melancholy reflections, if it was not for so frequently hearing from you. That is a consolation to me, tho a cold comfort in a winter's Night."[20] To a friend she wrote, "It has been a relief to my mind to drop some of my sorrows through my pen."[21] To her husband she confessed: "I have scarcly ever taken my pen to write but the tears have flowed faster than the Ink."[22] She told John, "I love to amuse myself with my pen, and pour out some of the tender sentiments of a Heart over flowing with affection."[23] Although she knew that "Many things may be said, which it is improper to commit to paper,"[24] yet she also found that her pen was "always freer than my tongue." She told John, "I have wrote many things to you that I suppose I never could have talk'd."[25] Sometimes she approached eroticism, embarrassing her relatively prudish husband, who advised her to be more cautious. She would have none of it. She could relieve "the anxiety of my Heart" only by "a frequent intercourse by Letters unrestrained by the apprehension of their becoming food for our Enemies. The affection I feel for my Friend is of the tenderest kind, matured by years, sanctified by choise and approved by Heaven. Angels can witness to its purity, what care I then for the Ridicule of Britains should this testimony of it fall into their Hands, nor can I endure that so much caution and circumspection on your part should deprive me of the only consolor of your absence."[26]

After John left a second time for diplomatic service abroad, Abigail wrote, "My candle and my pen are all my companions. I send my thoughts across the broad Atlantick in search of my associate and rejoice that thought and immagination are not confined like my person to the small spot on which I exist."[27] The correspondence she exchanged with loved ones sustained her throughout a life shadowed by illness and "the pangs of seperation from near and dear Friends."[28]

Although Abigail Adams was not formally educated, her letters are brilliant. They capture historical events and everyday life over a period of fifty momentous years. They reveal a woman of truly admirable strength, insight, and wisdom. In 1794, while he was serving as vice president and presiding over the U.S. Senate, John told Abigail that her letters gave him "more entertainment than all the speeches I hear. There is more good Thoughts, fine strokes and Mother Wit in them than I hear in the whole Week. An Ounce of Mother Wit is worth a pound of Clergy." He rejoiced that at least one of their children (John Quincy) had "an Abundance of not only Mother Wit, but his Mother's Wit."[29] It is from this wonderful correspondence that we two centuries later can profit; it is from these letters that the following quotations have been compiled.

Notes

1. To Mercy Otis Warren, Boston, December 5, 1773.
2. To Harriet Welsh, Quincy, March 9, 1815.
3. To Mercy Otis Warren, Braintree, April 27, 1776.
4. To Mercy Otis Warren, Boston, December 5, 1773.
5. To Charles Adams and JQA, July 22, 1780.
6. To JA, Weymouth, April 12, 1764.
7. To JA, Braintree, June 25, 1775.
8. To JQA, Quincy, February 27, 1814; to John Adams, Braintree, May 27, 1776.
9. To JA, Braintree, c. July 15, 1778. To her son Thomas she wrote: "I never feel so great a propensity to write as when I have just received a Letter." Quincy, March 10, 1796.
10. To JQA, London, June 26, 1785.
11. To JA Quincy, February 20, 1796.
12. To JA, December 13, 1778.
13. To JA, Braintree, September 20, 1776.
14. To JA, Braintree, July 16, 1775.
15. To Mary Cranch, Philadelphia, June 19, 1798.
16. To Elizabeth Cranch, London, September 2, 1785.
17. To Louisa Catherine Adams, Quincy, September 30, 1815.
18. To Louisa Catherine Adams, February 18, 1811.
19. To JA, April 2, 1777.
20. To JA, Braintree, April 17, 1777.

21. To James Lovell, Braintree, c. December 15, 1777.
22. To JA, Braintree, October 21, 1778.
23. To JA, Sunday Evening, December 27, 1778.
24. To JQA, Quincy, April 1808.
25. To JA, Braintree, October 22, 1775.
26. To JA, Braintree, November 12–13, 1778.
27. To JA, June–July 1779.
28. To Louisa Catherine Adams, Quincy, September 22, 1810.
29. JA to AA, Philadelphia, February 4, 1794.

— Introduction

Abigail Adams was born on November 11, 1744, in Weymouth, Massachusetts, about fourteen miles southeast of Boston. Her father, William Smith, was a prominent Congregational minister; her mother, Elizabeth Quincy, was the daughter of John Quincy, who was regularly elected speaker of the colonial Massachusetts House of Representatives. The Quincy family had been public officials, landowners, and merchants throughout Massachusetts history. Abigail had two sisters and a brother: Mary, three years older; William, two years younger; and Elizabeth, nine years younger.

Abigail's recurring illnesses kept her from school. Her parents, her older sister, and her grandparents, resident at Mount Wollaston four miles from Weymouth, provided her education. Abigail was surrounded by books and encouraged to read. When in 1762 Mary Smith married Richard Cranch, a watchmaker fifteen years her senior, he supervised Abigail's education and directed her reading. Abigail read widely; her letters often quote from works of literature and from the Bible. She greatly enjoyed the novels of Samuel Richardson, especially the seven-volume *Sir Charles Grandison,* in which Richardson lauded the importance of female education and the intellectual role women played in their marriages. It is likely that because she was kept out of school, she received a broader education than was typical for most New England girls.

As the daughter of a Congregational minister, Abigail had strongly held religious beliefs. She adhered to the liberal Congregationalism espoused by her father, which eschewed the harsh predestination of John Calvin, the distant God of the deists, and the fire and brimstone of the evangelical enthusiasts spawned by the Great Awakening. Abigail believed that each individual should have a personal relationship with God. Alluding to the Sermon on the Mount, Abigail believed that those who practiced good deeds could expect to be rewarded in this life and in the hereafter; those who were evil would likewise be punished. She believed that those who had gained the most knowledge and virtue during their earthly lives would receive favored status in the stratified society of heaven. Because God's divine plan was impenetrable by man, believers must be resigned to the will of God. Death, illness, and other trials and tribulations were to be borne stoically. As the divine word of God, the Bible was to be studied and used to cultivate a moral conscience. Both Abigail and John Adams became Unitarians in their later years.

John Adams was born in Braintree in 1735. After graduating from Harvard, he disappointed his father (a farmer, shoemaker, and local official) by abandoning the ministry in favor of the law. John had met the Smith family in about 1759. As John increasingly came in contact with the Smiths—especially after his friend Richard Cranch began courting Abigail's older sister, Mary—his interest in Abigail intensified. Soon the young lawyer became completely enamored of Abigail. She too came to feel passionately about him.

Initially, because of his comparatively humble origins, the Smith family thought John was not the best suitor for Abigail. Soon, however, John's abilities overcame their objections. As John approached his thirtieth birthday, he decided that it was time to marry. He and Abigail were married on October 25, 1764, in the Weymouth parsonage in a ceremony officiated by her father. They left Weymouth for their home in Braintree.

The Adamses resided in the hundred-year-old saltbox-style cottage on Braintree's main road at the base of Penn's Hill, about two miles from the ocean. John had inherited the cottage from his father. The two-story cottage had four rooms on each floor. A large room downstairs had been converted into John's law office by replacing one of the windows with a door. A parlor and a kitchen with a gigantic fireplace occupied the first floor along with a servant's bedroom. The upstairs had two large bedrooms and two small rooms. John's widowed mother lived across the lane in a similar cottage, in which John had been born.

Along with the cottage, John had also inherited ten acres of adjacent farmland and another thirty acres of orchards, pasture, and timber. Periodic purchases of parcels of land added to their holdings. The produce raised on the farm, generally consumed by the family rather than sold for cash, consisted of seasonal fruit and vegetables and animal feed. Soon the young couple had three cows from whose milk they made butter and cheese. They also raised sheep and chickens, until the latter were sold off because they became too mischievous. Apples were pressed into cider, one of the Adamses' favorite drinks. By 1766, the Adamses had two horses and two yearlings. While home, John and a hired hand planted, weeded, and harvested the crops and pruned the orchards. When John was away, Abigail hired farmhands or rented out the land to other farmers.

Throughout her marriage Abigail always had servants. At first there was only one, a black woman named Judah hired by John's mother. By 1767 Abigail had four servants. Although she depended on them, she frequently complained about their cost, inebriety, untrustworthiness, laziness, and repeated illnesses. When she became attached to one or another servant, she did everything she could to retain his or her services.

Marriage did not lessen Abigail's voracious appetite for reading. She avidly read the books in her husband's library. When newspapers arrived, the newlyweds read them together and discussed the important issues of the day. They regularly walked up and down and around Penn's Hill, which afforded a spectacular panorama of the countryside and the sea. They frequently visited relatives: Abigail's parents and younger sister, Betsy, were only five miles away; her grandparents, only four. Her sister Mary Cranch lived in an area of Braintree called Germantown. And John's mother, who developed a loving relationship with her daughter-in-law, was just across the lane.

Throughout the first decade of their marriage, John was gone about a third of every month, riding the circuit in Massachusetts and neighboring colonies. On July 14, 1765, their first child was born—a girl they named Abigail but who was always called Nabby. John was not home for the birth; he was off attending court. Abigail's mother and sister assisted in the delivery. Two years later, on July 11, 1767, a boy was born and named after his dying great-grandfather, John Quincy.

In April 1768 the family moved to Boston to be closer to John's clients and to the unfolding political developments dividing the colonies from the mother country. Abigail now read four Boston weekly newspapers. She daily witnessed British soldiers, recently stationed in Boston, as they drilled past the Adams home on Brattle Street. She regularly hosted the colony's opposition leadership—men such as Samuel Adams, John Hancock, and Joseph Warren. Here another daughter, Susanna (Suky), was born in late 1768, but lived only fourteen months. A second boy, named Charles, was born in May 1770.

With a lull in the political conflict with Parliament and with John exhausted from his efforts to keep mob activities from prematurely provoking a powerful imperial response, John and Abigail moved back to Braintree in April 1771. The law office, however, remained in Boston. John would leave early in the morning and often not return home until after nine in the evening. As he devoted more time to his growing practice and to his unfolding political activities, Abigail was left with far more responsibility for raising the children and supervising the farm.

In September 1772, a third son, Thomas Boylston, was born. Four youngsters were enough for Abigail to handle even with the aid of servants. No more pregnancies would occur for five years. After nineteen months in Braintree, the family returned to Boston in November 1772, residing in a substantial brick house purchased by John that was located on South Queen Street opposite the courthouse and near his law office. Although committed to avoiding politics, John found his life was filled with revolution. Abigail, meanwhile, had to attend to the children. The older ones were now ready to begin reading. Abigail started their lessons each day by reading a chapter from the Bible. As political events escalated, the family again moved back to Braintree in early 1774. John purchased his father's "homestead" and the large farm that accompanied it from his brother, who had inherited the property.

Starting in 1761 and then escalating after the end of the French and

Indian War in 1763, Parliament and the king's ministers pursued a new imperial policy toward colonial America. The colonies were to be administered as a conquered people in the same manner as Ireland was administered. At first the "policy" was indecipherable. The writs of assistance (general search warrants) issued by Massachusetts's governor to combat widespread smuggling by merchants were denounced in the famous Paxton's Case. John Adams praised James Otis, Jr., for his forceful arguments against the writs, and later asserted that the child Independence was born then and there. Its birth, however, was far from apparent at the time.

The Proclamation Line of 1763, which forbade colonists from settling beyond the crest of the Appalachian Mountains, was ignored. The Sugar Act of 1764, with its tax on molasses and its establishment of a vice admiralty court in Halifax, was condemned and went unimplemented. But then in 1765 the Stamp Act was passed, the stamps were sent to America, and stamp agents were appointed to collect this new form of taxation, which was used to support the occupying troops. Opposition mounted throughout the colonies. John Adams and his cousin Samuel Adams became the leaders of the Boston opposition and Abigail was soon enlisted in the revolutionary cause. In fact, Samuel, John, and Abigail Adams were among the very few who early in the 1760s secretly advocated independence instead of reconciliation with the mother country.

With the passage of the Tea Act in 1773, tension between the colonies and Parliament mounted further. Although the act actually lowered the price of tea on the open market, colonists objected to it on two grounds: it would establish Parliament's right to tax Americans in principle and it would give the financially strapped East Indies Company a monopoly to sell its huge inventory of tea. When ships loaded with tea arrived in Boston Harbor, Abigail anticipated violence. Less than two weeks later, angry Bostonians dumped the tea into the sea. Parliament responded swiftly by closing the Port of Boston, dissolving the colonial legislature, and appointing a military governor.

Parliament's harsh retribution for the Boston Tea Party spread alarm throughout the colonies. A Continental Congress was called to meet in Philadelphia in September 1774 to respond. The Massachusetts legislature appointed John Adams as one of five delegates to represent the colony. On August 10, John Adams left for Philadelphia. Abigail would not hear from him for five weeks. John returned from Philadelphia in late October 1774 and for the next six months remained active in Massachusetts politics in Cambridge and in Boston. Usually he would spend the evenings in Braintree. But in May 1775, after the outbreak of warfare between the colonies and Britain, John again traveled to Philadelphia for the Second Continental Congress and a much longer absence from home.

On June 17, Abigail wrote John of the dreadful news of the Battle of Bunker Hill and the burning of the town of Charlestown by naval incendiary bombs. The cannon started to roar at 3:00 A.M. on Saturday and continued as she was writing at 3:00 P.M. on Sunday. Everyone lived in fear.

The Second Continental Congress recessed during August and September 1775. John came home to Massachusetts but immediately began attending the provincial congress then meeting in Watertown. He went home on weekends. Abigail visited John during the final three days of the session before he returned to Congress in Philadelphia, only to leave Abigail to fight a more deadly personal foe. A virulent dysentery epidemic broke out that killed many, including Abigail's mother and John's brother Elihu and his child. Abigail brought Elihu's orphaned daughter Susanna into her home.

On March 17 the British evacuated Boston. By now, Abigail felt that the conflict with Britain could never be peacefully resolved. She eagerly awaited word of a declaration of independence accompanied by a new code of laws for women. Abigail did not seek equality with men. She believed that men and women had different roles assigned to them by nature. Women were destined to be wives and mothers and express themselves in these roles. No man could achieve his full potential without the support of a loving and encouraging wife. Abigail did not argue for the right of women to vote and hold office—not that she felt women incapable of such political expressions. She sought only what she felt was immediately pressing and achievable: property and judicial rights for women and protection from physical abuse from tyrannical husbands. No such relief would come from Congress.

John kept Abigail informed about Congress's movement toward independence. On July 3, he wrote to her about the momentous events that had occurred on the previous day, when Congress declared independence without a dissenting colony. Two days after the vote on independence Congress approved a formal Declaration of Independence submitted by a committee of five. John Adams was on the committee, but the poetic declaration was written by Thomas Jefferson, a thirty-three-year-old delegate from Virginia. Abigail thanked John for the wonderful news.

Abigail was writing from Boston, where she and the children had gone to be inoculated for smallpox. John had wanted the family inoculated but Abigail hadn't consulted with him about the timing. Abigail's inoculation went well, and John Quincy and Thomas had mild reactions. Charles had to be re-inoculated before having it take. But poor Nabby reacted violently with hundreds of painful eruptions all over her body.

In mid-October 1776 Congress approved a leave of absence and John returned home. He was again elected a delegate to Congress but with six colleagues, it seemed apparent he would not be expected to stay away from home long. He left Braintree on January 9, 1777, for what would be his last congressional tour of duty. Abigail felt especially vulnerable when John left because she was pregnant for the sixth time. Abigail started having forebodings about the pregnancy. On the evening of July 8, 1777, she suffered a "shaking fit" and sensed that the baby had died. Three days later Abigail gave birth to a still-born baby girl. John was informed of the death and that Abigail was in no danger herself. Both were heartbroken.

The second year of war was difficult for Abigail on the home front. Hired farmhands were hard to come by because the state militia and Continental Line offered attractive bounties to enlistees. Inflation became rampant as the continental printing presses poured out endless streams of almost worthless paper currency. Prices skyrocketed while some goods were not available at any price.

In early November 1777 Congress gave John and Samuel Adams leave of absence to visit their families. By the end of the month they were home. Immediately John set about to restore his law practice, taking on a lucrative admiralty law case in Portsmouth, New Hampshire. This would be his last appearance in a courtroom as a practicing attorney.

While he was off in Portsmouth, a letter arrived from Congress appointing John a commissioner at Versailles, instructing him to join Benjamin Franklin and Arthur Lee in negotiating alliances and commercial treaties with European and North African countries. Abigail was distressed. She knew John could not refuse the appointment and she could not stand in the way. Abigail suggested that John might take the boys along with him to Europe. In the end, only ten-year-old John Quincy would accompany his father overseas. In mid-February 1778, father and son were on their way to France aboard the *Boston*, a 24-gun Continental frigate. Abigail waited for word from John, but nothing arrived for almost five months. Her imagination ran wild, feeding on rumors that Franklin had been assassinated and that the *Boston* had been sunk or captured. Where was her husband; what was he doing? What about little Johnny? Were they safe? Finally she received word that her husband and son had arrived in France safely after a six-week voyage punctuated with thunderstorms, a hurricane, and close encounters with the British navy. After more than a year's absence, John and John Quincy returned to Braintree on August 2, 1779. For two months the family was happy. John and Abigail did many of the things they had done as newlyweds, but now with four children in tow.

In August, Braintree elected John its representative to the state constitutional convention, which was to meet on September 1, 1779, in Cambridge. John found himself elected a subcommittee of one to draft a new constitution. Diligently working during the week, he came home for weekends. The constitution was submitted to the towns and ratified in 1780.

While John was at Cambridge, word arrived in Braintree that Congress had appointed him to draft treaties of peace and commerce with Great Britain and to serve as minister to the Court of St. James's after hostilities ended. What an honor! The man who above all others had led the way toward declaring independence was now appointed to negotiate the peace.

When John returned to Europe he started sending Abigail a variety of goods that she could barter or sell to her neighbors. With inflation rampant and the worth of paper currency diminishing daily, European goods were more valuable than money. Soon Abigail had a thriving little business that she greatly enjoyed managing. She informed John that small articles had the best profit. Gauze, ribbons, feathers, and flowers for women's fashion sold best.

Ineffective in Paris, John traveled to the Netherlands hoping to obtain a loan from prominent Dutch bankers and to conclude a treaty with the government. After almost a year, the loans were arranged and on October 8, 1782, Adams signed a treaty of amity and commerce with the Netherlands. He then returned to Paris to join John Jay, who had been conducting peace negotiations with British commissioners for several months. Franklin had been too ill with the gout and kidney stones to attend these opening sessions. For the next year negotiations continued, with Jay and Adams carrying the load.

After the preliminary peace treaty between Britain and the United States had been signed, Adams's official work in Europe was over. He waited for both countries to ratify the treaty and for Congress to decide whether he would be appointed as minister to Britain. At times John felt that his enemies back home would oppose his appointment; at other times he felt that they would gladly see him mired in a foreign assignment with little hope of success rather than come home where he would be more troublesome.

For more than a year both John and Abigail debated about Abigail's joining John in Europe. She felt it was her duty to be with her husband, to soften his cares, add to his happiness, and prolong his life. He begged her to make the journey. In principle Abigail wanted to go; in practice she had grave doubts. Fear of the Atlantic crossing magnified as it approached and she worried that as the awkward, provincial wife of a diplomat she might embarrass her husband and her country.

Congress by now had appointed Franklin, Jefferson, and Adams to further two-year commissions to negotiate commercial treaties with European and North African countries. For months Abigail wrestled with the problem, finally deciding to sacrifice her feelings to be with her husband. Abigail and Nabby, accompanied by two servants, left Braintree on Friday, June 18, 1784. The next day they set sail aboard the *Active,* a copper-bottomed ship captained by Nathaniel Lyde, who had an unblemished record of forty-three Atlantic crossings. After a month at sea, they passed the cliffs of Dover and anchored near the town of Deals, seventy-two miles from London.

On July 23 Abigail wrote to John that they had arrived in London. John responded that he felt twenty years younger than yesterday. Unable to leave his post, John sent John Quincy to meet them, buy a carriage, and bring them all to The Hague, from which they would travel to Paris. When John Quincy arrived in London, Abigail did not recognize him: he had grown into a handsome young man. Viewing her son and daughter, Abigail felt exceedingly matronly. Two days later, John wrote telling Abigail that his plans had changed. He would join them in London and accompany them to France. On August 7, John and Abigail were reunited in London. Neither one committed their feelings to paper. Five months later, Abigail sent her travel journal to her sister to share with friends, but she refused to describe what happened when she met her husband after an absence of four years, except to say that they were once more a happy family.

It took time for Abigail to warm up to France in general and to Paris in particular. Her lack of conversational French inhibited her from socializing, but after five months' residency, "habititude" made her appreciate the refinements of French society. The end of April 1785 brought two important developments. First, it was decided that John Quincy Adams should return to America and finish his education and then go on to study law. On May 12, 1785, John Quincy left

Paris to attend Harvard College. Abigail and John would miss their son. Second, word finally arrived that Congress had appointed Adams as minister to Great Britain. Knowing that John had the best chance of succeeding in this difficult mission, Abigail reluctantly agreed to stay in Europe for several more years. The family arrived in London on May 26, 1785, where they rented an elegant house on Grosvenor Square, one of the finest squares in London. After three years had passed with no success in negotiating a commercial treaty, John Adams received permission from Congress to return to the United States. Abigail was eager to return home.

The Adamses left London for Portsmouth on March 30, 1788. Nabby, who on June 11, 1786, had married William Stephens Smith, the secretary to the American legation, had left London a week earlier to take up residence on Long Island, New York. After an exhausting seven-week voyage, the Adamses landed at Boston on June 17, to a tumultuous reception. Governor Hancock greeted them at the dock and entertained them at his mansion, which he offered for their comfort until they could move into their new house. The old family cottage was too small for a family with three grown boys, so the Adamses purchased an attractive old two-story building nearby that Abigail had long admired.

With a new Constitution adopted and George Washington the obvious choice to be the first president, it was soon agreed that John Adams should be elected vice president. On April 13, 1789, John Adams left Braintree for New York City to assume his new office. Abigail was again left alone at home.

In mid-May, John rented a "large, handsome house" called Richmond Hill, on a thirty-acre tract of land about two miles outside New York City. Abigail packed up more than a hundred boxes, including some of their furniture, to send to their new home, and then followed herself. Nabby and her family had already taken up residence at Richmond Hill when Abigail arrived on June 25 with her niece Louisa, two servants, and Charles, who was newly graduated from Harvard and would soon begin studying law. William Stephens

Smith, Nabby's husband, soon revealed himself to be an adventurer who frequently abandoned Nabby in pursuit of one unsuccessful speculative venture after another.

Although she missed her friends, Abigail was delighted with their new situation. Richmond Hill was beautiful and it was made more pleasant by the company of Nabby and the two grandchildren. The house overlooked the North River with commanding views of New York City, Long Island, and New Jersey. Soon Abigail became accustomed to New York's frenetic social life.

When the capital was moved to Philadelphia in the fall of 1790, Abigail did not relish the idea of boxing up all their belongings once again and having to establish another new set of friends and acquaintances. Abigail was very sick during the trip to Philadelphia. The brick house at Bush Hill, two and a half miles outside Philadelphia, had been unoccupied for four years. It needed a thorough cleaning and airing, but soon became comfortable. Within a few months, however, the inconvenience of its location became apparent and the family moved into a city house that rented for the enormous amount of $1,000 annually.

In April 1792, after Congress adjourned, John and Abigail traveled home to Quincy, the north precinct of Braintree that had become a separate town named after Abigail's grandfather. Feeling unwell, Abigail remained home when John returned to Philadelphia in November. Again she would feel the loneliness of a house without her family. John and Abigail would resort again to their correspondence for their "political Tittle tattle." Largely because of her health, Abigail spent all of John's second term as vice president in Quincy. John himself spent half of his four-year term at home as well. Concern for Abigail's health, the family's economy and the high cost of living, virulent partisan politics, and fear of the diseases rampant in Philadelphia all made Quincy a more palatable residence.

On January 5, 1796, John wrote to Abigail from Philadelphia with important news that had to remain secret. A cabinet member had told him that President Washington intended to retire at the end of his second term, and Martha Washington had implied the same. He and Abigail would have to decide if John should seek the office of president or retire as well. One thing was certain—he would not serve as vice president again. If John became president, Abigail worried whether she would be appropriate as the president's wife. She hoped that she could fill the position with as much dignity and grace as Martha Washington had done. John assured her that she could. His only concern was her health.

Adams and Jefferson emerged as the two contenders for the presidency in 1796. When Adams appeared to have a majority of the electors committed to him, Alexander Hamilton began intriguing to try to win a majority of electors for Thomas Pinckney of South Carolina. Pinckney, who had successfully negotiated a popular treaty with Spain two years earlier, would be obliged to Hamilton, and Adams would be relegated to the vice presidency again. Abigail condemned Hamilton as an intriguer with an unquenchable thirst for fame, and as ambitious as Julius Caesar. Abigail hoped instead that Jefferson would become vice president. When Vice President Adams opened the electoral ballots on the floor of the U.S. Senate, Adams had 71 votes, Jefferson 68, and Pinckney 59. The two old friends would be united in government again, but this time at the head of conflicting parties.

John Adams was inaugurated as president on March 4, 1797. Neither Abigail nor any of the Adams children attended the inauguration. Although Abigail's health had improved, it was still fragile enough so that she did not want to risk traveling during the winter. She also needed to arrange for tenants to lease their property and to hire servants to accompany her to Philadelphia.

Abigail wrote to John that she hoped to be a partner in his presidency. John repeatedly pleaded with her to hurry to Philadelphia, as he needed her support and advice. Abigail had already started advising her husband by suggesting that he support an increase in property taxes as opposed to other kinds of taxes, to compensate for the loss of tariff revenue caused by British and French depredations upon American merchantmen.

Abigail arrived in Philadelphia in mid-May 1797. She hated the partisan politics, the vicious press, and the high cost of living, especially with the entertaining required of the president and his wife. When Congress adjourned, the Adamses left Philadelphia on July 19, fearful of the capital's sickly season, an approaching war with France, and possibly a civil war at home. After stopping at Nabby's for a few days, they went on to Quincy, where they remained until the first week of October 1797. When they returned to the capital in November 1797, the political situation had calmed somewhat.

Abigail became increasingly disillusioned with national partisan politics. Not only did the Jeffersonians attack the president, his administration, and Congress, but they also attacked her son. John Quincy Adams had been appointed U.S. minister to Portugal. As he prepared to assume that post, he was reassigned as minister to Germany. The opposition press attacked John Quincy for double-dipping —getting two salaries and two diplomatic outfits (i.e., the furniture and trappings of office). In reality he received one salary and diplomatic outfit, and, in fact, lost some of his own money in preparing the embassy in Lisbon. Abigail's ire reached new heights. She had said that whenever her husband was wounded, she bled. She understood that, although she and her husband did not deserve the lies inflicted upon them in the press, they were fair game, but she would not stand for unfounded attacks on her son. The continued newspaper attacks on her husband and her son drove her into a frenzy. As the country moved ever closer to war with France, the president's popularity skyrocketed, but still the minority press continued its assault. Abigail pressed John for action, and finally in June and July 1798 Congress enacted the infamous Alien and Sedition Acts. The president, thicker-skinned than his wife, reluctantly signed the bills, and the federal district attorneys and courts avidly prosecuted Republican printers and one Republican congressman for their seditious libel. No one was prosecuted under the alien acts. In trying to protect her husband and her son, Abigail contributed to the most substantial blemish on her husband's illustrious career—a political misjudgment that contributed to his defeat when he ran for reelection.

Despite the nationwide clamor for war, President Adams tirelessly worked for peace. Against his own party's wishes, but with the wise counsel of Abigail, the president sent one peace commissioner after another to France to try to avoid war. Finally, the French realized that war with the United States would be foolish and the two former allies agreed to settle their differences peacefully. It was perhaps the greatest act of statesmanship in Adams's long career, and it contributed to his defeat in the election of 1800.

After the adjournment of Congress, John and Abigail returned to Quincy in July 1798. While in Quincy, Abigail became seriously ill with what was diagnosed as dysentery, intermittent fever, and diabetes. Fighting for her life, Abigail was bedridden for eleven weeks. John stayed until November 1798 before returning alone to Philadelphia. Abigail would not return to the capital for another year, until November 1799, when she resumed her social responsibilities. As the time neared for the capital to move from Philadelphia to Washington, Abigail felt regrets similar to when she left Paris and New York City.

For the last year of Adams's presidency, the campaign against John's reelection was relentless. The vitriolic attacks from the Jeffersonians were understandable, but Adams also felt the sting of his own party. Federalists were divided between those loyal to him and those who followed the beat of Alexander Hamilton's drum, often referred to as High Federalists. The "little general," as Abigail called Hamilton, again intrigued to be the king-maker by urging the presidential electors to vote for Charles Cotesworth Pinckney, a South Carolina lawyer and Revolutionary war hero who had recently served as an American diplomatic envoy to France. Hamilton publicly joined the assault on Adams with a fifty-four-page pamphlet claiming the president's character defects made him unsuitable for the job. Both Adams and Hamilton were discredited by the attacks. In the end, Jefferson and Aaron Burr received 73 electoral votes each, Adams 65, and Pinckney 64. After thirty-six ballots, the House of Representatives broke the tie and elected Jefferson president, making Burr his vice president.

In many respects, John's failure to be reelected was a relief to both

Abigail and John. Abigail especially looked forward to living without ceremony, at home with family and friends. She left for Quincy at the beginning of February 1801; John followed a month later, leaving Washington at 5:00 A.M. on March 4, seven hours before Jefferson's inauguration.

Life at Peacefield, the name John gave to their homestead, had its pleasures. John worked in the fields supervising his hired hands and kept up a voluminous correspondence. Abigail delighted in resuming her domestic chores. Now, at 5:00 in the morning she was occupied with skimming milk as a dairywoman rather than writing letters. Although frugally managed, the family farm barely turned a profit. The family relied on the savings that Abigail had squirreled away over the years and the investments she made in government securities. That was especially true when the Adamses lost a substantial sum when a European investment house went bankrupt.

Retirement brought sadness as well. Charles, the middle Adams son, had died in New York City in November 1800, an alcoholic in desperate financial straits. Abigail took in little Susan, Charles's daughter, to live at Quincy. Thomas, the youngest Adams son, recently returned from Europe, at first resided in Philadelphia, where he had a modest law practice. In 1803 Abigail convinced him to move to Quincy; in 1805 he married and lived at Peacefield until 1810, when he and his family moved into the original Adams cottage. Unfortunately, in 1812 his youngest daughter died.

John Quincy Adams had been abroad on diplomatic service for seven years before returning in late 1801 with a wife and a five-month-old son, George Washington Adams. After visiting Peacefield, he practiced law in Boston and taught at Harvard. Soon, however, he was back in public service, first as a state senator and then in 1803 as a U.S. senator from Massachusetts. Although saddened when John Quincy and his family left for Washington, it was through her son's career that Abigail was reborn to politics. She regularly corresponded with and advised him. Abigail was also able to develop a warm relationship with his wife, Louisa Catherine, through their correspondence—a relationship that was sometimes tense in person. In 1805 the two Adams boys stayed with their grandparents when their parents traveled to Washington.

Abigail, like John Quincy, supported James Madison for president in the election of 1808. In 1809 President Madison appointed John Quincy as U.S. minister to Russia. Abigail was devastated, fearing she might never see her son again. In August 1809 John Quincy, his wife, and their infant son, Charles Francis, left for St. Petersburg. The two older boys again stayed with their grandparents. In 1810 Abigail wrote to President Madison asking that her son be recalled. Madison acceded, and nominated him as an associate justice to the U.S. Supreme Court. Now, however, after a long absence from the law (which he never really enjoyed), John Quincy turned down the judicial appointment and stayed in Russia. In 1813, paralleling his father's career, he was appointed as a commissioner to Ghent, Belgium, to negotiate a peace between Great Britain and the United States to end the War of 1812. Three years later he was named U.S. minister to Great Britain. The two younger boys, who after two years at Peacefield had attended school in New Hampshire, were now sent to England to be with their parents. John Quincy finally returned to America in August 1817 to become secretary of state under President James Monroe.

The saddest part of Abigail's retirement was being apart from Nabby and the Smith grandchildren. While Nabby's husband continued his cavalier financial ventures, she was often left by herself. In 1808 Nabby, who with her daughter had been living at Peacefield, joined her husband on a small farm in the isolated village of Lebanon in upstate New York. Abigail was devastated at the separation. In 1811 Nabby was diagnosed with cancer and had one breast surgically removed with only opium for anesthesia. When the cancer reappeared, Nabby made a painful journey from upstate New York to Peacefield, where she died three months later in mid-August 1813.

Within days of Nabby's surgery in 1811, Abigail's brother-in-law Richard Cranch died, followed the next day by his wife, Mary, Abigail's older sister, who had been terminally ill for months. In 1812 infant daughters of John Quincy and Thomas both died. In 1815 Abigail's younger sister Elizabeth died, followed by Abigail's uncle Cotton Tufts and son-in-law William Stephens Smith. This stream of deaths, along with worsening arthritis and rheumatism, made life almost unbearable for Abigail, who wrote that old age was dark and unlovely. In October 1818, a month before she would have turned seventy-four, Abigail contracted typhoid fever. Sapped of strength, she died in her sleep on October 28. She had lived a long life nurturing her family and loving her country. She was, as her husband described her, an American heroine.

THE QUOTABLE Abigail Adams

⁓ Advice

Diffidence . . . should lead you to seek advice and instruction from
him, who is your natural guardian [your father], and will always
counsel and direct you in the best manner, both for your present and
future happiness.

To John Quincy Adams, June 10?, 1778

Advice is of little avail unless it is reduced to practise nor ought we
implicitly to give up our judgment to anyone what ever may be our
regard or esteem for them untill we have weighed and canvassed
that advice with our reason and judgment—then if it is right, agreable to virtue, expedient and prudent we ought strictly to adhere
to it.

To John Adams, June–July 1779

To become what you ought to be, and what a fond mother wishes to
see you, attend to some precepts and instructions from the pen of
one, who can have no motive but your welfare and happiness, and
who wishes in this way to supply to you the personal watchfulness
and care, which a separation from you deprived you of at a period of
life, when habits are easiest acquired and fixed; and though the advice may not be new, yet suffer it to obtain a place in your memory,
for occasions may offer, and perhaps some concurring circumstances
unite, to give it weight and force.

To John Quincy Adams, March 20, 1780

Whenever any difficulty encompasses me, my first thought is how
would my Friend conduct in this affair. I wish to know what his
mind would be and then to act agreable to it. If I err in my conduct
it is an error of the judgment, not of the Heart. Wholly deprived of
your aid, and even advice in domestick occurences, my next resource
is in that of my Friends.

To John Adams, April 25, 1782

Should you as I would fondly hope Religiously adhere to the precepts you have received from him [his father], and to the advice and instruction of your Friend and patron, then shall I see you become a usefull Member of Society, a Friend to your Country and a Guardian of her Laws and Liberties—for such is the example you have before you.

To John Quincy Adams, November 13, 1782

You have frequently flatterd me with an assurance that my advice is not unacceptable to you.

To Royall Tyler, June 14, 1783

Your favorite Rochefoucault* observes we may give advice, but we cannot give conduct. . . .

And why all this grave advice my dear Madam to one who so well knows his duty? Aya my dear sir who of us practise so well as we know? Nobody take a reproof so kindly as he who deserves most to be commended; we are always in want of a Friend who will deal plainly and gently with us. "Be to our faults a little blind, be to our virtues ever kind."**

To Royall Tyler, at sea, July 10, 1784

*One of over 500 maxims François de La Rochefoucauld published during his lifetime.   **Matthew Prior, "An English Padlock," lines 79–80.

It is an old Adage, that a man at 30 must be either a fool or a Physician. Tho you have not arrived to that age, you would do well to trust to the advice and experience of those who have. . . . thus do I give you Line upon Line, & precept upon precept.

To John Quincy Adams, London, October 12, 1787

I know I must sometime perplex you with domestick matters. I would not do it, but that I wish your advice and direction. . . . As you were always Remarkable at a difficult case, I wish you would direct me what to do with those which at present surround me.

> To John Adams, Braintree, May 5, 1789

I must request you in my absence to attend to your Brother Tom, to watch over his conduct & prevent by your advice & kind admonitions, his falling a prey to vicious Company.

> To John Quincy Adams, Braintree, May 30, 1789

Advising to a measure against which some objections arise, in case of failure the adviser must bear the blame.

> To John Quincy Adams, New York, September 9, 1790

You can do much service to your Sons by your Letters, and advice. You will not teach them what to think, but how to think, and they will then know how to act.

> To John Adams, Quincy, February 2, 1794

To confer freely with a confidential Friend, gives Strength and confidence to opinions, of which we may be doubtfull. King Solomon sanctiond this Sentiment when he declard that two were better than one.*

> To John Quincy Adams, Quincy, February 15, 1808

*Proverbs 11:14.

Receive every admonition from your Aunt with gratitude.

> To Susanna B. Adams, Quincy, September 12, 1808

Out of the abundance of the heart the mouth speaketh.*

> To Caroline Smith, Quincy, August 6, 1812

*Matthew 12:34.

It is a very difficult and hazardous undertaking to give advice in affairs of this kind* particularly where the affections are warmly interested, the adviser generally loses the Friendship of one or other of the parties.

To My Dear Young Friend, Quincy, c. 1812

*I.e., advice about a potential marriage.

It is said in a good Book that in a multitude of counsellors there is safety.* I wish it may be found in the counsels of our Nation, but at present they look very chaotic to me.

To William Stephens Smith, Quincy, January 25, 1815

*Proverbs 11:14.

I have often wished you were near to me, that I might assist at least by my advice in anything where you might feel as tho you wanted Age and experience to aid you.

To Abigail A. Shaw, Quincy, September 13, 1816

You will not I hope, consider me as taking improper Liberty with you—ground which I have traveled, is new to you: to find it safe is an arduous task.

To Louisa Catherine Adams, Quincy, February 20, 1818

Advice for Government Officials

As you have been calld in providence into the chair of Government, you did not accept it without knowing that it had its torments, its trials, its dangers and perplexities. Look steadfastly at them, arm yourself with patience and forbearance and be not dismayed, and may God and the people support you. Having put your Hand to the plough, you must not look back, nor ought You I think to wish you had not.

To John Adams, Quincy, February 19, 1797

Advice from Enemies

The abuse thrown out against you, and so liberally bestowed in anonymous publications in newspapers, or private Letters . . . I

would pay no further attention to them, than to see if any Truth was
contain in them, which might prove usefull as admonition or reproof, never refusing to profit even by the advice of an Enemy.

> To John Quincy Adams, Quincy, February 15, 1808

Be Strict to whatever Rules are directed in your Studies. You know
how to make yourself beloved. Attention & diligence & punctuality
will not fail to make you esteemed by preceptors & School mates.

> To John Adams 2nd, Quincy, September 17, 1817

— *America*

I know America capable of any thing she undertakes with spirit and
vigour. "Brave in distress, serene in conquest, drowsy when at rest, is
her true characteristick."*

> To John Adams, July 16, 1780

*Thomas Paine's "American Crisis," no. 9.

She possesses every requisite to render her the happiest Country
upon the Globe. She has the knowledge and experience of past ages
before her. She was not planted like most other Countries with a
Lawless Banditti, or an Ignorant savage Race who cannot even trace
their origin, but by an enlightend, a Religious and polished people.
The Numerous improvements which they have made during a Century and half, in what was then but a howling Wilderness, proves
their state of civilisation.

> To Elizabeth Cranch, London, September 2, 1785

We must struggle hard first, and find many difficulties to encounter,
but we may be a Great and a powerfull Nation if we will; industery
and frugality, wisdom, and virtue must make us so. I think America

is taking Steps towards a reform, and I know her Capable of whatever she undertakes.

To John Quincy Adams, London, September 6, 1785

I know they [Great Britain] abuse America because they fear her, and
every effort to render her unpopular is a proof of it. They go on de-
ceiving themselves, thinking they can keep us low and poor, but all
the time they are making us industrious, frugal, wise and Great I
hope.

To Elizabeth Shaw, London, September 15, 1785

I ought to love my Countrymen best, as I really think them possest
of a larger portion of virtue than any other Nation, I am acquainted
with, and my wish is that they had still more, and wisdom enough
added to it, to convince them of a necessity of a union of counsels
and conduct with regard to their publick measures. In vain will they
call for commercial Treaties, in vain will they look for respect in Europe, in vain will they hope for Peace with the Barbary states, whilst
their own citizens discover a jealousy of Congress and a reluctance
at enlarging their powers, a fear even to trust them with commercial
arrangements.

To Charles Storer, London, March 23, 1786

We have the means of being the freest and the happiest people upon
the Globe.

To Mary Cranch, London, January 20, 1787

How little cause of complaint have the inhabitants of the United
States, when they compare their situation, not with despotic monar-
chies, but with this land of freedom [i.e., Great Britain]! The ease
with which honest industry may acquire property in America, the
equal distribution of justice to the poor as well as the rich, and the
personal liberty they enjoy, all, all call upon them to support their

government and laws, to respect their rulers, and gratefully acknowledge their superior blessings, least Heaven in wrath should
send them a ——.

> To Mary Cranch, Grosvenor Square, September 15, 1787

Happy America, Land peculiarly blest: Long may it continue thus,
under an all glorious Providence.

> To John Adams, Quincy, December 12, 1794

What Nation or people have greater reason for gratefull acknowledgments to Heaven than America.

> To Julia Rush, Quincy, March 23, 1815

It is to be feared that visionary schemes and ambitious projects are
taking possession of men of property and science; but, before so
important an edifice as an established government is altered or
changed, its foundation should be examined by skillful artists, and
the materials of which it is composed, duly investigated.

America and the New Constitution

> To Mary Cranch, London, February 27, 1787

Our countrymen create most of the misfortune they feel, for want
of a disinterested spirit, a confidence in each other, and a union of
the whole. It is a great misfortune, when one State thwarts the measures of eleven or twelve, and thus injures the credit and reputation
of the whole.

> To Mary Cranch, London, April 28, 1787

I think we shall return to our Country at a very important period
and with more pleasing prospects opening before her than the turbulent Scenes which Massachusetts not long since presented.* May
wisdom Govern her counsels and justice direct her opperations.

> To John Adams, Bath Hotel, March 23, 1788

*Shays's Rebellion, 1786–87.

The union is compleat by the late Adoption of the constitution by Rhoad Island. Nothing hinders our being a very happy and prosperous people provided we have wisdom rightly to estimate our Blessings, and Hearts to improve them.

To Lucy Ludwell Paradise, September 6, 1790

America Compared with Europe

You may possibly think it much out of season, if I should now congratulate you upon your return to your native Country, but I never before could do it, with such a firm persuasion of the utility of it, or paint to myself the amaizing difference which subsists between those Countries which have passt the Zenith of their glory, saped by Luxury, and undermined by the rage for pleasure, and a Young, a flourishing, a free and I may add, a virtuous Country uncontrouled by a Royal Mandate, unshackled by a military police, unfearfull of the thundring anathamas of Ecclesiastic power, where every individual possest of industery and probity, has a sure reward for his Labour, uninfested with thousands of useless virmin, whom Luxery supports upon the Bread of Idleness, a Country where Virtue is still revered; and modesty still Cloaths itself in crimson. But you have lived too long in Europe to require any description from my pen, and I dare say have too often contrasted the difference not to wish a long long youth to America.

To John Thaxter, Auteuil, March 20, 1785

America at this time is the happiest and freest Country in the civilized World. She want or wish for more? I hope not a grateful heart, nor a suitable acknowledgment to that Being in whose hand is the destiny of Nations, and who has made us to differ.

To Louisa Catherine Adams, Quincy, April 24, 1816

America Endangered

No action however base or sordid, no measure however Cruel and Villainous will be matter of any Surprize.

The flame is kindled and like lightning it catches from Soul to Soul. Great will be the devastation if not timely quenched or allayed by some more Lenient Measures. Although the mind is shocked at the thought of shedding human blood, more especially the blood of our countrymen, and a civil war is of all wars the most dreadful.

To Mercy Otis Warren, Boston, December 5, 1773

Did ever any Kingdom or State regain their Liberty, when once it was invaded without Bloodshed? I cannot think of it without horror.

To John Adams, Braintree, August 19, 1774

We are told that all the Misfortunes of Sparta were occasioned by their too great Sollicitude for present tranquility, and by an excessive love of peace they neglected the means of making it sure and lasting. They ought to have reflected says Polibius* that as there is nothing more desirable, or advantage[ou]s than peace, when founded in justice and honour, so there is nothing more shameful and at the same time more pernicious when attained by bad measures, and purchased at the price of liberty.

To John Adams, Braintree, August 19, 1774

*Polybius, *Histories.*

The constant roar of the cannon is so distressing that we can not Eat, Drink or Sleep. . . . We live in continual Expectation of Hostilities.

To John Adams, Braintree, June 18 and 25, 1775

It is come to that pass now that the longest sword must decide the contest—and the sword is less dreaded here than the [British peace] commissioners.

To John Adams, Braintree, March 16, 1776

As "affliction is the good man's shining time"* so does America give proof of her Virtue when distressd.

To John Adams, July 5, 1780

*Edward Young, *Night Thoughts* (1742–1745).

We may truly say, we know not what a day will bring forth. From every side we are in Danger. We are in perils by Land, and we are in perils by sea, and in perils from false Brethren. Dr. Blair gave us an excelent discourse a Sunday or two ago. "Trust in the Lord, for in the Lord Jehovah is everlasting Strength."* If it was not for that trust and confidence our Hearts would often fail us.

To Mary Cranch, Philadelphia, July 6, 1797

*Isaiah 26:4.

Hastening to that period which in Scripture is termed the Life of Man, having every thing at stake which can render the remnant peacefull, or the future happy, reputation and honour, Life, Liberty, and property, is it possible to have a wish or desire which is not inter-woven with the present and future prosperity, freedom and independance of united America? It depends upon the people to say that they will remain a free and happy Republic.

To Mercy Otis Warren, Philadelphia, June 17, 1798

If ever we saw a day of darknes, I fear this is one which will be vis-ible untill kindled into flames.

To Mary Cranch, Washington, February 7, 1801

American Education

America is the Theatre for a young fellow who has any ambition of distinguishing himself in knowledge and Literature.

To Mary Cranch, Auteuil, December 12, 1784

American Revolution

A Cause . . . which is now become so serious to every American that we consider it as a struggle from which we shall obtain a release from our present bondage by an ample redress of our Grieveances— or a redress by the Sword. The only alternative which every ameri-can thinks of is Liberty or Death.

To Catharine Sawbridge Macaulay, 1774

Is it not better to die the last of British freemen than live the first of British slaves.

> To Mercy Otis Warren, Braintree, January 25, 1775

The Friends of Liberty, should any such remain will have one option still left, and will rather chuse no doubt to die the last British freemen, than bear to live the first of British Slaves, and this now seems to be all that is left to americans.

> To Mercy Otis Warren, Braintree, February 3?, 1775

I think upon the Maturest deliberation I can say, dreadful as the day would be I had rather see the Sword drawn. Let these truths says the admired Farmer* be indelibly impressed on our Minds that we cannot be happy without being free, that we cannot be free without being secure in our property, that we cannot be secure in our property if without our consent others may as by right take it away.

> To Mercy Otis Warren, Braintree, February 3?, 1775

*John Dickinson's *Letters from a Farmer in Pennsylvania,* published in Philadelphia in 1768.

We know not what a day will bring forth, nor what distress one hour may throw us into. Heitherto I have been able to maintain a calmness and presence of Mind, and hope I shall, let the Exigency of the time be what they will.

> To John Adams, Braintree, May 24, 1775

[On the Battle of Bunker Hill:] In the midst of sorrow we have abundant cause of thankfulness that so few of our Breathren are numbered with the slain, whilst our enemies were cut down like the Grass before the Sythe.

> To John Adams, Braintree, June 25, 1775

We live in continual Expectation of Hostilities.

> To John Adams, Braintree, June 25, 1775

I could not join today in the petitions of our worthy parson, for a reconciliation between our, no longer parent State, but tyrant State, and these Colonies. —Let us separate, they are unworthy to be our Brethren. Let us renounce them and instead of suplications as formerly for their prosperity and happiness, Let us beseach the almighty to blast their counsels and bring to Nought all their devices.

To John Adams, Braintree, November 12, 1775

Posterity who are to reap the Blessings, will scarcely be able to conceive the Hardships and Sufferings of their Ancesstors.

To John Adams, Braintree, March 8, 1777

The History and the Events of the present day must fill every Human Breast with Horrour. Every week produces some Horrid Scene perpetrated by our Barbarous foes. Not content with a uniform Series of cruelties practised by their own Hands, but they must let loose the infernal savages, those "dogs of warr," and cry Havock to them. Cruelty, impiety, and an utter oblivion of the natural Sentiments of probity and Honour, with the violation of all Laws Humane and Divine, rise at one view and characterise a George, a How, and a Burgoine.*

To Mercy Otis Warren, Braintree, August 14, 1777

*King George III and the British generals Sir William Howe and John Burgoyne.

No person possessed with common Humanity can be an inattentive unconcernd Spectator of the present contest. The suffering virtue of individuals if recorded upon the faithfull page of History will astonish future ages, and demands from the present gratitude and veneration.

To James Lovell, Braintree, September 17, 1777

We most sincerely wish for peace upon honorable terms. Heaven is our witness that we rejoice not in the Effusion of Blood, nor the

Carnage of the Humane Species but having forced us to draw the Sword we are determined never to sheathe it the Slaves of Britains.
To Isaac Smith, Jr., October 30, 1777

We have lived through dangerous Times, and have reason to be thankfull that we are still in possession of our Liberty & so much of our Property.
To Mary Cranch, Richmond Hill, September 1, 1789

The people of our Country have a Characteristic trait. Tho some times misled and deceived, they wish to know what is just and Right, and to conduct accordingly. In the 30 Years of my Life, in which I have attentively observed them, I have always found them return to the Right path, as soon as they have had time to Weigh, consider and reflect.
To Thomas Boylston Adams, Quincy, March 10, 1796

Americans

We have the virtues of patience, forbearance and long suffering if no others.
To Catherine Johnson, Quincy, May 4, 1810

We are a happy Land, but a grumbling Nation. We quarrel with our own Bread and Butter, abuse our Rulers by words, enjoy freedom even to licentiousness, grow fat and Rich.
To John Quincy Adams, Quincy, July 24, 1811

Americans must learn to become more National and respect themselves.
To Louisa Catherine Adams, Quincy, March 27, 1816

It is only Americans who forgive their Enemies and Hug them too!
To Louisa Catherine Adams, Quincy, September 2, 1815

America's Enemies

⟶ The Arts

As you view them oftner, You will find your taste for them increase.
I always derive a pleasure at this distance of Time from the recollection of many of the Paintings which I saw when abroad. . . . I found
the Wise man's observations true, that the Eye was not satisfied by
seeing,* and as Shakespeare said upon another occasion "increase of
Appetite grew from what it fed on."**

To Thomas Boylston Adams, Quincy, September 17, 1795

*Ecclesiastes 1:8.   **Shakespeare, *Hamlet* I:2.

That America has not acquired any great taste for the fine Arts, must
be allowed.

To William Cranch, Philadelphia, December 3, 1797

Books   With Books about me I have felt dismal and Lonely. You left the only
ones you intended to take; and an Inn seldom furnishes any entertainment of a literary kind.

To John Adams, Quincy, November 26, 1792

Books afford you entertainment, use them while you can, and memory is retentive. Time may come when what you read will scarcly
leave a trace behind.

To Harriet Welsh, Quincy, August 6, 1815

Literature   It is polite Literature which embellishes and enriches the understanding, which diffuses a delicacy and beauty over discourse, and
imparts a "charm beyond the reach of art."*

To John Adams Smith, Quincy, 1808

*Longinus, *A Grace Beyond the Reach of Art* (Genius and the Rules), 1729.

Music   The practise of Musick to those who have a taste and ear for it, must
be one of the most agreeable of Amusements. It tends to soften and
harmonize the passions, to elevate the mind, to raise it from earth to

Heaven. The most powerfull effects of Musick which I ever experienced was at Westminster Abbey. The place itself is well calculated to excite solemnity, not only from its ancient and venerable appearance, but from the dignified Dust, Marble and Monuments it contains. Last year it was fitted up with seats and an organ loft sufficiently large to contain six hundred Musicians, which were collected from this and other Countries. This Year the Musick was repeated. It is call'd the celebration of Handles Musick. The sums collected are deposited, and the income is appropriated to the support of decayed Musicians. There were 5 days set apart for the different performances. I was at the peice call'd the Messiah, and tho a Guinea a ticket, I am sure I never spent one with more satisfaction. It is impossible to describe to you the Solemnity and dignity of the Scene. When it came to that part, the Hallelujah, the whole assembly rose and all the Musicians, every person uncovered.* Only conceive six hundred voices and instruments perfectly chording in one word and one sound! I could scarcely believe myself an inhabitant of Earth. I was one continued shudder from the beginning to the end of the performance. Nine thousand pounds was collected, by which you may judge of the rage which prevaild for the entertainment.

To Elizabeth Cranch, London, September 2, 1785

*I.e., removed their hats as a sign of respect.

The art of dancing is carried to the highest degree of perfection that it is capable of; at the opera. The House is neither so grand, or Beautifull architecture as the French Theater, but it is more frequented by the Beau Mond,* who had rather be amused than instructed. The Scenary is more various, and more highly decorated, the dresses more costly and rich. And O! the Musick vocal and instrumental, it has a soft persuasive power and a dying Sound. Conceive a highly decorated building filled with Youth, Beauty, Grace, ease, clad in all the most pleasing and various ornaments of Dress which fancy can form; these objects Singing like Cherubs to the best tuned instruments most skilfully handled, the softest tenderest Strains, every at-

Opera

titude corresponding with the musick, full of the God or Goddess whom they celebrate, the female voices accompanied by an equal number of Adonises. Think you that this city can fail of becoming a Cytherea** and this House the temple of Venus?

"Where Musick Softnes, and where dancing fires"†

It requires the immortal Shield of the invincible Minerva to skreen youth from the arrows which assail them upon every side. How many of them resemble the Simple youth which Solomon describes as void of understanding, and when he drew the picture of his Heart he drew the portrait of a Parisian. She Caught him says the wise king and kissed him with an impudent face.‡ How often have I seen this upon the Stage?

As soon as a Girl sets her foot upon the floor of the opera, she is excommunicated by the Church and denied Burial in holy ground; she conceives nothing worse can happen to her, all restraint is thrown off and she delivers herself to the first who bids high enough for her.

To Mary Cranch, Auteuil, February 20, 1785

*Fashionable society.   **In Greek mythology, this island off the southern coast of Greece was the birthplace of Aphrodite (Venus).   †Paraphrased from Alexander Pope, "The Rape of the Lock," canto 1, line 76. ‡Proverbs 7:7, 13.

Poetry   I wonder Apollo and the Muses could not have indulged me with a poetical Genious. I have always been a votary to her charms, but never could ascend Parnassus* myself.

To Mercy Otis Warren, Braintree, April 27, 1776

*A mountain range in Greece, the seat for Apollo and the muses, from which poetry and song were inspired.

The Theater   Tho he [Molière] has drawn many pictures of real life, yet all pictures of life are not fit to be exhibited upon the Stage.

To Mercy Otis Warren, Boston, December 11, 1773

I wish, my dear, I could transport you in a balloon and carry you to the stages here; you would be charmed and enchanted with the scenery, the music, the dresses, and the action.

> To Elizabeth Cranch, Auteuil, December 13, 1784

The Theatre you know, has been call'd the pulse of the people.

> To Thomas Boylston Adams, Philadelphia, May 1, 1798

— *Cities, Countries, and Other Places*

A city is not the best calculated for study.   *Cities*

> To John Quincy Adams, London, November 22, 1786

Europe has no charms to attach me to it.   *Europe*

> To Royall Tyler, Auteuil, September 5, 1784

The Morals of Europe are depraved beyond conception. Love of Country and publick virtue, mere visions.

> To Mary Cranch, London, May 24, 1786

I shall quit Europe with more pleasure than I came to it, uncontaminated I hope with its Manners and vices. I have learnt to know the World, and its value. I have seen high Life, I have Witnessed the Luxury and pomp of State, the Power of riches and the influence of titles, and have beheld all Ranks bow before them, as the only shrine worthy of worship. Notwithstanding this, I feel that I can return to my little cottage and be happier than here, and if we have not wealth, we have what is better, Integrity.

> To Mary Cranch, London, February 25, 1787

The affairs of Europe are so surrounded with clouds, and enveloped in darkness, that the wisest politician with the most scientific Eye cannot penetrate their mazes, nor trace the regular confusion.

To John Quincy Adams, Philadelphia, November 23, 1797

European Education   A European life would, you say, be the ruin of our Children.

To John Adams, Braintree, June 20, 1783

The more my dear Madam that I see of Europe the more I am attached to the method of Education persued in the state of Massachusetts. If our Youth have not all those opportunities for improvement in some branches of Literature, and the fine Arts, which these old countries can boast, they have sufficient to qualify them for any departments they may be called to fill.

To Elizabeth Stoerr Smith, London, August 29, 1785

European Travel   An acquaintance with foreign Countries, is no doubt a benefit when properly improved, as it tends to remove prejudices, and enlarge the mind. But I question much whether out of the many Youth who come Anually from all parts of America, more of them do not return with corrupted morals, and a distaste to the purer manners of our own Country, than with improved understandings or wiser Heads.

To Elizabeth Storer Smith, London, August 29, 1785

France   You inquire of me how I like Paris? Why they tell me I am no judge, for that I have not seen it yet. One thing I know, and that is, that I have smelt it. If I was agreeably dissapointed in London, I am as much dissapointed in Paris. It is the very dirtyest place I ever saw. There are some Buildings and some Squares which are tolerable, but in general the streets are narrow, the shops, the houses inelegant, and dirty, the Streets full of Lumber and Stone with which they Build. Boston cannot Boast so elegant publick Buildings, but in every other respect, it is as much superiour in my Eyes to Paris, as London is to Boston.

To Lucy Cranch, Auteuil, September 5, 1784

[On dancing in France:] I have read, that "daily example is the most subtile of poisons." I have found my taste reconciling itself to habits, customs, and fashions, which at first disgusted me. The first dance which I saw upon the Stage shocked me; the Dresses and Beauty of the performers were enchanting; but, no sooner did the Dance commence, than I felt my delicacy wounded, and I was ashamed to be seen to look at them. Girls, cloathd in the thinest Silk and Gauze, with their peticoats short, Springing two foot from the floor, poising themselves in the air, with their feet flying, and as perfectly shewing their Garters and draws as tho no peticoat had been worn, was a sight altogether new to me. Their motions are as light as air and as quick as lightning. They balance themselves to astonishment. No description can equal the reality. They are daily trained to it from early infancy, at a Royal academy, instituted for this purpose. You will very often see little creatures, not more than 7 or 8 years old as undauntedly performing their parts as the eldest amongst them. Shall I speak a Truth and say that repeatedly seeing these Dances has worn off that disgust which I first felt, and that I see them now with pleasure. Yet, when I consider the tendency of these things, the passions they must excite, and the known Character, even to a proverb, which is attached to an opera Girl, my abhorrence is not lessend, and neither my Reason or judgment has accompanied my Sensibility in acquiring any degree of callousness. The art of dancing is carried to the highest degree of perfection that it is capable of; at the opera.

To Mary Cranch, Auteuil, February 20, 1785

I mourn more and more leaving this place, for it is daily more Beautifull, and I find too that six months more would make me tolerably expert in the Language. But all things must Yeald to Business.

To Elizabeth Shaw, Auteuil, May 10, 1785

When I was in Paris—for the last time! I took my leave of it, but without tears. Yet the thought that I might never visit it again gave me some pain, for it is as we say a dieing leave when we quit a place with that Idea.

To Charles Storer, Auteuil, May 18, 1785

I think I have somewhere met with the observation that nobody ever leaves Paris but with a degree of tristness.

> To Thomas Jefferson, London, June 6, 1785

In Europe all the lower class of women perform the most servile Labour, and work as hard with out door as the Men. In France you see them making hay, reaping, sowing, plowing and driveing their carts alone. It would astonish you to see how Labourious they are, and that all their gain is coars Bread and a little ordinary wine, not half so good as our cider. The Land is all owned by Marquisses, Counts and Dukes, for whom these poor wretches toil and sweat. Their houses through all the villages of France consist of thatched roof Huts, without one single pane of glass. When they have any business which requires light, they set out of Door, and this they usually do through the whole season, for Heaven has blesst them with an admirable Climate, and a soil productive of every necessary and delicacy that Luxery can pant for. But their Religion and Government Mar all heaven's Bounty.

> To Lucy Quincy Tufts, London, September 3, 1785

The French as a Nation do not wish our Prosperity more than the English, only as they have sense enough to See that every indulgence stipulated to us, is a thorn in the Side of the English.

> To Cotton Tufts, London, August 1, 1786

France to be sure was the first to acknowledge our independence, and to aid us with Men and money, and ought always to be first-rank'd amongst our Friends.

> To Mary Cranch, London, September 12, 1786

[On Paris:] *Sixty thousand* prostitutes in *one* city, Some of them the most Beautifull of their Sex!!!

> To Elizabeth Shaw, London, October 15, 1786

I wish, most ardently, that every arm extended against that unhappy country might be withdrawn, and they left to themselves, to form whatever constitution they choose; and whether it is republican or monarchical is not of any consequence to us, provided it is a regular government of some form or other, which may secure the faith of treaties, and due subordination to the laws, whilst so many governments are tottering to the foundations.

To Abigail Adams Smith, Quincy, February 3, 1794

When I have read the dreadfull Scenes which have past, and are still acting in France, when I behold so Numerous and powerfull a Nation overturning all their old established forms both of Government and of Religion opposing and baffeling so successfully so many powers, and that under no Government, that deserves the Name, I have been led to contemplate it, as no common or natural event, arrising from the pressure of any increasd burdens or any new infringement upon their priviledges, but the over ruling hand of providence fulfilling great designs. It is the Lord's work and it is Marvelous in our Eyes. The skirt of the cloud will pass over us, and thankfull may we be if justice and Righteousness may preserve us from its Artillery.

To John Adams, Quincy, May 10, 1794

The Greatest of all oppressors and usurpers. . . .

To Mercy Otis Warren, Philadelphia, April 25, 1798

Britain as usual has added insult to injustice and cruelty, by what she calls a conciliatory plan. From my Soul I despise her meaness; but she has long ago lost that treasure which a great authority tell[s] us exalteth a Nation,* and is receiving the reproaches due to her crimes.

Great Britain

To John Adams, May 18, 1778

*Proverbs 14:34.

That nation to which we were once united, as it has departed from justice, eluded and subverted the wise laws which formerly governed it, and suffered the worst of crimes to go unpunished, has lost its valor, wisdom and humanity, and, from being the dread and terror of Europe, has sunk into derision and infamy.

> To John Quincy Adams, June 10?, 1778

I hope your father will indulge you with a visit to England this winter. It is a country I should be fond of your seeing. Christianity, which teaches us to forgive our enemies, prevents me from enjoining upon you a similar vow, to that which Hamilcar obtained from his son Hanibal,* but I know not how to think of loving those haughty Islanders.

> To John Quincy Adams, Braintree, November 20, 1783

*Sometime before 237 B.C. Hannibal was made to swear eternal enmity toward Rome.

As to civility of behaviour, politeness of Manners, true Hospitality and Benevolence, this Country have much more need of going to America to learn from them, than our Country has of any establishment this can bestow.

> To Elizabeth Storer Smith, London, August 29, 1785

London, in the Summer season, is a mere desert; nobody of consequence resides in it, unless necessitated to by their Business. I think the Gentry quite right in every view to retire to their Country seats, residing upon them is generally a great benefit to the proprietor. Many noble men expend vast sums, anually, in improving and Beautifying their estates. I am told that one must visit some of these manors and lordships to form a just estimate of British grandeur and magnificence. All the villages that I have seen round London are mere gardens, and show what may be effected by culture; but we must not expect for many years to see America thus improved.

> To Elizabeth Cranch, London, September 2, 1785

Houses are built by the tenants, and taken at life-rents, which upon the decease of the lessees, revert back again to the owner of the soil. Thus is the landed property of this country vested in lordships and in the hands of the rich altogether. The peasantry are but slaves to the lord, notwithstanding the mighty boasts they make of liberty.

> To Mary Cranch, Grosvenor Square, September 15, 1787

If I was not present to see and hear it, I could scarcely credit that a whole people should not only tamely submit to the evils of war, but appear frantic with joy at the prospect; led away by false glory, by their passions and their vices, they do not reflect upon past calamities nor approaching destruction; and few of them have better reasons to offer for their conduct, than the lady with whom I was in company the other day, who hoped there would be a war. "Pray," said I, "how can you wish so much misery to mankind?" "O," said she, "if there is a war, my brother and several of my friends will be promoted."

> To John Quincy Adams, London, October 12, 1787

[On the English Channel:] That most horrid passage.

> To Thomas Jefferson, London, February 26, 1788

I esteem your friendship as one of the most valuable acquisitions that I made in your country: —a country that I should most sincerely rejoice to visit again, if I could do it without crossing the ocean. I have sometimes been suspected of partiality for the preference which I have given to England, but were I to live out of America, that country would have been my choice.

> To Thomas Brand-Hollis, New York, September 6, 1790

I know very well by experience the strong attractions which England possesses, and Should prefer it to any other country that I have seen America excepted.

> To Lucy Ludwell Paradise, September 6, 1790

A Country, for which I have ever since my residence in it, entertaind a fondness and partiality.

> To Thomas Boylston Adams, Quincy, November 30, 1794

In a Government like that of Great Britain, we know that many abuses exist, both in the Governors and Governed, but still in no Country, America excepted, has there ever existed so great a share of personal Liberty and Security of property.

To John Adams, Quincy, December 6, 1794

England you know, is the country of my greatest partiality.

To Thomas Boylston Adams, Quincy, February 11, 1795

Great Britain as surly as John Bull, tho he dare not Growl loud, hating our prosperity most cordially, and swelling to see our Navy rising in power and respectability. We have quite as much to guard against from that quarter, as from the Great Nation [i.e., France].

To Mary Cranch, Philadelphia, April 26, 1800

The British are very insolent and haughty—and exercise their power, without much regard to right.

To Abigail Adams Smith, Quincy, March 27, 1808

I wish to see a mutual Spirit of Love & good will, so honourable to humane Nature Substituted for that Spirit of bitterness which is too much encouraged upon both Sides of the Atlantic and which is so contrary to the precepts and example of him, who exhorted his followers, to prove themselves his disciples by Loving one another.*

To John Adams 2nd, Quincy, May 21, 1816

*John 13:34.

Great Britain
and France

In one Country, vice is like a ferocious Beast, seeking whom it may devour: in the other like a subtle Poison secretly penetrating and working destruction. [In England] you cannot travel a mile without danger to your person and Property yet Publick executions abound; [in France] your person and property are safe; executions are Rare. But in *a Lawful way, Beware* for with whomever you have to deal, you may rely upon an attempt to over reach [i.e., overcharge] you.

To Mercy Otis Warren, Auteuil, September 5, 1784

The rich variety of grass and grain with which that country was loaded, as I rode through it, exhibited a prospect of the highest cultivation. All nature looked like a garden. The villages around Paris are pleasant, but neither the land nor the cultivation equals the neighboring nation.

To Mercy Otis Warren, Auteuil, September 5, 1784

As a Husbandman you would be delighted with the rich verdure of the field, and the high cultivation of the Lands. In the Manufactory of many articles, the Country can boast a superiority over their Galician Neighbours. But when you come to consider the Man, and the social affections; ease, civility, and politeness of Manners, this people suffer by the comparison. They are more contracted and narrow in their sentiments notwithstanding their boasted liberality and will not allow their Neighbours half the Merrit they really deserve. They affect to despise the French, and to hate the Americans, of the latter they are very liberal in their proofs. So great is their pride that they cannot endure to view us as independent, and they fear our growing greatness. . . .

I have seen nothing that equals Parissian ease and grace. I should like to visit France once a year during my residence in Europe.

To Thomas Jefferson, London, August 12, 1785

They think much more of their titles here than in France. It is not unusual to find people of the highest rank there, the best bred and the politest people. If they have an equal share of pride, they know better how to hide it. Until I came here, I had no idea what a national and illiberal inveterancy the English have against their better behaved neighbours, and I feel a much greater partiality for them than I did whilst I resided among them. I would recommend to this nation a little more liberality and discernment; their contracted sentiments lead them to despise all other nations. Perhaps I should be chargeable with the same narrow sentiments, if I give America the preference over these old European nations. In the cultivation of the arts and improvement in manufactures, they greatly excel us; but we have native genius, capacity, and ingenuity, equal to all their improvements, and much more general knowledge diffused amongst us. You can scarcely form an idea how much superior our common people, as they are termed, are to those of the same rank in this country. Neither have we that servility of manners, which the distinction between nobility and citizens gives to the people of this country. We tremble not, either at the sight or name of majesty. I own that I never felt myself in a more contemptible situation, than when I stood four hours together for a gracious smile from majesty, a witness to the anxious solicitude of those around me for the same mighty *boon*.

To Elizabeth Shaw, London, August 15, 1785

In England the common people live more comfortably [than in France], but there is wretchedness and oppression enough here, to make a wise Man mad.

To Lucy Quincy Tufts, London, September 3, 1785

I believe they have as many spies here as the police of France.

To Mary Cranch, London, October 1, 1785

In houses, in furniture, in gardens and pleasure grounds, and in equipage, the wealth of France and England is displayed to a high pitch of grandeur and magnificence; but, the millions who are loaded with taxes to support this pomp and show, I look to my happier country with an enthusiastic warmth, and pray for the continuance of that equality of rank and fortune which forms so large a portion of our happiness.

To Mary Cranch, London, May 21, 1786

I wish I could say that a Change of Administration since the peace, had effected a change of sentiment with respect to America, but this Nation, sir, is still persueing measures which daily, more & more, alienate America from her, & force her into a closer connection with France: how much this will benefit England, time will discover.

To John Cranch, London, March 7, 1787

If they [i.e., France] are serious in their intended invasion of England, I think they must not delay the attempt much longer. I am sanguine that they will not succeed. I pray Heaven they may not. I consider England the only Barrier remaining against universal domination.

To Catherine Johnson, Philadelphia, May 4, 1798

God Grant the fate of Pharoah & his Hoast, to those who attempt to cross the channel. England is the only Barrier between France & universal domination.

To Mary Cranch, Philadelphia, June 4, 1798

The Schuykill is not more like the Hudson, than I to Hercules. *Hudson River*

To Cotton Tufts, Auteuil, March 8, 1785, and to
Abigail Adams Smith, Philadelphia, November 21, 1790

The city of London is pleasanter than I expected; the buildings more *London* regular, the streets much wider, and more sunshine than I thought to have found; but this, they tell me, is the pleasantest season to be in the city. At my lodgings I am as quiet as at any place in Boston; nor do I feel as if it could be any other place than Boston.

Travel Journal, July 24, 1784

I am better pleased with this city than I expected. It is a large magnificent and Beautifull city, most of the Streets 40 feet wide built strait, the houses all uniform, no [. . .] small tennaments, many fine open Squares where the nobility reside, and where most of the publick Buildings are Erected.

To Elizabeth Shaw, London, July 28, 1784

The suicide which is so frequent in London I have heard attributed to the everlasting fogs of that Island.

To Mary Cranch, Auteuil, January 7, 1785

I had lived so quietly in that Calm retreat [in Auteuil, France], that the Noise and bustle of this proud city almost turnd my Brain for

the first two or three Days. The figure which this city makes in respect to Equipages is vastly superiour to Paris, and gives one the Idea
of superiour wealth and grandeur. I have seen few carriages in Paris
and no horses superiour to what are used here for Hackneys.

To Thomas Jefferson, London, June 6, 1785

We are now really in the Gloomy Month of November Such as I
have heard it described, but did not last year experience. Now we
have it, all smoke, fog and darkness.

To Elizabeth Storer, London, November 21, 1786

I do not think I should draw a false picture of the Nobility and Gentry of this Metropolis, if I was to assert, that Money and pleasure are
the sole objects of their ardent persuit, publick virtue, & indeed all
virtue is exposed to Sale, and as to principle, where is it to be found,
either in the present administration, or opposition?

To Mercy Otis Warren, London, May 14, 1787

Mount Vernon   Mount Vernon is a retired spot, beautifull as a summer residence,
but not calculated for any intercourse in winter, there not being a
single house or Neighbour nearer than Alexandria which is nine
miles distant. The House has an ancient appearance and is really so.
The Rooms are small and low, as well as the Chambers. The greatest
Ornament about it, is a long piazza from which you have a fine view
of the River Potomac at the bottom of the Lawn. The grounds are
disposed in some taste, but they evidently show that the owner was
seldom an inhabitant of them, and that possessing judgment, he
lacked Guineys instead of acres. It required the ready money of
large funds to beautify and cultivate the grounds so as to make them
highly ornamental. It is now going to decay.

To Mary Cranch, Washington, December 21, 1800

The Netherlands   If politeness and attention could render a place agreeable, I have had
more reason to be pleased with this Country, than any other, that I

have visited, and when I get across the water again, I shall not regret the visit I have made here.

These people appear to think of the past, the present, and the future, whilst they do honour to their former Heroes, and patriots, by paintings, sculpture, and monuments, they are establishing wise institutions, and forming the minds and manners of their youth, that they may transmit to posterity, those rights, and liberties, which they are sensible have suffered infringements, but which they appear determined to regain, and are uniting in spirited and vigorous measures, for that purpose.

To Abigail Adams Smith, Amsterdam, August 23, 1786

As there was no settlement on any part of the continent Northward of Maryland except in Massachusetts for more than fifty years after the landing of our ancestors at Plimouth, That state may be considerd as the parent of all the other new England states. *New England*

To Charles Adams, London, c. February 16, 1786

If you find your Health Buffering come to Boston and you will find a journey to the Northward very agreable in the month of June. You must not however look for English turnpike Roads or Inns but you will find much of true English Hospitality.

To Catherine Johnson, Philadelphia, May 4, 1798

Our young Men like the wild geese are flocking to N. York to Baltimore to the Southard as the scene of Business lies there.

To John Quincy Adams, Quincy, October 6, 1815

No Southern Man quotes Scriptures. *North and South*

To Mary Cranch, Philadelphia, January 7, 1790

The North and South appear to be arranged very formidably against each other in politicks.

To John Adams, Quincy, May 10, 1794

I hope we may be held together, but I know not how long, for oil and water are not more contrary in their natures, than North and South. Yet I see so many evils arising from a division that I deprecate it during my day.

To Elizabeth Peabody, Philadelphia, February 13, 1798

Two Nations are not more different than the N. Englanders and many Natives of this city. I must not however be too local. Which has the preference I have not said—

To Mary Cranch, Philadelphia, March 5, 1798

Philadelphia   I believe Phyladelphia is an unfertile soil, or it would not produce so many unfruitfull women.

To John Adams, Braintree, December 1775

I am not confind, but am frequently obliged to decline going into company, of which this city is the General Resort during winter, and one continued Scene of Parties upon Parties, Balls & entertainments equal to any European city. The Publick amusements tis True are few, no Theatre here this winter, an assembly once a fortnight, to which I have not been this season but the more general method for those who have Houses calculated for it, is to give Balls at their own Houses.

To Mary Cranch, Philadelphia, February 5, 1792

I do not love that City so well as you do. I fear you will find it Changed for the worse when you return. It is more than any city the resort of Foreigners, who leave most of their virtues behind them, if they ever had any, and bring principles, and Manners into our Country by no means calculated to promote the order of our Government, or the purity of Our Morals. I would however make some exceptions to this Rule.

To Thomas Boylston Adams, Quincy, February 21, 1797

I believe this city is become as vile and debauched as the city of London, nay more so, for in the lower classes, much more respect is had to Character there.

> To Mary Cranch, Philadelphia, May 24, 1797

As it respects the independence and happiness of the Country, a removal from this sink of corruption and depravity would be a very happy and fortunate circumstance. I speak of the city only.

> To William Cranch, Philadelphia, July 20, 1797

These Philadelphians are a strange set of people, making pretentions to give Laws of politeness and propriety to the union. They have the least feeling of real genuine politeness of any people with whom I am acquainted.

> To Mary Cranch, Philadelphia, February 15, 1798

This City, which was formerly torpid with indolence, and fettered with Quakerism; has become *one* Military School, and every morning, the Sound of the drum and fife, lead forth "A Band of Brothers joind."* The Martial Spirit resounds from one end of the Country, to the other.

> To John Quincy Adams, Philadelphia, June 12, 1798

*Shakespeare, *Henry V,* IV:3.

Philadelphia has shown a Spirit of Patriotism which does them great honour.

> To John Quincy Adams, Philadelphia, July 20, 1798

Philadelphia is very gay.

> To Catherine Johnson, Philadelphia, March 13, 1800

The Streets here are all upon strait lines crossd like a checker board, the width of them add greatly to the Elegance, convenience and beauty of the City, and admit of trees upon each side of them, paved with brick upon each side upon which passengers always walk, so that you never see a person in the middle of the Street but with Waggons or carriages. Since Congress first sat here, the City has grown one third. Most of the Elegant Houses have been built within the last ten years.

To Mary Cranch, Philadelphia, April 16, 1800

It is the last time that I shall reside in this city, and as present appearances indicate, the last time I shall visit it; The people are led blind fold by those who will ride them without saddle, but well curbed and bitted.

To Mary Cranch, Philadelphia, May 5, 1800

Switzerland   That unhappy Country is such an instructive lesson and warning to us that we shall be hardned and stupified not to profit by it.

To Cotton Tufts, Philadelphia, June 8, 1798

Virginia   Virginia by some of her resolves plainly shews what manner of spirit She is of.

To John Adams, Quincy, January 12, 1794

I read the News papers you send. The old Dominion makes me sick. What are they about? They would do well to ponder.

To William Smith Shaw, Quincy, February 8, 1799

The old dominion is progressing fast by her politicks to a State of Warfare against the federal Government.

To John Quincy Adams, Philadelphia, February 28, 1800

The White House   This House is built for ages to come.

To Mary Cranch, Columbia City of Washington, November 21, 1800

~ Communications

Bad news has swifter wings than good.

> To John Quincy Adams, Quincy, September 24, 1813

To communicate pleasure, is reflecting happiness.

> To Mary Cranch, Philadelphia, March 3, 1798

What would I give for an hour's conversation.

> To John Adams, Quincy, April 5, 1797

Accept this hasty Scrawl warm from the Heart of Your Sincere Diana.

> To John Adams, Weymouth, August 11, 1763

But after all, notwithstanding we are told that the giver is more blessed than the receiver.* I must confess that I am not of so generous a disposition, in this case, as to give without wishing for a return.

> To John Adams, Weymouth, September 12, 1763

*Luke 18:17.

Received the pacquet you so generously bestowed upon me. To say I Fasted after such an entertainment, would be wronging my Conscience and wounding Truth. How kind is it in you, thus by frequent tokens of remembrance to alleviate the pangs of absence, by this I am convinced that I am often in your Thoughts, which is a satisfaction to me.

> To John Adams, Weymouth, April 12, 1764

The Nest of Letters which you so undervalue, were to me a much more welcome present than a Nest of Baskets, tho every stran[d] of those had been gold and silver. I do not estimate everything according to the price the world set upon it, but according to the value it is of to me, thus that which was cheapest to you I look upon as highly valuable.

To John Adams, Weymouth, April 12, 1764

My pen, which I once loved and delighted in, has for a long time been out of credit with me. Could I borrow the powers and faculties of my much valued friend, I should then hope to use it with advantage to myself and delight to others. Incorrect and unpolished as it is, I will not suffer a mistaken pride so far to lead me astray as to omit the present opportunity of improvement. And Should I prove a tractable scholar, you will not find me tardy.

To Mercy Otis Warren, Boston, December 5, 1773

Don't fail of letting me hear from you by every opportunity, every line is like a precious Relict of the Saints.

To John Adams, Braintree, June 16, 1775

I want some sentimental Effusions of the Heart. I am sure you are not destitute of them, or are they all absorbed in the great publick. Much is due to that I know, but being part of the whole I lay claim to a Larger Share than I have had. You used to be more communicative a Sundays. I always loved a Sabeth days letter, for then you had a greater command of your time—but hush to all complaints.

To John Adams, Braintree, July 16, 1775

My Heart is as light as a feather and my Spirits are dancing. I received this afternoon a fine parcel of Letters and papers . . . it was a feast to me. I shall rest in quiet I hope this Night.

To John Adams, Braintree, May 27, 1776

I never think your Letters half long enough.

To John Adams, Braintree, September 20, 1776

I know not How I should support an absence already tedious, and many times attended with melancholy reflections, if it was not for so frequently hearing from you. That is a consolation to me, tho a cold comfort in a winter's Night.

> To John Adams, Braintree, April 17, 1777

I generally endeavour to write you once a week, if my Letters do not reach you, tis oweing to the neglect of the post. I generally get Letters from you once a week, but seldom in a fortnight after they are wrote.

> To John Adams, June 8, 1777

It has been a relief to my mind to drop some of my sorrows through my pen.

> To James Lovell, Braintree, c. December 15, 1777

My Heart overflows, and longs to give utterance to my pen.

> To John Adams, Braintree, c. July 15, 1778

I have scarcly ever taken my pen to write but the tears have flowed faster than the Ink.

> To John Adams, Braintree, October 21, 1778

A short Letter always gives one pain as well as pleasure since a few lines only from such a distance looks as if the Friend we wrote to possessd but a small share of our attention and regard.

> To John Adams, December 13, 1778

I love to amuse myself with my pen, and pour out some of the tender sentiments of a Heart over flowing with affection . . . for the sympathetick Heart that Beats in unison with Portia.

> To John Adams, Sunday Evening, December 27, 1778

Next to the pain of not receiving is that of not being able to send a token of remembrance and affection.

> To John Adams, April 23, 1779

My candle and my pen are all my companions. I send my thoughts across the broad Atlantick in search of my associate and rejoice that thought and immagination are not confined like my person to the small spot on which I exist.

To John Adams, June–July 1779

Letters are always valuable from those we Love, if they contain nothing but an account of their Health.

To Charles and John Quincy Adams, July 22, 1780

Letters . . . were your great delight when they did not censure, or complain, when they did they were your greatest punishment.

To John Adams, November 13, 1780

My pen must be the faithfull confident of my Heart. I could not say to a stranger, that which I could not write, nor dare I even trust to my pen the fullness of my Heart. You must measure it, by the contents of your own when softned by recollection.

To John Adams, May 28, 1781

When ever any opportunity occurs write, and write me a volume to amuse, to comfort and inform me. I turn to the loved pages of former days and read them with delight. They are all my comfort, all my consolation in the long long interval of time that I have not received a line. Should I name my dear Boys a tear will flow with the Ink—not a line have I received from them for more than a Year.

To John Adams, August 1, 1781

There is not any thing in this Life, now my Dear Friend is seperated from me, that can communicate equal delight and pleasure to that which I feel upon the Sight of Letters written in the well known Hand of my Friend. My Heart Leaps forward to meet them, whilst the trembling Hand uncloses the Seals, and my eager Eyes devour the contents; tho unwilling to reach the close.

To John Adams, June 17, 1782

Let me hear from you by every opportunity, as the correspondence of my Friends is the only compensation I can receive for the loss of their Society.

> To Mercy Otis Warren, Auteuil, September 5, 1784

Letters from my Friends are a cordial to my Soul.

> To Cotton Tufts, Auteuil, January 3, 1785

My pen will always run greater lengths than I am aware of when I address those who are particularly dear to me and to whom I can write with unreserve.

> To John Quincy Adams, London, June 26, 1785

I seldom feel a stimulus for writing until I hear that a vessel is just about to sail, and then I find myself so deep in debt, that I know not where to begin to discharge the account; but it is time for me to be a little more provident; for, upon looking into my list, I find I have no less than eighteen correspondents, who have demands upon me. One needs to have a more fruitful fund than I am possessed of, to pay half these in sterling bullion. I fear many will find too great a quantity of alloy to be pleased with the traffic.

> To Elizabeth Shaw, London, March 4, 1786

Your kind letter, my dear niece, was received with much pleasure. These tokens of love and regard which I know flow from the heart, always find their way to mine, and give me a satisfaction and plea-sure beyond any thing which the ceremony and pomp of courts and kingdoms can afford.

> To Lucy Cranch, London, April 2, 1786

There are no days in the year so agreable to me, nor any amuse-ments this Country can boast so gratifying to my Heart and mind as those days which bring me Letters from my Dear Friends. In them I always find the law of kindness written, and they solace my mind in the separation.

> To Elizabeth Cranch, London, July 18, 1786

To many of them [i.e., her friends] I owe Letters, but I really hate to touch a pen. I am ashamed to say how laizy I am grown in that respect.

> To Mary Cranch, Richmond Hill, January 24, 1789

Pray burn all these scribles for fear you should leave or drop any of them any where.

> To John Adams, Braintree, April 26, 1789

Pray burn all my Letters.

> To John Adams, Braintree, May 5, 1789

We shall hear often from one another, and the Separation be renderd less painfull by that means—

> To Mary Cranch, Providence, June 19, 1789

You know very well that when a person is fixed to any particular spot, that very few subjects worth communicating can occur.

> To Mary Cranch, Richmond Hill, October 4, 1789

Gentlemen are not half as particular as the Ladies are in their details.

> To John Adams, Quincy, December 20, 1795

I can seldom find more to say than one Letter contains. Upon some subjects I think much more than I write.

> To John Adams, Quincy, February 20, 1796

The very Sight of a Letter exhilirates my Spirits, and I tread back Ten Years in an instant.

> To John Quincy Adams, Quincy, February 29, 1796

I never feel so great a propensity to write as when I have just received a Letter.

> To Thomas Boylston Adams, Quincy, March 10, 1796

I think you observe that a few Lines are better than none at all.
To John Quincy Adams, Quincy, June 10, 1796

I have much upon my mind which I could say to you; prudence forbids my committing it to writing.
To Thomas Boylston Adams, Quincy, November 8, 1796

There is a kind of communication and intercourse which is a relief to the burdend mind.
To John Adams, Quincy, March 12, 1797

When we get together, we may say to each other what would not be proper to write.
To Mary Cranch, Philadelphia, July 21, 1797

Your Letters are the reviving cordials of my Spirits. They administer consolation for your absence.
To Thomas Boylston Adams, East Chester, N.Y., November 7, 1797

I yesterday about 11 oclock went into the President's Room to see if John had returned from the post office. My good Gentleman was soberly standing at the fire with your Letter open and very gravely reading it. I scolded and very soon carried it off. I thank you for all your communications. The P[resident] says one of Sister Cranch's Letters is worth half a dozen others. She allways tells us so much about home.
To Mary Cranch, Philadelphia, November 15, 1797

The President has agreed that he will not open any more Letters to me, and will be satisfied with such parts as I am willing to communicate. Accordingly he has not opend any since I scolded so hard about it.
To Mary Cranch, Philadelphia, December 26, 1797

My pen, I think, is scarcly ever dry.
To Mary Cranch, Philadelphia, April 26, 1798

I know how good and how sweet it is to hear from our far distant
Friends.

>   To John Quincy Adams, Philadelphia, May 3, 1798

I who have more leisure, and no care of Family affairs, but my orders can, and do devote almost every morning in writing to some
Friend or other.

>   To Mary Cranch, Philadelphia, June 19, 1798

I hope to hear from you frequently as a solace to me.

>   To John Adams, Quincy, November 22, 1798

This Letter may serve in lieu of the talkative wife. I hope you put
them all in the fire after you have read them. It would mortify me to
have one of them found upon your table.

>   To John Adams, Quincy, December 23, 1798

The pleasing Emotions excited by the Sight of a Letter, in your
Hand writing, were similar to those we experience at meeting a long
absent Friend doubly endeard to us by the perils and dangers
through which they have past.

>   To Mercy Otis Warren, Quincy, October 5, 1799

I find the best time for writing, is to rise about an hour earlier than
the rest of the family; go into the President's Room, and apply myself to my pen. Now the weather grows warmer I can do it. His
Room in which I now write has three large windows to the South.
The Sun visits it with his earliest beams at the East window, and
Cheers it the whole day in winter. All my keeping Rooms are North,
but my forenoons are generally spent in my own Chamber tho a
dark one, and I often think of my Sun Shine Cottage at Quincy.

>   To Mary Cranch, Philadelphia, March 15, 1800

Whenever a reluctance to the pen commences, it increases with
time, untill it becomes irksome.

>   To Sarah Adams, Quincy, January 20, 1808

A letter from a travelling friend is a great treat to those who sit by their firesides.

> To Caroline Smith, Quincy, January 24, 1808

The writing Spirit is not always present, and it is shy and coy. If you do not frequently solicit it, neglect is sure to be followed by indifference, and indifference by disgust.

> To Louisa Catherine Adams, Quincy, April 4, 1808

Many things may be said, which it is improper to commit to paper.

> To John Quincy Adams, Quincy, April 1808

William must continue to write. Tell him it is a habit the pleasure of which increases with the practise, but becomes irksome by neglect.

> To Abigail Adams Smith, Quincy, May 8, 1808

What is the reason I do not get a Letter from my Mother I think I hear you say? Why I will tell you Child. I have Sat down more than once, got through one page, been interrupted, laid it by—untill it seemed of no value. I love to be by myself when I write and that is a difficult thing in the winter season. The parlour your Father occupies all the forenoon in reading or writing. It is proper he should have it to himself. My own chamber is compleatly full this winter, and I know not how to write in the Evening, so that I can only snatch a few moments at a time, and then with various interruptions. Since I began these few lines I have been twice calld away.

> To Abigail Adams Smith, Quincy, December 28, 1808

I always feel most disposed to write when I have just received a Letter. Yet that is not the case now, but what is very similar to it. I have just read one from you to your Grandfather.

> To John Adams Smith, Quincy, 1808

How very wretched should I be but for the intercourse which Letters afford to soften the pains of absence and mitigate the pangs of seperation from near and dear Friends?

> To Louisa Catherine Adams, Quincy, September 22, 1810

I always call Duplicates of Letters, the Disappointment; yet the duplicate often reaches before the original. We have experienced several of these disappointments of late. When I expected a new treat, I have found only a Repition of the old one, altho that was exquisite when new, we thirsted for more originals from the same fountain.

> To Catherine Johnson, Quincy, December 29, 1810

Your Letters are a cordial to the Heart of your Friend.

> To Julia Rush, Quincy, December 21, 1813

Like cold water to a thirsty Soul would a refreshing Letter be from you.

> To John Quincy Adams, Quincy, February 27, 1814

I know how gratefull it is, to absent Friends to hear from each other, especially when to learn, that they are living, can be added the agreable circumstance of their being in health.

> To John Quincy Adams, Quincy, June 10, 1816

I know full well, that if the pen is not kept in constant practise, writing becomes irksome.

> To Julia Rush, Quincy, October 15, 1817

Let me hear from you, it lessens the distance that separates us.

> To Caroline deWindt, Quincy, January 29, 1818

Good-Byes   Shall I come and see you before you go. No I won't, for I want not again, to experience what I this morning felt, when you left Your A. Smith

> To John Adams, Weymouth, April 7, 1764

When you write again don't tell us one dismall Story. Let us have   *Good News*
sun shine from some quarter, if it is only imaginary.
> To Charles Storer, London, May 22, 1786

As Water to a thirsty Soul, so is good News from a far Country.
> To Catherine Johnson, Philadelphia, January 19, 1800

What a cordial for low Spirits agreable news from a far Country is.
> To Catherine Johnson, Quincy, December 19, 1809

As news like the Snow Ball, always gathers according to the distance   *News*
it passes.
> To Eunice Paine, Braintree, June 3, 1775

There is a pleasure I know not whence it arises nor can I stop now to
find it out, but I say there is a degree of pleasure in being able to tell
news—especially any which so nearly concerns us as all your proceedings do.
> To John Adams, Braintree, July 5, 1775

In a distant land far seperated from our Friends and connexions triv-
ial circumstances of a domestick kind become interesting.
> To Louisa Catherine Adams, Quincy, January 12, 1810

Domestic occurences . . . are always interesting to families when seperated from each other.
> To Abigail Adams Smith, Quincy, February 11, 1810

I do not Love to see the News writers fib so. . . . Yet the News writers   *Newspapers*
will fib to answer particular purposes.
> To Mary Cranch, Richmond Hill, August 9, 1789

I can read them all with a true Phylosophical contempt, and I could
tell them what the President says, that their praise for a few weeks
mortified him, much more, than all their impudent abuse does.
> To Mary Cranch, Philadelphia, June 3, 1797

The Jacobin printers seazd it with the eagerness of sharks, and circulated it, with the greediness of vultures.

To Thomas Boylston Adams, East Chester, N.Y., November 7, 1797

Of all the vehicals of falshood, lies fabricated only to injure the Nation and deceive them, our federal papers are the most detestable! They are a crying abomination of our Land.

To Elizabeth Peabody, Quincy, February 14, 1814

I regret any low ribalding should disgrace our papers, whether it respects foreign countries or our own.

To John Quincy Adams, Quincy, June 30, 1816

Sharing Bad News   Well why should I torment you. Why because when one feels fretted, it is an ease to the Mind when it has cast off.

To John Adams, Quincy, March 28, 1796

— Death

How great the mind that can overcome the fear of Death! How anxious the Heart of a parent who looks round upon a family of young and helpless children and thinks of leaving them to a World full of snares and temptations which they have neither discretion to foresee, nor prudence to avoid.

To John Adams, April 17, 1777

Yet must the common Lot of Man one day take place whether we dwell in our own Native Land, or are far distant from it. That we rest under the shadow of the Almighty is the consolation to which I resort, and find that comfort which the World cannot give.

To John Adams, June 8, 1779

How trifling, and of how little importance does such a scene, make all the wealth, power and greatness of the world appear.

> To John Adams, Braintree, September 20, 1783

How soon may our fairest prospects be leveld with the dust and shew us that Man in his best estate is but vanity and dust?

> To Mary Cranch, Philadelphia, March 21, 1792

I must not close this Letter without informing you that our Parent remains much in the State as when I wrote last. Exhausted nature appears to be seeking repose and the setting sun will go down calmly and serenely, and rise to a more perfect day, freed from the clogs of Mortality which now encumber it. For that inevitable lot may You and I my dear Friend ever be ready.

> To John Adams, Quincy, February 1794

Death . . . is no distinguisher of persons or Character.

> To John Quincy Adams, Quincy, November 15, 1798

Death, thou are no Respecter of persons.

> To Mary Cranch, Philadelphia, December 18, 1799

It used to be a petition of my Father's that he might not outlive his usefullness. His prayers were answerd, and I think it would be the wish and desire of every good Christian.

> To William Smith, March 3, 1800

The ways of providence are never more inscrutable to us, than when we see the early promising Blossom witherd, and cut off in its Bloom, e'er it reach maturity. We are ready to inquire, wherefore it is? whilst many who to us appear encumberers of the ground are left to fill up the measure of their iniquity. Yet it becomes us weak, feeble, short sighted beings, to consider all events as under the controul and direction of a supreem, all wise and beneficent Being, who knows what is best for his Creatures, and whom we are assured does not willingly afflict his Children. Whom the Lord Loveth, he chastneth.*

> To Hannah Smith, Quincy, February 14, 1806

*Proverbs 13:24; Hebrews 12:6.

We are told that at the death of Lazerus Jesus wept. If possesst with the power of raising him from the dead as we are assured he did, he wept as a proof of his affection and Sorrow, surely he must look with compassion upon those of his Creatures from whom he sees fit to take the nearest and dearest connexion, with the assurance only that they shall rise hereafter—by his example we are permitted to shed tears of sorrow to ease the swoln heart; and we must be less than humane Beings not to feel the hand which strikes us.

> To Hannah Cushing, Quincy, March 1808

The old Actors are gone off the Stage.

> To Mercy Otis Warren, Quincy, January 16, 1803

There is no Situation in Life from the Throne to the footstool which exempts us from its troubles in this respect all things come alike to all men.

> To Hannah Cushing, Quincy, March 1808

Death at any time, and in any form, is a solemn event.

> To Caroline Smith, Quincy, February 2, 1809

[On God's allowing John Quincy Adams to be sent away as U.S. minister to Russia:] Our hearts were "garnered up in him,"* perhaps too closely, and we were called to this trial to wean us from too strong an attachment to this earth.

> To Caroline Smith, Quincy, August 12, 1809

*Shakespeare, Othello, IV:2.

That no inroad has been made by death amongst any of my near and dear connections, is a sincere source of grateful remembrance; may the lives and health of every branch be prolonged, until, like a shock of corn fully ripe, we may be gathered to our fathers.

> To Caroline Smith, Quincy, December 9, 1809

It is lawfull to wish for Life whilst we can serve God and our generation! Who but our heavenly Parent shall say when that period ends. The lives of some are prolonged to try the virtues of those arround them. Their fillial gratitude and affection of Children to those parents whose tender solicitude nurtured and cherished them, when they hung upon the Breast incapable of helping themselves, who laboured, watched and prayed for their welfare, untill they arrived at Maturity.

> To Elizabeth Peabody, Quincy, October 10, 1810

Neither Age, Youth or Sex are exempt from this warfare.

> To Hannah Cushing, Quincy, May 22, 1811

[On the deaths of Richard and Mary Cranch:] Their deaths were such as is desirable. They did not outlive their usefullness, nor exhibit a second Childhood so humiliating in Age. Their minds were vigoras to the last periods of existance and together their Spirits have joind the Angelic Choir and will I trust receive the sentence of well done good and faithfull servants, enter into the joy of the Lord.*

> To John Quincy Adams, Quincy, November 17, 1811

*Matthew 15:21.

We see that neither Innocense or Beauty, Infancy or Age are exempt from the King of Terror—nor can we fathom the depth of that wisdom which takes the lovely Infant, unconscious either of good or Evil, just as the bud begins to expand and open its leaves to the rising Sun—It is our duty in Silent Submission to bow to the awfull mandate and receive it as a lesson full of instruction both to the Young and the Aged.

To Abigail L. S. Adams, Quincy, March 5, 1812

Thus fall, the Young, the Aged; and all Ranks, Nations and kindred bow to that great leveller—who can refrain from this inquiry? Where goes the unembodied Spirit?

Adieu my dear Sister, may we meet in a happier world and be permitted to recognize each other. Will not that be one of the joys of the Blessed.

To Elizabeth Peabody, Quincy, February 16, 1814

It is the order of nature, that as some pass off the Stage, others should succeed and supply their places.

To Louisa Catherine Adams, Quincy, December 21, 1814

At the Age to which I have arrived I must naturally look for the fall and decay of my early Friends and associates. All the ravages of the great destroyer have not been limited to Age. The Infant Bud, the blooming Youth, and the Mature in Life have fallen around me, even to the only Twig of the third generation which appertained to me. Why should I complain? He who knows our Frame, and that we are but dust, knows best at what period of our Lives it is most consistant with his wise designs to recall us and unto his infinate wisdom let us commit, The hour, the day, the Year.

To Louisa Catherine Adams, Quincy, September 30, 1815

Condolences   [On the death of Isaac Smith's mother:] I wipe the selfish tear from my Eye, "and look through nature up to Nature's God"* and in that Mansion not made with Hands I view the Departed Spirit, disencumberd from the Clogs of Mortality, earnestly desirous of receiving and welcoming her Friends into those happy Regions of Security and Bliss where She is safely landed, and there perfecting all those virtuous Friendships which were but commenced on Earth.

"Angels from Friendship, gather half their joy."**

These are consolations which Christianity offers to the afflicted mind. You sir who have for a course of years made those sacred doctrines your study and delight cannot fail to find them a Support under your present affliction. Those doctrines do not call for a Stoical insensibility or forbid us to feel as Humane Creatures, but so to lead us into any excesses that would discover an impotence of mind, and a diffidence of providence.

To Isaac Smith, Jr., London, December 30, 1786

*Alexander Pope, *An Essay on Man,* Epistle IV, line 332.   **Edward Young, *Night Thoughts* (1742–1745).

[On the death of John Adams's mother and the fatal illness of the Adamses' niece:] I think through all the most trying conflicts of my life, I have been called to pass through them separated from the personal condolence and support of my bosom friend, I have been taught to look for support and aid from superior power than man: there is a state of mind, when affliction dries up the source of tears, and almost bids the swollen heart burst. I have left one of those distressing scenes, and come from the house of sorrow, and bitterness, and wo, to the house of silent mourning. The venerable remains of our parent, yet lie uninterred, and the distressing pangs of dissolution of an agonizing nature, are separating the soul from the body of my dear niece, whilst her senses are perfect, and alive to every attention, willing to go, praying to be released, yet requesting her friends and sisters not to leave her dying bed; but to remain by her until she breathes her last. O it is too much to bear! my heart is too big for my bosom; it rends my frame, and you will find me, when I reach you, more emaciated than with a fit of sickness. Tomorrow I have the last duties to pay to our venerable parent. I have taken upon me the care and charge of the funeral; and tomorrow she will, for the last time, enter our doors. I have requested Mr. Whitney to attend. It is not for me to say when I will leave here [to go to Philadelphia]; the will of heaven has detained me; I must not complain.

To John Adams, Quincy, April 23, 1797

Whilst in unison with the sympathetic sorrow of a Nation; I unite in deploring the Loss; it has sustained of a Father, Friend and Benefactor. I intreat Madam, that you would permit a Heart deeply penetrated with your loss, and sharing personally in your Grief; to mingle with you, the Tears which flow for the partner of all your joys and Sorrows.

Deep as the Wound you have Sustained is, and irreparable as the Stroke must be, May that Religion to which you have ever been an ornament afford you Support, and from that Being who has promised to be a Husband to the Widow, may you derive Consolation is the fervent prayer of Your truly Sympathizing Friend.

To Martha Washington, Philadelphia, December 25, 1799

With the only and beloved daughter of my late venerable and respected Friend, I pour the tear of sympathy, and with a full Heart participate in the sorrowfull event which has deprived her of one of the most tender and affectionate of parents, one of the best of Mothers, one of the kindest Friends, one of the pleasantest companions and one of the most exemplary of women. To me she "was a Friend of more than 50 years ripening," my earliest, my constant, and my oldest Friend.

Dear departed Spirit will thou still be my Friend in those Regions of immortal Bliss to which I trust thou art translated, and whither I hope e'er long to follow thee.

To Ann Quincy Packard, Quincy, March 11, 1805

Next to the Support of Religion is the Sympathy of Friends in affliction. Of the first you have abundant Sources in the belief of an all wise Governour and dispenser of events in whose goodness you can confide and upon whose word you can repose. As the Husband of the Widows and the Father of the Fatherless,* unto that Being I commend you and your dear Children most sincerely Sympathezing with you in the Berevement you have been calld upon to sustain.

To Mary Otis, Quincy, May 13, 1814

*Psalms 68:5.

Sympathy from those we Love, when affliction assails us, is balm to the Bleading bosom, and assuages the wound it cannot heal and which is opened affresh.

> To Louisa Catherine Adams, Quincy, September 30, 1815

We must remember that our Children are but short favours borrowed now, to be returned anon. We may feel as parents, but submit in silence as Christians. Shall not the Lord of all the earth do right?

I have felt the pangs of loosing an Infant, but the still severe anguish when calld to part with a dear and only daughter, the delight of my Eyes, and my companion and Friend—but I cannot dwell upon the subject. My duty is to be still.

> To Abigail H. Adams, Quincy, September 7, 1813

Even tho not unexpected yet when we are calld to the trial of resigning our dear Friends to the grave Nature will recoil, and the Belief of a Glorious immortality can only support the anguish of a bleading Heart, or bring the mind quietly to submit to the allotments of Heaven.

> To Mercy Otis Warren, Braintree, December 10, 1778

We console ourselves however by the reflection which tends to molify our grief for our departed Friends; that they are gone to a better Country, and a Society more congenial to the benevolence of their minds.

> To Thomas Jefferson, London, July 3, 1786

When we reach the Meridian of Life, if not before one Dear Friend or other is dropping off, till we lose all that makes life desirable.

> To Cotton Tufts, London, August 1, 1786

I think of all my Friends with an unabated affection, & hope the period is not far distant when I shall meet them again. Some alass, I shall miss—but this is the portion of mortality.

> To Mary Cranch, London, October 8, 1787

I can say with Pope upon a similar occasion, "that my constant attendance upon her has indeed affected my mind very much, and lessened my desire of long life, since the best that can come of it is a miserable benediction."* "Nothing," says Seneca, "is so melancholy a circumstance in human life, or so soon reconciles us to the thought of our own death, as the reflection and prospect of one friend after another dropping around us. Who would stand alone, the sole remaining ruin, the last tottering column of all the fabric of friendship, seemingly so strong, once so large, and yet so suddenly sunk and buried?"**

To Abigail Adams Smith, Quincy, March 8, 1794

*Alexander Pope to Jonathan Swift, November 29, 1729.   **Quoted in
The Works of Alexander Pope, III (London, 1752), 43.

I feel these ligaments giving way one after another. I feel their loss to society and the warning voice to myself, "This Life's a dream, an empty Show."*

To Mary Cranch, Philadelphia, April 4, 1798

*Isaac Watts, *The Psalms of David* (1719).

It is some consolation that as one old Friend and acquaintance drops off, one after the other, others who are taking their place, inherit their virtues, and reconcile the aged Survivors to a longer continuence in a world, from which nothing tends so effectually to wean us, as the loss of near and dear connections.

To William Smith, Philadelphia, April 6, 1798

If any thing can effectually wean & detach us from this world, it is the loss of those who render Life pleasant and agreable to us. Yet we are apt to cling to those which remain.

To Mary Cranch, Philadelphia, May 7, 1798

We must live all the days of our appointed time, and when our change commeth, may it be happy to us.

To Mary Cranch, Washington, January 15, 1801

When each of us looking back upon the past, have reason to say, Thus far the Lord hath helped us—and it is of his Mercy that we are yet amongst the living, whilst nearly all of our early acquaintance are numberd with the great Congregation. Our Fathers & our Mothers where are they? With the Spirits of the just made perfect I trust anticipating our arrival at no distant period. . . .

As our Lamp of Life is nearly burnt out, I feel a Sympathy drawing me nearer & nearer to those dear Surviving Friends who began the race with me, and who are yet upon the ground—every year lessens the Number and who as Mr. Pope says would wish to stand the last Surviving column of the whole fabrick of Friendship.*

To Hannah Green, Quincy, 1809

*The Works of Alexander Pope, III (London, 1752), 43.

Those who have lived in the world three score years and ten, may literally be said to "be alone on earth" as it respects their cotemporaries. How few, how very few of my much loved early acquaintances remain? and every year diminishes the number.

To Abigail Adams Smith, Quincy, April 27, 1813

Like the Leaves of Nature, our Friends fall arround us, and shall they fall in vain? Let it be a loud call for the Surviving to apply their hearts to Wisdom.

To Elizabeth Peabody, Quincy, December 12, 1814

I find every year lessening the number of my cotemporaries until I am left almost alone.

To Louisa Catherine Adams, Quincy, December 21, 1814

Untill you arrive at old Age you can not realize the sensation caused by the removal of a Friend of many years growth—so ripened by our side, so endeard to us by every virtue.

To John Quincy Adams, Quincy, December 24, 1815

One of the afflictions to which long Life is Subject; nearly all our early associates, and many of our mature years, leave us, like Trees Striped of their leaves, its branches, a witherd Stock.

To John Quincy Adams, Quincy, June 10, 1816

When the Aged fall, it is the Course of Nature, but when the Young and promising are cut down e'er they reach the meridian of Life, we are led to inquire Wherefore, and it is only in the belief of a Being of unerring wisdom and goodness from whom the afflicted Heart can derive consolation—or can say,

> *"He gave and blessed be his name*
> *He takes but what he gave."**

You and your Family have in so many instances been calld to practice the great virtue of Resignation, and have so frequently exhibited such firmness under heavey trials. That you fully experienced the truth of "Whom the Lord Loveth he chasteneth"** as we descend the vale of Life, more particularly if we arrive at three Score & ten, we have nearley outlived our cotemporaries and feel less reluctance at quitting a scene already made desolate by the loss of our early Friends and companions, now reviveing the Thought that we may again join them, free from the clogs of mortality in purer Regions, in homes not made with hands, eternal in the Heavens—

To François Adriaan Vanderkemp, Quincy, April 28, 1818

*Job 1:21.   **Proverbs 13:24; Hebrews 12:6.

Mourning It becomes us then to be silent, and adore the hand which strikes our comforts dead. To be insensible to our loss is not requird of us by Him who made and knows our Frame, and whom we are told in holy writ wept at the loss of a Friend,* to mourn is the State of humanity. But we have comfort in this that we mourn not as those who have no hope. Tho our dear young Friend [. . .] have gone before us we have a rational hope from their lives and conversation, that the period of their duties were compleat, what tho short their date:

"Virtue, not rolling Suns, the mind matures,
*That life is long which answers Life's great End."***

To Susanna Warner Tufts, Philadelphia, May 8, 1798

*John 11:35.   **Edward Young, *Night Thoughts* (1742–1745).

Let not gloom and melancholy take root in your mind. The wounded Breast must have time to recover from the stroke which has pierced it. There are duties which you are calld upon to discharge to yourself, Your Family, and your Country, and to them devote your mind and your attention. Your heavenly Father, when he removed your Babe, knew what was best for you.

To John Quincy Adams, Quincy, February 27, 1813

The wound which has lacerated my Bosom, cannot be healed. The broken Heart may be bound up; and religion teach submission and Silence, even under the anguish of the Heart, but it can not cure it. The unbidden sigh will rise. And the bitter tear flow long after the Tomb is closed.

To John Quincy Adams, Quincy, October 22, 1813

Religion teaches me, Silence and Submission, this can assuage, but can never suppress the deep drawn Sigh, which recollection forever brings up, and which will endure, until recollection and Life are extinguishd together.

To Louisa Catherine Adams, Quincy, October 24, 1813

Bitter is the loss of a sweet Infant. But how much increased are the pangs which rend the Heart of a Mother, when calld to part with the Head of a Family, in the midst of her days, and usefulness? Endeared by a thousand Strong ties?

The hour, the day, the year are all before me and can never be effaced from my memory until Life and recollection expire together.

Yet how great is the sum of the Blessings still left me?

To Louisa Catherine Adams, Quincy, December 6, 1813

— Dreams, Imagination, Memories

Daydreaming   How many are the solitary hours I spend, ruminating upon the past, and anticipating the future.

          To John Adams, Braintree, May 7, 1776

Dreams   Tis only in my Night visions that I know any thing about you.

          To John Adams, Braintree, October 21, 1775

Expectations   Expectation has so long and so often been combatted by dissappoint-ment that I feel myself unhappy, my Spirits which were naturally cheerfull are depressed and the enjoyments of life are growing very insipid to me.

          To John Adams, Braintree, September 29, 1778

Our highest expectations are sometimes cut off, and that in a morti-fying manner.

          To John Thaxter, October 26, 1782

One month of daily expectation is more tedious than a year of cer-tainty.

          To John Adams, Braintree, November 11, 1783

Tis expectation makes the blessing sweet.

          To Thomas Boylston Adams, Quincy, February 21, 1797

As I had formed no expectations, I met with no disappointment.

          To Mercy Otis Warren, Quincy, March 4, 1797

Every wind may waft as tidings of vast importance.

          To Louisa Catherine Adams, Quincy, April 4, 1808

I feel gratified with the immagination at the close of the Day.   *Imagination*
>
> To John Adams, Weymouth, December 30, 1773

Tis true I never close my Eyes at night till I have been to Philadelphia, and my first visit in the morning is there.
>
> To John Adams, Braintree, September 20, 1776

The Hazards which if not real, my immagination represents so.
>
> To John Adams, January 26, 1777

Could I see my Friend in reality as I often do in immagination I think
I should feel a happiness beyond expression.
>
> To John Adams, July 23, 1777

I . . . rejoice that thought and immagination are not confined like my
person to the small spot on which I exist.
>
> To John Adams, June–July 1779

My Heart sickens at the recollection. O for the wings of a dove that I
might flie away.*
>
> To James Lovell, Braintree, June 23, 1781

*Psalms 55:6.

How gladly would I visit you and partake of your Labours and cares,
sooth you to rest, and alleviate your anxieties were it given me to
visit you even by moon Light, as the faries are fabled to do.
>
> To John Adams, April 10, 1782

[Referring to Shays's Rebellion:] I think I should not feel more anxious if I was in the midst of all the disturbances, than I do at this distance, where imagination is left at full liberty.
>
> To Mary Cranch, London, February 25, 1787

Immagination paints higher than reality, and the danger appre-
hended is always worse than that which is experienced.

To Elizabeth Shaw, London, March 10, 1787

I . . . wish that I could visit you more than in Idea, but at present I do
not see any prospect of the kind.

To Abigail Adams Smith, Braintree, August 6, 1788

The imagination is fruitfull in uncertainty.

To Cotton Tufts, New York, March 7, 1790

Immagination has full scope in the wide feild of conjecture, it moves
from one object to another, fixing sometimes upon one, and sometimes upon another; puzzeld in mazes, and perplexd with errors,
lost and bewilderd in the search.

To William Smith Shaw, Quincy, March 4, 1799

That the fire of imagination should be checked, that the effusions
of genious should be stifled, through want of leisure to display
them, is sometimes the lot of those who seem born to shine in
higher Spheres of Life, the mind which is necessarily imprisoned in
its own little tenement, and the Book of knowledge is closely clasped
against those who must fulfil their daily task of manual labour.

To Elizabeth Peabody, Philadelphia, February 4, 1800

[On women's revealing dresses:] I wishd that more had been left to
the imagination, and less to the Eye.

To Mary Cranch, Philadelphia, April 26, 1800

A strong immagination is said to be a refuge from sorrow, and a
kindly solace for a feeling Heart.

To Mary Cranch, Norfolk, Conn., May 26, 1800

My Imagination frequently visits you, and always finds you occupied.

To Abigail Adams Smith, Quincy, May 8, 1808

To bring home to your remembrance Scenes in which you once delighted, cannot fail in a mind like yours to excite pleasing Sensations.

Memories

To John Quincy Adams, Quincy, March 3, 1797

Why does the mind Love to turn to those painfull scenes and to recollect them with pleasure?

Painful Memories

To John Adams, November 13, 1780

I do not wish to prolong painfull recollections in the minds of others.

To John Quincy Adams, Quincy, October 22, 1813

— *Duty, Honor, Citizenship*

The Honour does not consist so much in the Trust reposed, as in the able, the Honest, the upright and faithfull discharge of it.

Duty

To John Adams, October 8, 1780

I will sacrifice my present feelings and hope for a blessing in persuit of my duty.

To John Adams, February 11, 1784

All that is well intended is not well received. The consciousness of doing our duty is however a support, but the designing Jack daw will sometimes borrow the plumes of the Jay, and pass himself off to those who judge only by appearances.

To Mercy Otis Warren, London, May 24, 1786

I consider myself following where duty leads and trust the Event. . . . Such appears to me the situation in which I am placed, enviable no doubt in the Eyes of some, but never envy'd by me. That I may discharge my part with honour, and give satisfaction is my most earnest wish.

To Mary Cranch, Springfield, Mass., April 30, 1797

When duty calls my own happiness has always been with me, but a secondary consideration.

> To John Quincy Adams, Quincy, November 15, 1798

"No Man liveth for himself."* The Tour of duty falls harder upon some than others and he to whom ten talents is given, must expect if he would receive the precious Reward "of Good and *Faithfull* Servant"** to improve them ten fold. To endure and suffer in a Good cause has been the Lot of the Greatest Law givers, Statesmen, Heroes and Phylosophers, nor is their any Charm or Tallissman, Sheild or defence for similiar Characters even in this age of the world.

> To John Adams, Quincy, December 21, 1798

*Romans 14:7.   **Matthew 25:21.

Altho you must expect that it will raise a Hornet's nest around you, the Consciousness of having uprightly discharged your duty to your country, will serve to shield you from their Sting.

> To John Quincy Adams, Quincy, April 1808

With regard to the path of duty before me, I have not any hesitation.

> To James Monroe, Quincy, April 20, 1813

Eventful Times

These are times in which a Genius would wish to live. It is not in the still calm of life, or the repose of a pacific station, that great characters are formed. Would Cicero have shone so distinguished an orator, if he had not been roused, kindled and enflamed by the Tyranny of Catiline, Millo, Verres and Mark Anthony.

> To John Quincy Adams, January 12, 1780

Leadership

He who as an individual is cruel, unjust and immoral, will not be likely to possess those virtues necessary in a General or Statesman. Yet in our Infant Country, Infidelity and debauchery are so fashionably prevalent that less attention is paid to the characters of those

who fill important offices, wise Legislators of old, are the surest pre-
servatives of publick happiness.

To John Adams, January 28, 1781

Perhaps there has been no juncture in the publick affairs of our
country; not even in the hour of our deepest distress, when able
statesmen and wise Counsellors were more wanted than at the present day. . . . We want a Soloman in wisdom, to guide and conduct
this great people: at this critical era, when the counsels which are
taken, and the measures which are persued, will mark our future
Character either with honour, and Fame, or disgrace and infamy.
In adversity, we have conducted with prudence and magninimity.
Heaven forbid, that we should grow giddy with prosperity, or the
height to which we have soared, render a fall conspicuously fatal.

To John Adams, Braintree, June 20, 1783

There is a position in Machiavel* says a late elegant writer that a
country should sometimes be without order, and over run with all
sorts of calamities, that Men of great Genius may distinguish themselves by restoring it.

To John Adams, July 21, 1783

*Machiavelli, *The Prince,* chapter 26.

No Man is fit to be trusted who is not diffident of himself. Such is
the frailty of humane Nature, & so great a flatterer is Self Love, that
it presents false appearances, & deceives its votaries.

To Mary Cranch, London, July 16, 1787

Any pilot may Navigate in smooth water. He who can conduct a
Ship in a Storm, tho he has harder labour, will feel more Satisfaction
when he reflects, that his Labours have largely contributed to her
Safety.

To William Smith Shaw, Quincy, December 14, 1788

How few of the Sons of Men are qualified for bold decisive action when danger threatens?

To William Smith, Philadelphia, July 7, 1798

When on Board a ship, who feels at ease without a skillfull pilot? If tempests threaten us, we look for judgment, prudence, calmness and intrepidity in the commander.

To Catherine Johnson, Philadelphia, May 9, 1800

A sensible writer observes, that there are certain Epochs in the History of every Country, when the best and brightest Men are overwhelmed by a general combination in favour of stupidity, avarice or faction. In such cases it is vain to look for much patriotism in individuals.

To Eliza Susan Quincy, Quincy, March 24, 1806

It is an observation of a "Statesman that Some periods produce many great Men and few great occasions. On the contrary great occasions and few great Men!" I believe that great occasions will make great Men, all out of tallents which would otherways be dorment. The Revolution in France, the cruelties committed by Robespeare, Marat and many others made a Napolean—a mighty conqueror—a wonderfull Man—to whom History gives us not a parallel raised up, continued, and supported for ends and designs not yet fathomed.

To Catherine Johnson, Quincy, August 18, 1810

Patriotism The proceedings of our Citizens have been United, Spirited and firm. The flame is kindled and like Lightning it catches from Soul to Soul.

To Mercy Otis Warren, Boston, December 5, 1773

A patriot without religion in my estimation is as great a paradox, as an honest Man without the fear of God. Is it possible that he whom no moral obligations bind, can have any real Good Will towards

Man, can he be a patriot who by an openly vicious conduct is undermining the very bonds of Society, corrupting the Morals of Youth, and by his bad example injuring that very Country he professes to patrionize more than he can possibly compensate by his intrepidity, Generosity and honour?

To Mercy Otis Warren, Braintree, c. November 5, 1775

All domestick pleasures and injoyments are absorbed in the great and important duty you owe your Country "for our Country is as it were a secondary God, and the First and greatest parent. It is to be preferred to Parents, Wives, Children, Friends and all things the Gods only excepted. For if our Country perishes it is as impossible to save an Individual, as to preserve one of the fingers of a Mortified Hand."* Thus do I suppress every wish, and silence every Murmur, acquiescing in a painfull Seperation from the companion of my youth, and the Friend of my Heart.

To John Adams, Braintree, May 7, 1776

*James Burgh, *Political Disquisitions* (London, 1774), Vol. II.

Justice, humanity, and benevolence are the duties you owe to society in general. To your country the same duties are incumbent upon you, with the additional obligation of sacrificing ease, pleasure, wealth, and life itself for its defence and security.

To John Quincy Adams, March 20, 1780

I feel a pleasure in being able to sacrifice my selfish passions to the general good, and in imitating the example which has taught me to consider myself and family, but as the small dust of the balance when compaired with the great community.

To John Adams, December 23, 1782

Patriotism and that noble love of your country . . . will teach you to despise wealth, titles, pomp, and equipage, as mere external advantages, which cannot add to the internal excellence of your mind, or compensate for the want of integrity and virtue.

> To John Quincy Adams, Braintree, December 26, 1783

Everything I have yet seen, serves to endear my own Country more and more to me.

> To Cotton Tufts, Auteuil, September 8, 1784

I could not have believed if I had not experienced it, how strong the Love of Country is in the humane mind.

> To Mary Cranch, Auteuil, May 8, 1785

I must congratulate you upon setting your foot again upon American ground. To Say that I love it above all other countries is only imitating the passion common to all Nations, each of which has something to endear it to its Natives, something which he prizes beyond what he can find elsewhere.

> To Abigail Bromfield Rogers, London, July 30, 1786

It is indeed a pleasing presage of future good, when the most promising youth shrink not from danger, through a fondness for those delights which a peaceful, affluent life bestows.

> To Mercy Otis Warren, London, May 14, 1787

The eagerness with which the Youth of Family fortune and Education enter the Navy, and Army, is a Surety for our Country, that the Spirit of the Fathers, live in their Sons.

> To John Quincy Adams, Philadelphia, June 12, 1798

Even every Tree, plant and flower finds an Imperious interest in our bosoms if they are the natives of our own Soil; altho not half so beautifull, or fragrant as those of a foreign Country. This is an instinctive Love of Country. The frozen Laplander, and the burning affrican feel the same partiality.

> To Louisa Catherine Adams, Quincy, May 15, 1810

So long as we are inhabitants of this earth and possess any of our faculties, we cannot be indifferent to the state of our country, our posterity and our friends.

> To Mercy Otis Warren, Quincy, December 30, 1812

Where is the true Native American Spirit? It dwells in the breasts of our uncorrupted orators, in our yeomanry, in our Sailors, and in our few remaining old Patriots.

Where dwells British influence? In our Banks, in our warehouses, in our commerce.

> To John Quincy Adams, Quincy, April 5, 1813

Can it be that the Love of gain like the rod of Aron* has swallowd up all public spirit and Love of Country?

> To John Quincy Adams, Quincy, July 1, 1813

*Exodus 7:12.

I long impatiently to have you upon the Stage of action.   *Public Service*

> To John Adams, Braintree, August 19, 1774

You cannot be, I know, nor do I wish to see you an inactive Spectator.

> To John Adams, Braintree, October 16, 1774

I feard much for your Health when you went away. I must intreat you to be as careful as you can consistant with the Duty you owe your Country.

> To John Adams, Braintree, June 16, 1775

All those who act in publick life have very unthankful offices and

> "will often sigh to find the unwilling Gratitude of base Mankind."*

. . . The post of honour is a private Station. Tis certainly the most comfortable Station. Yet in these days of peril whilst the vessel is in a storm, it would be guilt in an able passenger not to lend his assistance.

To Mercy Otis Warren, Braintree, January ? 1776

*Alexander Pope, *Second Book of Horace.*

He who can retire from a publick Life to a private Station, with a self approveing conscience, unambitious of pomp or power has little to dread from the machinations of envy, the snares of treachery, the Malice of Dissimulation, or the Clandestine stabs of Calumny. In time they will work their own ruin.

To John Adams, February 26, 1780

The firm patriot whose views extend to the welfare of Mankind tho obstructed by faction and vice, tho crossed by fortune, tho wounded by calumny and reproach, shall find in the end that his generous Labour is not lost—even tho he meets with no other reward than that self approving hour, which the poet tells us outweighs whole years of stupid starers and loud Huzzas.*

To John Adams, August 1, 1781

*Alexander Pope, *An Essay on Man,* Epistle IV, line 256.

Why should I indulge an Idea, that whilst the active powers of my Friend remain, they will not be devoted to the Service of his country? Can I believe that the Man who fears neither poverty or dangers, who sees not charms sufficient either in Riches, power or place to tempt him in the least to swerve from the purest Sentiments of Honour and Delicacy; will retire, unnoticed, Fameless to a Rustick cottage there by dint of Labour to earn his Bread. I need not much examination of my Heart to say I would not willingly consent to it.

To John Adams, Braintree, April 10, 1782

Public business . . . must always be done by somebody. —it will be done by somebody or other—If wise men decline it others will not: if honest men refuse it, others will not. A young man should well weigh his plans. Integrity should be preserved in all events, as essential to his happiness, thro every stage of his existence. His first maxim then, should be to place his honor out of the reach of all men: In order to do this he must make it a rule never to become dependant on public employments for subsistence. Let him have a trade, a profession, a farm, a shop, something whereby he can honestly live, and then he may engage in public affairs, if invited, upon independant principles.

To Thomas Boylston Adams, Richmond Hill, September 2, 1789

When we see the intrigues, the Ambition, the Envy, the malice and ingratitude of the World, who would not rather retire and live unnoticed in a country village, than stand the Broad Mark for all those arrows to be shot at placed upon a pinnicle. But I have done. Upon my pillow I shall reflect, fear and tremble, and the President of the United States [i.e., George Washington] may long long continue to hold the Reigns of Government, and that his valuable Life may be prolonged for that purpose.

To John Adams, Quincy, January 21, 1796

I am anxious for the proper discharge of that share [of work] which will devolve upon me. Whether I have patience, prudence, discretion sufficient to fill a Station so unexceptionably as the Worthy Lady who now holds it. I fear I have not. As Second I have had the happiness of steering clear of censure as far as I know. If the contemplation did not make me feel very serious I should say that I have been so used to a freedom of sentiment that I know not how to plane so many guards about me, as will be indispensable, to look at every word before I utter it, and to impose a silence upon myself, when I long to talk.

To John Adams, Quincy, February 20, 1796

No Man even if sixty Years of Age ought to have more than three Months at a Time from his Family, and our Country is a very hard hearted tyrannical niggardly Country. It has committed more Robberies upon me, and obliged me to more sacrifices than any other woman in the Country and this I will maintain against any one who will venture to come forward and dispute it with me. As there never can be a compensation for me, I must sit down with this consolation that it might have been worse.

To John Adams, Quincy, March 2, 1796

Military Services make a greater eclat in the World [than civil service].

To John Quincy Adams, July 11, 1796

I have been so long a witness to the scenes which have been acted for years past, and know too well what must be endured, to have any other sensations, when I look to an elevated seat, than painful solicitude and anxiety. It is a mark at which envy, pride and malevolence will shoot their envenomed arrows. Joy dwells in these dear silent shades at Quincy; and domestic pleasures, in peace and tranquility.

To Thomas Boylston Adams, Quincy, November 8, 1796

As to a Crown my dear Madam I will not deny, that there is one which I aspire after, and in a Country where envy can never enter to plant thorns beneath it. The fashion of this world passeth away. I would hope that I have not lived in vain, but have learnt how and what value to place upon the fleeting and transitory enjoyments of it. I shall esteem myself peculiarly fortunate, if at the close of my publick Life, I can retire, esteemed, beloved and equally respected with my predecessor.

To Mercy Otis Warren, Quincy, February 28, 1797

Publick service becomes urksome to all men of talents and to men in Years who are worn out by continual opposition and by constant exertions to support order, Harmony and peace against ambition, disorder and anarchy.

To Elizabeth Peabody, Philadelphia, February 13, 1798

The Service of this Government is not a Bed of Roses, in any department of it.

> To Catherine Johnson, Philadelphia, March 2, 1798

The publick service of our Country my dear Madam, is a service of Labour, but not of profit, as my best Friend has for 35 years experienced, and every other Gentleman who has been engaged in it, and done his duty.

> To Catherine Johnson, Philadelphia, June 9, 1798

I early learnd the lesson of sacrificing to the publick.

> To John Quincy Adams, Quincy, December 2, 1798

To lose the talents of a Man well fitted for the Station merely through a mistaken parsimony, is not giving an equal chance to merit. It is creating an aristocracy of Wealth, for if no man can be Governour, but such as can afford it, Wealth and not merit will be sought for.

> To William Smith, Philadelphia, February 5, 1800

If my future peace & tranquility were all that I considered, a release from public life would be the most desirable event of it—I feel perfectly tranquil upon the subject, hoping and trusting that, the Being in whose Hands are the Hearts of all Men, will guide and direct our national counsels for the peace & prosperity of this great people.

> To Mary Cranch, Columbia City of Washington, November 21, 1800

I have seen and known that much of the conduct of a public ruler, is liable to be misunderstood and misrepresented.

> To Thomas Jefferson, Quincy, August 18, 1804

There are Situations and circumstances in which a Country may be placed, when it becomes the duty of a good citizen to hazard, not only property, but even his Life, to Serve and save it.

> To James Madison, Quincy, August 1, 1810

I wish Congress could be convinced, unawed by constituents, that parsimony to their public officers is neither wise, just or prudent. In the Eyes of foreign Nations, it is contemptable—as well as in those of our own Countrymen who know our means and what is expected from those in high places. . . . Those who devote their time and talents to the public Service ought not to want Bread for their children—be destitute of the means of giving them an Education—and in their old Age, have nothing to leave them. Professional Men, who in private Life would have been much better provided for, but why do I scrible to you but that I know you are & will be one of the sufferers.

To Richard Rush, Quincy, April 24, 1816

From experience I know how to estimate popular favour & while the volumes of History are open before me, I am not so dazzled by the brightness or glare of high Station as to forget, that a "Breath can Create, and a Breath destroy." When called to fill an important office, an approving conscience is its best Reward, one hour of which, says Pope, "whole years out weighs" "of Stupid Starers, and of loud Huzzas."*

To John Quincy Adams, Quincy, April 13, 1817

*Alexander Pope, *An Essay on Man,* Epistle IV, line 256.

There is not one of all the presidents who have held that office; "and Strutted their Hour upon the Stage,"* who have not carried poverty home with them. Subjected by the Station they have held to Company from all quarters—and expences from which as private Gentlemen they would not be exposed. I speak feelingly—and let the American Republic Blush.

It is true "that I want but little here below

*Nor Shall want that little long."***

But I Should have been happy to have left to my Family an Independence, which the long and unremitted Service of the Head of it, intitled him to.

The Blessings and prosperity which have coverd the Nation, are the fruits which we can taste, with the consciousness that they have ripened, and grown to maturity in our day. May the succeeding generation prove worthy of them.

To Louisa Catherine Adams, Quincy, February 1, 1818

*Shakespeare, *Macbeth*, V:5.   **Oliver Goldsmith, *The Vicar of Wakefield* (1766).

Let not the popular torrent, which at present sets against your worthy partner, distress you. Time will convince the world who are their approved and unshaken friends, whatever mistaken judgments they at present form. . . . The consciousness of doing our duty is, however, a support; but the designing jackdaw will sometimes borrow the plumes of the jay, and pass himself off to those who judge only by appearances.

To Mercy Otis Warren, London, May 24, 1786

Public Approbation

How happy should I esteem myself could the dear Friend of my Heart join us. I think I make a greater Sacrifice to the publick than I could by Gold and Silver, had I it to bestow.

To Mercy Otis Warren, Braintree, November 1775

Sacrifice

Tis no small Satisfaction to me that my country is like to profit so largely by my sacrifices.

To John Adams, October 8, 1782

I feel a pleasure in being able to sacrifice my selfish passions to the general good, and in imitating the example which has taught me to consider myself and family, but as the small dust of the balance when compaired with the great community.

To John Adams, December 23, 1782

— *Economics*

Banks   Pernicious Banks will undoe us.

To John Adams, Quincy, December 29, 1792

That multiplied Banks are productive of many of those evil consequences which he enumerates I both see and feel, that many persons are making fortunes from them I believe, that they are an indirect tax upon the community, I fully credit.

To John Adams, Quincy, February 2, 1794

Our Country flourishes beyond any former period. Cannals, Bridges, Roads, and Buildings are daily increasing and improving. There is one evil which calls loudly for a remedy. I mean the multiplicity of Banks, which opperate very injuriously by raising the price of the necessaries of Life, which affects the most defenceless part of the Community, the Clergy, the widow and the orphan. The Day Labourer does not feel it so much as he rises in proportion in his Labour: but whatever oppresses any part of the community is an Evil.

To Thomas Boylston Adams, Quincy, March 10, 1796

Credit   If one has a little credit and reputation we hate to part with it.

To Elizabeth Shaw, London, July 29, 1784

The less credit we can obtain the better it will in the end prove for our Countrymen.

To Thomas Welsh, London, July 22, 1786

Debt   No person thinks of paying any thing, and I do not chuse to run in debt. I endeavour to live in the most frugal manner possible, but I am many times distressed.

To John Adams, Braintree, July 16, 1775

I mean that I might always have it in my power, to answer the first demand of a Creditor, a Dun was always my abhorance; nor will I ever involve my partner if oeconomy and frugality will prevent it.

To John Thaxter, April 9, 1778

Debts are my abhorrance. I never will borrow if any other method can be devised.

To John Adams, Braintree, c. July 15, 1778

I do not dread want, but I dread debt, and for that reason I would contract no debt which I do not see a way clear to pay.

To Thomas Boylston Adams, Quincy, April 26, 1803

When a man gets embarrassed in his circumstances he seems to lose all moral feelings.

To Thomas Boylston Adams, Quincy, January 23, 1799

Financial Embarrassments

When a Man gets embarrassed in his circumstances it seems to stiffel all Moral feelings, and he permits himself to do things which he would have started at, if he had been thought capable of them.

To John Quincy Adams, Quincy, February 1, 1799

You and I, who know what value to place upon a durable and lasting attachment, know also, that without it, a palace would be dreary, and the most luxurious living tasteless and insipid—yet Man cannot live upon that alone, nor woman either. There must be Solid food, and we must look beyond the present moment and calculate for futurity. We have some Family warnings which ought to show the folly nay the cruelty, of entering into engagements without the means of support.

To Susanna B. Adams, Quincy, April 12, 1817

Financial Well-Being

I endeavour to live with as great frugality as possible.

To John Adams, June 1, 1777

Frugality

Frugality and oeconomy are, or ought to be considerd as virtues.

To Isaac Smith, Sr., Auteuil, May 8, 1785

It is no disadvantage to young people to be obliged to innure themselves at first setting out in Life to habits of frugality, and industery. On the contrary I believe it usefull. It is much more pleasing to rise gradually than to descend from the Summit of wealth and ease, to penury and want. It is desirable however to be able with an equal mind to bear the reverses of fortune which all are subject to.

To Catherine Johnson, Philadelphia, July 14, 1798

Inflation   Every thing bears a very great price. The Merchant complains of the Farmer and the Farmer of the Merchant. Both are extravagant. Living is double what it was one year ago.

To John Adams, Braintree, June 3, 1776

Every thing Here is extravagantly high, but more tolerable than with you. A Dollar now is not eaquel to what one Quarter was two years ago, and there is no sort of property which is not held in higher estimation than money.

To John Adams, June 1, 1777

It cost me as much to live one month as it used to in a year.

To John Thaxter, Braintree, September 29, 1778

Family expences in the course of 3 months have brought me some in debt, every article having risen instead of falling.

To John Adams, Quincy, March 23, 1797

Interest on Debt   Interest is a canker worm which will knaw to the vitals.

To John Thaxter, Auteuil, March 20, 1785

Investments   I do not know of any person's property so unproductive as ours is. I do not believe that it yealds us one pr cent pr Annum. . . . I never desired so much Land unless we could have lived upon it. The money paid for useless land I would have purchased publick securities with. The interest of which, poorly as it is funded, would have been less troublesome to take charge of than Land and much more productive. But in these Ideas I have always been so unfortunate as to differ from my partner, who thinks he never saved any thing but what he vested in Land.

To Mary Cranch, New York, October 10, 1790

As I know what money you have must be saved by a rigid oeconomy, I wish you might have it placed in safe and productive funds.

To John Quincy Adams, East Chester, N.Y., November 3, 1797

I wish he [i.e., John Adams] did not Love Land so well because I know we have enough to torment us. When we come to look to that for support, we shall find it difficult enough to procure it and very much swallowed up by taxes and Labour. I am for having as little trouble as possible. As we pass down the vale of years we shall want repose if we live.

To Cotton Tufts, Philadelphia, May 23, 1798

The circumspect use of money, arising, not from any avaricious principle, but from the wise practise of applying means to ends, will keep a man in that state of independence which is the Rock of Life. On that foundation he can stand firm, return the haughty look, smile at the supercilious frown, give truth its due force, and scorn the embroidered lie.

To Thomas Boylston Adams, Quincy, May 16, 1801

I cannot avoid sometimes repineing that the gifts of fortune were not bestowed upon us, that I might have enjoyed the happiness of spending my days with my Partner. But as it is, I think it my duty to attend with frugality and oeconomy to our own private affairs, and if I cannot add to our Little Substance yet see that it is not dimin-

Living within One's Means

ished. I should enjoy but little comfort in a state of Idleness and use-lessness. Here I can serve my partner, my family and myself, and in-joy the Satisfaction of your serving your Country.

To John Adams, Braintree, June 3, 1776

You know my situation, and that a rigid oeconomy is necessary for me to preserve that independancy which has always been my ambi-tion.

To John Thaxter, April 9, 1778

Without fortune it is more than probable we shall end our days.

To John Adams, April 10, 1782

I am sure you will suppose that we live very differently from what we really do, when I assure you that I am obliged to Economize not to be in debt at the close of every Month.

To Cotton Tufts, Auteuil, March 8, 1785

I know your Prudence & oeconomy has carried you along, tho not in affluence, yet with decency & comfort, and I hope you will still be able to live so.

To Mary Cranch, Richmond Hill, July 12, 1789

Bringing our minds to our circumstances is a duty encumbent upon us.

To Mary Cranch, Richmond Hill, September 1, 1789

I hate to complain. No one is without their difficulties, whether in High, or low Life, & every person knows best where their own shoe pinches—

To Mary Cranch, New York, March 21, 1790

It will be sometime before we can ourselves credit how near we must calculate, to preserve that independance which I always hope to maintain by living within our income.

To Cotton Tufts, Washington, December 15, 1800

I have not a regreet at quiting my station personally. I believe it best both for your Father and for me. As to our prospects that is another subject. We have not made a fortune in the service of the public, that the world knows. We will live in independance, because we will live within our income. If that is mean and much below the rank we ought to move in, the fault is not ours. The Country which calld into Service an active, able and meritorious citizen, placed him in various conspicuous and elevated situations, without the power or means of saving for himself or family what his professional business would have enabled him to have done, at advanced years can dismiss him to retirement (and poverty in the world's sense). That Country must bear the disgrace, which it will do with as much indifference and apathy, as the cold Massaleum can feel which that Country is raising to commemorate the virtues, the Services and *sacrifices* of really a great and good man.*

> To Thomas Boylston Adams, Washington, January 15, 1801

*Congress planned to build a masoleum in the Capitol for George Washington.

The President retains his Health, and his Spirits beyond what you could imagine; he has the consciousness of having served his Country with pure intentions; with upright views and from the most disinterested motives, as his own pecuniary affairs manifest, tho free from debts, or embarrassments of that nature. His income will oblige us to a strickt oeconomy, in order to preserve that independance upon which our future tranquility rests.

> To John Quincy Adams, Washington, January 29, 1801

After near fifty years devoted to public Service, a rigid oeconomy is necessary for us to preserve that independence; which asks no favours; and Solicits no recompence.

> To James Madison, Quincy, August 1, 1810

I must renew my means before I multiply wants.

> To Harriet Welsh, Quincy, March 5, 1815

Labour with my hands, I have never declined, and although I was reduced to earn my Bread, I could submit to it, but to Beg—I am ashamed.

> To Louisa Catherine Adams, Quincy, December 12, 1817

Luxuries   Wherever luxury abounds, there you will find corruption and degeneracy of manners. Wretches that we are, thus to misuse the bounties of Providence, to forget the hand that blesses us, and even deny the source from whence we derived our being.

> To Lucy Cranch, London, April 2, 1786

When a people become Luxurious, is there anything that will reclaim them but dire necessity?

> To Thomas Welsh, London, July 22, 1786

Luxury, dissipation and vice, have a natural tendency to extirpate every generous principle, and leave the Heart susceptable of the most malignant vices, to the total absence of principle.

> To Mercy Otis Warren, London, May 14, 1787

Success crowned our efforts and gave us Independence. Our misfortune is that there we became indolent and intoxicated; Luxury with ten thousand evils in her train, exiled the humble virtues, Industry and frugality, were swallowed up in dissipation.

> To Mercy Otis Warren, London, May 14, 1787

Manufactures   Every manufactor which will render us less dependent, is a valuable acquisition.

> To Abigail Adams Smith, Quincy, May 8, 1808

Material Things   By how many instances are we taught, not to place our affections too firmly upon earthly objects.

> To Elizabeth Shaw, Auteuil, January 11, 1785

Monopoly   A monopoly of any kind is always envidious.

> To Mary Cranch, London, April 28, 1787

I am anxious for your welfare,* and Solicitious for your success in
Business. You must expect however to advance slowly at first and
must call to your aid Patience and perseverence, keeping in mind the
observation of that great Master of Life and manners who has said,
"that there is a tide in the affairs of Men."** It must be some dire
misfortune or calamity, if I judge not amiss, that will ever place you
in the shallows.

*Occupational
Success*

> To John Quincy Adams, New York, July 11, 1790

*JQA was just beginning his law practice.   **Shakespeare, *Julius Caesar*,
IV:3.

A Young man who depends upon a profession for support, must
stick close to it, for if he quits that, that will quit him.

> To Harriet Welsh, Quincy, June 6, 1815

Business once lost, does not easily return to the old hands.

> To Harriet Welsh, Quincy, June 6, 1815

A Young Gentleman at his time of Life, ought to be establishing
himself in some profession, whereby he may serve himself and his
generation.

Occupations

> To Elizabeth Storer Smith, London, August 29, 1785

I had rather a son of mine should follow any mechanical trade whatever than be a gentleman at large without any occupation.

> To Mary Cranch, Jamaica, Long Island, December 18, 1788

I always wish every gentleman to have a profession whatever may be
his fortune. If he does not practice, it will qualify him for civil employments and render him more respectable amongst men of Letters.

> To Harriet Welsh, Quincy, December 8, 1814

Cautious as tis necessary you should be, methinks you need not be
so parsimonious.

Parsimony

> To John Adams, Braintree, c. July 15, 1778

While on the one hand, I would not recommend parsimony on the other I would avoid extravagance; for you will only excite envy—
To Louisa Catherine Adams, Quincy, February 20, 1818

Prosperity   To the blessings of Peace, we have, that of plenty added. The Earth yealds in abundance, Ceres* flourishes with her sheaves and her cornicopia. Pomona** cannot boast of being so richly laiden.
To John Adams, August 24, 1783

*Roman goddess of grain.   **Roman goddess of fruit.

Prosperity and success is more dangerous than adversity.
To John Quincy Adams, Quincy, December 7, 1804

Speculation   I most sincerely wish a stop could be put to the Rage of speculation, yet I think it is an Evil that will cure itself in Time.
To Mary Cranch, Philadelphia, March 29, 1792

There will be Speculators whilst there is Commerce.
To John Adams, Quincy, May 23, 1794

Such is the folly and madness of speculation and extravagance.
To Mary Cranch, Philadelphia, May 16, 1797

Speculation in Property, in politicks and in Religion have gone very far in depraving the morals of the higher classes of the people of our Country.
To Mary Cranch, Philadelphia, May 24, 1797

What a Besom* of destruction is this Spirit of Speculation?
To Mary Cranch, Philadelphia, May 7, 1798

*Broom.

Stocks   Tho Stocks have fallen, I would not advise to selling out; nay if I had money to spair, I would vest it in them. I think they will rise again.
To Thomas Boylston Adams, Washington, January 3, 1801

Wealth, Wealth is the only thing that is looked after now.
> To Hannah Lincoln, Weymouth, October 5, 1761

Riches always create Luxery, and Luxery always leads to Idleness, Indolence and effeminacy which stiffels every noble purpose, and withers the blossom of genious which fall useless to the ground, unproductive of fruit.
> To John Quincy Adams, London, March 20, 1786

But such are the vissitudes of Life and the Transitory fleeting state of all sublinary things; of all pride that which persons discover from Riches is the weakest. If we look over our acquaintance, how many do we find who were a few years ago in affluence, now reduced to real want.
> To Mary Cranch, Richmond Hill, February 20, 1790

Better is a little contentment than great Treasure; and trouble therewith.
> To Mary Cranch, Richmond Hill, February 20, 1790

"Make not haste to be rich"* is a maxim of Sound policy tho contrary to the Sentiments of Mankind, yet I have ever observed that wealth suddenly acquired is seldom balanced with discretion, but is as suddenly dissipated, and as happiness is by no means in proportion to Wealth, it ought to make us content even tho we do not attain to any great degree of it but to quit moralizing.
> To John Quincy Adams, New York, July 11, 1790

*Proverbs 28:20: A faithful man shall abound with blessings, but that maketh haste to be rich shall not be innocent.

Pride and insolence too often accompany wealth and very little happiness is to be expected from sordid souls of earthly mould.*
> To John Quincy Adams, Richmond Hill, August 20, 1790

*Isaac Watts, "Few Happy Matches," line 13.

Many of my particular acquaintance whose affluence was great & well founded when I lived here, and even when I past through last winter, are now in Ruinous circumstances, thousands worse than nothing. Such is the wheel of fortune.

To Mary Cranch, New York, April 29, 1792

I have no contempt of Riches. They are tallents which are given to the possessor to be used for the benefit of individuals, and upon which allso the community have claims, and when so improved, become blessings, but they are generally attended with so many allurements to Luxury and dissipation, that food and raiment, with a competence to the Situation in which we are placed in Life, is more desirable than great wealth, in which there must be great trouble.

To Hannah Cushing, Philadelphia, April 1800

By no means think wealth an absolute ingredient in the composition of happiness. I cannot believe it attainable destitute of a competence.

To My Dear Young Friend, Quincy, c. 1812

Too much consequence is not [to be] given to wealth, to swell and look down contemptuously upon those who are less fortunate.

To Elizabeth Peabody, Quincy, November 20, 1814

— Education

Education alone I conceive Constitutes the difference in Manners.

To John Adams, Braintree, April 20, 1771

That knowledge which is obtain in early Life becomes every day more usefull, as it is commonly that which is best retaind.

To Elizabeth Shaw, Auteuil, January 11, 1785

The idea that their success in life depends upon their diligence and application to their studies, and a modest and virtuous deportment, cannot be too strongly impressed upon their minds. The foolish idea in which some of our youth are educated, of being born gentlemen, is the most ridiculous in the world for a country like ours. It is the mind and manners which make the gentleman, and not the estate.

> To Mary Cranch, London, May 21, 1786

We are daily more and more confirmed in the opinion, that the early period of every American's Education, during which the mind receives the most lasting impressions; ought to be in his own Country, where he may acquire an inherent Love of Liberty and a thorough acquaintance with the Manners and taste of the Society and country of which he is a Member.

> To Elizabeth Shaw, London, October 15, 1786

It is a maxim here, that he who dies with studying dies in a good cause, and may go to another world much better calculated to improve his talents, than if he had died a blockhead. Well, knowledge is a fine thing, and mother Eve thought so; but she smarted so severely for hers, that most of her daughters have been afraid of it since.

> To Elizabeth Shaw, Bush Hill, March 20, 1791

One great mistake in the education of youth is gratifying every wish of their hearts. Children should know how to suffer want. They are little capable of knowing how to abound. Their enjoyments are much lessened by it.

> To Abigail Adams Smith, Quincy, August 14, 1795

Education and example may do allmost any thing.

> To Mary Cranch, Philadelphia, April 26, 1800

The more we cultivated and improved our intellectual powers, the more capable we should be of enjoyment in a higher and more perfect state of existence; the nearer we should be allied to angels, and the spirits of just men made perfect.

To Caroline Smith, Quincy, January 24, 1808

Dangers of College I have a thousand fears for my dear Boys as they rise into Life, the most critical period of which is I conceive, at the university; there infidelity abounds, both in example and precepts. There they imbibe the speicious arguments of a Voltaire, a Hume and Mandevill. If not from the fountain, they receive them at second hand. These are well calculated to intice a youth, not yet capable of investigating their principals, or answering their arguments. Thus is a youth puzzeld in Mazes and perplexed with error untill he is led to doubt, and from doubting to disbelief. Christianity gives not such a pleasing latitude to the passions. It is too pure. It teaches moderation, humility and patience, which are incompatible with the high Glow of Health, and the warm blood which riots in their veins. With them, "to enjoy, is to obey."* I hope before either of our children are prepaired for colledge you will be able to return and assist by your example and advice, to direct and counsel them; that with undeviating feet they may keep the path of virtue.

To John Adams, Braintree, November 11, 1783

*Psalms 119:16.

Education in New England One only visit have I made, and that to my sister in New Hampshire. I fulfilld two duties, that of visiting a very dear Sister, which I had not done before, since her residence and marriage in that State, and placing my two Grandsons at an accademy there, and in her Family and under her inspection, that they may receive a Genuine New England education which I am Yankey enough to prefer to any other I have yet seen.

To Mercy Otis Warren, Quincy, October 1, 1797

Knowledge Learning is not attained by chance, it must be sought for with ardour and attended to with diligence.

To John Quincy Adams, May 8, 1780

If you have made some small attainments in knowledge, yet when you look forward to the immense sum; of which you are still Ignorant, you will find your own, but as a grain of sand, a drop, to the ocean.

To Charles Adams, May 26, 1781

I am glad to see your mind so much engaged in the pursuit of knowledge. It is a young Man's best security against temptation and dissipation.

To John Adams Smith, Quincy, 1808

It is knowledge that inspires caution, as ignorance begets rashness.

To John Adams Smith, Quincy, after February 11, 1810

You have had a long vacation. I hope it has not all been Spent in amusement and dissipation. You know I used to wish you back to your School when the vacation was only a fortnight. You sometimes used to think hard of it. You will not think so, when you know the value of Time, and the brevity of Life. From ten to 50, which is the period best suited for improvement and for retaining what is acquired, is but a short space to obtain knowledge, in any of the Arts, Sciences, Languages or Literature. Of these forty years—contemplate, as you are a good arithematician, how much of it, must be absorbed in Sleep, in Nourishment of the Body, and necessary relocation—then say what proportion remains for close application?

To John Adams 2nd, Quincy, October 24, 1816

I hold it as a maxim; that the mind is acquiring knowledge through Life.

To Louisa Catherine Adams, Quincy, April 15, 1818

I hope to make the journey usefull to me by further observations.

To John Adams, Hartford, November 16, 1788

Learning by Observation

— Family and Home

Abodes

Could I, you ask, return to my (Rustick) cottage, and view it with the same pleasure and Satisfaction I once enjoy'd in it? I answer I think I could, provided I have the same kind Friends and dear Relatives to enhance its value to me. It is not the superb and magnificent House nor the rich and Costly furniture that can ensure either pleasure or happiness to the possessor. A convenient abode Suteable to the station of the possessor, is no doubt desirable, and to those who can afford them, Parks, Gardens, or what in this Country is call'd an ornamented Farm, appears to me an Innocent and desirable object. They are Beautifull to the Eye, pleasing to the fancy, and improving to the Imagination.

To Elizabeth Cranch, London, July 18, 1786

Our publick buildings should be of stone, and as magnificent as the Age and State of our Country will countenance. Private buildings moderate should be in their Size, convenient in their arrangement, and proportioned to the State and ability of the owner. I think our Citizens have in several instances surpassed the bounds, of oeconomy and discretion in building too expensely. Old Hudibras had a right Idea of the Subject when he said,

> Who Builds a House
> And wants where with to pay
> Provides a home, from which to run away.*

To Hannah Storer, Philadelphia, March 21, 1798

*Samuel Butler, Hudibras.

Childbearing

I believe Philadelphia is an unfertile soil, or it would not produce so many unfruitfull women. I always conceive of these persons as wanting one addition to their happiness, but in these perilous times I know not whether it ought to be considerd as an infelicity, since they are certainly freed, from the anxiety every parent must feel for their rising offspring.

> To John Adams, Braintree, December 10. 1775

I wish the day passt, yet dread its arrival.

> To John Adams, June 23, 1777

I was last night taken with a shaking fit, and am very apprehensive that a life was lost.

> To John Adams, July 9, 1777

Slow, lingering and troublesome is the present situation.

> To John Adams, July 10, 1777

I hope you are not in the increasing way, as I think your Health ill able to bear it. We have none of us nursing constitutions—twice my life was nearly sacrificed to it.

> To Elizabeth Shaw, Braintree, February–March 1782

I have been much engaged in assisting Mrs. Smith. I wish for a sister as the time draws near. I shall find myself of little use. She seems to have good Spirits and knowing nothing fears nothing.

> To Mary Cranch, London, February 25, 1787

Mrs. Norton is getting Health & strength I hope fast. I pray she may not have children as fast as Mrs. Smith. It is enough to wear out an Iron constitution.

> To Mary Cranch, Richmond Hill, June 27, 1790

[On Mrs. Cranch, Abigail's niece:] She, poor thing, has had a mishap [i.e., a miscarriage]. I rather think it good than ill luck however, for it is Slavery to have children as fast as she has. She has recovered tho she is thin & weak.

> To Mary Cranch, Philadelphia, April 7, 1800

Your Brother has not been out this fortnight. He is waiting Madam's confinement which is daily expected. He looks as anxious as tho he had the trouble himself to pass through. She is very well for so feeble a Body as she is.

To Thomas Boylston Adams, Quincy, June 20, 1803

The circumstances attendent upon a child bed death have ever appeared to me one of the most awful dispensations of providence.

To Catherine Johnson, Quincy, January 19, 1811

Abbe Johnson was deliverd of a son upon the 3rd of this Month. . . . Mother and Babe well. . . . The Mother was Seventeen Years of Age! Too young to be a Mother, tho Solid as 25—

To Louisa Catherine Adams, Quincy, October 13, 1815

Child Rearing   I have always thought it of very great importance that children should in the early part of life be unaccustomed to such examples as would tend to corrupt the purity of their words and actions that they may chill with horrour at the sound of an oath, and blush with indignation at an obscene expression. These first principals which grow with their growth and strengthen with their strength neither time nor custom can totally eradicate.

To John Adams, Braintree, September 16, 1774

Habits early fixed, and daily inculcated, will I hope render them usefull and ornamental Members of Society.

To John Adams, April 10, 1782

Your Children have a demand upon You, they want [i.e., need] your care, your advice and instruction.

To John Adams, October 19, 1783

No humane foresight can effectually preserve them from the contagion of vice; true, but I have a great opinion of early impressions of virtue, and believe that they take such hold of the mind, as neither time, or temptations can wholy subdue. . . .

I have hitherto been able to obtain their Love, their confidence and obedience, but I feel unequal to the task of guiding them alone, encompassed as I know they must be with a thousand snares and temptations.

To John Adams, Braintree, November 11, 1783

The equanimity of your disposition will lead you to a patient submission to the allotments of Providence. The education of your children will occupy much of your time, and you will always keep in mind the great importance of first principles, and the necessity of instilling the precepts of morality very early into their minds. Youth is so imitative, that it catches at every thing. I have a great opinion of Dr. Watts's "Moral Songs for Children."* They are adapted to their capacities, and they comprehend all the social and relative duties of life. They impress the young mind with the ideas of the Supreme Being, as their creator, benefactor, and preserver. They teach brotherly love, sisterly affection, and filial respect and reverence. I do not know any book so well calculated for the early period of life; and they may be made as pleasant to them, by the method of instructing, as a hundred little stories, which are taught them, containing neither a rule of life, nor sentiment worth retaining, such as little John will now run over, or "Jack and Jill," and "Little Jack Horner." As a trial of their memory, and a practice for their tongues, these may be useful, but no other way.

To Abigail Adams Smith, Philadelphia, February 21, 1791

*Isaac Watts's *Divine and Moral Songs for Children,* published in numerous editions since 1715, most recently in the United States in 1788.

As to the other little Gentleman whom you, and Mrs. Adams describe as very fractious, time may cure that tendency to irritability, but it requires much care and attention to rear such a child or his temper may be spoiled for Life.

To John Quincy Adams, Quincy, December 30, 1804

It is an observation of a judicious writer, that if we expect Boys should make valuable Men, they must continue, some time, in the State of Boys, or they will never make men worth forming. It is further said, that against learning, against talents of any kind, nothing can Steady the head, unless the heart is fortified with real Christianity. In raising the Moral Edifice, we must sink deep in proportion as we build high. Great thoughts make great minds.

To John Quincy Adams, Quincy, May 20, 1815

An active Spirit requires a Rein.

To Louisa Catherine Adams, Quincy, December 12, 1817

Children Nabby, Johnny, Charly, Tommy all send duty. Tom says I wish I could see *par.* You would laugh to see them all run upon the sight of a Letter—like chickens for a crum, when the Hen clucks.

To John Adams, Braintree, June 25, 1775

How anxious the Heart of a parent who looks round upon a family of young and helpless children and thinks of leaving them to a World full of snares and temptations which they have neither discretion to foresee, nor prudence to avoid.

To John Adams, Braintree, April 17, 1777

[On her two sons John Quincy and Charles, who were on their way to Europe with their father:] My dear sons I can not think of them without a tear, little do they know the feelings of a Mother's Heart!

To John Adams, November 14, 1779

May they be their Father's comfort and their Mother's delight.

To John Adams, August 1, 1781

What is it that affectionate parents require of their Children for all their care, anxiety, and toil on their accounts? Only that they would be wise and virtuous, Benevolent and kind.

To John Quincy Adams, November 20, 1783

You and I Love to praise our children and why when deserving
should we not?

> To Mercy Otis Warren, Auteuil, May 10, 1785

How little do Children know the solicitude and anxiety of a Parent's
Heart, or how tenderly their conduct affects them.

> To Mary Cranch, London, September 11, 1785

Can Life afford a higher satisfaction to a Parent than that of seeing
their Children persuing the paths of virtue and rectitude? It is a pleasure which the Almighty himself enjoied, when he lookd upon the
Works which his hands had formed and pronounced that all was
Good.*

> To Mary Cranch, London, January 10, 1786

*Genesis 1.

I will not say that all my Geese are swan. I hope however that I have
no occasion to Blush for the conduct of any of my Children. Perhaps
I build more expectation upon the rising Fame and Reputation of
one of them, than of another, but where much is given, much shall
be required.* I know their virtues and I am not blind to their failings.
Let him who is without cast the first stone.**

> To John Adams, Quincy, May 27, 1794

*Luke 12:48.   **John 8:7.

You know how good and how sweet it is to receive good tidings
from a far Country, but you do not know the lively sensations, or the
glow of pleasure which a parent feels at hearing from a Dear and
long absent child.

> To Thomas Boylston Adams, Quincy, March 10, 1796

I think we have great cause of pleasure and satisfaction in our Children. I hope you feel very proud of them; I do I assure you.

> To John Adams, Quincy, March 28, 1796

This is the Anniversary of that day when as the poet expresses it,

"To me a Son was given
*Such as in fondness, parents ask of Heaven."**

To John Quincy Adams, July 11, 1796
The Odyssey of Homer, translated by Alexander Pope, book 18.

I do not consider G. W. [George Washington] at all a happier Man because he has not Children. If he has none to give him pain, he has none to give him pleasure, and he has other Sources of anxiety, in full proportion.

To John Adams, Quincy, January 12, 1799

[On children reunited with parents:] I Received yours of the 16th on Wedensday, and participated in the Joy and pleasure you must have experienced in meeting a dear and amiable son after a four years seperation. How happy should I have been to have folded him at the same time to my Bosom, and felt a pleasure which the Childless can never experience. I have already written both to you, and to him, respecting his comeing to Quincy. I know so well your lonely Situation, and your need of some Solace, from the weight and cares of your office, that I can restrain my impatience to see him; whilst I know he is affording comfort to you.

To John Adams, Quincy, January 25, 1799

There can be no higher enjoyment to a parent than to see their Children deserving, and prosperous, beloved and honourd.

To Thomas Boylston Adams, Quincy, August 4, 1799

To be so far distant and know that a dear child is ill, and that we cannot render any aid to them is painfull in the extrem.

To Mary Cranch, Philadelphia, April 24, 1800

We have been a scatterd family. If some of my Children could now be collected round the parent Hive it appears to me, that it would add much to the happiness of our declining Years.

> To John Quincy Adams, Washington, January 29, 1801

They are so grown, that they will make you feel old.

> To Louisa Catherine Adams, Quincy, October 24, 1813

The eyes of the world are always placed upon those whose situation may possibly subject them to censure, and even the friendly attentions of one's acquaintance are liable to be misconstrued, so that a lady cannot possibly be too circumspect.

> To Abigail Adams Smith, Philadelphia, January 8, 1791

Children of Celebrities

We neither wish on the one hand to be lavish nor on the other Parsimonious. . . . I know it is critical and too much is apt to do more harm than too little.

> To Mary Cranch, London, October 12, 1786

Children's Allowance

I am happy in a daughter who is both a companion and an assistant in my Family affairs and who I think has a prudence and steadiness beyond her years.

> To John Adams, June 8, 1777

Daughters

However kind sons may be disposed to be, they cannot be daughters to a Mother.

> To John Adams, February 11, 1784

Into the Bosom of a Mother, a daughter may repose her confidence.

> To Harriet Welsh, Quincy, March 18, 1815

I know not how to think of their [Charlie and Tommy Adams] leaving Home. I could not live in the House were it so deserted. If they are gone only for a day, it is as silent as a Tomb.

> To John Adams, July 17, 1782

The Empty Nest

Family   I cannot omit any opportunity which presents of telling you what I know always makes you happy—that I am well, that our children are so, and the rest of our Friends. Uninteresting as this is to the rest of the World, it is sweet musick to those who love and are beloved. I know nothing which could make me happier than such an assurance from you which I daily hope and pray for.

To John Adams, December 30, 1782

I cannot be unhappy surrounded by my own family. Without it no country would be pleasing.

To Elizabeth Cranch, London, August 1, 1784

This day, two months ago, we removed here, where I should be much delighted, if I could have my Sisters, my Cousins and connections round me; but for want of them every Country I reside in, lacks a principal ingredient in the composition of my happiness.

To Elizabeth Cranch, London, September 2, 1785

What are common Schools compared to a family where Manners and Morals are equally an object of attention, where Love, and not Morossness is the Preceptor.

To Elizabeth Shaw, London, October 15, 1786

A Father's House is still the most desirable place.

To Mary Cranch, Philadelphia, January 9, 1791

A family harmony would make so essential a part of my happiness that I could never enjoy myself without it.

To Abigail Adams Smith, Quincy, August 14, 1795

It has always been a subject of regreet to me that my Family have always been seperated more or less from me; but still more distressing thought, that I cannot have joy in them all, tho so few in Number.

To Thomas Boylston Adams, Quincy, August 4, 1799

I have scarcely ever been able to collect my Family together tho so
small a Number at these Annual festivals—they have been scatterd
over the Globe. I had the largest collection of them together the last
Sunday you dinned with us—all my Children, and all but one of my
Grandchildren—which have ever met before. It is a pleasing and [. . .]
sensation to parents to see them thus assembled like a live plant
round about the table—yea to see as the psalmist expresses it, to see
our children's Children.*

> To Louisa Catherine Adams, Quincy, November 30, 1807

*Psalms 128:6.

Remember that your wife and Children have the first claim upon
you.

> To William Cranch, Quincy, 1817

I know more injury may be done to furniture in one year than a
House can easily sustain in several. A Hundred dollers goes but a little way in good furniture.

> To Mary Cranch, New York, August 29, 1790

Furniture

My Grandson grows a fine Boy, and will get too much of my Heart I
fear. He stood his journey very well, and was a great amusement to
us.

> To Elizabeth Shaw, London, October 12, 1787

Grandchildren

You will e'er long know that a Grandchild is almost as near to your
Heart as your own children; my little Boys delight me and I should
feel quite melancholy without them.

> To Mary Cranch, Richmond Hill, September 1, 1789

I congratulate you and my dear Neice upon the late happy event in
your Family. Can you really believe that you are a Grandmamma?
Does not the little fellow feel as if he was really your own? If he does

not now, by that time you have lived a year with him, or near you, I question if you will be able to feel a difference.

To Mary Cranch, Richmond Hill, April 3, 1790

I never had any of my own children so much under my eye, and so little mixed with other children or with servants, as this little boy of yours. Whatever appears is self-taught, and, though a very good boy and very orderly, he frequently surprises me with a new air, a new word, or some action, that I should ascribe to others, if he mixed with them at all. He is never permitted to go into the kitchen. Every day, after dinner, he sets his grandpapa to draw him about in a chair, which is generally done for half an hour to the derangement of my carpet and the amusement of his grandpapa.

To Abigail Adams Smith, Philadelphia, February 21, 1791

I feel many anxieties for my Grandsons. I wish them so to cultivate their Genious, and improve their understandings, that there may be a prospect of their future usefullness.

To Elizabeth Peabody, Philadelphia, February 4, 1800

I always feel gay, when I take my pen to write to you. It is the recollection of your ardour, your intrepidity and your Sparkling Eyes; and rosy cheeks which appeard to me the other Night, heightned by your return to your Native State & Country which animated your whole frame when you ran eagerly into the Arms of your Grand Mother, which so gratified me, that I regreted when I awoke and found it was but a dream—

To John Adams 2nd, Quincy, May 21, 1816

Grandparents   In April tis probable your Sister may be a Grandmama. New Relations create new anxieties.

To Mary Cranch, London, January 20, 1787

Tis time to think of being venerable when tis probable a few Months will make her a *Grandmamma* and she has now got to look out a

Nurse and make Baby linnen &c &c. A thousand New cares and anxieties as well as pleasures attend new Relatives.

To Elizabeth Shaw, London, January 20, 1787

Perhaps the Next time I write you I may be turnd into a grandame as it is now a fine sunshine day, and my spirits tolerably, good; I do not feel so ancient as that event will make me.

To Elizabeth Shaw, London, March 10, 1787

I write you a few lines my dear Lucy to thank you for your kind Letter, and to inform you that I am a *Grandmamma!** my Grandson be sure is a fine Boy, & I already feel as fond of him as if he was my own son, nay I can hardly persuade myself that he is not.

To Lucy Cranch, London, April 26, 1787

*AA became a grandmother for the first time when her daughter gave birth to a son on April 2, 1787.

I will not close this letter without informing you that I am—a grand —o no! that would be confessing myself old, which would be quite unfashionable and vulgar; but true, it is. I have a fine grandson. I regret a little that it was not a Daughter, for then I would have claimed the little one for the great one.

To Mercy Otis Warren, London, May 14, 1787

Whenever you come to have Grandchildren, you will scarcly know any difference between them & your own children, particularly if you should be under the same roof with them.

To Mary Cranch, London, October 20, 1787

There is nothing that enlivens us so much as having these little creatures round us—

To Mary Cranch, Braintree, December 1790

In the venerable oaks, you must fancy you see the image of those grandparents you have left behind.

To Caroline Smith, January 24, 1808

I begin to think Grand parents not so well qualified to Educate Grandchildren as Parents. They are apt to relax in their Spirit of Government, and to be too indulgent. Yet that was not the case with my Grandmother whose memory I cherish with holy veneration whose maxims I have treasured up, whose virtues live in my memory—happy if I could say, they have been transplanted into my Life.

To Abigail Adams Smith, Quincy, December 28, 1808

Home   Tis natural I believe for every person to have a partiality for their own Country. Don't you think this little Spot of ours better calculated for happiness than any other you have yet seen or read of.

To John Adams, Braintree, April 20, 1771

[A] well ordered home is my chief delight, and the affectionate domestick wife, with the Relative Duties which accompany that character my highest ambition. . . . I do not wish you to accept an embassy to England, should you be appointed. This little Cottage has more Heart felt satisfaction for you than the most Brilliant Court can afford, the pure and undiminished tenderness of weded Love, the filial affection of a daughter who will never act contrary to the advise of a Father, or give pain to the Maternal Heart.

To John Adams, Braintree, June 20, 1783

Homesickness   I sigh (though not allowed) for my social tea parties which I left in America, and the friendship of my chosen few. Their agreeable converse would be a rich repast to me, could I transplant them round me in the village of Auteuil, with my habits, tastes, and sentiments, which are too firmly riveted to change with change of country or climate; and at my age, the greatest of my enjoyments consists in the reciprocation of friendship.

To Mercy Otis Warren, Auteuil, September 5, 1784

You cannot wonder that we all long for the Social Friends whom we left in America, whose places are not to be supplied in Europe.

To Mary Cranch, Auteuil, December 9, 1784

My Heart and Soul is more American than ever.

> To Cotton Tufts, Auteuil, January 3, 1785

What a sad misfortune it is to have the Body in one place, and the Soul in another.

> To Mary Cranch, Auteuil, February 20, 1785

My heart returns, like the dove of Noah,* and rests only in my native land.

> To Mary Cranch, Auteuil, May 8, 1785

*Genesis 8:8–12.

I want to come home and live amongst you, for with all your faults, I love you better than any other people.

> To Charles Storer, London, March 23, 1786

I want to return Home. . . . There we should find sentiments and opinions more agreeable to us, society and Friends which the European World knows not of.

> To Elizabeth Shaw, London, July 19, 1786

I long, my dear Madam, to return to my native land. My little Cottage encompassed with my Friends has more charms for me than the Drawing Room of St. James, where studied civility, and disguised coldness cover malignant Hearts.

> To Mercy Otis Warren, London, May 14, 1787

I believe it is true I know I was near home sick before. I think of a thousand things which I ought to be doing, and here I am near 300 miles distant.

> To John Adams, Jamaica, Long Island, December 15, 1788

Amidst these delightfull scenes of Nature, my Heart pants for the society of my dear Relatives and Friends who are too far removed from me.

> To Elizabeth Peabody, Richmond Hill, September 27, 1789

My Thoughts are continually like Noahs Dove, returning to the Ark I have left.* Whether like that I shall return no more, must be left with that Being, in whose hands my Breath is. I consider myself following where duty leads and trust the Event.

> To Mary Cranch, Springfield, Mass., April 30, 1797

*Genesis 8:8–12.

Housewives   A good House wife as I profess myself to be must be fully occupied.

> To Cotton Tufts, Philadelphia, December 18, 1791

Husbands   No friend can supply the absence of a good husband.

> To Abigail Adams Smith, Philadelphia, January 25, 1791

Ironing   Ironing is very bad for you.

> To Mary Cranch, London, October 12, 1786

Marital Infidelity   In a Country where . . . Marriage is esteemed holy and honorable, the seducer should be considerd as the worst of assassins.

> To Mary Cranch, London, January 20, 1787

Marriage   The Spirit of Barter and exchange predominates so much here that people dispose of their own Bodies. Matrimony prevails among all orders and Ages; the scarcity of the Commodity enhances the value. Men are a very scarce article to be sure.

> To John Adams, October 22, 1777

You will find a soft and tender Friendship, enlivened by taste, refined by sentiment, which time instead of destroying, will render every hour more dear and interesting.

> To John Thaxter, July 21, 1780

There is no Country where matrimony is held in higher estimation than your own, where the conjugal union is considerd in a more solemn and sacred light or adhered to with a stricter fidelity.

To John Thaxter, May 23, 1781

Heaven has yet in store for you some sweet female companion to smooth the Rugged road of Life, and sweeten the bitter cup—indeed you shall not live single. The greatest Authority pronounced that it was not good for Man to be alone.*

To John Thaxter, April 29, 1783

*Genesis 2:18.

[In France:] There is so little Regard paid here to the conjugal union that it naturally introduces every kind of licentiousness.

To Royall Tyler, Auteuil, January 4, 1785

How carefull ought young people to be, when they are about entering into connections for Life, to look to the Heart of those to whom they bind themselves. If that is false and deceitfull towards the Deity, they can have little hopes of fidelity towards themselves. In short there is nothing binding upon the Humane mind, but Religion.

To Mary Cranch, London, September 11, 1785

A soldier is always more expeditious in his courtships than other Men, they know better how to Capture the citidal.

To Charles Storer, London, March 23, 1786

No woman of sense will ever make her Husband an object of Ridicule; for in proportion as she lowers him she lessens herself.

To Mary Cranch, London, April 28, 1787

I will give you one peice of advise, never form connexions untill you see a prospect of supporting a Family, never take a woman from an Eligible situation and place her below it. remember that as some one says in a play "Marriage is chargeable"* and as you never wish to owe a fortune to a wife, never let her owe Poverty to you. Misfortunes may Surround even the fairest prospects. If so Humbly kiss the Rod in silence, but rush not upon distress and anxiety with your Eyes open—I approve your spirit. I should be ashamed to own him for a son who could be so devoted to avarice as to marry a woman for her fortune.

> To John Quincy Adams, Richmond Hill, August 20, 1790
>
> *Thomas Otway, *Venice Preserv'd; or, A Plot Discovered,* Act II, scene ii, line 42.

A too early marriage will involve you in troubles that may render you & yours unhappy the remainder of Your Life.

> To John Quincy Adams, New York, November 7, 1790

Time will Dim the Lustre of the Eye, and wither the bloom of the face, tho it may perfect and mature those mental attractions which yield a more permanent, and solid satisfaction, when the ardour of passion settles into the more lasting union of Friendship.

> To John Quincy Adams, Quincy, February 29, 1796

You have Years sufficient to judge for Yourself, and whom you call Yours shall be mine also. Only weigh well, consider maturely of the most important action of your Life.

> To John Quincy Adams, Boston, May 25, 1796

From some hints in his [i.e., John Quincy Adams's] last Letters, Cupid has new bent his Bow, nor misd his aim. . . . I hope however my dear Thomas You will be proof against his shafts untill You return to your Native Land, and then chuse a wife whose habits, tastes and sentiments are calculated for the meridian of Your own Country. May Your Choice be productive of happiness to Yourself, and then it cannot fail to give pleasure to Your ever affectionate Mother.

> To Thomas Boylston Adams, Quincy, June 10, 1796

You should learn to accumulate some solid property before you take upon you the charge of a Family. You are certainly old enough. Your Father was married nine days Younger than You now are.

> To John Quincy Adams, July 11, 1796

I want not the Authority of Milton* to pronounce the state, a perpetual fountain of domestic Bliss. To those who like yourself, seek for happiness and pleasure in the Bosom of virtuous Friendship, endeard by those engageing ties, of delicate sensibility, and sweetness of disposition, beauty will forever remain attractive and knowledge delightfull.

> To John Quincy Adams, East Chester, N.Y., November 3, 1797

*John Milton, *Paradise Lost*, book 4.

"Celibacy is existance thrown away, and every unmarried day is a blank in Life" said a great advocate for Matrimony. These expressions must be received with allowance, not implicitly follow'd. Yet the Man who voluntarily lives a Bachelor deprives himself of one great end of his Being, Social happiness. I do not however recommend very early Marriages. I am not displeased to find you disposed to return single to America.

> To Thomas Boylston Adams, East Chester, N.Y., November 7, 1797

I am a great friend to Matrimony and always like to promote it where there is a prospect of happiness and comfort.

> To William Smith Shaw, December 9, 1798

Mrs. Foster made me a short visit a few days since. She looks well, appears happy with a mind at ease. I call her a very fortunate Girl, and wish her Sister may be equally so. I call her fortunate that in these days of frivolity and licentiousness she should be united to a man of Sobriety, virtue and religion, with habits of industery and oeconomy. This is in my mind, much preferable to wealth and affluence without those qualities which I esteem essential to happiness.

> To Elizabeth Peabody, Quincy, December 30, 1798

I have not any fears for you myself, as they respect Your Heart. I know you have a Head to guide and Govern it. It was even predicted at our table yesterday, that Thomas would be a Batchelor. Now I do not believe this. Let him alone. Let him take his own way and time is the language of your ever affectionate Mother.

> To Thomas Boylston Adams, Quincy, August 4, 1799

When you take a wife, it must be for better or for worse, but a healthy and good constitution is an object with those who consider, maturely Very few *maturists* in the world tho.

> To Thomas Boylston Adams, Quincy, June 20, 1803

You are entering upon the most consequential, Solemn and important step you can take in this Life, and upon which hangs all your happiness in this World and much of that which extends beyond this transitory Scene.

> To Abigail L. S. Adams, Quincy, October 26, 1814

I presume your Husband will find you, what Soloman called a Good Thing,* and that you will do him good all the days of your Life.** For through all the visisitudes of Life and after fifty years of experience, I can say with Milton:

> *"Hail wedded Love, Mysterious Law*
> *Perpetual fountain of domestic sweets, &c."*†

May you ever find it such.

> To Abigail L. S. Johnson, January 6, 1815

*Proverbs 18:22.   **Proverbs 31:12.   †John Milton, *Paradise Lost,* book 4.

I can say with Themistocles,* when his daughter was asked in Marriage by a poor man "That in the choice of a son in Law, he would much rather have Merit without Riches, than Riches without merit."

> To Richard Rush, Quincy, November 23, 1816

*Plutarch's *Themistocles and Aristides.*

You [are] now embarked upon a new and untried scene, engaged in a new Relation with new duties and obligations upon you; much of your future happiness depends upon the early steps you take and the rectitude of your conduct, much delicacy of conduct is requisite, for more depends upon it "than meets the Eye." You have a critical observer now. You must respect even his whims some of which I know he has, but the way to conquer them, is to yeald to them, and by submitting, you may overcome them.

To Susanna B. Adams Clark, Quincy, August 6, 1817

The feelings of a Parent upon an event of this kind can only be known by experience, even where the most favourable prospect of happiness appears, to give away a Child is a Solemn peice of Business.

Marriage of a Daughter

To Mary Cranch, London, July 4, 1786

May Heaven Smile upon and bless their union is a petition in which I know you will join me. The only unpleasing Idea which attends it, is, that we must in all probability live in different states, perhaps in different Countries. But how small is this consideration, when compared with others? I gave her to him with all my Heart, he was worthy of her.

To Elizabeth Shaw, London, July 19, 1786

I suppose you must have heard the report respecting Col. [William Stephens] Smith—that he has taken my daughter from me, a contrivance between him and the Bishop of St. Asaph. It is true he tenderd me a Son as an equivalent and it was no bad offer, but I had three Sons before, and but one Daughter. Now I have been thinking of an exchange with you sir. Suppose you give me Miss Jefferson, and in some future day take a Son in lieu of her. I am for Strengthening the federal Union.

To Thomas Jefferson, London, July 23, 1786

Marriage Wish   Long may you live, mutual blessings to each other ameliorating the rugged path of Life.

        To Louisa Catherine Adams, Philadelphia, November 24, 1797

Long may they live in the full enjoyment of those domestick attachments which sweeten the cup of Life, and without which, paradise itself would yeald no solid pleasures.

        To Catherine Johnson, Philadelphia, May 20, 1798

I hope they will live to enjoy mutual happiness.

        To Mary Cranch, Philadelphia, April 13, 1798

Mothers   My dear sons, Little do they know how many veins of their Mother's Heart bled when she parted from them.*

        To John Adams, December 10, 1779

*Charles and John Quincy Adams left with their father for Europe in November 1779.

How much does the anxious Heart of a Mother feel.

        To John Adams, October 21, 1781

A Mother's Prayer   May the promiseing dawn of future usefullness grow with his Growth and strengthen with his Strength whilst it sweetens the declining Life of those to whom he is most dear.

        To John Adams, March 17, 1782

Moving Residences   Notwithstanding I have been such a Mover, I feel in every New place more & more the want of my own near & dear connexions.

        To Mary Cranch, New York, December 12, 1790

Parenting   I know your generosity is such, that, like a kind parent, you will bury in oblivion all my imperfections.

        To Hannah Lincoln, Weymouth, October 5, 1761

Our Little ones whom you so often recommend to my care and instruction shall not be deficient in virtue or probity if the precepts of a Mother have their desired Effect, but they would be doubly inforced could they be indulged with the example of a Father constantly before them.

> To John Adams, Braintree, May 7, 1776

The Education of my children is more at my Heart than any other object.

> To Mary Cranch, London, March 8, 1787

I flatter myself that what ever else may be our lot & portion in Life, that of undutifull and vicious children will not be added to it.

> To Thomas Boylston Adams, London, March 15, 1787

To your parents you owe love, reverence and obedience to all just *Parents* and equitable commands.

> To John Quincy Adams, March 20, 1780

What is it, that affectionate parents require of their children, for all their care, anxiety, and toil on their account? Only that they would be wise and virtuous, benevolent and kind.

Ever keep in mind, my son, that your parents are your disinterested friends, and that if, at any time, their advice militates with your own opinion or the advice of others, you ought always to be diffident of your own judgment; because you may rest assured, that their opinion is founded on experience and long observation, and that they would not direct you but to promote your happiness. Be thankful to a kind Providence, who has hitherto preserved the lives of your parents, the natural guardians of your youthful years. With gratitude I look up to Heaven, blessing the hand which continued to me my dear and honored parents until I was settled in life; and, though now I regret the loss of them, and daily feel the want of their advice and assistance, I cannot suffer as I should have done, if I had been early deprived of them.

> To John Quincy Adams, Braintree, November 20, 1783

Perhaps I discover the blind Partiality of a Parent.

To Elizabeth Shaw, London, July 19, 1786

There is no musick sweeter in the Ears of parents, than the well earned praises of their children.

To Cotton Tufts, London, October 5, 1787

Tho a state of dependance must ever be urksome to a generous mind, when that dependance is not the effect of Idleness or dissapation, there is no kind parent but what would freely contribute to the Support and assistance of a child in proportion to their ability.

To John Quincy Adams, Richmond Hill, August 20, 1790

Why do you feel alone in the world? I used to think that I felt so too; but, when I lost my mother, and afterwards my father, *that* "alone" appeared to me in a much more formidable light. It was like cutting away the main pillars of a building; and, though no friend can supply the absence of a good husband, yet, whilst our parents live, we cannot feel unprotected. To them we can apply for advice and direction, sure that it will be given with affection and tenderness. We know not what we can do or bear, till called to the trial.

To Abigail Adams Smith, Philadelphia, January 25, 1791

The desire you express, that no warmer encomium may be bestowed upon you, than a bare approbation, may restrain my pen, but cannot suppress my feelings.

To John Quincy Adams, Quincy, May 20, 1796

Relatives   The ties of Nature are powerfull bonds.

To Cotton Tufts, London, January 1, 1788

A Sick Child   The anxiety which you feel for the Health of a Beloved child, whom I pray God to restore to Health, and preserve to you, is I well know more exhausting to the spirits, and wearisome to the Body than labour.

To Elizabeth Peabody, Philadelphia, June 22, 1798

~ *Food and Drink*

A too frequent use of Spirits endangers the well being of Society.   *Alcohol*
To John Adams, Braintree, December 10. 1775

Bread, the staff of life and the chief reliance of the poor.   *Bread*
To Caroline Smith, Quincy, August 6, 1812

A great Student ought to be particularly carefull in the regulation of   *Diets*
his diet, and avoid that bane of Health, late suppers.
To John Quincy Adams, London, January 17, 1787

I wish whenever you return you would consult Dr. Rush upon the
State of your Health. I have a good opinion of Dr. May's practise.
Your dijestion is defective, your food does not nourish you, you do
not derive spirits or strength from it. I would recommend to you to
eat a hard Bisquit, and 3 figs daily, between meals. Make the experi-
ment, add a Glass of wine, and tell me after one month if you do
not feel the benefit of it.
To John Quincy Adams, Quincy, February 9, 1806

Famine is a Scourge with which Americans have never been afflicted.   *Famine*
God Grant they never may.
To John Quincy Adams, Boston, January 23, 1796

The tea, that baneful weed, is arrived. Great and I hope effectual op-   *Tea*
position has been made to the landing of it. . . . There has prevailed a
report that tomorrow there will be an attempt to land this weed of
slavery.
To Mercy Otis Warren, Boston, December 5, 1773

A little India herb would have been mighty agreable now.
To John Adams, Boston, July 14, 1776

I think you would find an advantage in drinking valerian & camomile Tea, for those spasms you complain of.

> To John Quincy Adams, Braintree, May 5, 1789

— *Foreign Affairs*

You are too well acquainted with Courts [of monarchs] not to know, that you must look behind the scenes to discover the real Characters of the actors, and their natural appearance, whilst the World see no further than the Stage.

> To John Thaxter, Auteuil, March 20, 1785

It is time to shake off the strong propensity we have, of loving our enemies better than our Friends, which is going a step further than Christianity itself enjoyns.

> To Cotton Tufts, London, February 21, 1786

Negotiations with other powers may be and have been effected; but with England there is not the least probability of a treaty, until the States are united in their measures, and invest Congress with full powers for the regulation of commerce. A minister here can be of very little service until that event takes place.

> To Mary Cranch, London, May 21, 1786

There are many things you know, which cannot and must not be told. The honour of America requires silence.

> To Charles Storer, London, May 22, 1786

Another lesson for America. I hope She will be wise enough to keep clear of the Blaize which threatens Europe. She may rise into power and consequence, even by the Calamities of other Nations if she improves their folly arright.

> To Cotton Tufts, London, October 5, 1787

In the general Flame which threatens Europe, I hope & pray, our own Country may have wisdom sufficient, to keep herself out of the Fire. I am sure she has been a sufficiently burnt child.

To John Quincy Adams, London, October 12, 1787

I hope & pray that our Country may be wise enough to keep out of it, and if they do they may milk the cow as it is termd, and it may prove beneficial to their Trade and Commerce.

To Mary Cranch, London, before October 18, 1787

It is high time that we had a Government who know how to conduct our affairs with steadiness, judgment, & equity that they may not make themselves contemptable in the Eyes of all Europe.

To Cotton Tufts, London, February 20, 1788

Partizans are so high, respecting English and French politicks, and argue so falsly and Reason so stupidly that one would suppose they could do no injury, but there are so many who read and hear without reflecting and judging for themselves and there is such a propensity in humane Nature to believe the worst, especially when their interest is like to be affected, that if we are preserved from the Calamities of war it will be more oweing to the superintending Providence of God than the virtue and wisdom of Man.

To John Adams, Quincy, December 31, 1793

I wish it were in our power to persuade all the Nations into a calm and steady disposition of mind, while Seeking particularly the quiet of our own Country and wishing for a total end of all the unhappy divisions of mankind by party-spirit, which at best, is but the Madness of many for the Gain of a few.

To John Adams, Quincy, April 18, 1794

This Whirligig of a World, tis difficult to keep steady in it.

To John Adams, Quincy, December 6, 1794

That we are in a very critical State with France every one must be sensible. Their insults to our Government and their depredations upon our Commerce ought not to be endured but upon the principle that it is better to bear wrong than do wrong.

> To John Quincy Adams, Quincy, February 5, 1797

We shall either be a united people, more strongly bound by common danger, or we shall become a prey to foreign influence.

> To John Adams, Quincy, April 5, 1797

The United States ought to know their Danger.

> To William Smith, Philadelphia, July 1, 1797

Happy for us that old ocean rolls between us [and Europe].

> To Thomas Boylston Adams, Philadelphia, April 4, 1798

If we become a united people, there is no doubt but we can withstand the storms which threaten us. United we stand, united we are formidable, and sufficient to ourselves, nor need we seek a *Foreign Aid,* or *dread a Foreign Foe.*

> To Mercy Otis Warren, Quincy, April 25, 1798

I wish the next President may be as independent of foreign attachments, to do Justice to all is the Rule, and to be partial to none.

> To Cotton Tufts, Quincy, November 22, 1799

Whether Commerce is ever again to shake off her Shackles, as respects America, is doubtfull. Not I fear untill she can do it, by the power of her own Navy, and the Thunder of her own Cannon. Britain is jealous of our prosperity and fears us, as a rival. She is determined to check us in every way which she can. France wishes to Embroil us with England, and to crush us in that way, least we should unite our power with hers, against France. Thus are we hemed in on every side. America is delirious of dealing justly by

Both, and extending her commerce as a Neutral Nation, to every part of the Globe. General [Jean Victor Marie] Moreau compares America to the trunk and limbs of a Giant, with the Muscles of an Infant.

> To Abigail Adams Smith, Quincy, November 3, 1808

Until our differences are adjusted and our wrongs in some measure redressed, both with France and England, it will be in vain to look for that union and harmony amongst ourselves which would give strength and energy to our government.

> To John Quincy Adams, Quincy, May 7, 1810

I hope the rage for foreign conquest will not ever seize upon Americans.

> To John Quincy Adams, Quincy, February 28, 1815

Every benevolent mind revolts at the Idea of Foreign powers forcing a Ruler upon a Nation, the majority of which reject him.

> To John Quincy Adams, Quincy, June 29, 1815

[On the salaries of foreign ministers:] The policy of our country has been, and still is, to be penny-wise and pound-foolish. . . . The system is bad; for that nation which degrades their own ministers by obliging them to live in narrow circumstances, cannot expect to be held in high estimation themselves.

Ambassadorships

> To Mary Cranch, Auteuil, September 5, 1784

A Minister who cannot keep a train of Servants, a publick table &c. is thought very little of.

> To Mary Cranch, Auteuil, April 15, 1785

The expences of persons in publick Life in Europe even upon the frugal plan in which we live, are beyond the conception of those who have not tried it, and what is worse is, that the importance of persons is Estimated by the show they make.

> To Isaac Smith, Sr., Auteuil, May 8, 1785

I suppose such a system of oeconomy will now get into their Heads, that they will rather think of curtailing more. Let them use at Home oeconomy where it is a virtue, but do not let them disgrace themselves abroad by narrowness.

> To John Quincy Adams, London, August 23, 1785

How difficult does our country render their foreign embassies by difficulties which unanimity and virtue, publick Spirit and some proper confidence might releive them from?

> To Cotton Tufts, London, October 5, 1785

There is no office more undesirable than Minister of the united States, under the present embarrassments, there is no reputation to be acquired, and there is much to lose.

> To Mary Cranch, London, May 21, 1786

The Laws of Nations require civility towards Publick Ministers. This we receive.

> To Charles Storer, London, May 22, 1786

A foreign Embassy is but an honorable Exile, yet is qualified for future usefullness; when rightly improved.

> To John Quincy Adams, Quincy, February 1, 1799

A foreign embassy is but an honorable banishment, and unless upon a special occasion, or any important Service, it is held up as an useless expence, an envidious station by one part of Society, and a mere out of Sight lucrative post by others.

> To Catherine Johnson, Quincy, August 20, 1800

Services renderd to a Country in a diplomatic line can be known only to a few; if they are important and become conspicuous they rather excite envy than gratitude.

To John Quincy Adams, Quincy, September 1, 1800

With respect to our foreign Ambassys our country has always been a penny wise and a pound foolish. A public minister is exposed to many mortifications upon this account, and few if any of his countrymen, who visit him, and wish to be noticed by him (many of whom ought so to be) can form an opinion of his true Situation or the pressing expences he is at to support his Station.

To William Steuben Smith, Quincy, August 30, 1815

— *Freedom, Liberty, and Equality*

Such is the constitution of the world that much of Life must be spent in the same manner by the wise & the Ignorant, the exalted and the low. Men however distiguish'd by external accidents or intrinsick qualities, have all the same wants, the same pains, and as far as the senses are consulted the same pleasures. The petty cares and petty duties are the same in every station to every understanding, and every hour brings us some occasion on which we all sink to the Common level. We are all naked till we are dressed, and hungry till we are fed. The General's Triumph and Sage's disputation, end like the Humble Labours of the smith or plowman in a dinner or a sleep—

Equality of Human Beings

To John Adams, Braintree, May 1, 1789

Genet* said that he never found any Republicans among the Ladies. If by Republicanism is meant that equality so much coveted by some I am of Mr. Pope's mind when he says all natural differences make all nature peace;** it is a hypocritical bait thrown out to catch Gulls.

To Catherine Johnson, Quincy, November 1809

*Edmond Genet, France's minister to the United States in 1793.
**Alexander Pope, *An Essay on Man,* Epistle IV, line 56.

That poetic french doctrine of Liberty and equality poisoned the minds of this people as much as it dazeld those of the french populace—a doctrine contrary to Nature, to Scripture and all civilizd Nations.

All Nature's difference, keeps all Nature's peace.* Not a goose in the yard who Erects his Head and Struts before the flock, but feels his preeminence—not a bee in the Hive but acknowledges its Sovereign, the [——] [–pants?] in the air who take their annual flight have their leader at their head.

Could we descend to the minute insect I doubt not we should discover the same Natural Law regulating throughout the creation—let all enjoy as much Liberty as is consistant with their happiness, but to talk of Equality is absurd—

To Richard Rush, Quincy, April 24, 1816

*Alexander Pope, *An Essay on Man,* Epistle IV, line 56.

Freedom   We enjoy freedom in as great a latitude as is consistent with our security, and happiness. God grant that we may rightly estimate our blessings.

To Thomas Brand-Hollis, New York, September 6, 1790

Liberty   For sure it were better never to have known the blessings of Liberty than to have enjoyed it, and then to have it ravished from us.

To John Adams, Braintree, April 20, 1771

Salutary restraint is the vital principal of Liberty, and that those who from a turbulent restless disposition endeavour to throw off every species of coercion are the real Enemies of freedom, and forge chains for themselves and posterity.

To John Quincy Adams, London, January 17, 1787

— *Friends and Enemies*

[On Vice President Adams residing in John Jay's home:] I hope it will not be long before you will be able to take a House, living upon a Friend cannot be long agreeable to you I know.

Dependence on Friends

To John Adams, Braintree, May 7, 1789

Give the devil his due, but lay no more than he deserves to his Charge.

Enemies

To Mary Cranch, Philadelphia, February 28, 1798

In Business or in pleasure the participation of a dear Friend, makes more than half the enjoyment.

Friends

To Cotton Tufts, New York, November 22, 1789

The society of a few friends is that from which most pleasure and satisfaction are to be derived.

To Abigail Adams Smith, Philadelphia, January 8, 1791

Old Friends can never be forgotten.

To Mercy Otis Warren, Quincy, February 28, 1797

To hear of the Health, and Welfare, of old, and Esteemed Friends, gives pleasure to her who sincerely rejoices, that the decline of Life, of all those whom she highly values, is renderd agreeable by the enjoyment of Health, Peace, and Competence. Blessings at all periods valuable but more particularly so, when active Life, yealds to the more tranquil and contemplative Scenes of Age.

To Mercy Otis Warren, Philadelphia, April 25, 1798

Faithfull are the wounds of a Friend.

To Thomas Jefferson, Quincy, July 1, 1804

There is a secret Sympathy in Souls whose minds are congenial to each other which draw them to communion.

To Unknown, Quincy, January 7, 1811

How much does the heart pant for the renewal of those affections, which once so cordially greeted an absent friend.

To Caroline Smith, Quincy, September 27, 1814

Congenial Souls will mingle.

To John Quincy Adams, Quincy, June 29, 1815

Friendship   So uncertain and so transitory are all the enjoyments of Life that were it not for the tender connections which bind us here, would it not be folly to wish for a continuance here? I think I shall never be wedded to the World, and were I to lose about a Dozen of my dearest Connections I should have not further realish for Life.

To John Adams, Braintree, September 17, 1775

Friendship and affection will suggest a thousand things to say to an intimate Friend.

To John Adams, Braintree, c. July 15, 1778

There is such a cheering influence, in the Bosom of a Friend, that those only who are deprived of it, can truly estimate its worth.

To Mercy Otis Warren, Braintree, December 10, 1778

At my age, the greatest of my enjoyments consisted in the reciprocation of Friendship.

To Mercy Otis Warren, Auteuil, September 5, 1784

I believe our social affections strengthen by age. As those objects and amusements which gratified our Youthfull Years lose their relish, the social converse and society of Friends becomes more necessary.

To Mary Cranch, London, September 30, 1785

O how my Heart Bounds towards you all, when I cast a retrospective look on times past, believe me I have never known the pleasures of society Since I left my native shoar.

> *"What is the World to me, its pomp its pleasures and its Nonsence all?"*★

Compared to the cordial Friendship and endearing ties of Country kindred and Friends?

To Mary Cranch, London, October 12, 1786

★James Thomson, *The Seasons.*

Only virtuous Souls are capable of true attachments, and sincere Friendships are more generally form'd at an early age, When the Heart is tender, soft and unsuspicious, before we have been jostled by the tumults of Life, and put out of humour and conceit of the World or the paltry competitions of Ambition and avarice freeze up the generous current of the Soul.

To John Quincy Adams, Quincy, February 29, 1796

⟶ Government

'Tis a Maxim of state that power and Liberty are like Heat and moisture; where they are well mixt every thing prospers, where they are single, they are destructive. A Government of more Stability is much wanted in this colony, and they are ready to receive it from the Hands of the Congress, and since I have begun with Maxims of State, I will add another, viz. that a people may let a king fall, yet still remain a people, but if a king lets his people slip from him, he is no longer a king. And this is most certainly our case, why not proclaim to the World in decisive terms your own importance?

To John Adams, Braintree, May 7, 1776

A Government of Good Laws well administerd should carry with them the fairest prospect of happiness to a community, as well as to individuals.

To John Adams, Braintree, May 9, 1776

The foundation of our new constitution [should] be justice, Truth and Righteousness. Like the wise Man's house may it be founded upon those Rocks and then neither storms or tempests will overthrow it.*

To John Adams, Boston, July 14, 1776

*Matthew 7:24–25.

Tis said by Pope that that government which is best administerd, is best.* I mean not to discuss this point, but this we feel, that a good government ill administerd is injurious to every member of the community.

To John Thaxter, October 26, 1782

*Alexander Pope, *An Essay on Man*, Epistle III, lines 303–4: "For forms of government let fools contest; / Whate'er is best administer'd is best."

Such times are approaching for our country, as require the skill, knowledge, experience and industry of all who regard peace and harmony, order, and regular government as blessings worth preserving, to be upon their guard, and to defend themselves, and their country against the machinations which are formed to destroy its tranquility and prosperity.

To Abigail Adams Smith, Philadelphia, May 11, 1800

I am for supporting the government and the laws; for respecting the rulers. If some laws are not so judicious or well calculated to promote the order of society as they might be, let the people petition for redress; not rise up in rebellion against them. I am opposed to all partialities for foreign nations.

To Abigail Adams Smith, Quincy, April 14, 1810

Give me a government even tho in some respects it may not be the
Best, rather than anarchy and confusion.

To Elizabeth Peabody, Quincy, April 23, 1810

This subject of appointments is one of the most difficult and delicate parts of the Executive department. Lewis the 14, it was I believe
who used to say, that when he made an appointment, he made 99
Enemies, and one ungratefull Man. I hope however he represented
Humane Nature worse than it really is, but it is extreemly difficult to
give satisfaction.

To John Quincy Adams, Philadelphia, June 23, 1797

Worthy men whose circumstances are distrest and whose property is
lost, are frequently urged upon the President for offices in which the
publick Revenue is concernd, but he has made it a rule against his
personal feelings and wishes, to put no such temptation or trust into
their hands. . . . It is indeed a painfull task assignd the President, and
his *patronage* will not weigh against the pain and anxiety and responsibility of it.

To Cotton Tufts, Philadelphia, June 29, 1798

I know from the observations which I have made that there is not a
more difficult part devolves upon a chief Majestrate, nor one which
subjects him to more reproach, and censures than the appointments
to office, and all the patronage which this enviable power gives him,
is but a poor compensation for the responsibility to which it subjects
him. It would be well however to weigh and consider Characters as
it respects their Moral worth and integrity. He who is not true to
himself, nor just to others, seeks an office for the benefit of himself,
unmindfull of that of his Country.

To Thomas Jefferson, Quincy, October 25, 1804

I am disposed to make every allowance for a president of the United
States, with respect to appointments. I know, for I have been witness
to enough of it. How eagerly every office is sought after, by both

parties. How urgent, how pressing, how importunate Candidates are for themselves and Friends, and often how painfull the task is, for a president to decide, between the Merits and qualifications of Rival Candidates. Much has been said of the dangers arising from patronage. Believe me there is more of torment, than pleasure or utility in it.

To Catherine Johnson, Quincy, March 6, 1811

It is impossible for a president with the best intentions to avoid mistakes in appointments as he must depend upon the opinion and judgment of those who recommend to office. He can not personally know one in a Hundred who hold offices civil and military.

To Elizabeth Peabody, Quincy, November 20, 1814

Aristocracy   Can it be, that one part of the Humane Species, and those a small proportion, were deignd to subjugate the rest of their fellow mortals, yet such is the use they make of their freedom, that one is led to the inquiry.

To Elizabeth Shaw, London, October 12, 1787

Balanced   Every day must convince our Countrymen more & more, of the ne-
Government   cessity of a well balanced Government and that a Head to it, is quite as necessary as a body & Limbs. The Name by which that Head is called is of very little consequence but they will find many Heads a Monster.

To Cotton Tufts, London, February 20, 1788

Banishment   No severer punishment need to be inflicted upon any mortals than that of banishment from their Country and Friends. Were it my case, I should pray for death and oblivion.

To Mary Cranch, Auteuil, December 9, 1784

Capital Punishment   Though every robber may deserve death, yet to exult over the wretched is what *our* country is not accustomed to. Long may it be free from such villanies, and long may it preserve a commiseration for the wretched.

Travel Journal, July 20, 1784

The attempts to destroy Boston by fire are daily, or rather Nightly repeated. Patroles are constantly kept. They have detected but few. The vile wretches have got into the Country. At Milton they keep a Nightly watch. It is really a distressing calamity, but we shall be infested with more vagabonds, if the states go on to abolish capital punishment.

To John Adams, Quincy, March 31, 1797

Civil dissensions never fail to spirit up the ambition of private Men. *Civil Dissension*

To John Quincy Adams, London, November 28, 1786

I have been much diverted with a little occurence which took place a   *Civil Rights*
few days since and which serve to shew how little founded in nature, the so much boasted principle of Liberty and equality is. Master Heath has opend an Evening School to instruct a Number of Apprentices Lads cyphering, at a shilling a week, finding their own wood and candles.

James desired that he might go. I told him to go with my compliments to Master Heath and ask him if he would take him. He did and master Heath returnd for answer that he would. Accordingly James went. After about a week, Neighbour Faxon came in one Evening and requested to speak to me. His errand was to inform me that if James went to School, it would break up the School for the other Lads refused to go. Pray mr Faxon has the Boy misbehaved? If he has let the Master turn him out of school. O no, there was no complaint of that kind, but they did not chuse to go to school with a Black Boy. And why not object to going to meeting because he does mr Faxon? Is there not room enough in the school for him to take his seperate forme. Yes. Did these Lads ever object to James' playing for them when at a dance. How can they bear to have a Black in the Room with them then? O it is not that I Object, or my Boys. It is some others. Pray who are they? Why did not they come them-selves? This mr Faxon is attacking the principle of Liberty and equal-ity of Rights. The Boy is a Freeman as much as any of the young Men, and merely because his Face is Black, is he to be denied instruc-tion. How is he to be qualified to procure a livelihood? Is this the Christian Principle of doing to others, as we would have others do to us?* O Mam, you are quite right. I hope you wont take any of-fence. None at all mr Faxon, only be so good as to send the young men to me. I think I can convince them that they are wrong. I have not thought it any disgrace to myself to take him into my parlour and teach him both to read and write. Tell them mr Faxon that I hope we shall all go to Heaven together. Upon which Faxon laugh'd, and thus ended the conversation. I have not heard any more upon the subject. I have sent Prince Constantly to the Town School for some time, and have heard no objection.

To John Adams, Quincy, February 13, 1797

*Matthew 7:12.

Congress There appears a dilatoryness, an indecision in their proceedings.

To John Adams, June 8, 1779

These slow sluggish wheels move not in unison with our feelings.

To John Adams, April 10, 1782

It is difficult to get Gentlemen of abilities and Integrity to serve in congress, few very few are willing to Sacrifice their Interest as others have done before them.

To John Adams, April 10, 1782

There are several Members of the House & some of the S[enat]e who are, to say no worse, wild as—Bedlammites but hush—I am speaking treason.

To Mary Cranch, Richmond Hill, October 4, 1789

You must be very sensible in such an assembly those only should speak who speak to the purpose. It is frequently the case that those who have least matter, ingrose most of the Time. They must be heard and frequently answerd, or they would complain of unfair dealing. . . . Men of Sense and industery complain here as loudly as their constituents, but untill Men of Superiour abilities compose publick assemblies, Business will be procrastinated.

To Cotton Tufts, New York, April 18, 1790

We hope that Congress will be *warmed* out of the city by the middle of July.

To William Smith, Philadelphia, June 10, 1797

We want more Men of *deeds,* and fewer of Words.

To William Smith, Philadelphia, June 10, 1797

Congress never get their Blood in motion untill after Christmas.

To Louisa Catherine Adams, Quincy, November 30, 1807

Before so important an Edifice as an Established Government is al-
terd or changed, its foundation should be examined by skilfull artists, and the Materials of which it is composed duly investigated.

*The Constitutional
Convention*

To Mary Cranch, London, February 25, 1787

I wish most sincerely that the meeting of our Convention which is to take place this month, may reform abuses, Reconcile parties, give energy to Government & stability to the States, but I sometimes fear we Must experience new Revollutions, before we shall set under our vines in peace.

To John Quincy Adams, London, May 6, 1787

I hope with you that the united Efforts of our wisest & ablest Coun-
trymen who are now convened, may prove Successfull in extricating us from our present enbarrassments, but they cannot work miracles,

& unless a Spirit of Economy, industery & frugality, can be diffused through the people they will find their labours a mere Penelopean web.*

To Mary Rutledge Smith, London, July 14, 1787

*The wife of Odysseus, Penelope by day spun a shroud that she unraveled by night.

Democracy   You know this people [in Massachusetts], they will Squabble a while but do right in the end, when once they comprehend the whole System and are rightly informd they will submit. . . . Who can withstand the Majesty of the people!

To John Adams, April 12, 1784

The common people, who are very ready to abuse Liberty, on this day are apt to take rather too freely of the good things of this Life.

To Mary Cranch, Richmond Hill, January 1, 1790

Unless mankind were universally enlightened, which never can be, they are unfit for freedom, nor do I believe that our Creator designed it for them. If such a Boon had been designed for them, all Ages and Nations from Adam to the present day would not have been one standing continued and universal proof to the contrary.

To John Adams, Quincy, February 26, 1794

The people will judge right, if they are left to act for themselves.

To John Adams, Quincy, April 5, 1797

Domination and   Let your observations and comparisons produce in your mind an
Power   abhorrence of Domination and power, the Parent of Slavery, Ignorance, and barbarism, which places Man upon a level with his fellow tenants of the woods;

*"A day, an hour of virtuous Liberty
is worth a whole eternity of Bondage."**

You have seen Power in its various forms—a Benign Deity, when exercised in the supression of fraud, injustice, and tyranny, but a Demon, when united with unbounded ambition: a wide wasting fury, which has destroyed her thousands. Not an age of the World but has produced Characters, to which whole humane Hecatombs have been sacrificed.

What is the History of mighty kingdoms and Nations but a detail, of the Ravages and cruelties of the powerfull over the weak?

To John Quincy Adams, Braintree, December 26, 1783

*Joseph Addison, *Cato,* II:1.

It is a very just observation, that those who have raised an empire have always been grave and severe; they who have ruined it have been uniformly distinguished for their dissipation.   *Empires*

To Mary Cranch, London, February 27, 1787

Mrs. Tufts once stiled my situation, splendid misery. She was not far from Truth.   *First Lady*

To Mary Cranch, Philadelphia, May 16, 1797

Poor France! what a state of confusion and anarchy is it rushing into? I have read Mr. Burke's letter,* and though I think he paints high, yet strip it of all its ornament and colouring, it will remain an awful picture of liberty abused, authority despised, property plundered, government annihilated, religion banished, murder, rapine and desolation scourging the land.   *The French Revolution*

To William Stephens Smith, Bush Hill, March 16, 1791

*Edmund Burke, *Reflections on the French Revolution* (1790).

Let our Country men look at France and ask themselves do the Rights of Men consist in the destruction & devastation of Private property do the Rights of Man consist in Murder & Massacre without distinction of Age or youth of sex or condition, Scenes which

Humanity Sickens at, the very recital of which at this distance from the scene of carnage, the Youthfull Blood is frozen, and each particular Hair as shakspear expresses it, stands on End, like quills upon the fretted Porcupine.*

To Thomas Welsh, Quincy, November 15, 1792

*Shakespeare, *Hamlet*, I:5.

Our publick affairs, as they respect the conduct of our Allies towards us, wear an unpleasant aspect. America is arousing from that delirium of enthusiasm which has enveloped her ever since the revolution of France commenced. Judgment and not justice, is dealt out to us, how much by our blind adulation we have merited the punishment is not for me to say.

To John Quincy Adams, Quincy, March 3, 1797

Frequent Elections   If any measures can drive our countrymen into a wish or desire for monarchy, it is the corruption of morals introduced by frequent Elections, the indecent calumny which tears to pieces the Characters and filches from the most meritorious, that which is dearer to them than Life, their good Names, that precious ointment which should embalm their memories; this prostration of truth and justice has been the cause in all Ages of producing tyrants, and our Country will in some future day smart under the same lash.

To Benjamin Rush, Quincy, October 18, 1800

Mr. [Elbridge] Gerry and Mr. [William] Gray have been the very Men, who have conducted the affairs of the Government with that moderation and justice which you recommended, and which certainly has had the benificial affect of softning the asperity of party animosity and harmonizing the discordent Strings by it. They have themselves enjoyed their short lived harmony in more tranquility than any of our chief Majestrates for a long period before. You will be confirmed in this opinion, when you read the Govr.'s Speech and the Replie of the Senate. But no Sooner has the waves subsided and a transcient calm succeeded, than a new Election comes to foment and agitate them again and to blow up all the turbulant passions into a Storm.

I am full in opinion with the British Statesman in the house of Lords, when a motion was made to repeal the Septennial Act.* "He observed that Frequency of Election had uniformly proved the curse of every State in which it was indulged. It renders the Annals of a Nation as flactuating as the popular will, and as flagitious as the popular will dispositions & substitutes in legislation for the energy of wisdom and the coolness of discretion, the violence of folly and the rashness of that party intemperance which it enkindles; & keeps a Nation perpetually heated by the ferment which it necessarily excites and lets loose to prey upon society the worst of human passions, & vitiates publick Morals and poisons individual Comfort."

Are we not in the daily experience of these Solid truths? Could it be that eagerness for publick employ and that hunger for office for which our countrymen are more notorious than any other, that could lead the Framers of our Constitution to leave so wide a Field, so open a common for the unbridled herd to range in, not only to display their wanton tricks of triping up each others heals, but Gladiators like to warring and tear each other to pieces? If they had foreseen the rapid increase and population of the Country and the wealth which has kept pace with it, not only new states springing up, but Foreign States purchased and incorporated with our own? Would they have left such a field open for corruption and intrigue as annual Elections for the Chief Majestrates? I mean the Framers of our Massachusetts Constitution?

To John Quincy Adams, Quincy, February 22, 1811

*Passed in 1716, the Septennial Act provided that no parliament could exceed seven years before a general election was called.

Pray is it prudent, discreet or wise, that the debates of the House should be publish'd in the crude, indigested manner in which they appear to be given to the publick?

House of Representatives

To John Adams, Braintree, April 26, 1789

When I read the debates of the House, I could not but be surprized at their permitting them to be open, and thought it would have been a happy circumstance if they could have found a Dr. [Samuel] Johnson for the Editor of them.

> To John Adams, Braintree, May 1, 1789

I was much surprizd to find their debates open. I cannot think any National advantage will arrise from this measure.

> To John Quincy Adams, Braintree, May 5, 1789

Their debates as given to the publick do not prove them all Solomans, forgive me if I am too sausy—tis only to you that I think thus freely.

> To John Adams, Braintree, May 7, 1789

Judges   A judge like the Wife of Ceasar, ought not to be suspected.*

> To John Quincy Adams, Quincy, November 29, 1795

*According to Plutarch, Caesar divorced his wife Pompeia when she was indirectly connected in the trial of Publius Clodius.

I can only say, thinking as I do, I can never cease to regret . . . a decision in favour of the Removal of the Judges, by a petition from both Houses of Congress. If through Age or imbecility, some judges may continue upon the Bench, longer than the powers and faculties of their minds are equal to their Situations, is it not a less evil, than would result, from making them dependent upon Legislative power?

You must have considerd this Subject upon a larger Scale than I have: yet I have been taught to consider an independent judiciary as our Surety against arbitrary power, our best Security for Life, Liberty and property.

> To John Quincy Adams, Quincy, February 15, 1808

A judge like the wife of Ceasar ought not to be suspected, either of immorality or party animosities.

> To Hannah Cushing, Quincy, September 1810

When Law and justice are laid prostrate, who or what is Secure? *Law and Justice*
To Mary Cranch, London, February 25, 1787

Too much Lenity will prove our ruin. *Lenity*
To John Adams, May 6, 1777

I wish a general Spirit of Liberality may prevail towards all Mankind. *Liberality in*
Let them be considerd as one Nation equally intitled to our regard *Governing*
as Breathren of the same universal Parent. Let Learning, personal
Merit and virtue create the only distinctions, and as we have taken
the Lead of all other Nations with respect to Religious toleration, let
us shew ourselves equally Liberal in all other respects. Then will our
Nation be a Phenomenon indeed, and I am Sure the more we cultivate peace and good will to Man, the happier we shall be.
To Elizabeth Shaw, London, July 19, 1786

A people may let a king fall, yet still remain a people, but if a king let *Monarchy*
his people slip from him, he is no longer a king.
To John Adams, Braintree, May 7, 1776

Courts like Ladies stand upon Punctilio's and chuse to be address'd
upon their own ground.
To Mercy Otis Warren, Auteuil, December 12, 1784

Human nature is much the same in all countries, but it is the govern- *National Character*
ment, the laws, and religion, which form the character of a nation.
To Lucy Cranch, London, April 2, 1786

One cannot refrain from being affected by the disgraces brought *National*
upon their Country from the evil conduct of its Members, tho they *Embarrassments*
abhor the measures & detest the Authors.
To John Cranch, London, March 7, 1787

National Respect   Dignified conduct, and united measures, is the only basis of National Respectability: and honesty is the best policy for a Nation, as well as an individual.

> To Elizabeth Shaw, London, October 15, 1786

A Nation which does not respect itself, cannot expect to receive it from others.

> To John Quincy Adams, Quincy, January 10, 1804

Negotiations   Altho encompassed with difficulties, honest hearts and upright minds upon both sides may effect it.

> To John Quincy Adams, Quincy, April 23, 1813

Neutrality   In the general flame, which threatens Europe, I hope and pray our own country may have wisdom sufficient to keep herself out of the fire.

> To John Quincy Adams, London, October 12, 1787

No Nation has more strictly adherd to neutrality, none sufferd so much, none borne with more patience the spoiling of their property.

> To Mary Cranch, Philadelphia, March 27, 1798

The Presidency   Considering it as the voluntary and unsolicited gift of a free and enlightened people, it is a precious and valuable deposit and calls for every exertion of the head and every virtue of the heart to do justice to so sacred a trust. Yet, however pure the intentions or upright the conduct, offences will come,

> *"High stations tumult but not bliss create."*★

> To Mercy Otis Warren, Quincy, March 4, 1797

★Edward Young, *Love of Fame: The Universal Passion*, Satire 1, p. 87.

The task of the President is very arduous, very perplexing and very hazardous. I do not wonder Washington wishd to retire from it, or rejoiced at seeing an old oak in his place.

To Mary Cranch, Philadelphia, June 23, 1797

If the people judge that a change in the chief Majestracy of the Nation is for its peace, safety and happiness, they will no doubt make it. The Station is an arduous and a painfull one, and may he who shall be calld to fill it have the confidence of the people and seek only their best interests.

To Samuel B. Malcolm, Philadelphia, May 18, 1800

I had witnessed enough of the anxiety, the solicitude, the envy, jealousy and reproach attendant upon the office as well as the high responsibility of the Station, to be perfectly willing to see a transfer of it. . . . Your experience I venture to affirm has convinced you that it is not a station to be envy'd.

To Thomas Jefferson, Quincy, July 1, 1804

The office of President has ever been stuck with thorns. It daily becomes a more difficult one to weild. A wise Man would find it a Herculean Task.*

To Abigail Adams Smith, Quincy, July 31, 1808

*The half-god, half-mortal Hercules was assigned twelve seemingly impossible tasks to atone for his sin.

. . . not that I consider it improper or unfit that the president's House should be magnificently furnished, the Stile of the Building, the Rank of the office, the wealth and opulence of the Country, and our connection with foreign Countries, all demand a very different establishment from the present to support the dignity of the first Majestrate of a great and powerfull Nation—when we consider how much mankind both high and low are influenced by appearance, I cannot be supposed to have any personal views when I say that I would give my vote for a hundred Thousand dollars as a Sallery to the chief Majestrate, and have him Elected only once in 12 years—I believe it would give more Stability to our Government, and be less productive of intrigue and cabal than the frequent Elections which keep us always at variance and in a warfare of Ambition and intrigue—do not however let those whom conduct it in conformity to these opinions, lack of republican Simplicity.

> To Catherine Johnson, Quincy, November 1809

I trust the president is not to be intimidated by the Spirit of party or by the Anglo faction. It is a persecuting Spirit, I know sufficiently the dangers, difficulties and embarrassments of the office he sustains, to commisserate every Man who holds it, with a desire to do justly and love mercy.

> To Catherine Johnson, Quincy, February 23, 1810

With regard to another office—neither you or I shall live to see it filled by a New England Man again. I have not any ambition to see a Son of mine elevated to a Station, the torments of which, I have been too well acquainted with—

> To Catherine Johnson, Quincy, December 29, 1810

No Man has more of my compassion and commiseration than he who Stands upon the giddy height of the pinnacle.

> To Catherine Johnson, Quincy, July 31, 1811

Presidencies of Adams and Jefferson Compared

Time must determine, and posterity will judge, with more candor and impartiality, I hope, than the conflicting parties of our day, what measures have best promoted the happiness of the people; what raised them from a state of depression and degradation to wealth, honor, and reputation; what has made them affluent at home and respected abroad; and to whomsoever the tribute is due, to them may it be given.

> To Thomas Jefferson, Quincy, October 25, 1804

I was pleasd with a Toast drunk by some scholars at Cambridge. *Presidential Election*
Adams and *Jefferson* or Checks and balances. *of 1796*

> To John Adams, Quincy, March 18, 1797

The power which makes a Law, is alone competent to the repeal. *Repealing*
Legislation

> To Thomas Jefferson, Quincy, August 18, 1804

The Senate are secret and silent. *The Senate*

> To Mary Cranch, New York, June 25, 1795

I believe our Legislatures when they made the House tax were not *Taxation*
aware of the trouble attendant upon the execution of it. To measure
every House, Barn, out House, count every Square of Glass, collect
every peice of Land, and its bounds and then apprize the whole is a
Labour indeed. . . . I sat a silent hearer upon all but one Subject
which was the apprizement of this House. The Major was loth that
it should appear that the president had not the best House in Town.
I laught at him and told him I should have no objection to owning
the best House, but if the fact was otherways did the Law say, that
the owner of the House was to be taken into consideration or the
House prized according to what it would in his judgment sell for.

> To John Adams, Quincy, December 23, 1798

The purse strings are those which pull at the Heart of the populace
and can be made use of to raise a clamour.

> To Harriet Welsh, Quincy, June 12, 1818

The experience of ages, and the Historick page teach us, that a pop- *Tyranny*
ular Tyrranny never fails to be followed by the arbitrary government
of a Single person.

> To John Quincy Adams, November 28, 1786

Tyrants stick at nothing.

> To Mary Cranch, Philadelphia, January 5, 1798

Union   Union is what we want, but that will not be easily obtaind.

To Mary Cranch, Philadelphia, March 27, 1798

If we become a united people, there is no doubt but we can withstand the Storms which threaten us. United we stand. United we are formidable, and sufficient to ourselves. Nor need we seek a *Foreign Aid,* or dread a *Foreign Foe.*

To Mercy Otis Warren, Philadelphia, April 25, 1798

A union of Sentiment is pervading all parts of the union, and common danger will again cement us. If *we do not* at present all we ought, we shall do a great deal, and all we ought will follow.

To Thomas Boylston Adams, Philadelphia, May 7, 1798

In the present State of our Country, Union is essentially necessary to our very existance.

To Abigail Adams Smith, Quincy, March 18, 1808

America—the only Land of freedom left upon the Globe. What a call upon her for union, for strength to hold fast that anchor of safety. All Nations will envy us and Strive to divide us, the only means by which we can ever be subdued or conquerd. May Heaven in mercy avert so great calamity.

To Thomas B. Johnson, Quincy, November 9, 1815

Vice Presidency   Much of the tranquility and happiness of the Government depends upon having in that Station, an establishd Character for firmness, integrity and independence, and Such must be the Character who can divest himself of personal feelings, and do equal justice to those who are declaredly in opposition to his principles, as to those who unite in Sentiment with him.

To John Adams, Quincy, December 29, 1792

That the Halcion days of America are past I fully believe, but I cannot agree with you in sentiment respecting the office you hold; altho it is so limited as to prevent your being so actively usefull as you have been accustomed to. Yet those former exertions and Services give a weight of Character which like the Heavenly orbs silently diffuse a benign influence. Suppose for Instance as things are often exemplified by their contraries, a Man, in that office, of unbridled Ambition, Subtle, intriguing, warped and biased by interested views, joining at this critical crisis, his Secret influence against the Measures of the President, how very soon would this Country be involved in all the Horrours of a civil war.

To John Adams, Quincy, December 31, 1793

When the people are fully informd and convinced of what is Right, they will execute, but the danger is, that from partial evidence, they will be led astray.

The Will of the People

To William Smith, Philadelphia, April 6, 1798

The President [i.e., John Adams] had frequently contemplated resigning; I thought it would be best for him to leave to the people to act for themselves; and take no responsibility upon himself.

To Mary Cranch, Washington, January 15, 1801

— Health, Medicine, and Exercise

I would advise you upon the approach of Spring to lose some Blood. The Headacks and flushing in your face with which you used to be troubled was occasiond by too great a Quantity of Blood in your Head.

Bleeding

To John Quincy Adams, London, January 17, 1787

Tell Cousin Betsy if her cough does not soon mend, to lose a few ounces of Blood. She can spair it well, and it may prevent dangerous consequences.

To Mary Cranch, Philadelphia, March 13, 1798

I hope, my dear Sister, that my friends will conquer the aversion to the Lancet, which I believe is not used sufficiently early in inflamitory diseases. But this climate calls for it more than ours.

To Mary Cranch, Philadelphia, July 9, 1798

I hope your illness has terminated without any long confinement: I would not have you too free with the lancet. I have found *emetics* more salutary than bleeding unless the lungs and head are much affected.

To Thomas Boylston Adams, Washington, January 2, 1801

The account of your Health and your debility gives me much allarms. The frequent bleedings your Physician thinks proper for you, quite allarms me. I am sure Louisa could not have survived if any Blood had been taken from her.

To Susanna B. Adams, Quincy, May 5, 1817

Coughs

Coughs are dangerous if of long continuance.

To Louisa Catherine Adams, Quincy, January 27, 1805

Depression

I do not like to hear you complain so much of Lowness of spirits. A Cheerfull Heart doth good like a medicine.* . . . I must say to you, as Lord Lyttleton wrote to his Father, "Suffer not a depression of spirits to rob you of that pleasing hope which both supports and nourishes. Think less of those circumstances which disquiet you,"** and rejoice in those which ought to gladden you.

To John Adams, Quincy, December 26, 1794

*Proverbs 17:22. **Works of George Lyttleton, Letters to Sir Thomas Lyttleton, Letter VI.

Melancholy thoughts will frequently get the better of me.

To John Adams, Quincy, November 18, 1798

Permit not your Spirit to be deprest. Your Family calls for your exertions, and you must not give way to lowness of Spirits, or despondency.

To William Cranch, Quincy, [1798]

I hope you will not be induced by any means to over exert yourself, *Disease* or try your strength beyond its bearing, a relapse being often more fatal than an original disease.

To Mary Cranch, Washington, December 1, 1800

I hope you will not apply so constantly to your Studies as to injure *Exercise* your Health: exercise is very necessary for you.

To John Quincy Adams, London, November 28, 1786

As you and I are both inclined to corpulence we should be attentive to exercise. Without this a Sedantary Life will infalliby destroy your Health, and then it will be of little avail that you have trim'd the midnight Lamp. In the cultivation of the mind care should be taken, not to neglect or injure the body upon which the vigor of the mind greatly depends.

To John Quincy Adams, London, January 17, 1787

I fear you will grow too indolent. I very Seldom hear of you at Boston or any where out of colledge. Your Blood will grow thick & you will be sick. Your Pappa is sure of it. He is always preaching up exercise to me and it would be a very usefull doctrine if I sufficiently attended to it.

To John Quincy Adams, London, March 20, 1787

Our Bodies are framed of such materials as to require constant exercise to keep them in repair, to Brace the Nerves and give vigor to the Animal functions.

To John Quincy Adams, London, October 12, 1787

You must not let the mind wear so much upon the Body. Your disposition to a Sedentary Life prevents you from taking that regular exercise which the Body requires to keep it in a healthy State. I used frequently to remind you of it during your stay here. You eat too little; and studied too much.

To John Quincy Adams, Quincy, December 18, 1804

Exercise is better than bleeding if he can take it.

To Louisa Catherine Adams, Quincy, February 27, 1818

I believe as much exercise as you can take without fatigue salutary.

To Louisa Catherine Adams, Quincy, April 15, 1818

Eyes I did not say enough to you about your Eyes. . . . If lost Health may be restored, lost Eyes cannot.

To John Quincy Adams, Brookfield, October 9, 1791

Health The Fabrick often wants repairing and if we neglect it the Deity will not long inhabit it, yet after all our care and solicitude to preserve it, it is a tottering Building, and often reminds us that it will finally fall.

To John Adams, Weymouth, August 11, 1763

I am very fearful that you will not when left to your own management follow your directions—but let her who tenderly cares for you both in Sickness and Health, intreet you to be careful of that Health upon which depends the happiness of Your A. Smith

To John Adams, Weymouth, April 8, 1764

If we have many troubles we have also many blessings, amongst which and not the least I consider Health. . . . but the constant care, application, and anxiety will wear out the firmest constitution.

To Mary Cranch, Philadelphia, April 4, 1798

Husband your Health as well as your time, for without Health from experience I tell you, Life has no enjoyments.

To William Smith Shaw, Quincy, January 3, 1799

Health will suffer when the mind is anxious and distrest.

> To Elizabeth Peabody, Quincy, April 9, 1799

Above all worldly goods, I wish you Health, for destitute of that great Blessing, few others can be enjoyed.

> To Thomas Boylston Adams, Quincy, June 2, 1799

I sensibly feel that the Health of the Body depends very much upon the tranquility of the mind.

> To Catherine Johnson, Philadelphia, January 19, 1800

Without Health, Life has few enjoyments.

> To Mary Cranch, Philadelphia, February 27, 1800

I thank you my dear Son for the solicitude you express for my Life and Health. Without the latter in a tollerable degree, the former would soon be a burden to myself and others.

> To John Quincy Adams, Quincy, December 18, 1804

Your affectionate Letter of December 19th reachd me a few days since, and found me and the rest of the family in good Health, and Spirits, blessings for which we ought to be truly thankfull. As all the Gifts of providence are enhanced and enjoyed with tenfold pleasure when attended by them, we can never so justly appreciate the blessings we enjoy, as when we are deprived of them.

> To John Quincy Adams, Quincy, December 30, 1804

When a Man enjoys good Health, good Spirits are a natural attenant.

> To John Quincy Adams, Quincy, March 24, 1806

I am frequently reminded that here I have no abiding place. I bend to the blast, it passes over for the present and I rise again.

> To Mercy Otis Warren, Quincy, March 9, 1807

Illness   Your son is some afflicted with what I may properly stile our Family infirmity, the Rheumatism.

> To Mary Cranch, Philadelphia, April 16, 1800

A Sick Man Should lay aside all business if possible.

> To William Smith Shaw, Quincy, January 23, 1811

Late Hours   O, I must chide you for such late hours. You will injure your Health. Do not practise them. The midnight Lamp is too late. Husband your Health as well as your time, for without Health from experience I tell you, Life has no enjoyments. From early rising there is no danger, but late hours of Study, or dissipation are Hurtfull if practised too frequently.

> To William Smith Shaw, Quincy, January 3, 1799

Medications and   [For rheumatism:] I have a great opinion of cabbage leaves. I would
Treatments   apply them to the feet, to her neck & to her Head.

> To Mary Cranch, Philadelphia, February, 6, 1798

Near-Death Illness   The world looks very different to us when surrounded with its pleasures and allured by its temptation than what it does when the world of spirits opens to our view, then all things and objects are as nothing before us.

> To Sarah Adams, Quincy, January 20, 1808

Seasickness   [By 2:00 the captain] sent word to the Ladies to put on their Sea cloths and prepare for sickness. We had only time to follow his directions before we found ourselves all sick. To those who have never been at Sea or experienced this disspiriting malady tis impossible to discribe it, the Nausia arising from the smell of the Ship, the continual rolling, tossing and tumbling contribute to keep up this Disorder, and once it seazeis a person it levels Sex and condition.

> Sea Journal, June 20, 1784

No person, who is a stranger to the sea can form an adequate idea of the debility occasioned by sea-sickness. The hard rocking of a ship in a storm, and the want of sleep for many nights, altogether reduces one to such a lassitude that you care little for your fate.

> Sea Journal, July 6, 1784

I have been in Bed it is true but the multitude of my Thoughts have *Sleeplessness* allowed me but a small portion of Sleep.

> To John Adams, Quincy, April 6, 1797

For a sprain when first done, a Tea Kettle of cold water poured upon *Sprained Ankles* it in a stream; is the best thing, I ever saw used, tho painfull it is salutary.

> To Abigail Adams Smith, Quincy, August 29, 1808

I have walked out today, for the first time, and a jaunt Mr. Storer has *Walking* led me. I shall not get the better of it for a week. The walking is very easy here, the sides of the street being wholly of flat stones; and the London ladies walk a great deal, and very fast. My walk out and in was only four miles; judge you then, what an effect it had upon me. I was engaged to dine out. I got home at one, but was obliged to lie upon the bed an hour, and have not recovered from it yet.

> Travel Journal, July 28, 1784

As to my own health, it is much as usual. I suffer through want of exercise, and grow fat. I cannot persuade myself to walk an hour in the day, in a long entry which we have, merely for exercise; and as to the streets, they are continually a quagmire. No walking there without boots or wooden shoes, neither of which are my feet calculated for. Mr. Adams makes it his constant practice to walk several miles every day, without which he would not be able to preserve his health, which at best is but infirm.

> To Elizabeth Shaw, Auteuil, December 14, 1784

You have not mentiond your own Health; how is it? Your Friends write me that you do not look so well as when you first arrived and they think that the walk twice a day is too much for you. In the morning when the weather is fine it might not be an injury to you;

but when, exhausted by attention, or perplexd by Business; or vext by ignorance or stupidity, a tedious long walk with an empty Stomachk is very unhealthy you may depend upon it. It serves to irritate the whole nervous system; which wants soothing and calming with the oil and wine of comfort and consolation, instead of ploding along on foot a three miles trudge. Beside the very look of it will be attributed to a cause which has no foundation. Some will call it parsimony, others will call it odity, but all this I should not heed so much as the real injury I conceive it will be to your Health. Pray assure me that you will ride in all bad weather, and I shall be easier in my mind, and go rest more tranquil at night.

To John Quincy Adams, Quincy, January 9, 1806

— History

[On the American Revolution:] Many very many memorable events which ought to be handed down to posterity will be buried in oblivion, merely for want of a proper Hand to record them; whilst upon the opposite Side many venal pens will be imployed to misrepresent facts and render all our actions odious in the eyes of future generations. I have always been sorry that a certain person who once put their Hand to the pen, should be discouraged, and give up so important a service. Many things would have been recorded by the penetrating genious of that person which, thro the multiplicity of events and the avocations of the times, will wholly escape the notice of any future Historian.

To Mercy Otis Warren, Braintree, August 14, 1777

I would recommend it to you to become acquainted with the History of their Country [i.e., the Dutch]; in many respects it is similar to the Revolution of your own. Tyranny and oppression were the original causes of the revolt of both Countries. It is from a wide and extensive view of mankind that a just and true Estimate can be formed of the powers of Humane Nature. She appears enobled or deformed, as Religion, Government, Laws and customs Guide or direct her.

Fierce, rude, and savage in the uncultivated desert, Gloomy, Bigoted and Superstitious where Truth is veiled in obscurity and mistery. Ductile, pliant, Elegant and refined—you have seen her in that dress, as well as the active, Bold, hardy and intrepid Garb of your own Country.

Inquire of the Historick page and let your own observations second the inquiry, whence arrises this difference? And when compared, learn to cultivate those dispositions and to practise those Virtues which tend most to the Benefit and happiness of Mankind.

To Charles Adams, May 26, 1781

Attend to the Historians you read, and carefully observe the Springs and causes that have produced the rise and fall of Empires.

To John Quincy Adams, November 13, 1782

What is the History of mighty kingdoms and Nations but a detail of the Ravages and cruelties of the powerfull over the weak? Yet it is instructive to trace the various causes, which produced the strength of one Nation, and the decline and weakness of another; to learn by what arts one Man has been able to Subjugate millions of his fellow creatures; the motives which have put him upon action, and the causes of his Success—Sometimes driven by ambition and a lust of power; at other times swallowed up by Religious enthusiasm, blind Bigotry, and Ignorant Zeal; Sometimes enervated with Luxury, debauched by pleasure, untill the most powerfull Nations have become a prey, and been subdued by these Syrens, when neither the Number of their Enemies, nor the prowess of their Arms, could conquer them.

History informs us that the Assyrian empire sunk under the Arms of Cyrus with his poor but hardy Persians. The extensive and opulent empire of Persia fell an easy prey to Alexander and an handful of Macedonians; and the Macedonian empire when enervated by the Luxury of Asia, was compelled to receive the yoke of the victorious Romans. Yet even this mistress of the World, as she is proudly stiled, in her turn, defaced her glory, tarnished her victories, and became a prey to Luxury, ambition, faction, pride, Revenge, and avarice.

To John Quincy Adams, Braintree, December 26, 1783

Let me recommend to you, my dear girl, to make yourself perfect mistress of the history of your own country, if you are not so already. No one can be sufficiently thankful for the blessings he enjoys, unless he knows the value of them.

To Elizabeth Cranch, London, September 2, 1785

I am very glad you have engaged in the reading of History. You recollect I dare Say how often I have recommended to you an acquaintance with the most important events both of ancient and modern times. You have begun properly by attending to that of your own Country first.

To Charles Adams, London, c. February 16, 1786

Yet notwithstanding the Pencil of a Trumble [John Trumbull], and the Historick Pen of a Gorden [William Gordon] and others, many of the componant parts of the great whole, will finally be lost. Instances of Patience, perseverance, fortitude, magninimity, courage, humanity and tenderness, which would have graced the Roman Character, are known only to those who were themselves the actors, and whose modesty will not suffer them to blazon abroad their own fame. These however will be engraven by Yorick's recording Angel upon unfading tablets;* in that repositary where a just estimate will be made both of principals and actions.

To Elizabeth Shaw, London, March 4, 1786

*Laurence Sterne, *A Sentimental Journey through France and Italy by Mr. Yorick* (1768).

I leave to posterity to reflect upon the times past, and I leave them Characters to contemplate upon.
> To Thomas Boylston Adams, Washington, December 13, 1800

History I hope will impartially recount the truth.
> To Caroline deWindt, Quincy, February 19, 1815

The American Historian will do, I most ardently hope, justice to the valour and Heroic deeds of all parties, and Nations, who united in defence of New Orleans. From Great Britain we cannot expect either candour, truth or Justice, if what Cobbet writes is true, for he tells us that in the village where he resides, not a person belonging to it, but what fully believes that the British gave the Yankees a heavy drubing, and this is the opinion of the common people throughout the Kingdom who are kept in ignorance of the Truth.
> To Thomas B. Johnson, Quincy, November 9, 1815

Adams Papers

Have you read the two Letters written 63 years since? published in Nantucket. What will they not rake up—I believe I will make a bond fire of mine, least they should some hundred years hence be thought of consequence enough to publish—
> To Harriet Welsh, Quincy, March 9, 1815

Genealogy

It is a subject which young people scarcely think of, but as they advance in years they become more inquisitive about their Ancestors.
> To Caroline Smith, Quincy, April 18, 1811

— *Human Nature*

To you, you have so thoroughly looked through the deeds of men, and developed the dark designs of a rapacious soul, no action however base or sordid, no measure however cruel and villanous, will be matter of any surprise.

To Mercy Otis Warren, Boston, December 5, 1773

It seems Humane Nature is the same in all ages and Countrys.

To John Adams, November 5, 1775

Man is a dangerous creature, and that power whether vested in many or a few is ever grasping, and like the grave cries give, give. The great fish swallow up the small, and he who is most strenuous for the Rights of the people, when vested with power, is as eager after the perogatives of Government. You tell me of degrees of perfection to which Humane Nature is capable of arriving, and I believe it, but at the same time lament that our admiration should arise from the scarcity of the instances. . . . I fear the people will not quietly submit to those restraints which are necessary for the peace, and security, of the community; if we separate from Britain, what Code of Laws will be established. How shall we be governd so as to retain our Liberties? . . . but whatever occurs, may justice and righteousness be the Stability of our times, and order arise out of confusion.

To John Adams, Braintree, November 27, 1775

It is from a wide and extensive view of mankind that a just and true estimate can be formed of the powers of human nature.

To John Quincy Adams, Braintree, May 20, 1781

I have seen many of the Beauties and some of the Deformities of this old World. I have been more than ever convinced that there is no Sumit of virtue, and no Depth of vice, which Humane Nature is not Capable of rising to, on the one hand, or sinking into, on the other.

To Mary Cranch, Auteuil, February 20, 1785

The human mind is an active principle, always in search of some gratification; and those writings which tend to elevate it to the contemplation of truth and virtue, and to teach it that it is capable of rising to higher degrees of excellence than the mere gratification of sensual appetites and passions, contribute to promote its mutual pleasures, and to advance the dignity of our natures.

To Lucy Cranch, London, August 27, 1785

There must be frailty in all human characters, and it should teach us in judging of the actions of others, to remember the weakness of Humane Nature and to examine the tenor of our own minds as well as the Strength of our own virtue, before we pass a rigid sentence upon their conduct.

To Mary Cranch, London, July 4, 1786

To our mortification we find, that humane nature is the same in all ages. Neither the dread of Tyrants, the fall of Empires, the Havock and dessolation of the Humane Species, nor the more gloomy picture of civil Discord, are sufficient to deter Mankind from persuing the Same Steps which have led others to ruin; Selfishness and spite, avarice and ambition, pride and a *levelling* principal are qualities very unfavourable to the existance of civil Liberty.

To Mary Cranch, London, February 25, 1787

The more I see of Mankind, and of their views and designs, (the more Sick I am of publick Life) and the less worthy do they appear to me, and the less deserving of the Sacrifices which Honest men make to serve them.

To Cotton Tufts, New York, March 7, 1790

I am sometimes led to think that human nature is a very perverse thing, and much more given to evil than good.

To Abigail Adams Smith, Philadelphia, February 21, 1791

There is such a propensity in humane Nature to believe the worst, especially when their interest is like to be affected.

To John Adams, Quincy, December 31, 1793

Unless mankind were universally enlightened, which never can be, they are unfit for freedom, nor do I believe that our Creator designed it for them. If such a Boon had been designed for them, all Ages and Nations from Adam to the present day would not have been one standing continued and universal proof to the contrary.

To John Adams, Quincy, February 26, 1794

Society and Interest and dissapointed ambition will have their influence upon most minds.

To John Adams, Quincy, June 15, 1795

How weak is Humane Nature.

To Thomas Boylston Adams, Philadelphia, January 3, 1798

I am surprizd at the want of knowledge of Human Nature.

To William Smith, Philadelphia, July 7, 1798

Pride, envy and ambition are the predominant passions of man.

To Abigail Adams Smith, Quincy, March 5, 1809

In all countries the populace are much alike.

To Catherine Johnson, Quincy, December 29, 1810

Ambition How unbounded is ambition and what ravages has it made among the human Species. It was that which led Alexander to weep for more Worlds to conquer, and Caesar to say that he had rather be the first man in a village than the second in Rome and the arch Fiend himself to declare he had rather Reign in Hell than serve in Heaven.* But that Ambition which would establish itself by crimes and agrandize its possessor by the ruin of the State and by the oppression of its Subjects, will most certainly defeat itself. When Alexander Weep't he degraded himself. He would certainly have acquired much greater Glory by a wise and prudent government of those kingdoms he had conquerd than [by] childishly blubering after new Worlds. This passion of Ambition when it centers in an honest mind possess'd of great Abilities may and often has done imminent Service to the World. There are but few minds if any wholy destitute of it and tho in itself it is Laudable yet there is nothing in Nature so amiable but the passions and interest of Men will pervert to very base purposes.

To Mercy Otis Warren, ante February 27, 1774

*John Milton, *Paradise Lost.*

How hard is it to divest the Humane mind of all private ambition, and to sacrifice ourselves and all we possess to the publick Emolument.

To Mercy Otis Warren, Braintree, July 24, 1775

O Ambition, how many inconsistent actions dost thou make poor mortals commit!

To Mercy Otis Warren, Braintree, c. November 5, 1775

Let your ambition lead you to make yourself Master of what you undertake, do not be content to lag behind others, but strive to excell.

To Charles Adams, January 19, 1780

Let your ambition be engaged to become eminent, but above all things support a virtuous character, and remember that "an Honest Man is the Noblest work of God."*

To John Quincy Adams, Braintree, January 21, 1781

*Alexander Pope, *An Essay on Man,* Epistle IV.

Have you not Ambition, let it warm you to Emulation, let it fire you to rise to a Superiour height.

To Royall Tyler, June 14, 1783

Ambition is a very wild passion.

To Mary Cranch, London, July 16, 1787

What will not disappointed ambition Stick at?

> To Mary Cranch, Richmond Hill, September 1, 1789

Oh how many passions are set at work by ambition, by an asspiring Genious.

> To William Smith, Philadelphia, July 7, 1798

Ambition often over shoots the mark.

> To Abigail Adams Smith, Washington, January 17, 1801

There is a Spanish proverb, "If you are well, Stand still," but Ambition and enterprize forbid it.

> To Richard Rush, Quincy, February 24, 1816

Ardor Ardour and generosity are the qualities of a mind raised and animated in the conduct of Scenes that engage the Heart, not the Gifts of reflections or knowledge.

> To Jonathan Mason?, Braintree, August 1778

Curiosity I want to know all that passes, curiosity you see natural to me as a ——,* but I know who has as much and therefore can excuse a reasonable share of it in her Friend.

> To Mercy Otis Warren, Braintree, October 19, 1775

*"As a woman." AA is echoing Warren's comment about female curiosity in her letter of January 28, 1775.

I want to know how the world passes, tho I cannot gain admittance now into the Cabinet.

> To John Adams, Quincy, December 15, 1798

Diffidence The most amiable and most useful disposition in a young mind is diffidence of itself.

> To John Quincy Adams, June 10?, 1778

No man is fit to be trusted, who is not diffident of himself.

> To Mary Cranch, London, July 16, 1787

Genius is always eccentrick I think. Superiour talents give no secu- *Genius*
rity for propriety of conduct.

> To John Quincy Adams, Quincy, December 30, 1804

What is bred to the bone will never be out of the flesh.* *Inbred*

> To John Adams, Weymouth, April 16, 1764

*Michel de Montaigne, *Essays,* Book III, chapter xiii.

The human mind is an active principle, always in search of some *Intellect*
gratification; and those writings which tend to elevate it to the contemplation of truth and virtue, and to teach it that it is capable of
rising to higher degrees of excellence than the mere gratification of
sensual appetites and passions, contribute to promote its mental
pleasures, and to advance the dignity of our natures.

> To Lucy Cranch, London, August 27, 1785

— Human Relations

How long is the space since I heard from my dear absent Friends? *Absence*
Most feelingly do I experience that sentiment of Rousseaus' "that
one of the greatest evils of absence, and the only one which reason
cannot alleviate, is the inquietude we are under concerning the ac-
tual state of those we love, their health, their life, their repose, their
affections. Nothing escapes the apprehension of those who have every thing to lose."* Nor are we more certain of the present condition than of the future. How tormenting is absence! How fatally ca-
pricious is that Situation in which we can only enjoy the past
Moment, for the present is not yet arrived.

> To John Adams, November 13, 1780

*Jean-Jacques Rousseau, *La Nouvelle Héloïse* (Paris, 1761), Letter XVI.

I fancy the pains of absence increase in proportion to distance, as the
power of attraction encreases as the distance diminishes. Magnets

are said to have the same motion tho in different places. Why may not we have the same sensations tho the wide Atlantick roll between us?

> To John Adams, November 24, 1780

If I know you are happy, it will tend to alleviate the pains of absence.

> To John Adams, July 17, 1782

Neither Time or distance have in the Least diminished that Maternal Regard, and affection which I bear you. You are ever upon my heart and Mind, both of which take no Small interest in your advancement in Life.

> To John Quincy Adams, November 13, 1782

Absence heightens rather than diminishes those affections which are strong and Sincere.

> To Mercy Otis Warren, Auteuil, September 5, 1784

Accommodation

We will endeavour to do every thing that falls to our share with as much calmness & composure as possible, & where they do not go according to our minds, we will bring our minds to go according to them if possible.

> To John Adams, Braintree, June 14, 1789

Accomplishments

We ought never to despair of what has been once accomplished. How many things have the Idea of impossible been annexed to, that have become easy to those who knew how to take advantage of Time, opportunity, lucky Moments, the Faults of others, different dispositions and an infinite Number of other circumstances.

> To John Adams, Braintree, May 27, 1776

Actions

Our actions must not only be right, but expedient, they must not only be agreable to virtue but to prudence.

> To John Adams, June–July 1779

I should enjoy but little comfort in a state of Idleness and uselessness.

> To John Adams, Braintree, June 3, 1776

We were formed for a scene of active virtue.

> To John Thaxter, December 8, 1780

A State of inactivity was never meant for Man.

> To John Thaxter, Braintree, July 1, 1783

I begin to think that a Calm is not desirable in any situation in life.
Every object is most Beautifull in motion; a ship under full sail, trees
Gently agitated with the wind, and a fine woman dancing, are 3 instances in point. Man was made for action and for Bustle too, I believe. I am quite out of conceit with calms.

> Sea Journal, July 15, 1784

I detest still life—and had rather be jostled, than inanimate.

> To John Adams, Quincy, March 28, 1796

I have frequently said to my friends, when they have thought me
overburdened with care, I would rather have too much than too
little. Life stagnates without action. I could never bear merely to
vegetate.

> *"Waters stagnate when they cease to flow."*

> To Elizabeth Shaw, Quincy, June 5, 1809

I have sometimes found great address necessary to carry a point.

> To John Quincy Adams, New York, September 9, 1790

I have lived long enough, and seen enough of the world, to check expectations, and to bring my mind to my circumstances.

> To Thomas Jefferson, London, February 26, 1788

Aim at Perfection   It is an old & just observation, that by aiming at perfection we may approach it much more nearly than if we sat down inactive through despair—

>   To Thomas Boylston Adams, London, March 15, 1787

Alertness   It is well to observe, to watch and to attend to consequences.

>   To John Adams, Quincy, April 5, 1797

Anticipation   I believe we always find, that we have enjoyed more pleasure in the anticipation than in the real enjoyment of our wishes.

>   To Hannah Lincoln, Weymouth, October 5, 1761

Appearances   Mankind both high and low are influenced by appearance.

>   To Catherine Johnson, Quincy, November 1809

Appreciation   It is not in humane Nature, to regard those we despise.

>   To James Lovell, February 13, 1780

Appropriateness   Cut your coat according to your Cloth.

>   To Mary Cranch, Columbia City of Washington, November 21, 1800

Bearing Arms   You will do well to join the military company as soon as you are qualified. Every citizen should learn the use of arms & by being thus qualified he will be less likely to be calld to the use of them.

>   To Thomas Boylston Adams, London, March 15, 1787

Blame   Hear before you blame, is a good maxim.

>   To Mary Cranch, Philadelphia, May 21, 1798

Candlelight   Candle Light is a great improver of Beauty.

>   To Cotton Tufts, Philadelphia, February 6, 1791

Cause and Effect   The same cause will produce the same effect.

>   To Elizabeth Peabody, Philadelphia, December 18, 1797

What cannot be help'd must be endured.   *Circumstances*

To John Adams, April 17, 1777

Let no person say what they would or would not do, since we are
not judges for ourselves untill circumstances call us to act.

To John Adams, Boston, May 25, 1784

When circumstances are known, it greatly alters appearances.

To Mary Cranch, London, April 28, 1787

It is natural to mourn the loss of any comforts in proportion to the   *Comfort*
pleasure and satisfaction we derived from them.

To John Adams, Braintree, October 25, 1775

Our comforts are strewd amidst our perplexities, and we have a
Share of enjoyment and Satisfaction which we should most keenly
feel, if we were deprived of them.

To John Adams, Quincy, December 21, 1798

Be a comfort to me in my advanced Age—and you will reap a sweet
reward—the consciousness of having fullfilld your duty.

To Susanna B. Adams, Quincy, September 12, 1808

The two most important Lessons in life for a young person to ac-   *Companions*
quire is a knowledge of themselves and of the connections they
form. As the latter determines and establishes the character, too
much attention cannot be paid to this important matter. Who can
touch pitch and not be defiled?

To Winslow Warren, May 19, 1780

It is not good for man to be alone.*   *Companionship*

To Cotton Tufts, London, April 29, 1787

*Genesis 2:18.

What pleasure do the delightfull secrets of Nature afford to those, who have no one, to whom they can say How pleasant it is? Participation is the Root of pleasure, in reading a fine passage, how greatly is the enjoyment heightned by communicating it to one who can equally share in it? It is Sterne who says he would have a companion if it was only to say how the shadows lengthen as the sun declines.* All the reasoning and Eloquence of Zimmerman** could never reconcile me to solitude. It is a cold unsocial feeling.

> *"For where are the charms*
> *which Sages have seen in thy face?†*
> *Eden was tasteless till an Eve was there."*

To John Quincy Adams, Quincy, May 9, 1816

*Laurence Sterne, *A Sentimental Journey through France and Italy by Mr. Yorick* (1768).   **Johann Georg Zimmerman, *Solitude.*   †William Cowper, *The Solitude of Alexander Selkirk.*

Comparativeness It is said of Hannibal, that he wanted nothing to the completion of his martial virtues, but that, when he had gained a victory, he should know how to use it. It is natural to the human heart, to swell with presumption, when conscious of superior power; yet all human excellence is comparative, and he, who thinks he knows much today, will find much more still unattained, provided he is still eager in pursuit of knowledge.

To John Quincy Adams, London, October 12, 1787

Comparisons Comparisons are odious.

To John Quincy Adams, London, February 16, 1786

Complaints I hate to complain.

To Mary Cranch, Richmond Hill, March 21, 1790

Heretofore I have had spirits which would surmount & rise above bodily infirmity; whether they will be continued to me, I know not;

I hope they may, for a groaning, whineing, complaining temper I deprecate.

> To Mary Cranch, Washington, January 15, 1801

A mutability of temper and inconsistency with ourselves is the *Consistency* greatest weakness of Humane Nature, and will render us little and contemptable in the Eyes of the World. There are certain principals which ought to become unchangeable in us—justice, temperance, fortitude hold the first rank—he who possesses these will soon have all others added unto him.

> To John Adams, June–July 1779

I come to place my head upon your Bosom and to receive and give *Consolation* that consolation which sympathetick hearts alone know how to communicate.

> To John Adams, Quincy, April 30, 1797

Whilst I mingle my tears with yours over the remains of your much loved sister, I would lead your mind to the only source of consolation, from whence you can draw comfort to sooth and calm your agitated bosom. To that resignation which teaches submission to the will of heaven and that confidence in the supreme being which assures us that all his ways are just and right, however hidden in mazes and perplexed to us short sighted mortals. It becomes us to say of love divine

> *Teach us the hand of love divine*
> *In evils to discern*
> *Tis the first lesson which we need*
> *The latest which we learn.*

> To Louisa Catherine Adams, February 18, 1811

There is nothing which a person will not sooner forgive, than contempt. *Contempt*

> To John Quincy Adams, London, July 21, 1786

Who is hardy enough to brave contempt?

> To John Quincy Adams, Philadelphia, November 23, 1797

Contentment I am determined to be content whatever it may be, because I know it will be the result of Love and affection.

> To John Adams, December 30, 1782

I dare say, you have not been so inattentive an observer as to suppose, that Sweet peace and contentment cannot inhabit the lowly roof and bless the tranquil inhabitants, equally guarded and protected in person and property in this happy Country as those who reside in the most elegant and costly dwellings.

> To John Quincy Adams, Braintree, November 20, 1783

True contentment is never extremely gay or noisy. My own Ideas of pleasure consist in tranquility.

> To John Quincy Adams, c. March 15, 1784

It is the duty of every one to strive to be content, in whatever state they may be placed, and to be useful as far as their abilities extend.

> To Abigail Adams Smith, Philadelphia, March 9, 1800

I am determined to be satisfied and content.

> To Mary Cranch, Columbia City of Washington, November 21, 1800

Criticism But altho it is vastly disagreeable to be accused of faults, yet no person ought to be offended when such accusations are deliverd in the Spirit of Friendship.

> To John Adams, Weymouth, April 19, 1764

Customs Much however must be allowed for Forms and Customs which render even disagreeable practises familiar.

> To John Adams, Braintree, c. July 15, 1778

Custom which reconciles us to many untoward events, has renderd our habitation more tolerable.

> To Royall Tyler, at sea, July 10, 1784

Every Country has its customs and manners peculiar to it.

> To Cotton Tufts, Auteuil, January 3, 1785

Manners are very catching I assure you, and dissagreeable as I found many customs when I first came here, 5 months habitude have made them less so. . . . I believe however there are some practices which neither time nor Custom will ever make me a convert to.

> To Royall Tyler, Auteuil, January 4, 1785

If we Live in the world and mean to serve ourselves and it, we must conform to its customs, its habits and in some measure to its fashions.

> To Louisa Catherine Adams, Quincy, December 8, 1804

Decorum alone is necessary.   *Decorum*

> To John Thaxter, May 23, 1781

There are delicacies to be observed towards those who are in distress   *Delicacies*
which every person you know does not feel. I need not add any thing further.

> To John Quincy Adams, Quincy, February 27, 1807

I have to combat my own feelings in leaving my Friends.   *Departures*

> To John Adams, Boston, May 25, 1784

There is something always melancholy in the Idea of leaving a place for the last time. It is like burying a Friend.

> To Mary Cranch, Philadelphia, February 27, 1800

In proportion as a person becomes necessary to us we feel their loss.   *Dependence*

> To Mary Cranch, Auteuil, April 15, 1785

A state of dependance must ever be urksome to a generous mind.

> To John Quincy Adams, Richmond Hill, August 20, 1790

Descriptions   No description can equal the reality.

> To Mary Cranch, Auteuil, February 20, 1785

Differing Opinions   Good people cannot always think alike.

> To Elbridge Gerry, Philadelphia, July 8, 1797

Encouragement   Keep your Spirits up, and I make no doubt you will do well eno'.

> To John Adams, Weymouth, April 7, 1764

It is an observation of Pliny's that no Man's abilities are so remarkably shining, as not to stand in need of a proper opportunity, a patron, and even the praises of a Friend to recommend them to the Notice of the World.*

> To John Thaxter, April 29, 1783

*Pliny the Elder, *The Letters of Pliny the Council.*

End Results   Blame is too often liberally bestowed upon actions, which if fully understood, and candidly judged would merit praise instead of censure. It is only by the general issue of measures producing banefull or benificial effects that they ought to be tested.

> To Thomas Jefferson, Quincy, August 18, 1804

Error   We now see where our errors lay, but a people must feel to be convinced.

> To John Adams, January 15, 1781

Exaggeration   One swallow makes no Summer.

> To Catherine Johnson, Quincy, July 31, 1811

I know how easily a mole Hill Swells to a mountain in some people's estimation.

> To Harriet Welsh, Quincy, June 2, 1816

It is very wrong to magnify a mole Hill to a mountain and to suffer prejudice to blind our Eyes; frailties and infirmities we all have; let us then learn to be candid where we can, and each of us search our own Hearts, we shall find enough to mend there.

To Susanna B. Adams Clarke, Quincy, October 5, 1817

It is an observation not the less true for being common, that example is more forcible.

Example

To Chandler Robbins, Jr., c. January 10, 1783

Precept without example is of little avail, for habits of the mind are produced by the exertion of inward practical principles.

To Elizabeth Shaw, London, March 4, 1786

It is a sad misfortune when example can be plead to satisfy scruples—

To Mary Cranch, New York, March 21, 1790

A good excuse is better than a precious ointment.

Excuses

To Caroline Smith, Quincy, February 21, 1813

There are two ways . . . of acquiring improvement and instruction, the first by one's own experience, and secondly by that of other men. It is much more wise and usefull to improve by other men's miscarriages than by our own.

Experience

To John Adams, September 24, 1777

Wisdom and penetration are the fruits of experience, not the Lessons of retirement and leisure.

To John Quincy Adams, January 19, 1780

Experience has . . . taught me more patience.

To John Adams, April 15, 1780

Age and experience should teach wisdom.

To Charles Storer, London, March 23, 1786

Youth are seldom wise, but by experience.

> To John Quincy Adams, London, January 17, 1787

Experience is the best school.

> To Elizabeth Peabody, Quincy, February 10, 1797

What is past cannot be remedied. We seldom learn experience untill we get too old to use it, or we grow callous to the misfortunes of the world by Reiterated abuse.

> To Mary Cranch, Philadelphia, March 13, 1798

Wisdom [is] taught by experience.

> To Mary Cranch, Philadelphia, June 8, 1798

Every person must have wisdom by experience.

> To Elizabeth Peabody, Quincy, April 9, 1799

Experience may teach.

> To Abigail Adams Smith, Philadelphia, May 11, 1800

We shall learn wisdom by Chastisement and skill by experience.

> To John Quincy Adams, Quincy, December 30, 1812

Let Sober reason advise and experience teach.

> To My Dear Young Friend, Quincy, c. 1812

Fashion   A little of what you call frippery is very necessary towards looking like the rest of the world.

> To John Adams, May 1, 1780

Here is the stay maker, the Mantua maker, the hoop maker, the shoe maker, the miliner and hair dresser all of whom are necessary to transform me into the fashionable Lady. I could not help recollecting Moliere's fine Gentleman with his dancing master, his musick Master &c.* nor despising the tyranny of fashion which obliges a reasonable creature to submit to Such outrages.

> To Elizabeth Shaw, London, July 28, 1784

*Molière, *Le Bourgeois Gentilhomme* (Paris, 1769, and London, 1784).

Fashion is the Deity every one worships in this country [France] and from the highest to the lowest you must submit. . . . To be out of fashion is more criminal than to be seen in a state of Nature to which the Parissians are not averse.

> To Mary Cranch, Auteuil, September 5, 1784

The Parissians . . . have established a tyranny of fashion, which is above Law and to which there must be an implicit obedience.

> To Cotton Tufts, Auteuil, September 8, 1784

It requires some time you know, before any fashion quite new becomes familiar to us. The dress of the French laidies has the most taste and variety in it, of any I have yet seen.

> To Mary Cranch, Auteuil, December 9, 1784

Dress and appearance are the index of the mind.

> To Hannah Lincoln Storer, Auteuil, January 20, 1785

I have had a buisy time getting my House in order and procuring a thousand little necessaries for different countries have different fashions and what suits in one will not answer in another.

> To Mary Cranch, London, c. July–August 1785

Fancy dresses are more favourable to Youth, than the formality of an uniform.

> To Lucy Cranch, London, April 2, 1786

Pray does the fashion of Merry *thoughts, Bustles* and *protuberances* prevail with you. I really think the English more ridiculous than the

French in this respect. They import their fashions from them; but in order to give them the mode Anglois, they divest them both of taste and Elegance. Our fair Country women would do well to establish fashions of their own; let Modesty be the first ingredient, neatness the second and Economy the third. Then they cannot fail of being Lovely without the aid of olympian dew, or Parissian Rouge.

To Elizabeth Cranch, London, July 18, 1786

What new fashions may be introduced by the admission of French Millinary during the summer, is past even the art of devination, but as that is a matter which my Country women will concern them-selves very little with *I hope.*

To Mary Cranch, London, February 25, 1787

How various a dame Fashion is.

To Elizabeth Shaw, London, May 2, 1787

The fashion of this world passeth away.

To Mercy Otis Warren, Quincy, February 28, 1797

The fashions . . . are as various as the Changes of the moon.

To Mary Cranch, Philadelphia, March 14, 1798

She has all the appearance and dress of a Real French woman, Rouged up to the Ears.

To Mary Cranch, Philadelphia, March 15, 1799

I have heard of once a Man & twice a child, and the Ladies caps are an exact coppy of the Baby caps.

To Mary Cranch, Philadelphia, March 15, 1799

At my Age I think I am priviledged to set a fashion.

To Mary Cranch, Philadelphia, December 4, 1799

Ladies . . . wear their Cloaths too scant upon the body, and too full upon the Bosom for my fancy. Not content with the *Show which* na-

ture bestows, they borrow from art, and litterally look like Nursing
Mothers. —To disguise the strait appearance of the Gowns before,
those Aprons, which you say look like fig leaves, were adopted.

To Mary Cranch, Philadelphia, March 18, 1800

I could not but lament, that the uncoverd bosom should display
what ought to have been veild, or that the well turnd, and finely pro-
portiond form, should not have been less conspicuous in the dance,
from the thin drapery which coverd it. I wishd that more had been
left to the imagination, and less to the Eye.

To Mary Cranch, Philadelphia, April 26, 1800

To reason and expostulate against the strong arm of fashion, are but
weak and feeble weapons; she is as powerfull in her dominion as
Bonaparte is in his. She levels all distinctions, decency submits to her
sway, and modesty looses all her Blushes. Even a fig leaf is thought
too cumbersome and untransparent for the vestals of the present
day. . . . All, allmost all, may be seen, from the crown of the Head, to
the Sole of the foot, but as in early Life they have not been innured
to this Mode, and fashion, the most delicate and fragile constitutions, fall early and premature sacrifices.

To Louisa Catherine Adams, Quincy, December 17, 1805

A kind turn will not be considerd as a burden.   *Favors*

To Ann Harrod Adams, Quincy, February 2, 1806

The Heart is long, very long in receiving the conviction that is forced *Feelings*
upon it by reason.

To Thomas Jefferson, Quincy, October 25, 1804

[On the election of Adams as Vice President:] I enjoyed, the Tri- *Fickleness*
umph tho I did not partake the Gale, and perhaps my mind might
have been a little Elated upon the Late occasion if I had not lived
Long enough in the world to have seen the fickleness of it, yet to
give it, its due, it blew from the right point on that day.

To John Adams, Braintree, April 22, 1789

First Impressions   There are persons, there are countenances, there is a deportment, which strike at first sight, and create an interest which it is impossible to account for. It is the great hand of nature which engraves upon the external appearance the internal Spirit and Character. Lavater the great physiognomist* has given a Number of Rules for judging of the Character by the countenance. They are more fancifull than just I believe, and much depends upon Education. It is Tom Jones I think who says a good face is a Letter of recommendation.**

To Caroline Smith, Quincy, November 17, 1808

*Johann Caspar Lavater, a Swiss minister, had written three major works on physiognomy.   **Henry Fielding, *The History of Tom Jones*.

Flattery   Who can withstand flattery and admiration?

To John Quincy Adams, London, February 16, 1786

Praises are often so many inquisitors and always a tax where they are lavishd.

To Elizabeth Shaw, London, March 4, 1786

You say so many handsome things to me regarding my Letters that you ought to fear making me vain. Since however we may appreciate the enconiums of the World the praises of those whom we Love, and esteem, are the more dangerous because we are led to believe them the most sincere.

To John Adams, Quincy, February 1794

A young man should be modest and diffident, but praise and adulation are great corrupters of the Heart, and a man is never in so much danger from his Enemies, as from his flatterers.

To William Smith Shaw, Quincy, December 23, 1798

Follies of Man   [We should have] a certain respect for the follies of Mankind. For there are so many fools whom the opinion of the world entittles to regard; whom accident has placed in heights of which they are unworthy, that he who cannot restrain his contempt or indignation at the sight, will be too often Quarrelling with the disposal of things to realish that Share, which is allotted to himself.

To John Adams, Braintree, December 15, 1783

It does not look well to tell the price of any thing which is for a present, but that you may know its real value, I will tell you that it was six dollars.

Gifts

To Mary Cranch, Philadelphia, May 13, 1798

Do not look upon the gloomy side only, how easily might your situation be changed for the worse.

Gloominess

To Mary Cranch, Richmond Hill, July 12, 1789

Gloom is not part of my Religion.

To Mary Cranch, Philadelphia, November 26, 1799

When the rain subsides and the sun shines, it will dispell some of the gloom which hangs heavey at my heart.

To Mary Cranch, Norfolk, Conn., May 26, 1800

Love and the desire of glory as they are the most natural, are capable of being refined into the most delicate and rational passions.

Glory

To John Thaxter, Braintree, July 1, 1783

When a Man enjoys good Health, good Spirits are a natural attenant, and he is more disposed to attend to his personal appearance. Now this is a subject that I have not hinted at this winter. Indeed I found so much real cause for it last Summer, that I was fearfull you would get callous to my admonitions.

Good Appearances

"A good Coat is tantamount to a good Character; and if the world be a stage it's as necessary to dress as to act your part well,"* says [. . .] in the play. . . . I recollect a story in the Spectator, Mr. Bicker-staff remarks that his servant always bowed lower to him, and was more attentive whenever he had his full bottomd wig on, than when he wore his night Cap. Now I hope you never appear in Senate with a Beard two days old, or otherways make, what is calld a shabby appearance. Seriously I think a man's usefullness depends much upon his personal appearance. I do not wish a Senator to dress like a Beau, but I want him to conform to the fashion, as not to incur the Character of singularity, nor give occasion to the world to ask what kind of Mother he had? or to Charge upon a wife neglegence and inattention when she is guiltless.

To John Quincy Adams, Quincy, March 24, 1806

*Thomas Holcroft, *The Man of Ten Thousand: A Comedy* (London, 1796), p. 33.

Gratefulness   I wish our Gratitude may be any ways proportionate to our Benefits.

To John Adams, Braintree, December 10, 1775

How much more gratefull are the feelings, which spring from benevolence and kindness to our fellow Creatures, than all the Triumphs of conquerors.

To John Quincy Adams, Quincy, May 20, 1815

Great Thoughts   Great thoughts make great minds.

To John Quincy Adams, Quincy, May 20, 1815

Grief   Grief is no incurable disease; but time, patience and a little philosophy with the help of humane frailty and address will do the Business.

To Elizabeth Shaw, Braintree, February–March 1782

Religion my Friend does not forbid us to weep and to mourn for our departed friends. But it teaches us to cast our Sorrows upon that Being in whose hands and at whose disposal we are and who can heal the wounded bosom and bind up the broken heart.

To Unknown, January 19, 1811

You my dear son have learnt from the Scriptures which you so faithfully study those lessons of . . . duty and of submission to the dispensations of heaven. Yet this does not forbid us to sorrow for our great Teacher wept, altho cloathed with the power of raising him whom he loved from the dead and this to shew his disciples and followers that he took our infirmities upon him.*

> To John Quincy Adams, January 25, 1813

*John 11:35.

The full Heart loves to pour out its sorrows, into the Bosom of sympathizing Friendship.

> To Thomas Jefferson, Quincy, September 20, 1813

Grievous words Stir up Wrath.   *Grievous Words*

> To Cotton Tufts, Auteuil, April 26, 1785

It will be harder to erase them [i.e., faults] when habit has strength-   *Habit*
ened and confirmd them.

> To John Adams, Weymouth, April 19, 1764

If you look into your own Heart, and mind, you will find those amiable Qualities, for which you are beloved and esteemed, to result rather from habit and constitution, than from any solid, and settled principal. But it remains with you to Establish, and confirm that by choice and principal which has hitherto been a natural impulse.

> To Charles Adams, May 26, 1781

I have felt the force of an observation which I have read, that "daily example is the most subtle of poisons." I have found my taste reconciling itself to habits, customs and fashions, which at first disgusted me.

> To Mary Cranch, Auteuil, February 20, 1785

I know you want your own Bed & pillows, your Hot coffe & your full portion of kian.* Where habit has become Natural, how many of these little matters, make up a large portion of our happiness & content.

> To John Adams, Braintree, May 31, 1789

*Cayenne pepper, used medicinally as a stimulant.

We are all, in a measure, children of habit, and are apt to contract the manners and habits of those we most frequently see and converse with.

> To Abigail Adams Smith, Quincy, May 21, 1809

Halfway Invitations   I cannot accept a half way invitation.

> To John Adams, September 5, 1782

Harsh Words   I have drawn a lesson . . . never to say a severe thing because to a feeling heart they wound too deeply to be easily cured.

> To John Adams, Boston, October 4, 1764

Hindsight   What Signifies looking back—let us look forward.

> To John Quincy Adams, New York, September 12, 1790

Hope and Fear   My hopes and fears rise alternately.

> To John Adams, November 14, 1779

My Hopes and fears are at varience.

> To John Adams, June 17, 1782

Hope and Fear have been the two ruling passions of a large portion of my Life, and I have been banded from one to the other like a tennis Ball.

> To John Adams, August 24, 1783

Humanity   Humanity obliges us to be affected with the distresses and Miserys of our fellow creatures. Friendship is a band yet stronger, which causes us to feel with greater tenderness the afflictions of our Friends.

> To John Adams, Weymouth, August 11, 1763

Impossibilities   How many things have the Idea of impossible been annexed to, that have become easy to those who knew how to take advantage of

time, opportunity, Lucky moments, the faults of others, different
Dispositions, and an infinate Number of circumstances.

>To John Thaxter, August 26, 1778

Providence has kindly orderd, that every step of improvement
whether moral or Mental, should be attended with complacency,
and that industry in laudible persuits should be a never failing
source of satisfaction.

>To William Cranch, Philadelphia, December 3, 1797

Improvement

My own inclinations must not be followed—to Duty I sacrifice
them.

>To John Adams, Weymouth, April 20, 1764

Inclination

Would that my ability was equal to my inclination.

>To John Quincy Adams, London, February 16, 1786

My Indignation is too big for utterance.

>To John Adams, Braintree, August 1, 1781

Indignation

'Tis said Plato thought, if Virtue would appear to the world, all
mankind would be enamoured with her,* but now interest governs
the world and men neglect the golden mean.

>To Hannah Lincoln, Weymouth, October 5, 1761

Interest

*Quoted in Jonathan Swift, *A Critical Essay upon the Faculties of the Mind.*

It is the Character of the whole people I find, "get what you can, and
keep what you have got." My advice to you is among the Romans,
do as the Romans do. This is a selfish world you know. Interest governs it, there are but very few, who are moved by any Spring. They
are Generous, Benevolent and Friendly when it is for their interest,
when any thing is to be got by it, but touch that tender part, their Interest, and you will immediately find the reverse, the greater half the
World are mere Janases.

>To Mary Cranch, Braintree, October 6, 1766

Intimidation   I am not apt to be intimidated you know. . . . I have slept as soundly since my return not withstanding all the Ghosts and hobgoblins, as ever I did in my life.

> To John Adams, Braintree, September 20, 1776

Intrigue   Intrigue is substituted for wisdom, judgment, justice, truth and gratitude.

> To Samuel B. Malcolm, Philadelphia, May 18, 1800

Joy and Grief   So near akin are joy and grief, that the effect is often similar.

> To John Quincy Adams, London, September 6, 1785

Judgment   Reflection and observation must form the judgment. We must compare past event with the present in order to form a just estimate of Truth never taking any thing merely from the opinion of others, but weigh and judge for ourselves.

> To Charles Adams, London, c. February 16, 1786

More people fail for want of Judgment, than deficiency in any other quality—that sense which is calld Common Sense.

> To Louisa Catherine Adams, Quincy, November 12, 1817

Just   Let us be just, and we shall not be miserable.

> To Catherine Johnson, Quincy, July 31, 1811

How sweet is the memory of the just.

> To Julia Rush, Quincy, December 21, 1813

Just Pursuits   Those pursuits only are worth a reasonable Man's attention which will neither disgust by possession, nor sting with remorse.

> To John Thaxter, July 21, 1780

Just Rewards   How difficult the task to quench out the fire and the pride of private ambition, and to sacrifice ourselfs and all our hopes and expectations to the publick weal. How few have souls capable of so noble an undertaking—how often are the lawrels worn by those who have had no share in earning them, but there is a future recompense of reward to which the upright man looks, and which he will most assuredly obtain provided he perseveres unto the end.

To John Adams, Braintree, July 16, 1775

A man whose mind is so engrosd with great objects—cannot descend to the minutiae of an odd sock—a raggid ristband &c &c.

To Elizabeth Peabody, Quincy, June 10, 1807

Large and Small Issues

I never knew a Man of great talants much given to Laughter.

To John Quincy Adams, c. March 15, 1784

Laughter

I have not been able to write oweing to an inflamation first in my Eyes and then upon my Lungs, which deprived me of my Speech, and this you know, to a person who loves to be sociable, as much as your Friend, was a great privation. This disposition to loquacity with which you know we are charged by the other sex, appears, by the tradition of the Jewish doctors that we are entitled to. Eve, say they, comes from a word which signifies to talk and she was so called, because, soon after the creation, there fell from heaven twelve Baskets full of Chit chat, and She picked up Nine of them; while her husband was gathering the other three. A good story much better then some of their Legends.

To Mary Smith Gray Otis, Quincy, January 12, 1812

Loquacity

Instead of repining at what is taken, I will rejoice and be glad with that which remains. . . . It is too frequently by the loss only, that we learn to estimate the daily bounties of providence, or are taught to acknowledge the Hand from which they flow.

To Thomas Boylston Adams, Quincy, June 20, 1803

Losses

Time past, cannot be recalled.

To Cotton Tufts, Auteuil, March 8, 1785

Lost Opportunities

Manners If Evil communications corrupt good Manners, why may not those which are virtuous, have as great a tendency to enlighten the Mind and rectify the Manners?

> To Cotton Tufts, Weymouth, April 9, 1764

If you can preserve good Breeding and decency of Manners you will have an advantage over the agressor and will maintain a dignity of character which will always insure you respect even from the offender.

> To John Quincy Adams, March 20, 1780

The Humane mind is easily intoxicated with pleasure and the purest Manners soon sullied.

> To Winslow Warren, May 19, 1780

It is manners more than conversation which distinguishes a fine woman in my Eye.

> To Royall Tyler, Auteuil, September 5, 1784

Manners differ exceedingly in different countries. I hope, however, to find amongst the French ladies manners more consistent with my ideas of decency, or I shall be a mere recluse.

> To Lucy Cranch, Auteuil, September 5, 1784

I pray Heaven to preserve us from that dissoluteness of manners, which is the bane of society, and the destroyer of domestic happiness.

> To Abigail Adams Smith, Quincy, March 10, 1794

We are so much the beings of habit, that we cannot avoid partaking of manners to which we become habituated. Where there is mind, there will be manners and where the natural temper is mild and generous, deep impulsions of integrity and early habits of benevolence must communicate to the manners the unconstrained air of open

Rectitude and that animated Softness which a disinterested wish to please always produces.

> To Abigail Adams Smith, Quincy, May 20, 1809

Where there is mind there is manners; but even in a college, we see that although science may form and enlighten the understanding, it is only by mixing with polished society that the rust is rubbed off, and the manners embellished and refined.

> To Abigail Adams Smith, Quincy, May 21, 1809

I fully agree with you in opinion respecting propriety of behaviour and the weight true politeness carries with it. I rank it amongst the virtues. Its influence upon the manners is constant and uniform. How many fine tallents have been lost to the world, merely through a deficiency of good Breeding, a proper respect and deference for the opinions of others, and a modest distrust of their own.

> To Louisa Catherine Adams, Quincy, May 9, 1815

When a man is down, why trample upon him?   *Meanness*

> To Harriet Welsh, Quincy, July 7, 1818

When the means are so inadequate to the end, it requires great skill   *Means and Ends*
and judgement to shape the course.

> To Louisa Catherine Adams, Quincy, May 15, 1810

May . . . Mercy temper justice where it can.   *Mercy*

> To Abigail Adams Smith, Philadelphia, April 27, 1800

As we hope for mercy, so may we extend it to others.

> To Mary Cranch, Philadelphia, May 3, 1800

Mercy and judgment are the mingled cup allotted me.

> To Mary Cranch, Philadelphia, November 10, 1800

"Mercy is twice blest, it blesseth him that gives and him that takes."*

To John Quincy Adams, Quincy, May 20, 1815

*Shakespeare, *The Merchant of Venice*, IV:1.

Blessed are the mercifull, for they shall find mercy.*

To Thomas B. Johnson, Quincy, November 9, 1815

*Matthew 5:7.

Merit   Modest Merit must be its own Reward.

To John Adams, September 5, 1782

Merit I know will ever be the first consideration with you.

To John Adams, December 30, 1782

Mean are those arts indeed which would derogate from the Merit of a Man, upon accounting of the honest occupation of his parents. The truly noble mind spurns the Idea.

To John Adams, June 30, 1783

It is an observation of Swift's,* that persons of transcendent merit force their way in spight of all obstacles, but that those whose merit was of a second, third or fourth rate, were seldom able to perform anything; because the Knaves and dunces of the World, had all the imprudence, assiduity, flattery, and servile compliance divided among them; which kept them continually in the Way; and engaged every body to become their Solicitors. Swift's observations generally carry a Sting with them—yet he had too much reason for his severity.

To John Adams, July 21, 1783

*Jonathan Swift's *Letters to Narcissus Marsh,* Letter XI.

Merit, not title, gave a man preeminence in our country.

Sea Journal, July 16, 1784

Let Learning, personal Merit and virtue create the only distinctions.
> To Elizabeth Shaw, London, July 19, 1786

Faction . . . may turn every Innocent action to evil.   *Misrepresentation*
> To Mary Cranch, Richmond Hill, July 27, 1790

In moderation of enjoyment consists the most perfect felicity of the   *Moderation*
humane mind and there is a certain point which I term tranquility,
beyond which is disgust or pain—and I know from experience that
sudden and excessive joy will produce tears sooner than Laughter.
> To John Quincy Adams, c. March 15, 1784

Moderation in all things is condusive to human happiness, tho this is
a maxim little heeded by Youth whether their persuits are of a sensual, or a more refined and elevated kind.
> To John Quincy Adams, London, October 12, 1787

Moderation and Judgment, prudence and discretion go hand in
hand.
> To Elizabeth Peabody, Quincy, November 20, 1814

Is it not better to show your moderation to all men? than by a precipitate Slip, plunge yourself and those whose happiness you are
seeking into difficulties?
> To John Quincy Adams, Quincy, November 5, 1816

A woman may forgive the man she loves an indiscretion, but never a   *Neglect*
neglect.
> To Mary Cranch, London, August 15, 1785

Never suffer the natural flow of your Spirits to degenerate into noisy   *Noisiness*
mirth. Tis an old observation that empty vessels sound the loudest.
> To John Quincy Adams, c. March 15, 1784

Observance   It is often observd that the Spectator sees more of the Game than the actors.

> To William Stephens Smith, Quincy, September 6, 1812

Offenses   However pure the intentions, or upright the conduct, offences will come.

> To Mercy Otis Warren, Quincy, March 4, 1797

Opinion   There is no despotism like that practised by the rulers of opinion.

> To Abigail Adams Smith, Quincy, May 23, 1809

Optimism   Think you that the phylosopher who laught at the follies of mankind did not pass thro' life with more ease and pleasure, than he who wept at them, and perhaps did as much towards a reformation.

> To John Adams, Boston, October 4, 1764

Keep up a good Heart.

> To Mary Cranch, Richmond Hill, March 21 and April 21, 1790

I am determined to be very well pleased with the world, and wish well to all its inhabitants. Altho in my journey through it, I meet with some who are too selfish, others too ambitious, some uncharitable, others malitious and envious. Yet these views are counterbalanced by opposite virtues—and therefore this is a very good world, and I always thought the laughing phylosopher a much wiser Man, than the Sniveling one—as he who enjoys must be happier than he who suffers.

> To John Quincy Adams, Quincy, November 5, 1816

Order   Order is heaven's first Law. If there was not a much greater proportion of good than evil predominating in the World, who could suffer being here below? If as a good divine observed those objects which administer to our delight and comfort, had been created merely to annoy & harrass us, then we might have had some reason to complain that the evils we sufferd were not oweing to our blindness and folly; if that had been the design of providence, the Bee would have been without her Honey & the rose devoid of its fragrance, the feilds would have been destitude of their Chearfull green & gay flowers, the Fire would have scorched instead of warming us, and the Light of day dazzeld without cheering us. Every Breath of air would have cut us like the point of a sword, every taste would have been a bitter & every sound a Scream, every sense would have been a torment instead of a pleasure, but the real state of things is totally different, & the Benificent Creator made all things good. Tis man alone who perverts his Laws & creates the evils which he justly suffers.

To Elizabeth Shaw, London, March 10, 1787

In order to cultivate our faculties to advantage, we must have order and method in all our affairs.

To Caroline Smith, Quincy, January 24, 1808

You see what a good thing order is. Pope says it is heaven's first Law.*
Therefore respect it in all things.

To George Washington Adams, Quincy, August 7, 1815

*Alexander Pope, *An Essay on Man*, Epistle IV, line 49.

Those who see but, in part, and know but in part are not the most competent judges. **Outsiders' Opinions**

To Louisa Catherine Adams, Quincy, April 4, 1808

I would not put too many Irons at once in the fire. **Overcommitment**

To Mary Cranch, Philadelphia, April 26, 1798

But gold may be bought too dear. **Overpriced Goods**

To John Adams, Quincy, March 1, 1797

A String too long Stretched will Break. **Overwork**

To Louisa Catherine Adams, Quincy, May 20, 1818

Partialities   Certain partialities will bias the mind.

To William Smith, Philadelphia, July 3, 1798

Parting   I must commit my dear Friends to a kind providence, and with a heavy heart leave them.

To John Adams, Quincy, October 18, 1800

Passions   Ungoverned passions have aptly been compared to the boisterous ocean, which is known to produce the most terrible effects. "Passions are the elements of life," but elements which are subject to the control of reason. Whoever will candidly examine themselves, will find some degree of passion, peevishness, or obstinacy in their natural tempers. You will seldom find these disagreeable ingredients all united in one; but the uncontrolled indulgence of either is sufficient to render the possessor unhappy in himself, and disagreeable to all who are so unhappy as to be witnesses of it, or suffer from its effects. . . . Few persons are so subject to passion, but that they can command themselves, when they have a motive sufficiently strong; and those who are most apt to transgress will restrain themselves through respect and reverence to superiors, and even, where they wish to recommend themselves, to their equals. The due government of the passions, has been considered in all ages as a most valuable acquisition. Hence an inspired writer observes, "He that is slow to anger, is better than the mighty; and he that ruleth his spirit, than he that taketh a city."* . . . and learn betimes, from your own observation and experience, to govern and control yourself. Having once obtained this self-government, you will find a foundation laid for happiness to yourself and usefulness to mankind.

To John Quincy Adams, March 20, 1780

*Proverbs 16:32.

I hate an unfealing mortal. The passions are common to us all, but the lively sweet affections are the portion only of a chosen few.

To James Lovell, September 20?, 1781

What restraint have mankind upon their Appetites and Passions?
>To Mercy Otis Warren, Auteuil, September 5, 1784

What is past cannot be remedied. *The Past*
>To Mary Cranch, Philadelphia, March 13, 1798

Having put your Hand to the plough, you must not look back, nor *Perseverance*
ought You I think to wish you had not.
>To John Adams, Quincy, February 19, 1797

Objects appear different, according to the different positions in *Perspective*
which they are placed, or the point from which you view them.
>To Charles Storer, Auteuil, January 3, 1785

Anticipated evils have often as much power over the mind as real *Pessimism*
ones. To guard against this imbecility of the mind an ancient Author
observes "that sufficient unto the day was the Evil thereof."*
>To John Thaxter, March 2, 1780

*Matthew 6:34.

I am sick of that conversation which spends itself in railing at the
times we live in. I am apt to think they are not made better by these
complaints; and I have often times occasion to know they are made
worse by those very persons who are loudest to complain of them.
—If this be really one of the habits of Age, it is high time for every
Man who grows old to guard against it, for there is no occasion to
invite more peevish companions for the last hours of Life than time
and decrepitude will bring in their train.
>To John Quincy Adams, Quincy, November 5, 1816

Tell Lucy I would give a great deal for one of her Cats. I have abso- *Pets*
lutely had an inclination to buy me some little Images according to
the mode of this country that I might have some little creatures to

amuse myself with, not that I have turnd worshiper of those things, neither.

To Elizabeth Cranch, Auteuil, March 8, 1785

I have bought a little Bird lately, and I really think I feel more attached to that, than to any object out of my own family animate, or inanimate. Yet I do not consider myself in the predicament of a poor fellow who not having a house, in which to put his Head, took up his abode in the stable of a Gentleman; but tho so very poor he kept a Dog, with whom he daily divided the small portion of food which he earnd. Upon being ask'd why when he found it so difficult to live himself, he still kept a Dog. What Says the poor fellow part with my Dog! Why who should I have to Love me then?

To Mary Cranch, Auteuil, May 8, 1785

I do not wonder as I formerly used to, that persons who have no children substitute cats, dogs and Birds in their stead.

To Elizabeth Shaw, London, July 19, 1786

The Bird and dog are both in fine health and spirits. We tolerate them for the Love we have to John [their grandson]. The Bird is under no controul and Sings so loud, especially if we are reading as to be quite a nuisance—he is a true worshiper of the rising sun.

To Louisa Catherine Adams, Quincy, February 27, 1818

Pleasantness   Sweetness of temper, easiness of behaviour, and kindness of disposition, are peculiarly engaging in youth, and when found in age, adorn life's decline.

To Caroline Smith, Quincy, August 30, 1808

Polite Society   Polite circles are much alike throughout Europe. . . . I shall never have much society with this kind of people, for they would not like me any more than I do them.

To Elizabeth Shaw, London, August 15, 1785

How is it possible that the love of Gain and the lust of domination   *Power*
should render the Humane mind so callous to every principle of
honour, Generosity and Benevolence.

> To John Adams, Braintree, July 25, 1775

I am more and more convinced that Man is a dangerous creature,
and that power whether vested in many or a few is ever grasping,
and like the grave cries give, give. The great fish swallow up the
small, and he who is most strenuous for the Rights of the people,
when vested with power, is as eager after the perogatives of Government.

> To John Adams, November 27, 1775

As all Men of Delicacy and Sentiment are averse to Exercising the
power they possess, yet as there is a natural propensity in Human
Nature to domination, I thought the most generous plan was to put
it out of the power of the Arbitrary and Tyranick to injure us with
impunity by Establishing some Laws in our favour upon just and
Liberal principles.

> To Mercy Otis Warren, April 27, 1776

'Tis a Maxim of state That power and Liberty are like Heat and
moisture; where they are well mixt every thing prospers, where they
are single, they are destructive.

> To John Adams, Braintree, May 7, 1776

Power without right will never do.

> To John Quincy Adams, Quincy, July 25, 1810

The love of power is a lust in Man no charm can tame.

> To John Quincy Adams, Quincy, February 28, 1815

Praise is a Dangerous Sweet unless properly tempered. If it does not   *Praise*
make you arrogant, assuming and self sufficient, but on the contrary
fires your Breast with Emulation to become still more worthy and

engaging, it may not opperate to your Disadvantage. But if ever you feel your Little Bosom swell with pride and begin to think yourself better than others; you will then become less worthy, and lose those Qualities which now make you valuable. Worthy and amiable as I hope you are, there are still imperfections enough in every Humane Being to excite Humility, rather than pride.

> To Charles Adams, May 26, 1781

The sweetest of all praise is that which is given to those we best love.

> To John Adams, August 5, 1782

Prating　　Some Men prate* too much and it is too evident that it is to be admired.

> To John Adams, Quincy, January 13, 1799

*Prating is idle chitchat.

Preeminence　　Preeminence is a crime not to be forgiven—and are you not ashamed said a philosopher to his Son or daughter, to done so well? Even distinction in amusement excites envy.

> To Harriet Welsh, Quincy, February 18, 1818

Preferments　　*All distinction* you know is unpopular.

> To Mary Cranch, Philadelphia, January 5, 1790

Preparedness　　I cannot bear to go to a place unprovided, when a little forethought and care would save me much trouble.

> To Mary Cranch, Bush Hill, April 18, 1791

Provincialism　　There are certain tastes, and Habits which we contract in early Life, which grow up with us, and lead us to think that they have no equal. A free intercourse with the world, and observation upon the Habits and customs of other states, Nations, & Kingdoms, tends in a great measure to wear off these local attachments, to enlarge our Ideas, and Liberalize our Sentiments, and teach us that the Bountifull

Hand of Providence has Strewed comforts and Blessings within the reach of all his creatures, and that it is civilisation, cultivation and improvement which enhances their value to us.

> To Hannah Lincoln Storer, Richmond Hill, January 29, 1790

It is much more pleasing to serve a people whose willing and general suffrage accompanies their Choice, than when spairingly given.

> To John Adams, Quincy, December 23, 1792

Public Approbation

The greatest evil we now suffer is the want of public credit, and this is felt throughout the Union. Every Limb sharing and suffering through the want of confidence in the Head. How it is to be re-stored, I am not casuist enough to determine.

> To John Quincy Adams, Quincy, November 29, 1814

Public Confidence

Dr. Franklin says if it was not for the Eyes of other people we should not want a fine Horse, fine furniture, or fine cloaths. Respect to pub-lick opinion ought not to be disregarded—not to subject yourself to it is the Safest course be sure.

> To Harriet Welsh, Quincy, May 30, 1817

Public Opinion

A sudden exhilaration of the spirits, has proved of vast service in many disorders.

> To Elizabeth Shaw, Auteuil, January 11, 1785

Quick Changes

The Author of Common Sense* some where says that no persons make use of quotations but those who are destitute of Ideas of their own. Tho this may not at all times be true, yet I am willing to ac-knowledge it at present.

> To John Adams, April 2, 1777

Quotations

*Thomas Paine.

[Speaking] of the celebrated actress, Mrs. Siddons.* . . . The first piece I saw her in was Shakespeare's "Othello." She was interesting

Racial Prejudice

beyond any actress I had ever seen; but I lost much of the pleasure of the play, from the sooty appearance of the Moor. Perhaps it may be early prejudice; but I could not separate the African color from the man, nor prevent that disgust and horror which filled my mind every time I saw him touch the gentle Desdemona; nor did I wonder that Brabantio thought some love potion or some witchcraft had been practised to make his daughter fall in love with what she scarcely dared to look upon.

To Elizabeth Shaw, London, March 4, 1786

*Sarah Siddons, who dominated the English theatrical scene for thirty years.

Reality No description can equal the reality.

To Mary Cranch, Auteuil, February 20, 1785

Reflections will not alter the Situation.

To Elizabeth Peabody, Philadelphia, February 4, 1800

Reasoning Sound reason and cool Argument will prevail in the end.

To John Adams, Quincy, December 31, 1793

Reasoning and not railing will have the effect.

To Mary Cranch, Philadelphia, November 15, 1797

Recollection Recollection is more Sweet than painfull.

To John Adams, Braintree, December 15, 1783

Recommendations There are some men who will get much said in their favour when they do not merit it.

To Mary Cranch, Richmond Hill, August 9, 1789

Recrimination In the most Intimate of Friendships, there must not be any recrimination.

To John Adams, November 13, 1780

Reflection becomes all ages. *Reflection*
> To Caroline Smith, Quincy, December 9, 1809

Repentance may come too late. *Repentance*
> To John Quincy Adams, London, January 17, 1787

Tis in vain to repine. *Repine*
> To John Adams, Braintree, November 27, 1775

My resolution often fails me; and my fortitude wavers. *Resolution*
> To John Adams, January 3, 1784

Retaliation is a painfull task to the Humane breasts of Americans yet *Retaliation*
is certainly due in justice to the worthy suffering citizens.
> To Mercy Otis Warren, Braintree, March 5, 1781

When an object is to be ridiculed, tis generally exagerated. *Ridicule*
> To Elizabeth Cranch, London, July 18, 1786

Ten thousand reports are passing vague and uncertain as the wind. *Rumors*
> To John Adams, Braintree, June 8, 1775

To report the vague flying rumours would be endless.
> To John Adams, Braintree, July 16, 1775

I believe slowly, and rely more upon the information of my Friend,
than all the whole Legend [i.e., legion] of stories which rise with the
sun, and set as soon.
> To John Adams, March 20, 1779

It is said to be one of the enigmas of Pythagoris, "When the winds
rise, worship the Echo,"* which has been thus interpreted: When ru-

mours increase, and when there is abundance of Noise and Clamour, believe the second report.

> To John Adams, Quincy, February 1794

*Quoted by Alexander Pope in his letter to Sir William Trumbull, November 29, 1715.

Rumour at a distance magnifies and Seldom reports truth.

> To Mary Cranch, Philadelphia, May 10, 1798

You will hear many a Goblin story.

> To Mary Cranch, Philadelphia, May 20, 1798

The Rumour of yesterday ends in vapour but tho not true, I hope it will be soon.

> To Mary Cranch, Philadelphia, June 8, 1798

Unfounded reports . . . circulated wantonly, can create but a trancient unhappiness to those connections who can soon discover the truth; but to those who are far distant, the falsehood has all the power of reality, and gives an equal portion of unhappiness.

> To Catherine Johnson, Quincy, May 8, 1801

Sarcasm The low sarcasm of these people affect me no more at this day than the idle wind.

> To Caroline deWindt, Quincy, March 22, 1818

Satire Satire in the hands of some is a very dangerous weapon yet when it is so happily blended with benevolence, and is awakened only by the Love of virtue, and abhorance of vice, when Truth is inviolably preserved, and ridiculous and vicious actions are alone the Subject, it is so far from blameable, that it is certainly meritorious; and to suppress it would be hiding a talent like the slothful Servant in a napkin

*"Who combats virtue's foe is virtue's friend"**

and a keen Satire well applied, has sometimes found its way when persuasions, admonitions of humane nature when it deviates from the path of rectitude, to be represented in its true coulours.

> To Mercy Otis Warren, Braintree, February 3?, 1775

*Alexander Pope, *Essay on Satire,* Part 1, line 130.

Good humored satire, which tho it partakes of the caustic; leaves not a Scar behind.

> *"Thus in Smooth oil, the Razor best is Whet*
> *So Wit is by politeness, Sharpest Set."**

> To John Quincy Adams, Quincy, August 7, 1816

*Edward Young, *Love of Fame: The Universal Passion,* Satire II.

One Man ought not to have everything.   *Satisfaction*

> To John Adams, Quincy, February 19, 1797

If we have not all we may wish, we have all that is best for us.

> To Abigail Adams Smith, Quincy, April 10, 1809

Pray burn this Letter, dead men tell no tales. It is really too bad to   *Secrecy* Survive the Flames.

> To John Adams, Quincy, January 28, 1797

Tho secrecy is sometimes necessary, . . . the fate of a Nation may be involved in a disclosure of measures.

> To Eliza Susan Quincy, Quincy, March 24, 1806

I have ever made it a rule in life never to seek for a Secret which con-   *Secrets* cernd the honour of a person to withhold, and have been too proud to divulge one when once confided in.

> To James Lovell, Braintree, December 13, 1779

Sedentariness   A sedentary Life is not favourable to Health.

> To John Quincy Adams, Quincy, August 7, 1816

Sedition   You know what an Engine the press has been in France, in sewing the Seeds of Sedition and, aiding all their Sanguinary Machinations. God forbid that Americans should become imitators of their examples.

> To John Quincy Adams, Quincy, October 8, 1795

In a quotation from the Chronicle [the Boston *Independent Chronicle*] you cannot expect truth. Falsehood and malevolence are its strongest features. It is the offspring of faction, and nursed by sedition, the adopted bantling of party.

> To Thomas Boylston Adams, Quincy, November 8, 1796

Scarcely a day passes but some such scurrility appears in [Benjamin Franklin] Bache's paper, very often unnoticed, and of no consequence in the minds of many people, but it has like vice of every kind a tendency to corrupt the morals of the common people. Lawless principles naturally produce lawless actions.

> To Mary Cranch, Philadelphia, December 12, 1797

The Liberty of the press is become licentious beyond any former period. The Good sense of the American people in general directs them Right, where they can see and judge for themselves, but in distant and remote parts of the union, this continued abuse, deception, and falsehood is productive of great mischief, and tends to destroy that confidence and Harmony which is the Life, Health and Security of a Republick.

> To Mercy Otis Warren, Quincy, April 25, 1798

The wrath of the public ought to fall upon their devoted Heads.

> To Mary Cranch, Philadelphia, April 26, 1798

I wish the Laws of our Country were competant to punish the Stirer up of Sedition, the writer and printer of base and unfounded calumny. This would contribute as much to the peace and harmony of our Country as any measure, and in times like the present, a more carefull and attentive watch ought to be kept over foreigners.

To Mary Cranch, Philadelphia, May 26, 1798

Why, when we have the thing, should we boggle at the Name.

To Mary Cranch, Philadelphia, July 9, 1798

When such vipers are let lose upon Society, all distinction between virtue and vice are levelled, all respect for Character is lost in the overwhelming deluge of calumny—that respect which is a necessary bond in the social union, which gives efficacy to laws, and teaches the subject to obey the Majestrate, and the child to submit to the parent.

To Thomas Jefferson, Quincy, July 1, 1804

That some restraint should be laid upon the assassin, who stabs reputation, all civilized Nations have assented to. In no Country has calumny, falshood, and revileing stalked abroad more licentiously, than in this. No political Character has been secure from its attacks, no reputation so fair, as not to be counted by it, untill truth and falshood lie in one undistinctioned heap. If there are no checks to be resorted to in the Laws of the Land, and no reperation to be made to the injured, will not Man become the judge and avenger of his own wrong, and as in a late instance, the sword and pistol decide the contest?* All the Christian and social virtues will be banished the Land. All that makes Life desirable, and softens the ferocious passions of Man will assume a savage deportment, and like Cain of old,** malevolent uncandid, ungenerous, unjust and unforgiving.

To Thomas Jefferson, Quincy, August 18, 1804

*A reference to the duel between Aaron Burr and Alexander Hamilton in which the latter was killed.   **Genesis 4.

I cannot agree, in opinion, that the constitution ever meant to withhold from the National Government the power of self defence, or that it could be considered an infringement of the Liberty of the press, to punish the licentiousness of it.

To Thomas Jefferson, Quincy, October 25, 1804

Self-Analysis It will greatly tend to improve our wisdom, to promote our piety, and increase our pleasure, to take frequent and particular views of our lives, and to observe the changes which have taken place in our circumstances, from time to time, in connection with the means and instruments which have been employed, and through which we have succeeded or failed in our enterprises, that by experience we may learn wisdom; and put our trust and confidence in that Being who holds the lives and fortunes of individuals in his hands, as well as the fate of kingdoms and nations.

To Abigail Adams Smith, Quincy, April 10, 1809

Self-Condemnation There is something which makes it more agreeable to condemn ourselves than to be condemned by others.

To John Adams, Weymouth, April 19, 1764

Self-Deception Mankind are prone to deceive themselves.

To Mary Cranch, Richmond Hill, July 12, 1789

What we wish, we are very apt to believe.

To Harriet Welsh, Quincy, July 7, 1818

Self-Defense Self defence is the first Law of Nature.* Give us peace in our day** is a petition I most devoutly join in, but fear it will not be in our power to determine that question for ourselves. May we be prepared to meet with whatever is allotted for us with becoming fortitude, patience and firmness, and never tamely resign that independence for which so many of our Countrymen have fought and bled.

To Esther Black, Philadelphia, March 30, 1798

*Oliver Goldsmith, *The Vicar of Wakefield* (1766).   **The Evening Prayer in *The Book of Common Prayer*.

Whoever thinks too highly of himself will discover it, and just in   *Self-Importance*
proportion as he overvalues his abilities, will mankind endeavour to
mortify and lessen them nor will they suffer him to take that as a
right, which they claim the privelege of bestowing as a reward.

To Elizabeth Shaw, London, July 19, 1786

Self, Self is very often the first Consideration.

To Harriet Welsh, Quincy, April 18, 1816

Such is the frailty of humane Nature, & so great a flatterer is Self   *Self-Love*
Love, that it presents false appearances, & deceives its votaries.

To Mary Cranch, London, July 16, 1787

You must be your own monitor.   *Self-Regulation*

To George Washington Adams and John Adams 2nd,
Quincy, July 12, 1815

God helps them that help themselves as King Richard said* and if we   *Self-Reliance*
can obtain the divine aid by our own virtue, fortitude and perseverance we may be sure of releaf.

To John Adams, Braintree, September 17, 1775

*Traditional saying often ascribed to Poor Richard (Benjamin Franklin).

The more we are qualified to help ourselves, the less dependent we
are upon others.

To Caroline Smith, Quincy, December 9, 1809

It has been made a question with some writers, whether an exquisite   *Sensibility*
sensibility is a blessing or a misfortune. For myself: I could easily decide, yet allow that it is a great source of misiry when closely united,
"to logs of Green wood that quench the coals."*

To John Quincy Adams, Philadelphia, February 8, 1800

*Isaac Watts, "Few Happy Matches," line 28.

Separation   Tis a hard thing to be weaned from anything we Love, time nor distance has not yet had that Effect upon me.

> To Mary Cranch, Braintree, October 13, 1766

Alass! How many snow banks devide thee and me and my warmest wishes to see thee will not melt one of them.

> To John Adams, Weymouth, December 30, 1773

The great distance between us, makes the time appear very long to me.

> To John Adams, Braintree, August 19, 1774

We are told the most dissagreable things by use become less so. I cannot say that I find the truth of the observation verified. I am sure no seperation was ever so painfull to me as the last. Many circumstances concur to make it so—the distance and the difficulty of communication, the Hazards which if not real, my immagination represents so, all conspire to make me anxious, as well as what I need not mention.

> To John Adams, January 26, 1777

May the joy of meeting again be eaquel to the pain of seperation.

> To John Adams, June 8, 1777

I have some times melancholly reflections, and immagine these seperations as preparatory to a still more painfull one in which even hope the anchor of the Soul is lost, but whilst that remains no Temporary absence can ever wean or abate the ardor of my affection.

> To John Adams, June 8, 1777

Tis almost 14 years since we were united, but not more than half that time have we had the happiness of living together.

The unfealing world may consider it in what light they please, I consider it as a sacrifice to my Country and one of my greatest misfortunes [for my husband] to be seperated from my children at a

time of life when the joint instructions and admonition of parents
sink deeper than in maturer years.

To John Adams, Braintree, August 5, 1777

I have ever thought that in the seperation of near and Dear Friends,
and you know I have often experienced it, that the one who was left
behind was the greatest sufferer, for the Mind must necessarily accompany the Body, and while that is in motion, it feels a kind of rotation too. Diversity of objects take off the attention, whilst the
Lonely Being who is left behind, has no other amusement but to sit
down and brood over the dangers and hazards to which the other
may be exposed, *the Hair Breadth Scapes,* to which they are incident.

To John Thaxter, March 2, 1780

Those only who know by experience what a Seperation is from the
tenderest of connextions, can form adequate Ideas of the happiness
which even a literary communication affords.

To John Adams, August 23, 1780

No situation was more delicate, more critical or more liable to censure than that of a Lady whose Husband has been long seperated
from her.

To James Lovell, March 17, 1781

O that I could realize the agreable reverie of the last Night when my
dear Friend presented himself and two Sons safely returnd to the
Arms of the affectionate wife and Mother. Cruel that I should wake
only to experience a renual of my daily solicitude. The next month
will compleat a whole year since a single Line from your Hand has
reachd the longing Eyes of Portia.

To John Adams, Braintree, August 1, 1781

If I know you are happy, it will tend to alleviate the pains of absence.

To John Adams, July 17, 1782

I think every Seperation more painfull as I increase in Years. . . . If these cold Nights last a little vital Heat must be wanting. I would recommend to you the Green Baize Gown, and if that will not answer, you recollect the Bear Skin.

> To John Adams, Jamaica, N.Y., December 3, 1788

You cannot regret your separation more than I do, for morn, noon, and night, you rest upon the mind and heart.

> To Abigail Adams Smith, Bush Hill, December 26, 1790

I agree with Mr. Izzard,* that we are grown too old to live seperate, and I could literally construe that part of the Marriage Service, which says, "What God has put together, let No man put assunder,"** for in Youth most people are too young to be seperated, and he understood Humane Nature well; who pronounced that it was not good for Man to be alone.†

> To John Adams, Quincy, January 12, 1794

*Ralph Izard of South Carolina.   **Matthew 19:6.   †Genesis 2:18.

If oceans do not rool [roll] between us, mountains have arrisen. The late sevear Snow Storm has shut me in, as close as a mouse in a trap, and that so early in the Season, that no probability appears, of any comfortable travelling this winter. The Banks are so high, so hardly compacted together that they will not be removed untill Spring; I am well persuaded, so that I must sigh at Quincy, and you at Philadelphia, without being able to afford each other any personal comfort, or Genial warmth.

> To John Adams, Quincy, December 15, 1798

I have no Groans or complaints to make, but that of being seperated from you. Every day however shortens the period.

> To John Adams, Quincy, January 20, 1799

Shortcomings   Let him who is without cast the first stone.*

> To John Adams, Quincy, May 27, 1794

*John 8:7.

There are cases where silence is prudence, and I think without flat-
tering myself I have attaind to some share of that virtue. We live in a
world where having Eyes we must not see, and Ears we must not
hear.

Silence

> To Mary Cranch, Richmond Hill, January 5, 1790

I want to acquire an habit of silence, or of saying unimportant
things.

> To John Adams, Quincy, January 15, 1797

There is an old proverb, The least Said is soonest mended. So I take
the hint.

> To John Quincy Adams, Quincy, July 1, 1813

The pomp, pagentry magnificence or splendour of a Court can
wean or alienate your affections from your dear adopted Country—
there is so much more ease and comfort in Simplicity and quiet that
all who are condemnd to endure the former, Seek the latter as a
Boon & a Blessing.

Simplicity

> To Louisa Catherine Adams, Quincy, June 8, 1811

I have the Authority of my son for saying that Studied correctness is
always cold. I had rather have one warm line from the Heart, than
20 correctly cold from the head.

Sincerity

> To Elizabeth Peabody, Quincy, February 26, 1811

You well know that the Love of Slander is the prevailing passion of
many in this place, and the spirit of levelling all characters has
prompted them to strike at the best, and the most unexceptionable.

Slander

> To John Thaxter, December 8, 1780

I cannot . . . protect you from the Slanderous arrow that flieth in
Secret.

> To John Adams, August 1, 1781

I do not think female Slander has been the busyest—you might possibly find it in the city where you reside.

To James Lovell, September 12, 1781

I received a letter to-day from Mr. Jefferson, who writes me that he had just received a parcel of English newspapers; they "teem," says he, "with every horror of which nature is capable; assassinations, suicide, thefts, robberies, and, what is worse than thefts, murder, and robbery, the blackest slanders! Indeed, the man must be of rock who can stand all this. To Mr. Adams it will be but one victory the more. It would illy suit me. I do not love difficulties. I am fond of quiet; willing to do my duty; but irratable by slander, and apt to be forced by it to abandon my post. I fancy," says he, "it must be the quantity of animal food eaten by the English, which renders their character unsusceptible of civilization. I suspect that it is in their kitchens, and not in their churches, that their reformation must be worked, and that missionaries from hence would avail more than those who should endeavour to tame them by precepts of religion or philosophy."*

To Mary Cranch, London, October 1, 1785

*Thomas Jefferson to Abigail Adams, Paris, September 25, 1785.

Sleep I am very well & sleep soundly—when I am not vexed.

To Mary Cranch, Philadelphia, April 15, 1800

Small Beginnings From what small causes, do great effects frequently arise?

To John Quincy Adams, Quincy, March 10, 1815

Small Means Great deeds may be performed by a Small means.

To John Quincy Adams, Quincy, November 8, 1813

Small Problems Mole hills I always Expect to find, but them I can easily surmount.

To Mary Cranch, Braintree, July 15, 1766

Life is too short to have the dearest of its enjoyments curtaild. The
Social feelings grow Callous by disuse and lose that pliancy of affection which Sweetens the cup of Life as we drink it. The Rational
pleasures of Friendship and Society, and the still more refined sensations to which delicate minds only are susceptable like the tender
Blosom when the rude Northern Blasts assail them shrink within,
collect themselves together, deprived of the all chearing and Beamy
influence of the Sun. The Blosom falls, and the fruit withers and de-
cays—but here the similtude fails—for tho lost for the present—the
Season returns; the Tree vegetates anew; and the Blossom again puts
forth.

But alass with me; those days which are past, are gone forever;
and time is hastning on that period, when I must fall, to rise no
more; untill Mortality shall put on immortality, and we shall meet
again, pure and unimbodied Spirits.

To John Adams, November 13, 1782

Large mixed companies are not calculated for true Social converse.
It is an observation of Rochfoucault's that a company to be truly
agreable should not consist of more than the number of the Muses,
nor less than the Graces.*

To John Thaxter, Braintree, July 1, 1783

*Thus between three (the Graces) and nine (the Muses).

As you know I am fond of sociability.

To Elizabeth Cranch, London, August 1, 1784

I sigh (though not allow'd) for my social tea parties which I left in
America, and the friendship of my chosen few, and their agreeable
converse would be a rich repast to me, could I transplant them
round me in the Village of Auteuil, with my habits, tastes and Sentiments, which are too firmly rivetted to change with change of
Country or Climate, and at my age the greatest of my enjoyments
consisted in the reciprocation of Friendship.

To Mercy Otis Warren, Auteuil, September 5, 1784

I go from home but very little, yet I do not find my time hang heavy upon my hands. You know that I have no aversion to join in the cheerful circle, or mix in the world, when opportunity offers. I think it tends to rub off those austerities which age is apt to contract, and reminds us, as Goldsmith says, "that we once were young."*

To Abigail Adams Smith, Quincy, February 3, 1794

*Oliver Goldsmith, *The Vicar of Wakefield*.

I love Sociability.

To John Adams, Quincy, February 20, 1796

Social Graces   I should fear you would become rusticated, and lose that polish, which is of some value in the polite world, and without which, I have known many a talent hidden under a bushel, instead of shedding a lustre all around.

To Caroline Smith, Quincy, August 30, 1808

Society   Justice, humanity, and benevolence are the duties you owe to society in general.

To John Quincy Adams, March 20, 1780

The social affections are, and may be made the truest channels for our pleasures and comforts to flow through. Heaven form'd us, not for ourselves, but others.

To Lucy Cranch, London, April 2, 1786

Chastity, Modesty, decency, and conjugal Faith are the pillars of society. Sap these, and the whole fabrick falls sooner or later.

To Elizabeth Shaw, London, October 15, 1786

Solitude   There are times when the heart is peculiarly awake to tender impressions, when philosophy slumbers, or is overpowered by sentiments more conformable to Nature. It is then that I feel myself alone in the wide world, without any one to tenderly care for me, or lend me an assisting hand through the difficulties that surround me, yet my cooler reason dissaproofs the repining thought, and bids me bless the hand from whence my comforts flow.

> To John Adams, December 25, 1780

No Man liveth for himself.*

> To John Adams, October 25, 1782

*Romans 14:7.

Man was not made to be alone. There is more force in that expression than I once conceived there was, for I did not then suppose a person might be alone tho in a croud.

> To Mary Cranch, London, May 25, 1786

There is no temper of mind which I wish to Strive harder against, than a sour discontented complaining disposition.

> To Thomas Boylston Adams, Quincy, April 22, 1801

Sour Dispositions

Steady habits are a presage of future excellence which consist not in resolutions, much less in pretensions, but in action.

> To Caroline Smith, Quincy, February 21, 1813

Steadiness

What cannot be help'd must be endured.

> To John Adams, April 17, 1777

Stoicism

I hope and hope till hope is swallowed up in the victory of Dispair. I then consider all my anxiety as vain since I cannot benifit any one by it, or alter the established order of things.

> To John Adams, August 1, 1781

I wish you to form an easy correct stile. It is necessary to you as a Scholar and gentleman & as a professional Man. . . . In Letter writing, never abreviate your words as thus—twas—instead of it was—twould instead of it would. Study your own language correctly or you can never write elegantly.

> To John Adams Smith, Quincy, after February 11, 1810

Style

Success   I most sincerely wish you a success, proportionate to your Merrits, and ample as your wishes.

To William Cranch, Philadelphia, December 3, 1797

Suffering   I should rather be the Sufferer . . . than the agressor, rather Suffer wrong, than do wrong. This is however but a poor consolation to the oppressed—

To Louisa Catherine Adams, Quincy, April 24, 1816

Sufficiency   Tho I do not abound, I am not in want. I have neither poverty nor Riches but food which is convenient for me and a Heart to be thank-full and content.

To John Adams, April 17, 1777

Suicide   It is not for us to say, or judge, the self immolater—we have all reason enough to say, God be merciful to us.

To Louisa Catherine Adams, Quincy, September 30, 1817

Superiority   The finest tuned instrument is the soonest put out of Tune, but who that possesses them, notwithstanding all the suffering to which they subject them, would drether have a common Tune or a common instrument?

To François Adriaan Vanderkemp, Quincy, April 10, 1817

Superstition   Am I superstitious enough for a good Catholick?

To John Adams, December 25, 1780

Superstition I do believe inherent in the Humane Character, and there is not any person wholly free from it in some shape or other.

To John Quincy Adams, Quincy, September 30, 1816

Sympathy   A similarity of circumstances will always lead to Sympathy.

To James Lovell, Braintree, February–March 1779

Sympathy is a Solace which Friendship can bestow.

To Catherine Johnson, Quincy, September 22, 1811

Where much is given, much shall be required.   *Talents*
> To John Adams, Quincy, May 27, 1794

Every expression of tenderness is a cordial to my Heart. Unimport-   *Tenderness*
ant as they are to the rest of the world, to me they are *every Thing*.
> To John Adams, Boston, July 14, 1776

I know your mind is susceptible of tender impressions; these were
implanted in the human breast for wise purposes.
> To Caroline Smith, Quincy, February 2, 1809

I never trust myself long with the terrors which sometimes intrude   *Terrors*
themselves upon me.
> To John Adams, Braintree, June 16, 1775

You and I think much more than we say.   *Thinking*
> To Abigail Adams Smith, Philadelphia, March 9, 1800

Every Moment of your time is precious, if trifled away never to be   *Time*
recalled. Do not spend too much of it in recreation, it will never afford you that permanent satisfaction which the acquisition of one
Art or Science will give you.
> To John Quincy Adams, March 2, 1780

Time which is said to soften and alleviate Sorrow, encreases anxiety
when connected with expectation.
> To John Adams, October 21, 1781

Who shall give me back Time?
> To John Adams, October 25, 1782

Time and reflection dispelld the mist and illusion.
> To John Quincy Adams, London, June 13, 1786

Time, which improves youth, every year furrows the brow of age.
> To Thomas Boylston Adams, Quincy, November 8, 1796

That time which waits for none may be lost.

To John Adams, Quincy, March 23, 1797

As our time is not our own I cannot say when we may hope to be at liberty.

To William Smith, Philadelphia, July 1, 1797

Tranquility   My own Ideas of pleasure consist in tranquility.

To John Quincy Adams, c. March 15, 1784

Truth   Truths are not always to be spoken.

To Benjamin Rush, August 1794

Truth is truth: as we say, let it come as it will, but how Sweet, "when truths divine come mended from the Tongue."*

To Harriet Welsh, Quincy, March 5, 1815

*Alexander Pope, *Eloisa to Abelard* (1717).

Uniformity   The country round has too much of the level to be in my style. The appearance of uniformity wearies the eye, and confines the imagination.

To Elizabeth Shaw, Bush Hill, March 20, 1781

Usefulness   I have enjoyed for a year past a greater proportion of health, than has fallen to my lot in many preseeding ones, thanks to the Giver of every good and perfect Gift. I fear I have not made so good a use of it as I ought to have done, but shall be calld an unprofitable Servant. May my future days be those of more usefullness, more devoted to the Service of my Maker.

To Abigail Adams Smith, Quincy, May 20, 1808

Value   I do not estimate everything according to the price the world set upon it, but according to the value it is of to me, thus that which was cheapest to you I look upon as highly valuable.

To John Adams, Weymouth, April 12, 1764

I will not Build upon other people's judgment.   *Value Judgment*
To James Lovell, September 20?, 1781

... variety, which Gentlemen are always fond of.   *Variety*
To John Thaxter, May 23, 1781

O dear variety! how pleasing to the human mind is change. I cannot find such a fund of entertainment within myself as not to require outward objects for my amusement. Nature abounds with variety, and the mind, unless fixed down by habit, delights in contemplating new objects, and the variety of scenes which present themselves to the senses were certainly designed to prevent our attention from being too long fixed upon any object.
Sea Journal, July 7, 1784

We stand in need of some variety to keep both body and mind in tune. The bountiful Parent of the universe has amply supplied our wants in this respect, by the succession of day and night, of seed time and harvest, of summer and winter, to which he has added social intercourse and the interchange of friendly offices.

> *"Heaven forming each on other to depend,*
> *A master, or a servant, or a friend."**

To Abigail Adams Smith, Quincy, April 10, 1810

*Alexander Pope, *An Essay on Man,* Epistle II.

It is in our Natures to resist confinement and to pine after variety.
To Hannah Cushing, Quincy, March 2, 1811

The importance of persons is Estimated by the show they make.   *Veneers in Society*
To Isaac Smith, Sr., Auteuil, May 8, 1785

Vicious conduct will always be a source of disquietude to me.   *Viciousness*
To John Adams, Quincy, January 12, 1799

Willingness to Fight   If Men will not fight and defend their own perticuliar spot, if they will not drive the Enemy from their Doors, they deserve the slavery and subjection which awaits them.

> To John Adams, October 20, 1777

Wisdom   I wish you . . . that wisdom which is profitable both for instruction and edification to conduct you in this difficult day.

> To John Adams, Braintree, August 19, 1774

May you be wise as Serpents.*

> To John Adams, September 15, 1776

*Matthew 10:16.

Wishful Thinking   I wish I had studied the prophecies. There seems to be so much pleasure in them.

> To John Adams, Quincy, January 4, 1799

Worry   Dont worry your face into wrinkles

> To John Quincy Adams, New York, September 12, 1790

— *Language, Grammar, and Penmanship*

Foreign Language   Having some small acquaintance with the French tongue, have attempted a translation of it, which I send, for your perusal and correction.

I am sensible that I am but ill qualified for such an undertaking, it being a maxim with me that no one can translate an author well, who cannot write like the original, and I find by Experience that tis more difficult to translate well, than to write well.

> To Isaac Smith, Jr., Weymouth, March 16, 1763

You will suppose I do not look forward with the most pleasureable Ideas, to my visit and residence in a Country the language of which I am a Stranger.

> To Elizabeth Cranch, London, August 1, 1784

Nothing can be more dissagreeable than living in a Country, the language of which you cannot speak.

> To Mary Cranch, Auteuil, April 15, 1785

I feel your embarrassment in a foreign country, the language of which you cannot speak. I know by experience how unpleasant it is, but that is a difficulty which will daily diminish.

> To Thomas Boylston Adams, Quincy, February 11, 1795

Tis no small pleasure to me, to hear of the great proficiency you have made in the French tongue. A Tongue Sweet, and harmonious, a Tongue, useful to Merchants, to Statesmen; to Divines, and especially to Lawyers and Travellers; who by the help of it, may traverse the whole Globe; for in this respect, the French language is pretty much now, what I have heard the Latin formerly was, a universal tongue.

The French Language

> To Isaac Smith, Jr., Weymouth, March 16, 1763

As to Speaking French, I make but little progress in that; but I have acquired much more facility in reading it.

> To Mary Cranch, Auteuil, December 9, 1784

I have a little advice to give you respecting the French language. You had begun to learn it before I left America. Your good pappa, many years ago, gave me what is called a little smattering of it, but Indolence and the apprehension that I could not read it without a preceptor, made me neglect it. But since I came here, I found I must read French or nothing. Your uncle, to interest me in it, procured for me

Racine, Voltaire, Corneille, and Crebillon's plays, all of which are at times acted upon the French Theater. I took my dictionary and applied myself to reading a play a day, by which means I have made considerable progress, making it a rule to write down every word which I was obliged to look. Translating a few lines every day into English, would be another considerable help, and as your pappa so well understands the language he would assist in inspecting Your translation. By this means, and with the assistance of the Books which You may find in the office, you will be able to read it well in a little while.

To Elizabeth Cranch, Auteuil, December 13, 1784

Grammar It is not the studied sentence, nor the elaborate period, which pleases, but the genuine sentiments of the heart expressed with simplicity. All the specimens, which have been handed down to us as models for letter-writing, teach us that natural ease is the greatest beauty of it.

To Lucy Cranch, London, August 27, 1785

Penmanship Excuse a bad pen and cold hands.

To John Thaxter, April 9, 1778

And in the first place, my dear Lucy, shall I find a little fault with you? A fault, from which neither your good sister, nor cousin Abby, is free. It is that all of you so much neglect your handwriting. I know that a sentiment is equally wise and just, written in a good or bad hand; but then there is certainly a more pleasing appearance, when the lines are regular, and the letters distinct and well cut. A sensible woman is so, whether she be handsome or ugly; but who looks not with most pleasure upon the sensible beauty? "Why, my dear aunt," methinks I hear you say, "only look at your own handwriting." Acknowledged; I am very sensible of it, and it is from feeling the disadvantages of it myself, that I am the more solicitous that my young acquaintance should excel me, whilst they have leisure, and their fingers are young and flexible.

To Lucy Cranch, Auteuil, January 24, 1785

If you can get time to pay Some attention to your handwriting it will be an advantage to you. This part of Your Education has been too much neglected.

To Charles Adams, London, c. February 16, 1786

I am glad to find you mending in your hand writing, during the vacancies you & your Brother Charles would do well to attend to that. It is of more importance than perhaps you are aware of, more for a Man than a Woman, but I have always to lament my own inattention in this matter.

To Thomas Boylston Adams, London, March 15, 1787

I was much pleased with the improvement in your hand writing. I have had to regret all my Life time the want of that accomplishment. When I was young I was brought up in a Town where it was not at that time, customary for Girls to attend Schools for writing, and female Education was much less attended to than at the present day; indeed it was almost wholy neglected—when you get a little further advanced you must write a Letter to your Aunt Peabody in your best manner. She will be rejoiced to see your improvement. I shall not now be ashamed to have you write to your parents, which I could not before encourage. I felt so mortified at your hand writing.

To George Washington Adams, Quincy, January 9, 1813

— *Life's Blessings*

The Uneversal Parent has dispenced his Blessings throughout all creation, and tho to some he hath given a more goodly Heritage than others, we have reason to believe that a general order and harmony is maintained by apportioning each their proper station.

To Elizabeth Shaw, London, November 21, 1786

Our blessings are sometimes enhanced to us, by feeling the want of them.

To John Adams, Braintree, May 31, 1789

I feel grateful for the blessings which surround me, and murmur not at those which are withheld.

To Abigail Adams Smith, Philadelphia, January 25, 1791

I should rejoice if you had fewer perplexities, that you might have more agreable Sensations; yet if we look through the year which is past, we have abundant cause for gratitude and thankfullness to Heaven both for public and private Blessings and if we have not all we wish, we have perhaps as much as we ought. It would therefore give me great pleasure to receive a Cheerfull Letter from you.

To John Adams, Quincy, January 4, 1799

I hope I am not unmindfull or unthankfull for the blessings I possess.

To Thomas Boylston Adams, Quincy, August 4, 1799

We can never so justly appreciate the blessings we enjoy, as when we are deprived of them.

To John Quincy Adams, Quincy, December 30, 1804

How many blessings does the bountiful hand of providence scatter in various proportions to alleviate the sorrows and sufferings of a state only meant as the pathwath to felicity.

To Abigail Adams Smith, Quincy, May 23, 1809

When I think of my privations, I am silenced by a recollection of my many blessings.

To Caroline Smith, Quincy, August 6, 1812

I have my blessings—kind and sympathizing Friends and Neighbours, and my health altho feeble, yet I am able to attend the Sick,
and look to my Family.

> To Mercy Otis Warren, Quincy, August 8, 1813

I will remember with gratitude the Blessings I enjoy.

> To John Quincy Adams, Quincy, October 22, 1813

Adieu. Pray write in good Spirits. You know I never could bear to   *Good Spirits*
hear you groan and at this Distance it gives me the vapours.

> To John Adams, Quincy, December 6, 1794

I am sometimes led to question whether the fine and delicate sensi-   *Good Temper*
bilities of the Soul are a real blessing. They so often are wounded
by the insensible, by the unfealing beings which surround them of
which much the larger portion of Mankind are composed, that like
the Rose of Cowper they are shaken by the rude Blast, or witherd by
cold neglect, instead of having the tear of sorrow wiped away by the
sympathizing hand of congenial tenderness. Yet who possesses them
would be willing to exchange them for a cold hearted apathy, and a
stoical indifference. A fine tuned instrument is soonest put out of order, yet what lover of music would wish to possess in preference, an
ordinary, instrument?

> To Ann Harrod, Quincy, February 19, 1805

[With the British evacuation of Boston] I feel a gaieti de Cœur* to   *Happiness*
which before I was a stranger. I think the Sun looks brighter, the
Birds sing more melodiously, and Nature puts on a more chearfull
countenance.

> To John Adams, Braintree, March 31, 1776

*Gaiety of heart; lightheartedness.

I well know that real, true and substantial happiness depend not
upon titles, Rank and fortune; the Gay coach, the Brilliant attire, the

pomp and Etiquet of Courts, rob the mind of that placid harmony, that social intercourse which is an Enemy to ceremony. My Ambition, my happiness centers in him, who sighs for domestick enjoyments, amidst all the world calls happiness—who partakes not in the jovial Feast, or joins the Luxurious table, without turning his mind to the plain unadulterated food which covers his own frugal Board, and sighs for the Feast of reason and the flow of soul.

To John Adams, April 7, 1783

Let every one consider it as a duty which he owes to himself, to his country, and to posterity, to practise virtue, to cultivate knowledge and to revere the Deity, as the only means by which not only individuals but a people or a nation can be prosperous and happy.

To Elizabeth Cranch, London, September 2, 1785

I want to know all about the good folks in whose happiness I feel interested.

To Mary Cranch, Richmond Hill, March 21, 1790

Our portion of happiness is no doubt equal to our deserts.

To Mary Cranch, Philadelphia, April 20, 1792

To communicate pleasure, is reflecting happiness.

To Mary Cranch, Philadelphia, March 3, 1798

When you do all the good in your power, you enjoy all the happiness the practise of virtue can bestow, and long may you receive the Reward.

To Mary Cranch, Philadelphia, March 5, 1798

The mind has power over itself, and happiness has its set in the mind, not in external circumstances, for we frequently see the most affluent, the most discontented and unhappy.

To Abigail Adams Smith, Quincy, October 3, 1808

Much of our happiness in Life depends upon our connexions.

> To William Stephens Smith, Quincy, March 22, 1814

To be happy you must be good, for happiness is built only upon virtue.

> To Charles Francis Adams, Quincy, July 12, 1815

The more harmony and peace is cultivated amongst ourselves the Stronger we link ourselves together and discountenance every little internal bickering and jealousy. The more formidable we shall become to our enemies and better able to defend ourselves against them.

Harmony

> To Thomas Welsh, London, July 22, 1786

— Life's Difficulties

These are times in which a Genious would wish to live. It is not in the still calm of life, or the repose of a pacific station, that great characters are formed. Would Cicero have shone so distinguished an orator, if he had not been roused, kindled and enflamed by the tyranny of Cataline, Millo, Verres and Mark Anthony. The Habits of a vigorous mind are formed in contending with difficulties. All History will convince you of this, and that wisdom and penetration are the fruits of experience, not the Lessons of retirement and leisure.

Adversity

> To John Quincy Adams, January 19, 1780

The School of adversity is a usefull one, and tho not pleasant, her paths are strewed with instruction.

> To John Quincy Adams, Philadelphia, July 20, 1798

In the day of adversity, consider, is judicious advice.

> To Hannah Smith, Philadelphia, January 17, 1800

To rise with dignity, and fall with ease,* is a very desirable qualification; but such is the frailty of human nature; adversity is better calculated to call forth the virtues, than prosperity, which puffeth up, and is unseemly.

To Caroline Smith, Quincy, September 27, 1814

*Paraphrasing Alexander Pope, *An Essay on Man,* Epistle IV.

Afflictions Woe follows woe and one affliction treads upon the heel of another.

To John Adams, Braintree, September 25, 1775

In past years small has been my portion of the Bitter Cup in comparison with the many others. But there is now preparing for me I fear, a large draught thereof. May I be enabled to submit with patience and resignation to the rod and him who hath appointed it, knowing it is directed by unerring wisdom. The consolations of Religion are the only sure comforters in the day of affliction. They are not Buried in the dust, they journey not from us, nor can they be wrested from the mind by the lawless rapine of tyrants.

To John Adams, Braintree, September 29, 1775

It is .... from the Remembrance of the joys I have lost that the arrow of affliction is pointed.

To John Adams, October 25, 1782

Many are the afflictions of the righteous.* Would to Heaven that the clouds would disperse, and give them a brighter day.

To Lucy Cranch, Auteuil, January 24, 1785

*Psalms 34:19.

That I have been Supported, Sustaind and carried through one of the Severest trials of Life, is a subject of gratitude to that Being who saw fit thus to visit me.

To John Quincy Adams, Quincy, October 22, 1813

Twenty years you observe make great Alterations in all of us. So   *Aging*
does Seven. When we are travelling down the Gulfe. I found after an
absence of seven years from my country a great change, more visible, in those I left in middle Age, than those in more advanced Life.

To John Quincy Adams, Quincy, May 2, 1816

It costs me not much difficulty to suppose that my Friends who were
already grown old, when I Saw them last, are old still, but it costs me
a good deal sometimes to think of those who were at that time
young, as being older than they were, not having been an Eye Witness of the change which time has made on them.

To John Quincy Adams, Quincy, August 7, 1816

We have Some among us who love to fish in troubled waters, and   *Agitation*
who are more wroth at being neglected than at the measures of
Government on any other account.

To John Adams, April 12, 1784

My agitated mind wants repose.

To John Adams, Quincy, April 26, 1797

In vain do I strive to through [i.e., throw] off in the company of my   *Anxieties*
Friends some of the anxiety of my Heart, it increases in proportion
to my endeavours to conceal it.

To John Adams, Braintree, November 12–13, 1778

[About sailing to Europe:] My fears and anxieties are present; my
hopes and expectations, distant.

To John Adams, February 11, 1784

None of us live without our anxieties, tho some are of a much more
painfull kind than others.

To Mary Cranch, Richmond Hill, November 1, 1789

I know how to feel for you too the anxiety of a parent.

> To Mary Cranch, Richmond Hill, March 21, 1790

I know all my anxiety is of little avail. Yet I cannot divest myself of it.

> To John Adams, Quincy, December 23, 1798

Sure I have enough of public and private anxiety to humble a prouder Heart than mine.

> To Mary Cranch, Norfolk, Conn., May 26, 1800

Being a Burden I have too much pride to be a clog to any body.

> To John Adams, Weymouth, September 12, 1763

Dangers The Rocks and quick Sands appear upon every Side.

> To John Adams, Braintree, August 19, 1774

Danger they say makes people valiant.

> To John Adams, Braintree, July 5, 1775

Theory and practise are two very different things; and the object magnifies, as I approach nearer to it.

> To John Adams, Braintree, December 15, 1783

Common danger will more firmly unite the people.

> To John Quincy Adams, Philadelphia, March 17, 1798

Difficulties The Habits of a vigorous mind are formed in contending with difficulties. All History will convince you of this.

> To John Quincy Adams, January 12, 1780

I hate to complain. No one is without their difficulties, whether in High, or low Life, & every person knows best where their own shoe pinches.

> To Mary Cranch, Richmond Hill, March 21, 1790

Who is without their troubles?

> To Mary Cranch, New York, October 10, 1790

No station in Life was ever designd by providence to be free from trouble and anxiety. The portion I believe is much more equally distributed than we imagine.

> To Mary Cranch, Philadelphia, December 21, 1790

We know not what we can do or bear, till called to the trial. I have passed through many painful ones, yet have enjoyed as much happiness through life as usually falls to the lot of mortals; and, when my enjoyments have been damped, curtailed, or molested, it has not been owing to vice, that great disturber of human happiness, but sometimes to folly, in myself or others, or the hand of Providence, which has seen fit to afflict me. I feel grateful for the blessings which surround me, and murmur not at those which are withheld.

> To Abigail Adams Smith, Philadelphia, January 25, 1791

We must all have our trials, some of one kind & some of another.

> To Mary Cranch, Philadelphia, March 29, 1792

There must be a some thing to Mar all our enjoyments in a state of Probation like this Life, "a Cruel something unpossessd."*

> To John Adams, Quincy, February 1, 1793

*Matthew Prior, "The Ladle," line 165.

Heaven knows what is proper for our trials in this Life. I pray that I may be resigned, and submissive what ever I may be calld to endure. Heitherto, I may say, Goodness and mercy have followed me.*

> To Louisa Catherine Adams, Quincy, April 28, 1811

*Psalms 23:6.

Now do not deny my request on purpose to make me feel the weight of your observation, "that we are often disappointed when

Disappointment

we set our minds upon that which is to yield us great happiness." I know it too well already. Daily experience teaches me that truth. . . . Many of our disappointments and much of our unhappiness arise from our forming false notions of things and persons. We strangely impose upon ourselves; we create a fairy land of happiness. Fancy is fruitful and promises fair, but, like the dog in the fable,* we catch at a shadow, and when we find the disappointment, we are vexed, not with ourselves, who are really the impostors, but with the poor, in-nocent thing or person of whom we have formed such strange ideas. When this is the case, I believe we always find, that we have enjoyed more pleasure in the anticipation than in the real enjoyment of our wishes.

. . . Some disppointments are, indeed, more grievous than others. Since they are our lot, let us bear them with patience. That person that cannot bear a disappointment, must not live in a world so changeable as this, and 'tis wise it should be so; for, were we to enjoy a continual prosperity, we should be too firmly attached to the world ever to think of quitting it, and there would be room to fear, that we should be so far intoxicated with prosperity as to swim smoothly from joy to joy, along life's short current, wholly unmindful of the vast ocean, Eternity.

To Hannah Lincoln, Weymouth, October 5, 1761

*Aesop's *Fables*.

I hate Negatives when I have set my Heart upon any thing.

To Mary Cranch, Philadelphia, December 12, 1797

If my wishes are blasted I must submit to it, as a punishment, a trial, an affliction which I must bear and what I cannot remedy I must en-dure.

To John Adams, Quincy, January 12, 1799

We cannot always command just what we wish.

To Harriet Welsh, Quincy, August 6, 1815

Distress and difficulties in private life, are frequently Spurs to dilligence, so have we seen publick industery excited in the same manner.

Distress

> To Mercy Otis Warren, London, May 14, 1787

We have too many high sounding words, and too few actions that correspond with them.

Easier Said Than Done

> To John Adams, Braintree, October 16, 1774

Words are easy, but ways and means difficult to obtain.

> To John Adams, Quincy, April 25, 1794

May the triumph of the wicked be short.

Evil into Good

> To Elizabeth Shaw, London, January 20, 1787

The Devil is always easier raisd than laid.

> To John Adams, Quincy, December 12, 1794

That which was meant for evil, I hope may terminate in Good.

> To Mary Cranch, Philadelphia, April 7, 1798

I never was of a desponding nature. Whatever may be the allotments of providence for me or mine, my confidence in the Supreme Ruler will remain unshaken—and my belief that all partial Evil will terminate in universal good is firm—altho we cannot perceive how or when. The History of Joseph and his Brethrean is a lesson full of instruction.*

> To John Quincy Adams, Quincy, April 23, 1813

*Genesis 37:39–47.

To know how to be exalted and how to be abased; is a great attainment in the Christian Character.

Good and Bad Times

> To Hannah Lincoln Storer, Richmond Hill, January 29, 1790

In the midst of my afflictions I have my comforts to lighten the load, and remind me that the same hand which wounds can dispense blessings.

> To Elizabeth Peabody, Quincy, April 23, 1810

We must look to the bright Side, as well as to the dark Shade of the picture, and balance our Comforts, against our privations—and surely we shall have cause to rejoice.

> To Catherine Johnson, Quincy, March 6, 1811

Good and Evil The Beauty and fragrance of the Rose, would be but a small compensation for the wounds which might be felt in the gathering and wearing it.

> To John Adams, December 7, 1783

If there was not a much greater proportion of good than evil predominating in the World, who could suffer being here below?

> To Elizabeth Shaw, London, March 10, 1787

Is there no pleasure but in troubled waters?

> To John Adams, Quincy, December 26, 1794

Shall we receive Good and not evil? . . . Where is the situation in Life which exempts us from trouble? Who of us pass through the world with our path strewed with flowers, without encountering the thorns? In what ever state we are, we shall find a mixture of good and evil, and we must learn to receive these vicissitudes of life, so as not to be unduly exalted by the one, or depressed by the other. No cup so bitter, but what some cordial drops are mingled by a kind Providence, who knows how . . . to "temper the wind to the Shorn Lamb."*

> To Mary Cranch, East Chester, N.Y., October 31, 1799

*An ancient French proverb made popular by Laurence Sterne's *A Sentimental Journey through France and Italy by Mr. Yorick* (1768).

Shall I receive good and not evil? I will not forget the blessings which sweeten Life.

> To Mary Cranch, Norfolk, Conn., May 26, 1800

Mercy and judgment are the mingled cup allotted me. Shall I receive good and not evil?

> To Mary Cranch, Philadelphia, November 10, 1800

Shall we receive good and not evil?

> To Catherine Johnson, Quincy, January 19, 1811

You will suppose that I might have written to you long e'er this, but as my letters would only have been a detail of grievances and troubles I was reluctant at taking my pen, and put it off from day to day.

> To Mary Cranch, New York, December 12, 1790

Grievances and Troubles

We must all have our trials, some of one kind & some of another.

> To Mary Cranch, Philadelphia, March 29, 1792

Who of us can say, that we have not our troubles? Our portion of happiness is no doubt equal to our deserts.

> To Mary Cranch, Philadelphia, April 20, 1792

There must be a something to Mar all our enjoyments in a state of Probation like this Life, "a Cruel Something unpossessd."*

> To John Adams, Quincy, February 1, 1793

*Matthew Prior, *The Ladle,* II, line 165.

How consolatary the reflection, that whom the Lord loveth, he chasteneth.*

> To Mary Cranch, Springfield, Mass., April 30, 1797

*Proverbs 13:24; Hebrews 12:6.

Seldom comes a solitary woe.

> To John Quincy Adams, Philadelphia, June 15, 1797

It is a long lane which has no turn. Who of us is exempt from trouble, and sorrow of some kind?

> To William Cranch, Philadelphia, November 15, 1797

Woes are seldom solitary.

> To John Quincy Adams, Philadelphia, April 21, 1798

Who upon this Stage of existence can say he is without trouble? The Scripture assures us that Man is born to it,* and Religion alone teaches us to bear it like Christians.

> To Elizabeth Peabody, Philadelphia, July 7, 1798

*Job 5:7.

Everyone knows their own bitterness.

> To Elizabeth Peabody, Philadelphia, February 4, 1800

Loneliness How lonely are my days? How lonely are my Nights?

> To John Adams, Sunday Evening, December 27, 1778

My habituation, how disconsolate it looks! My table I set down to it but cannot swallow my food. O Why was I born with so much Sensibility and why possessing it have I so often been call'd to struggle with it? . . . My hopes and fears rise alternately. I cannot resign more than I do, unless life itself was called for. —My dear sons I can not think of them without a tear, little do they know the feelings of a Mother's Heart!

> To John Adams, Braintree, November 14, 1779

I shall wish to hear often from you. It is the only solace I shall have for your absence, but I will not add to your publick burdens personal glooms.

> To John Adams, Quincy, November 15, 1798

You complain that you are solitary. I know that must be your lot frequently. It is then you want the relief that your talkative wife cared to afford.

> To John Adams, Quincy, December 23, 1798

There are some maladies so deep rooted, that the most delicate hand dare not probe. The attempt might fix an incurable wound.

Maladies

> To Eliza Susan Quincy, Quincy, March 24, 1806

You should not forget what you learn that is valuable. That is the misfortune of old Age, which I too often find to my own mortification—

Memory

> To Charles Francis Adams, Quincy, March 28, 1816

A critical period of Life Augments my complaints.

Menopause

> To Mary Cranch, Philadelphia, April 20, 1792

Necessity will oblige . . . some desperate steps.

Necessity

> To John Adams, Weymouth, June 16?, 1775

Great necessities call out great virtues.

> To John Adams, June 8, 1779

Necessity has no law.

> To Elizabeth Shaw, on board the ship *Active*, July 10?, 1784

Necessity is without Law.

> To Mary Cranch, London, June 24, 1785

I am glad to learn from you that Luxery is in some measure retrenched, necessity itself may carry virtue in its train.

> To Charles Storer, London, March 23, 1786

Necessity knows no Law.

To Catherine Johnson, Philadelphia, March 13, 1800

Obstacles It has been my Lot to be fettered one way or another.

To Mary Cranch, Richmond Hill, October 4, 1789

Old Age I have made an important discovery, viz. that an old man is not a Young man.

To John Adams, Quincy, February 2, 1794

My constant attendance upon her [i.e., John Adams's mother] has very much lessend my desire of long life.

To John Adams, Quincy, February 26, 1794

Time, which improves youth, every year furrows the brow of age.

> *"Our years*
> *As life declines, speed rapidly away;*
> *And not a year but pilfers, as he goes,*
> *Some youthful grace that age would gladly keep,*
> *A tooth or auburn lock."**

Thus, my son, in the course of three years' absence, you will find many depredations of time upon those whom you left advanced in life, and in none more, perhaps, than in your mother, whose frequent indispositions hasten its strides and impair a frail fabric. But neither time, absence nor sickness have lessened the warmth of her affection for her dear children, which will burn with undiminished fervour until the lamp of life is extinguished together with the name of Abigail Adams.

To Thomas Boylston Adams, Quincy, November 8, 1796

*William Cowper, *The Task,* Book I, "The Sofa."

Of how uncertain a duration are all our worldly possessions and Earthly comforts? If we could not look for brighter Scenes and fairer prospects, who could wish to remain the victims of pain and sorrow?

> To John Adams, Quincy, April 17, 1797

Four or five years absence will make many Chasms amongst your acquaintance. It will give vigor to youth, but wrinkles to Age, and you will find Time has shed his hoary Honours upon the Heads of your parents. If he spairs their Lives to you, perhaps he will have so changed them, as to make the alteration painfull to you, but tho he may waist and decay these earthly Fabricks, whilst the Heart Beats, it will Beat for the welfare and happiness of those who are deservedly dear to their affectionate Mother.

> To Thomas Boylston Adams, East Chester, N.Y., November 7, 1797

I have seen too many instances of parents dependant upon Children. Tho there are instances which do honour to humane nature, there are more which disgrace it.

> To Mary Cranch, Philadelphia, February 21, 1798

"How the Shadows Lengthen, as the Sun declines,"* and this may be applied to the National as well as the natural system. As we descend the Hill of Life, our gay and visionary prospect vanish, and what gilded our Meridian days, our Zenith of Life, as the Shadows lengthen, we see through a different medium and may justly estimate many of our persuits as vanity and vexation of spirit.

"But there's a Brighter world on high" which opens to us prospects more permanent and pleasure more durable. To that let us aspire in the sure and certain hope, that by a patient Continuence in the path of Religion and virtue, we shall assuredly reap, if we faint not, the happy fruits of a glorious immortality.

> To Mary Cranch, Philadelphia, March 27, 1798

*Laurence Sterne, *A Sentimental Journey through France and Italy by Mr. Yorick* (1768).

To hear of the Health, and welfare, of old and esteemed Friends, gives pleasure to her, who sincerely rejoices, that the decline of Life, of all those, whom she highly values; is renderd agreable by the enjoyment of Health, peace, and Competance. Blessings at all periods valuable but more particularly so, when active Life, yealds to the more tranquil and contemplative Scenes of Age. A scene to which your Friends are as rapidly hastning, as time can carry them.

> To Mercy Otis Warren, Quincy, April 25, 1798

The longer we live in the world, the more do troubles thicken upon us, yet we hug the fleeting shadow.

> To Mary Cranch, Philadelphia, June 1, 1798

Trials of various kinds seem to be reserved for our gray Hairs, for our declining years. Shall I receive good and not evil? I will not forget the blessings which sweeten Life.

> To Mary Cranch, Norfolk, Conn., May 26, 1800

Peace and esteem is all that age can hope.

> To Ann Quincy Packard, Quincy, March 11, 1805

I think a little journey would be of service to me; but I find, as years and infirmities increase, my courage and enterprise diminish. Ossian says, "Age is dark and unlovely."* When I look in my glass, I do not much wonder at the story related of a very celebrated painter, Zeuxis,** who, it is said, died of laughing at a comical picture he had made of an old woman. If our glass flatters us in youth, it tells us truths in age. The cold hand of death has frozen up some of the streams of our early friendships; the congelation is gaining upon our vital powers and marking us for the tomb. "May we so number our days as to apply our hearts unto wisdom."†

"The man is yet unborn who duly weighs an hour."‡

> To Elizabeth Shaw, Quincy, June 5, 1809

*Ossian, *Cathon: A Poem.*   **Zeuxis, who lived around 400 B.C.
†Psalms 90:12.   ‡Edward Young, *Night Thoughts* (1742–1745).

Old age with its infirmities assail me.

> To Caroline Smith, Quincy, December 9, 1809

When we get so far advanced in years as your Father & I are, the keepers of the house Fumble and we know not what a day may bring forth.

> To Abigail Adams Smith, Quincy, February 11, 1810

After three Score years and ten, few persons have any right to look for much enjoyment.

> To Abigail Adams Smith, Quincy, February 11, 1810

[On the death of William Cushing:] When it is painfull to behold the powers of the Body and the noble faculties of the mind Sinking into apathy of Age the Glory is to wish to die. That wish is praise and promise, it applauds past Life and promises our future bliss. Of that bliss you have every well grounded hope which Religion inspires us as your solace, your consolation and your anchor.

> To Hannah Cushing, Quincy, September 15, 1810

It is a sad thing to outlive our usefullness, our faculties and hang like a dead branch upon a Tree.

> To Elizabeth Peabody, Quincy, October 10, 1810

Old Age is a Disease which time does not cure, and I must say I would not live always if I could.

> To John Quincy Adams, Quincy, April 8, 1811

Your Father and myself [are] as well as old Age can expect to be, neither of us deaf, dumb or blind as yet, trembling and shakeing however, and every week almost loosing some one of our ancient Friends and acquaintance, who with warning voices call us to be ready to follow, not only the Aged, but those much Younger, we are called to mourn over before half their days are Numberd to the Age of Man. . . . Yet how preferable is it, how desirable to be calld out of Life before the days come in which a Grasshopper shall be considerd as a burden, and we become burdensome to all around us?

> To John Quincy Adams, Quincy, May 15, 1811

What a wreck does age and sickness make of the human Frame.

> To Elizabeth Peabody, Quincy, July 10, 1811

Personally we have arrived so near the close of the drama that we can experience but few of the evils which await the rising generation.

> To Mercy Otis Warren, Quincy, December 30, 1812

We are all in usual health. Age and infirmities will come, but we have had our day, and as yet are neither Blind or deaf, which I consider amongst many other blessings not the least.

> To Louisa Catherine Adams, Quincy, July 24, 1813

Years and affliction have made such depredations upon your parents, more particularly upon your Mother, that should she live to see you again you would find her so changed in person that you would scarcly know her.

> To John Quincy Adams, Quincy, November 8, 1813

At my Age much is not to be looked for.

> To Louisa Catherine Adams, Quincy, December 19, 1813

It is easier to pull down an old building, than to repair or build it up again, and I most Sensibly feel my weakness.

> To Julia Rush, Quincy, December 21, 1813

What is Strength at my age but weakness?

> To John Quincy Adams, Quincy, December 24, 1813

The Glass, a faithfull mirror is a place that I do not like to look in. Yet why should I avoid what all must see and all know that this earthly fabrick must fall to decay before this mortal can put on immortality.

> To Elizabeth Peabody, Quincy, January 13, 1814

I am sometimes tempted to complain that at a period of Life, when we must retire from the active scene of it, we should be deprived by loss of sight, from the mental food, which we must need for support, when the World is receeding from us. But as it is the order of nature, and there is a morning and a noon, there must be an Evening, when the Lengthening Shadows admonish us of approaching Night and reconcile us to our destiny.

> To John Quincy Adams, Quincy, February 27, 1814

If we live to old Age, "string after string is severed from the heart" untill, as one expresses it, we have scarcly anything left to resign, but Breath.*

> To Mercy Otis Warren, Quincy, May 5, 1814

*James Thomson, *On the Death of a Particular Friend.*

Four score and ten is an age, when we can neither expect health, or much strength, when our strength is weakness. I cannot say that I have no pleasure in my days; I have abundant in this, my sickness. I have had kind, attentive friends, a skillful physician, and every human aid: is there not pleasure in all this? and unto the Great First Cause be the praise.

> To Caroline Smith, Quincy, September 27, 1814

I believe I told you this before, but old Age is forgetfull.

> To Harriet Welsh, Quincy, October 30, 1814

Old Age has less Security for Life than Youth. We know not what a day may bring forth.

> To Sarah A. Adams, Quincy, December 20, 1814

231

Old and decayed as I am, . . . sure my glass does not flatter me.

> To John Quincy Adams, Quincy, March 10, 1815

Four score years are not to be relied upon more than three score and ten. The depredations of time are daily visible and not less more seen than felt.

> To John Quincy Adams, Quincy, December 2, 1815

Since my last Letter to you, which I think was in January, I then wrote to you under an impression that it would prove my Last. But it has pleased Heaven to keep me yet longer from the Skies. I cannot say, but at times, I have felt regret at being like to return again to the world—of which I have more of a prospect than for months past. The desire of seeing my dear Children once more has been one of the strongest ligaments, which has bound me to Earth.

If I should recover Strength again to be usefull to myself and Family, I shall conclude that there are yet further duties for me to perform, or further trials for me to endure in either Situation "I trust the Ruler of the Skies."*

> To John Quincy Adams, Quincy, March 22, 1816

*Alexander Pope, *Imitations of Horace,* Book I, Epistle VI.

Old people cannot recover lost strength like young ones.

> To Harriet Welsh, Quincy, March 25, 1816

My dear Son, altho you left your parents Aged, if they Live to see you return, you will read in their decayed visages and see in their feeble Limbs, the ravages of Time. Yet has this universal destroyer Spaired to us, the Sense of hearing, which I esteem a great blessing, nor has he extinguished our Sight, tho his claws have impaired it. We both of us enjoy Society.

> To John Quincy Adams, Quincy, August 7, 1816

While some of us are passing off the Stage; others are coming on to take our places—Longevity is the lot of so few, and is so Seldom ren-

derd comfortable by the association of good health and Spirits, that
the Psalmist describes it, as days in which there are no pleasures, but
thanks to a kind providence, which has followed me, with goodness
and mercy all the days of my Life,* in none of which I can say, that
I had not some pleasure. To live comfortably while we do Live, is
every thing which can be wished for untill the curtain drops, that
hangs between Time & Eternity.

To Louisa Catherine Adams, Quincy, August 9, 1816

*Psalms 23:6.

Your Father and I have Lived to an Age to be Sought for as Curiosi-
ties—accordingly we have more Strangers to visit us and more company than for years past. Having the sense of hearing so well preserved to us, we can enjoy Society, which at our advanced period I
consider a great Blessing. And our Sight, tho much impaired, is still
such that we can read.

Altho as Mr. Jefferson expresses it, "Memory is constantly enlarging its frightfull blank, and parting with all we have ever seen and
known," reconciles us to the period, when it is reasonable we should
drop off, and make room for another growth, when we have lived
our generation out, we should not wish to encroach on another. He
adds (what I feel and have seen, and what I deprecate) of all humane
contemplations, the most abhorrent is "body without mind."* What
ever Humiliation is destined for us in this respect, is submitted to a
higher power to that Being whose disposition has given no understanding.

To John Quincy Adams, Quincy, August 27, 1816

*Jefferson to John Adams, August 1, 1816.

With Years & old Age, the little which can be acquired soon vanishes
—it is necessary that all the good we can do and all the knowledge
we can obtain should be applied for the benefit of those who are to
succeed us. No Man liveth for himself.*

To John Adams 2nd, Quincy, October 24, 1816

*Romans 14:7.

If it were not for our Books, which we can yet read, and our pens, we should find some heavy hours in these long evenings.

To John Adams 2nd, Quincy, October 24, 1816

If either of you live to 70 Years, You will find your fingers grow Stiff, your faculties dull, your memory treacherous, and your immagination decayed and blunted by the tooth of old Time—

To John Adams, Jr., Quincy, March 16, 1817

My Glass will neither flatter or lie—and that tells me I am aged, wrinkled & decayed. Thanks to a kind providence that I can hear & see so well, and enjoy so large a share of health.

To Harriet Welsh, Quincy, December 1, 1817

I hope my dear Son that you will come and see us, indeed you must, if only for a short time. If Life should still be continued to us. Yet every day steals something from us and Nature cannot long Sustain herself against the depredations of time—I think with Mr. Jefferson that one of the most humiliating Spectacles is Body without mind.*
Come then and see us, while something of that remains.

To John Quincy Adams, Quincy, May 30, 1818

*Jefferson to John Adams, August 1, 1816.

As I do not Copy, and am an old woman may relate twice over the same storys, for memory is treacherous.

To Harriet Welsh, Quincy, June 12, 1818

Perplexities Perplexitys surround me which ever way I look.

To John Adams, Quincy, March 23, 1797

I have my perplexities. . . . I shall not however trouble you with them. I will surmount those which are to be conquered, and submit to those which are not.

To John Adams, Quincy, April 9, 1797

I hate Negatives when I have set my Heart upon any thing.

Rejections

To Mary Cranch, Philadelphia, December 12, 1797

There is a period of Life too, when neither business or pleasure can be persued with the ardour of Youth. Then it is that we feel more sensibly the want of domestick tranquility and retirement. May your declining years my dear sir be as repleat with happiness as the visisi-tudes of Humane Life will permit, and when this transitory scene ends, may you meet the Reward of a good and Faithfull Servant.*

Retirement

To Cotton Tufts, New York, November 22, 1789

*Matthew 25:23.

I feel that retirement, and domestic pleasures, are those only which I expect to receive pleasure from.

To Catherine Johnson, Quincy, August 20, 1800

[Contemplating a transatlantic voyage:] Theory and practice are two very different things; and the object magnifies, as I approach nearer to it.

Theory vs. Practice

To John Adams, Braintree, December 15, 1783

We know not what we can do or bear, till called to the trial.

To Abigail Adams Smith, Philadelphia, January 25, 1791

I am for having as little trouble as possible. As we pass down the vale of years we shall want repose if we live.

To Cotton Tufts, Philadelphia, May 23, 1798

What right have I to be exempted from trouble of some kind or other, when a whole world is filld with evils of all sorts.

Troubles

To John Adams, Quincy, December 23, 1798

I make it my rule, not to repine, but to bear, as becomes one who has much to be gratefull and thankfull for, that portion of Sorrow and unhappiness which Providence sees fit to allot me. If all is not according to my wishes, I still have more than my deserts.

To Elizabeth Peabody, Quincy, December 30, 1798

Man is born to trouble as the sparks file upwards, we daily experience this truth; both your public and domestic occurencies; and every one knows their own bitterness when they are the result of the dispensations of providence, it becomes us to kiss the Rod, but when they are brought upon us, by our own indiscretion, folly and wickedness, we deserve all the wretchedness they intail; but it is a bitter portion when tho innocent ourselves we suffer from those, too closely connected with us, not to wound us in the sharpest manner; how often when the Heart is sorrowfull are we called upon to assume the smile of cheerfulnes, and the aspect of content? You can trace my thoughts, to their source.

To Elizabeth Peabody, Quincy, April 9, 1799

God tempers the wind to the shorn Lamb, says Sterne,* all our troubles in this Life are no doubt intended for salutary purposes: with them is blended goodness and mercy, and with Job I would say although he slay me I will trust in him.**

To Lucy Cranch Greenleaf, Quincy, July 1813

*An ancient French proverb made popular by Laurence Sterne's *A Sentimental Journey through France and Italy by Mr. Yorick* (1768).   **Job 13:15.

The calamities which afflict our family . . . have rolled in wave after wave.

To John Quincy Adams, Quincy, September 13, 1813

Every heart knows its own bitterness.

To Louisa Catherine Adams, Quincy, September 30
and November 12, 1817

This life is well termed a checkered state; tis wisely ordered so, since with all the visisitudes we pass through we are still strongly attached to it.

To Mercy Otis Warren, Braintree, December 10, 1778

Looking back for 20 years and exclaiming what a change! but such are the visisitudes of Life, and the Transitory fleeting state of all sublinary things; of all pride that which persons discover from Riches is the weakest. If we look over our acquaintance, how many do we find who were a few years ago in affluence, now reduced to real want but there is no Family amongst them all whose schemes have proved so visionary, and so abortive as the unhappy one we are now commisirating. Better is a little with contentment than great Treasure; and trouble therewith.

To Mary Cranch, Richmond Hill, February 20, 1790

— *Life's Uncertainties*

Our Lot is a checkerd one.

To Catherine Johnson, Quincy, July 31, 1811

Chance governs many actions of my life.

To Abigail Adams Smith, Philadelphia, November 21, 1790

The way to command Fortune is to be as independent of her as possible.

To Abigail Adams Smith, Philadelphia, February 21, 1791

That Life is long, which answers life's great end. I am often led to inquire, why are the gifts of fortune so unequally distributed? Why is there so many thorns scattered in the path of those, who by their lives and conduct appear to deserve more easy and eligible situations, whilst the heart or disposition to use them for the benefit of their fellow creatures. But the ways of heaven are unsearchable, and the dispositions of providence wise and equitable.

To Elizabeth Peabody, Quincy, June 22, 1810

Heaven from all overtures hides the Book of Fate.

To Elizabeth Peabody, Quincy, October 22, 1811

What a pity that fortune does not follow the Brave, and favour the virtuous—yet maybe they owe their very virtues to her frowns.

To Harriet Welsh, Quincy, October 24, 1816

The Future   Great Events are most certainly in the womb of futurity.

To John Adams, Braintree, May 7, 1775

We cannot see into futurity.

To John Adams, April 10, 1782

The Book of fate is wisely closed from the prying Eye of man.

To Elizabeth Cranch, Auteuil, January 3, 1785

It is not permitted us to look into futurity, nor can we say with certainty what will be the Lot of any one.

To Mary Cranch, London, January 10, 1786

The Book of futurity is wisely closed from our Eyes.

To Mary Cranch, London, February 26 and June 13, 1786

Heaven only knows how we are to be disposed of.

To Thomas Jefferson, London, February 26, 1788

We see so little Way before us, that I think it best to submit all futurity into the hands of the great Disposer of Events, who has directed us not to be anxious over much. "To enjoy is to obey."* I will therefore with gratitude reflect upon the large portion of comfort and happiness which has fallen to my lot, without repining at that which is denyd me.

To John Adams, Quincy, December 24, 1794

*Psalms 119:16.

We see but a little way into futurity, and we know not what is before us. So we will hope for the Blessings of Peace and plenty, and thankfull Hearts to enjoy them.

To William Smith, East Chester, N.Y., October 23, 1797, and to
Elizabeth Peabody, Quincy, June 10, 1807

As yet sufficient light has not reached us to enable us to judge of the future—I cannot say System, for where can that be found, when Revolution succeeds revolution, like wave following wave.

To John Quincy Adams, Philadelphia, February 8, 1800

Time only can disclose what the future will be.

To John Quincy Adams, Philadelphia, February 28, 1800

We see but a little way before us. The curtain is draped between us and the future.

To Abigail Adams Smith, Philadelphia, March 9, 1800

I leave to time the unfolding of a drama.

To Thomas Boylston Adams, Washington, December 13, 1800

What is before us God only knows.

To Cotton Tufts, Washington, December 15, 1800

What is to be our future Lot—Heaven only knows. May the Righteous few save our Land.

To Abigail Adams Smith, Quincy, August 29, 1808

The longer I live, the more wrapt in clouds and darkness does the future appear to me.

> To Mercy Otis Warren, Quincy, December 30, 1812

Goods of Fortune   Why why are the goods of fortune so niggardly bestowed upon the deserving, and so wantonly scatterd upon fools and knaves?

> To Thomas Boylston Adams, Quincy, June 20, 1803

Uncertainty   What course you can or will take is all wrapt in the Bosom of futurity. Uncertainty and expectation leave the mind great Scope.

> To John Adams, Braintree, August 19, 1774

Tis a day of doubtfull expectation. Heaven only knows our destiny.

> To John Adams, October 5, 1777

A dissagreable certainty is preferable to a painfull suspence.

> To John Thaxter, May 21, 1778

One month of daily expectation, is more tedious than a year of certainty.

> To John Adams, Braintree, November 11, 1783

We may truly say, we know not what a day will bring forth—from every side we are in Danger. We are in perils by Land, and we are in perils by Sea; and in perils from false Brethren.

> To Mary Cranch, Philadelphia, July 6, 1797

We live in critical Times. I hope the vessel will be conducted in safety through the Rocks and quicksands and protected from all warring Elements.

> To Ruth Dalton, c. July 18, 1797

Every day brings up Something.

> To Cotton Tufts, Philadelphia, June 29, 1798

Time & Chance happen to all men.
>   To William Cranch, Philadelphia, February 4, 1800

Rocks & Shoals are before us—Heaven knows where we shall be landed we see as yet but in part.
>   To Catherine Johnson, Philadelphia, May 9, 1800

What is before us Heaven only knows. Time only can unfold.
>   To John Quincy Adams, Washington, January 29, 1801

We know not one day what another will bring forth the whole world is in a turmoil.
>   To Abigail Adams Smith, Quincy, July 31, 1808

All things are uncertain and fluctuating in this world.
>   To Edward Miller, August 15, 1812

Are not the politicks of the world at this day beyond calculation or prophecy?
>   To François Adriaan Vanderkemp, Quincy, February 23, 1814

We know not what a day may bring forth.
>   To François Adriaan Vanderkemp, Quincy, April 10, 1817

Pleasing Ideas must Yeald to new arrangements.   *Unforeseen Events*
>   To John Adams, Quincy, April 6, 1797

— Love

There is a tye more binding than Humanity, and stronger than Friendship, which makes us anxious for the happiness and welfare of those to whom it binds us. It makes their Misfortunes, Sorrows and afflictions, our own. Unite these, and there is a threefold cord—by this cord I am not ashamed to own myself bound, nor do I believe that you are wholly free from it.

> To John Adams, Weymouth, August 11, 1763

Love is an intellectual pleasure, and even the senses will be weakly affected where the Heart does not participate.

> To John Thaxter, July 21, 1780

The indissoluble Bond which affection first began and my security depends not upon your passion, which other objects might more easily excite, but upon the sober and settled dictates of Religion and Honour. It is these that cement, at the same time that they ensure the affections.

> To John Adams, Braintree, November 13, 1780

Assurances of unabating Love and affection, which tho a thousand times told, will never diminish of their value.

> To John Adams, Quincy, March 25, 1797

From the abundance of the heart the stream flows.

> To John Adams, Quincy, April 26, 1797

Affection Affection and intimacy will cover a multitude of faults.

> Sea Journal, July 6, 1784

Beauty Time will Dim the Lustre of the Eye, and wither the bloom of the face, tho it may perfect and mature those mental attractions which yield a more permanent, and solid satisfaction, when the ardour of passion settles into the more lasting union of Friendship.

> To John Quincy Adams, Quincy, February 29, 1796

Expressions of Love Your Letters are always valuable to me, but more particularly so, when they close with an affectionate assurance of regard, which tho I do not doubt, is never repeated without exciting the tenderest sen-

timents—and never omitted without pain to the affectionate Bosom
of Your Portia.

To John Adams, July 16, 1780

To the great Physician both of body and soul I committed you and
yours, and set out with an anxious mind and heavey Heart.

To Mary Cranch, Philadelphia, November 2, 1800

Leaving Loved Ones

Tis Natural to feel an affection for every thing which belongs to
those we love, and most so when the object is far—far distant from
us.

To John Adams, February 13, 1779

Loved Ones

A Heart agitated with the remains of a former passion is most susceptable of a new one.

To John Quincy Adams, London, February 16, 1786

*Love on the
Rebound*

Lovers . . . you know are *all the World* to each other, and to whom
the company of a third person is disagreable, or if it is not it is seldom fit that a third person should be witness, to what they cannot
be actors in, for if I recollect aright, there are a thousand little ten-
dernesses, which pass between persons of this character, which can
make no one but themselves happy.

To John Thaxter, Braintree, July 1, 1783

Lovers

The desires and requests of my Friend are a Law to me. I will Sacrifice my present feelings and hope for a blessing in pursuit of my
duty.

To John Adams, Braintree, February 11, 1784

Lover's Duty

[We] wanted no mediating power to adjust the difference, we no
sooner understood each other properly, but as the poet says, "The
falling out of Lovers is the renewal of Love."*

Reconciling Lovers

"Be to my faults a little Blind.
Be to my virtues ever kind."**

To John Adams, Braintree, November 13, 1780

*Samuel Richardson, *The History of Sir Charles Grandison,* III (1753). Richardson probably took the phrase from Robert Burton's *Anatomy of Melancholy* (1621), part III, sec. 2. **Matthew Prior, "An English Padlock," lines 79 and 81.

Reuniting with Loved Ones

What is past, and what we suffered by sickness and fatigue. . . . It is all done away in the joyfull hope of soon holding to my Bosom the dearest best of Friends.

To John Adams, London, July 23, 1784

You will chide me I suppose for not relating to you [the events of her meeting with John]. But you know my dear sister, that poets and painters wisely draw a veil over those Scenes which surpass the pen of the one and the pencil of the other. We were indeed a very very happy family once more met together after a Seperation of 4 years.

To Mary Cranch, Auteuil, December 11, 1784

— The Military

Military Leadership

Tis Natural to estimate the military abilities of a man according to his Success.

To Mercy Otis Warren, January 1777

That the inquiry will be made I make no doubt, and if Cowardice, Guilt, Deceit, are found upon any one How high or exalted soever his station, may shame, reproach, infamy, hatred, and the execrations of the publick be his portion.

I would not be so narrow minded as to suppose that there are not many Men of all Nations possessd of Honour, Virtue and Integrity; yet tis to be lamented that we have not Men among ourselves sufficiently qualified for War to take upon them the most important command.

> To John Adams, July 30, 1777

Good officers will make good Soldiers.

> To John Adams, September 24, 1777

If you want your Arms crownd with victory you should not appoint what General [Horatio] Gates calls dreaming deacons to conduct them.

> To John Adams, November 16, 1777

I had rather see my descendents cultivating the civil Arts and forming themselves for the Cabinet, than the field.

> To Louisa Catherine Adams, Quincy, October 20, 1815

Military Service

We wish for a Naval force superiour to what we have yet had, to act in concert with our Army.

> To John Adams, May 25, 1781

Navy

My Love to Thomas. I hear he is for fighting the Algerines, but I am not sure that would be the best economy, tho it might give us a good pretence for Building a Navy that we need not be twichd by the Nose by every sausy Jack a Nips.

> To John Adams, Quincy, December 31, 1793

Every exertion is making to get our Frigates to Sea. We have some 20 Gun vessels out. Newburyport has set an example, by voting and raising money to Build a 20 Gun Ship and loaning it to Government. Newyork have voted 2 and this City 2; the Sea ports will all follow the example and we shall have a Navy Spring up like the Gourd of Jonah; I hope however that it will not wither, as soon.*

> To John Quincy Adams, Philadelphia, June 12, 1798

*Jonah 4:6.

The Navy of our Country is rising to respectability.

> To John Quincy Adams, Philadelphia, July 20, 1798

A powerfull Navy will be our best Security for the faithfull performance of any treaty which may be formed, as well as to command respect from the Mistress of the Ocean.

> To Hannah Cushing, Philadelphia, April 1800

Our seventy-fours* are building; our little navy shows what we should have done if it had not been impeded in its growth.

> To Caroline Smith, Quincy, August 6, 1812

*U.S. naval vessels with 74 guns.

The Glory which our Navy has acquired and the same of our Gallant Commanders must surely have been wafted to you upon the wings of the wind.* . . . Generous in conquest, modest in victory. These are the characteristic traits of our Naval commanders. They have redeemed the honour of our Country and coverd themselves with Glory. Altho they may experience a reverse and be compelld to yeald to Superiour force, Hull, Perry, Decatur, Bainbridge and Lawrence will never be forgotten by Britain or America.

You may easily suppose the pleasure your Father experiences in the Laurels they have won. They were most if not all, officers of his appointment, when the power rested with him—and they hail him as the Father of the Navy.

> To John Quincy Adams, Quincy, April 23, 1813

*Psalms 104:3.

I congratulate you upon the noble and brilliant victory of Commodore Perry upon Lake Erie—Such victories will be our most able Negotiators.

> To Thomas B. Johnson, Quincy, October 3, 1813

I do not now wonder at the regard the Ladies express for a Soldier— *Soldiers*
every man who wears a cockade appears of double the importance
he used to, and I feel a respect for the lowest Subaltern in the Army.

> To John Adams, Braintree, June 16, 1775

Little Skirmishes seem trifling, but they serve to innure our Men and
harden them to Danger.

> To John Adams, Braintree, July 25, 1775

A soldier is always more expeditious in his courtships than other
Men, they know better how to Capture the citidal.

> To Charles Storer, London, March 23, 1786

We are not warlike people. If invaded we shall flie to Arms and re- *Standing Army*
pell the Enemy, but a Regular Army of native Americans we shall
never obtain. The field is too wide and our Dominions too extensive
and the priviledges of all men too equal for them to become Regular
Soldiers.

> To John Quincy Adams, Quincy, November 29, 1814

— Morality

Improve your understanding for acquiring usefull knowledge and *Character*
virtue, such as will render you an ornament to society, an Honour to
your Country, and a Blessing to your parents. Great learning and superior abilities, should you ever possess them, will be of little value
and small Estimation, unless Virtue, Honour, Truth and integrity are
added to them. Adhere to those religious Sentiments and principals
which were early instilled into your mind and remember that you
are accountable to your Maker for all your words and actions. Let
me injoin it upon you to attend constantly and steadfastly to the pre-

cepts and instructions of your Father as you value the happiness of your Mother and your own welfare. His care and attention to you render many things unnecessary for me to write which I might otherways do, but the inadvertency and Heedlessness of youth, requires line upon line and precept upon precept, and when inforced by the joint efforts of both parents will I hope have a due influence upon your Conduct, for dear as you are to me, I had much rather you should have found your Grave in the ocean you have crossed, or any untimely death crop you in your infant years, rather than see you an immoral profligate or a Graceless child.

To John Quincy Adams, June 10?, 1778

Be dutifull my dear Son, be thoughtfull, be serious, do not gather the Thorns and the Thistles, but collect Such a Garland of flowers as will flourish in your native climate, and Bloom upon your Brows with an unfading verdure.

To John Quincy Adams, September 29, 1778

When a mind is raised, and animated by scenes that engage the Heart, then those qualities which would otherways lay dormant, wake into Life, and form the Character of the Hero and the Statesman.

To John Adams, June 8, 1779

Let it be our study to cultivate the flowers, and root out the weeds, to nourish with a softening care and attention those tender Blossoms, that they may be neither blasted in their prime nor witherd in their bloom but as the blossom falls may the fruit yet green ripen into maturity untill the Beauty of its appearance, shall tempt some Fair hand to pluck it from its native soil and transplant it in one still more conducive to its perfection.

To John Adams, June–July 1779

These are the times in which a Genius would wish to live. It is not in the still calm of life, or the repose of a pacific station, that great

characters are formed. . . . The Habits of a vigorous mind are
formed in contending with difficulties. All History will convince
you of this, and that wisdom and penetration are the fruits of experience, not the Lessons of retirement and leisure. Great necessities
call out great virtues.

To John Quincy Adams, Braintree, January 12, 1780

Much depends upon a uniformity of conduct. There is a strength of
mind, a firmness and intrepidity which we look for in a masculine
character—an April countenance, now Sunshine and then cloudy,
can only be excused in a Baby faced girl—in your sex, it has not the
appearance of Nature, who is our best guide.

To Royall Tyler, June 14, 1783

A perserverance in the same steady course will continue to you the
regard and Esteem of every worthy character and what is of infinite
more importance your own peace of mind and the Approbation of
your Maker.

To Charles Adams, London, c. February 16, 1786

It is not rank, or titles, but Character alone which interest Posterity.

To Elizabeth Shaw, London, March 4, 1786

The Idea that their success in Life depends upon their diligence and
application to their studies, to a modest and virtuous deportment,
cannot be too Strongly impresst upon their minds. The foolish Idea
in which some of our Youth, are educated: of being born Gentlemen is the most ridiculous in the world for a Country like ours. It
is the mind and manners which make the Gentleman and not the
Estate.

To Mary Cranch, London, May 21, 1786

Few consider that the foundation stone and the pillar on which they
Rest, the fab[r]ick of their felicity must be in their own Hearts, oth-

erways the winds of dissipation will shake it and the floods of pleasure overwhelm it in ruins.

> To Mary Cranch, London, January 20, 1787

Time will unvail Characters.

> To John Adams, Braintree, May 26, 1789

Good characters & good abilities will make there way good in the
world—

> To Mary Cranch, Braintree, December 1790

There is no sure and certain dependance to be placed upon any Man,
however high and dignified his office, who has not solid principles of
Religion and virtue for their basis.

> To William Smith, Philadelphia, March 2, 1798

Charity I know not any pleasure equal to that which arises from feeding the
Hungry, cloathing the Naked and making the poor prisoner's Heart
sing for joy.

> To John Adams, August 5, 1782

I derive a pleasure from the regret of others, a pleasure which perhaps I might never have experienced if I had not been called to quit
my Country, the blessing and regret of the poor and the needy, who
bewail my going away. The World furnishes us with real objects of
Charity where ever we are placed, but the circle around me have
been particularly necessitous through this long and severe winter.
The real want of employment has multiplied the necessities of
those, who are disposed to industery; and willing to obtain a livelihood by their Labour; and the expence of fire wood through this
winter has far exceeded the ability of the widow, and the Fatherless.
Much happier should I be if my abilities were such as would enable
me to be more extensively usefull; that I might Streatch out my hand

to the needy, and manifest the Law of kindness which is written upon my Heart.

To John Adams, April 12, 1784

I regret that it is not in my power to assist my Friends more than I do.

To Mary Cranch, Richmond Hill, September 1, 1789

My Heart is much larger than my purse.

To Cotton Tufts, New York, January 17, 1790

I know you Love to be my almoner. I wish it was in my power to do more abundantly.

To Mary Cranch, Philadelphia, February 6, 1798

I am in full Charity with all Good Men.

To John Adams, Quincy, January 13, 1799

He who is not in some way or other useful to society, is a drone in the hive, and ought to be hunted down accordingly.   *Civic Virtue*

To Mary Cranch, London, May 21, 1786

I check every rising wish and suppress every anxious desire for your return, when I see how necessary you are to the welfare and protection of a Country which I love, and a people who will *one day* do justice to *your memory* the reflection however of always having done what you considered as your duty, will out weigh all popular Breath and virtue be its own reward.

To John Adams, Quincy, May 10, 1794

If humane nature is thus infirm & liable to err as daily experience   *Conscience*
proves let every effort be made to acquire strength. Nature has implanted in the humane mind nice sensibilities of moral rectitude and

a natural love of excellence & given to it powers capable of infinate improvement and the state of things is so constituted that Labour well bestowed & properly directed always produces valuable Effects.

To Thomas Boylston Adams, London, March 15, 1787

Guilt of conscience is the work of our own Hands and not to be classed with the inevitable evils of Humane Life.—

To Mary Cranch, Philadelphia, December 21, 1790

Conscience, that faithful monitor, has reprehended me very, very often.

To Elizabeth Shaw, Bush Hill, March 20, 1791

Consciences hold themselves accountable to a superior Tribunal than an earthly one.

To Abigail Adams Smith, Quincy, August 14, 1795

Creed of Life My hopes and Wishes for you are that you may be good, and do good, fear God and keep his Commandments for this is the whole duty of man.

To John Adams 2nd, Quincy, March 16, 1817

Doing What Is Let the consciousness of having acted right console you.
Right To John Quincy Adams, Quincy, February 29, 1796

When the people are fully informd and convinced of what is Right, they will execute, but the danger is, that from partial evidence, they will be led astray.

To William Smith, Philadelphia, April 6, 1798

Always remember to respect yourself, by which I mean neither to do or say any thing, which upon reflection you might be ashamed of.

To Susanna B. Adams, Quincy, October 19, 1810

Faithful are the wounds of a Friend.*

Faithfulness

To Thomas Jefferson, Quincy, July 1, 1804

*Proverbs 27:6.

I know the voice of Fame to be a mere weathercock, unstable as Water and fleeting as a Shadow.

Fame

To John Adams, December 9, 1781

Without fortune it is more than probable we shall end our days, but let the well earned Fame of having Sacrificed those prospects from a principal of universal Benevolence and good will to Man, descend as an inheritance to our offspring.

To John Adams, April 10, 1782

Conscious Rectitude is a grand support, but it will not ward off the attacks of envy, or secure from the assaults of jealousy. Both ancient and modern history furnish us with repeated proofs, that virtue must look beyond this shifting theatre for its reward; but the Love of praise is a passion deeply rooted in the mind, and in this we resemble the Supreem Being who is most Gratified with thanksgiving and praise. Those who are most affected with it, partake most of that particle of divinity which distinguishes mankind from the inferiour Creation; no one who deserves commendation can despise it, but we too frequently see it refused where it is due, and bestowed upon very undeserving characters.

To John Adams, October 19, 1783

Old men do not take so much pains to circulate their Fame as young ones.

To Mary Cranch, Philadelphia, June 23, 1797

I regret that it is not in my power to assist my Friends more than I do, but bringing our minds to our circumstances is a duty encumbent upon us.

Helping Hand

To Mary Cranch, Richmond Hill, September 1, 1789

Nothing would give me more pleasure than to be able to assist two worthy people.

> To Mary Cranch, Richmond Hill, February 20, 1790

Can there be a greater pleasure in Life than rendering kindness to those we love and esteem and who we know are every way worthy of our regard.

> To Mary Cranch, New York, October 17, 1790

Independent Character

My advice to my children, is to maintain an independant character, tho' in poverty and obscurity; neither riches nor illustration will console a man under the reflection that he has acted a mean, a mercenary part, much less a dishonest one.

> To Thomas Boylston Adams, Richmond Hill, September 2, 1789

The way to command Fortune is to be as independent of her as possible.

> To Abigail Adams Smith, Philadelphia, February 21, 1791

Integrity

Not only youth but maturer age is too often influenced by bad examples, and it requires much reason, much experience, firmness & resolution to stem the torrent of fashion & to preserve the integrity which will bear the Scrutiny of our own Hearts.

> To Thomas Boylston Adams, London, March 15, 1787

A young man should well weigh his plans. Integrity should be preserved in all events, as essential to his happiness, thro every stage of his existence.

> To Thomas Boylston Adams, Richmond Hill, September 2, 1789

The consciousness of holding fast your integrity, will solace you through Life.

> To John Quincy Adams, Quincy, February 24, 1804

So long as you live, may you hold fast your integrity.

> To John Quincy Adams, Quincy, February 15, 1808

I find myself advancing in years and the early sentiments and habits which I imbibed are daily more strongly impressed upon me. They are so old fashioned that though they make a part of my enjoyment, they are illsuited to modern style and fashion. Like other old people I am very apt to fancy they are the best.

> To Abigail Adams Smith, Quincy, August 14, 1795

Old Values

Lawless principles naturally produce lawless actions.

> To Mary Cranch, Philadelphia, December 12, 1797

Principles

It is in the power of every Man to preserve his probity; but no man living has it in his power to say that he can preserve his reputation.

> To John Adams, March 17, 1782

Reputation

Reputation, Reputation, Oh She who has lost her Reputation, has lost the immortal part of herself—lost that which not enriches the spoiler, and makes her poor indeed.

> To John Quincy Adams, Quincy, May 9, 1816

Let your reputation be unspotted and your character unblemished that it may descend with Credit to yourself to futurity.

> To John Adams 2nd, Quincy, October 24, 1816

A good name is better than a precious ointment; it is the immediate jewel of the soul.

> To Caroline deWindt, Quincy, March 22, 1818

— The Natural World

A lovely variety of birds serenade me morning and evening, rejoicing in their liberty and security, for I have as much as possible prohibited the grounds from invasion: and sometimes almost wished for game laws, when my orders have not been sufficiently regarded. The

Birds

partridge, the woodcock, and the pigeon are too great temptations to the sportsmen to withstand.

> To Thomas Brand-Hollis, New York, September 6, 1790

Climate   That a cold Country must be a dirty one and in a climate which requires much fire, to keep one from freezing. It is not to be wonderd at, that other than humane Beings take Shelter under them.

> To Louisa Catherine Adams, Quincy, January 15, 1811

I regret that you are destined to remain in a climate so harsh and so dismall as I should esteem it,* for to me the genial influence of the Sun is so necessary, both to my health and Spirits; that I deplore his absence if only hidden from me for a few days; and I feel anxious not only for your health but for that of my son, who is as sincere a Lover of the great Luminary as I am. When I was in England, I used frequently to Boast to our Brand Hollis of our fine clear skye and bright Sun Shine over his foggy Island. He replied to me, that he should not like to be dazzled with so much blew and gold. Every Country is and ought to be dear to the Natives of it.

> To Louisa Catherine Adams, Quincy, January 21, 1811

*Louisa Adams and her husband were living in St. Petersburg, Russia.

Dogs   As if you love me, proverbially, you must love my dog, you will be glad to learn that Juno yet lives, although like her mistress she is gray with age. She appears to enjoy life and to be grateful for the attention paid her. She wags her tail and announces a visitor whenever one appears.

> To Caroline Smith, Quincy, February 26, 1811

Flowers   Do not let my flowers be neglected.

> To Mary Cranch, Philadelphia, April 26, 1800

Gardens   The Garden Betsy! let me take a look at it. It is delightfull, such a Beautifull collection of flowers all in Bloom, so sweetly arranged with rows of orange Trees, and china vases of flowers. Why you would be in raptures.

> To Elizabeth Cranch, Auteuil, September 5, 1784

Tell me when you begin to garden. I can brag over you in that respect, for our flower pots were set out in February and our garden began to look smilling. The orange Trees were not however brought out of the House, and it was very lucky they were not, for since this month commenced came a nipping frost very unusual at this season, and stiffend all our flower roots. I really fear they are kill'd. O Betsy how you would delight in this Garden. . . . [Like their house] The Garden too is much out of repair and bespeaks the too extravagant provision of its owners who are not able to put it in order. The Garden is however a lime walk in summer and the beautifull variety of flowers would tempt you to tan yourself in picking and trimming them. The garden has a number of statues and figures, but there is none which pleases me more than one of a Boy who has robbed a bird of her nest of young; which he holds in one hand and in the other the old bird, who has laid hold of his finger with her Bill and is biting it furiously, so that the countanance of the lad is in great distress between the fear of loosing the young and the pain of his finger.

> To Elizabeth Cranch, Auteuil, March 8, 1785

Tis true the garden yields a rich profusion, but they are neither plants of my hand, or children of my care.

> To Mary Cranch, Auteuil, May 8, 1785

I derive much pleasure from your account of the Garden and rose Bush. I wish I could enhale the one and taste the other, but I fear not.

> To Mary Cranch, Philadelphia, July 6, 1797

The Beauties which my Garden now present to my view from the window at which I write tempt me to forget the month of rain cloudy and gloomy which I have past by. The full Bloom of the trees, and the rich luxiousnence of the Grass platts interspersed amongst them, the cowslip, the daffy & the collumbine all unite to render the Scene delightfull, the Crown Imperial tho an early flower has not yet found an assylum in my garden—it bears too monarchical a title to find admittance on the catalogue of an Humble citizen whose future occupations are destined to be, not amongst the Sons of Men; but the more innocent productions of Nature, the Grave! The Garden & the Field: these will gratefully return the labour and toil bestowed upon their cultivation; by the fruits they will offer, the fragrance they will yeald, and the coulours they will display; envy nips not their buds, calumny destroys not their fruits; nor does ingratitude tarnish their coulours.

To Catherine Johnson, Quincy, May 9, 1810

Nature   Nature . . . is our best guide.

To Royall Tyler, June 14, 1783

[Speaking of the ocean:] Nature all powerfull Nature!

To Elizabeth Shaw, on board the ship *Active*, July 10?, 1784

Nature is said to be the nurse of sentiment, the true source of taste; yet what misery, as well as rapture, is produced by a quick perception of the beautifull and sublime?

To John Quincy Adams, Philadelphia, February 8, 1800

The contemplation of nature and its history fills the mind with the greatest variety of Ideas and never brings weariness or disgust, and as an Elegant writer expresses it "The Study of Nature like the contemplation of Religion is" forever rising with the rising mind. Only reflect that the spacious oak once existed in a small acorn. Darwin in his Loves of the plants,* a Book I dare say which has not escaped your notice, thus expresses it—

> "The pulpy acorn e'er it swells, contains
> The oak's vast branches in its milky veins."

Who can contemplate the Heavens without breaking forth with the
Psalmist and proclaming them the Work of an Almighty hand?**

> To George Washington Adams, Quincy, May 25, 1812

*Erasmus Darwin, *The Loves of the Plants* (London, 1789).   **Psalms
102:25.

You might suspect me of partiality, if I was to say that nature shews   *Nature in America*
herself in a stile of greater magnificence and sublimity in America,
than in any part of Europe which I have yet seen. Every thing is
upon a Grandeur scale, our Summer's heats and Winter's colds,
form a contrast of great Beauty. Nature arising from a temporary
death, and bursting into Life with a sudden vegetation, yealding a
delicious fragrance and verdure which exhilarates the spirits and ex-
alts the imagination, much more than the gradual and slow advance
of Spring in the more temperate climates; and where the whole
summer has not heat sufficient to sweeten the fruit, as is the case in
this climate. Even our Storms and tempests, our thunder and lightning, are horibly Grand. Here nothing appears to leap the Bounds
of Mediocrity. Nothing ferocious but Man.

> To Elizabeth Cranch, London, July 18, 1786

Do you know that European birds have not half the melody of ours?
Nor is their fruit half so sweet, nor their flowers half so fragrant, nor
their manners half so pure, nor their people half so virtuous; but
keep this to yourself, or I shall be thought more than half deficient
in understanding and taste.

> To Elizabeth Shaw, London, November 21, 1786

Tis a vast tract of ocean which we have to traverse; I have contem-   *The Ocean*
plated it with its various appearances. It is indeed a secret world of
wonders, and one of the Sublimest objects in Nature.

> *"Thou mak'st the foaming Billows roar.*
> *Thou mak'st the roaring Billows sleep."**

They proclaim the deity, and are objects too vast for the controul of
feeble Man, that Being alone, who "maketh the Clouds his Chariots

and rideth upon the wings of the wind,"** is equal to the Government of this Stupendous part of Creation.

> To Mary Cranch, on board the ship *Active*, July 6, 1784

*John Wesley, *Journal*, September 1760.   **Psalms 104:3.

There is not an object in Nature, better calculated to raise in our minds sublime Ideas of the Deity than the boundless ocean. Who can contemplate it, without admiration and wonder. . . . I have contemplated it in its various appearances since I came to Sea, smooth as a Glass, then Gently agitated with a light Breize, then lifting wave upon wave, moving on with rapidity, then rising to the Skyes, and in majestick force tossing our ship to and fro, alternately rising and sinking; in the Night I have beheld it Blaizing and Sparkling with ten thousand Gems—untill with the devout psalmist I have exclaimed, "Great and Marvellous are thy Works, Lord God Almighty. In Wisdom hast thou made them all."*

> To Elizabeth Shaw, on board the ship *Active*, July 11, 1784

*Psalms 104:24.

Springtime   I turn from the painfull subject to the Rural delights which are just opening upon us here. The willow assumes its lost verdure and is cheering the prospect by its coulour so gratefull to the Eye. The peach blossom opens and the daisy and daffy adorn my Room. The brown here of the Feild is changed to a bright Green, and the spring songsters assume a cheering note. My spirits are exhilirated by the Scene, and for a moment I forget the disturbers of our Peace, and the destroyers of our pleasures. I can ride out daily and enjoy the air of the Country.

> To Mary Cranch, Philadelphia, April 9, 1798

The weeping willow, which is a great ornament to this City, putting on its first appearance of vegetation, a yellow aspect, which changes to a beautifull Green in a few weeks and is the first Harbinger of that Season, in which all nature is renovated.

> To Mary Cranch, Philadelphia, February 27, 1800

The season my dear sister is delightfull. The Grass and Grain have
spread over the late barren plains and feilds, a verdure which invigorates the Spirits, and gives pleasure to the Eye [. . .] which you behold the Trees all corresponding with their parent Earth, Streching
forth their luxurient Branches drest in nature's most pleasing livery.
The weeping Willow, which is a favorite tree with me, from the
gracefullness of its slender branches, which float and wave to every
breeze, intermixt with all strait and Elegant poplar, form a most
Charming assembledge planted and intermixt as they are throughout every Street in this large and populus city. As they are of quick
growth thousands of them have been planted out and grown to a
surprizing height since I first was a resident in this city and contribute greatly to the Beauty of it, releiving the Eye from the dead and
flat appearance of the brick walls of the Houses.

To Mary Cranch, Philadelphia, April 16, 1800

The weather has assumed the appearance of Spring, the Earth is
putting on a new suit, the trees corresponding with their parent, are
shooting their Branches and spreading their leaves whilst the lively
song of the Birds hail the welcome approach of the renovating Season; reminding me of my Garden at Quincy and that like Eden of
old it calls for culture, the pruning knife and the labourer.

To Hannah Cushing, Philadelphia, April 1800

To hear often from you is a great pleasure. One of the few left me in
the decline of Life. When the days approach in which we are told
there is no pleasure, there is an innocent pleasure to be derived from
the renovating Season of the spring which Charms us even in age. I
feel its influence in the vivid Green which cloaths the Earth, in the
beautious Blosom which adorn the trees, and in "the Charms of earliest Birds."* These are all before me. The Grass waves in the wind. I
never saw it more forward at this Season. On the 24 of April we cut
our first assparagass. On the 25 our Daffies Bloomd. Our peach and
pear and plumb trees are in full Bloom. Peas ready to stick. I did not
expect to hear from you, that your peas were up: I should like to
have you state the progress of your vegetation that we may compare

notes. Our Barley is also up. I am glad to find that you have been so successfull in making maple Sugar. Every manufactor which will render us less dependent, is a valuable acquisition.

To Abigail Adams Smith, Quincy, May 8, 1808

*John Milton, *Paradise Lost.*

Sunshine   There is no object in nature so exhilarating to the Spirits, or so invigorating to the animal as well as the Natural World, as that Glorious Luminary which was worshiped by the Heathens as a deity; and is truly one of the most magnificent productions of the Great architect.

To Mary Cranch, Auteuil, January 7, 1785

Weather   Air, Sun, and Water, the common blessings of Heaven; we receive as our just due, and too seldom acknowledge our obligations to the Father of the rain; and the Gracious dispencer of every good and perfect gift, yet if but for a very little while these blessings are withheld, or spairingly dealt out to us, we then soon discover how weak, how little and how blind, we are.

To Mercy Otis Warren, Boston, July 16, 1773

Tis a fine growing Season having lately had a charming rain, which was much wanted as we had none before for a forenight.

To John Adams, Braintree, May 24, 1775

I shudder at the approach of winter when I think I am to remain desolate.

To John Adams, Braintree, November 27, 1775

Winter set in with all its horrors in a week after you saild, and has continued with all its rigours ever since. Such mountains of snow have not been known for 60 years. No passing for this fortnight, only for foot travellers, [and] no prospect of any as one Storm succeeds another so soon that the roads are filld before a path can be made.

To John Adams, January 18, 1780

My hands freize by the fire.

> To Mercy Otis Warren, January 8, 1781

I love the cheerful sunshine of America and the clear blue sky.

> To Mercy Otis Warren, Auteuil, December 11, 1784

We have had very severe weather for several weeks; I think the coldest I have known since my return from abroad. The climate of Old England for me; people do not grow old half so fast there; two-thirds of the year here, we must freeze or melt.

> To Abigail Adams Smith, Philadelphia, January 8, 1791

Our weather is so changeable that it retards the kind of Business which I should be glad to have compleated. This week we have had floods of rain, which has carried off the chief of the heavy snow which fell the week before.

> To John Adams, Quincy, February 22, 1793

Thanks to the Father of the Rain, and the Bountifull dispencer of the dews of Heaven, who has plentifully waterd the dry and thirsty Earth. The Fields recover their verdure, and the little Hills rejoice, the drooping vine rears its head and the witherd flower Blooms anew. . . . Indeed my dearest Friend it would rejoice your Heart to behold the change made in the appearance of all Nature, after one of our old fashiond Election storms as we used to term them. I hope we may be further blessd by repeated Showers.

> To John Adams, Quincy, May 27, 1794

We have had a fine fall of snow which will enable our people to compleat getting home wood if it lasts.

> To John Adams, Quincy, January 21, 1796

The Cold has been more severe than I can ever before recollect. It has frozen the ink in my pen, and chilld the Blood in my veins.

> To John Adams, Quincy, January 15, 1797

The weather is exceeding cold and sour. Our dreadfull east winds prevail and peirces one through and through.

> To John Adams, Quincy, March 31, 1797

We are as well as the Hot weather will permit.

> To Mary Cranch, Philadelphia, July 11, 1797

The weather is Hot as we can bear. The whole city is like a Bake House. We have a House with large and airy Rooms, or I could not sustain it. I do bear it surprisingly well however, tho I long for a sea Breaze.

> To Mary Cranch, Philadelphia, July 21, 1797

A fine rain . . . is truly a blessing.

> To Mary Cranch, Philadelphia, May 29, 1798

Winter put on an early and formidable appeerence. I hope good will arrise from it and that it will effectually stay the plague in our cities.

> To John Adams, Quincy, November 22, 1798

I took a ride in the Sleigh yesterday afternoon towards Milton. The whole Earth looks like mid winter, and the Snow is 4 and 5 foot deep, in Banks driven together and consoladated so that it will lie at the Sides of the Road till next March or April.

> To John Adams, Quincy, November 25, 1798

I believe it was in some such cold weather as the present, that Solomon made the wise observation, if two lie together, they shall be warm, but how can one be warm alone?* Ever since Thursday the weather has been most severely cold, so as to freeze my ink in my warm Room; it has been as cold ever since Jan'ry came in, as it was intensely Hot last July. The Snow is very deep, and [. . .] is now adding to the quantity; tho whilst it is so cold there cannot be much.

> To John Adams, Quincy, January 6, 1799

*Ecclesiastes 4:11.

Our weather is so variable that one day we have it intencely cold and the next a thaw. The Ground is again covered with Snow of a foot depth. It is also very cold.

> To John Adams, Quincy, February 25, 1799

It looks so like the depth of winter that Spring appears far off.

> To John Adams, Quincy, February 27, 1799

We have had but one thing steady which is unsteadiness.

> To Louisa Catherine Adams, Quincy, January 27, 1805

Snow does not suit my constitution; it gives me the rheumatism.

> To Caroline Smith, Quincy, February 2, 1809

We have been abundantly blessed with plentifull rains which has revived the lanquishing fruits of the Earth, made the hills to rejoice, and the vallies to sing—the husbandman to rejoice and give thanks with a gratefull heart.

> To Elizabeth Peabody, Quincy, June 13, 1810

We have snow by the cargo this winter. Not a bird flits but a hungry crow now and then, in quest of prey. The fruit trees exhibit a mournful picture, broken down by the weight of the snow; whilst the running of sleighs and the jingle of bells assure us that all nature does not slumber.

> To Caroline Smith, Quincy, February 26, 1811

The gay parties in Boston, must have more charms for the young and Beautifull, than the Sombre & dreary view of a dead & brown carpet which covers the Earth at present & the leafless Trees so naked and bare. I want to See it put on the white mantle, so emblematical of innocence. But we are in some measure compensated by the fine weather.

> To Harriet Welsh, Quincy, January 1, 1817

March winds are intolerable, worse than the coldest we have had through the winter—and I am more afraid of them.

To Harriet Welsh, Quincy, March 14, 1817

Winter appears to have set in, with all its Beauties, for such I consider a covering of snow to the Earth.

To Louisa Catherine Adams, Quincy, January 17, 1818

— *Pain and Pleasure*

Like most of the scenes of life, the pleasure was mixed with pain.

To Mary Cranch, London, September 12, 1786

Fear   I know not that there is any pleasure in being feard.

To John Adams, Weymouth, April 19, 1764

Those who have most to lose have most to fear.

To Mercy Otis Warren, Braintree, February 3?, 1775

I have often heard that fear makes people loving.

To John Adams, Braintree, June 25, 1775

No state of mind is so painfull as that which admits of fear, suspicion, doubt, dread and apprehension.

To Mary Cranch, London, August 15, 1785

Fear often makes them desperate at last.

To Abigail Adams Smith, Washington, January 17, 1801

Pleasure and   Life is too short to have the dearest of its enjoyments curtaild.
Amusement

To John Adams, November 14, 1782

The love of pleasure and amusement overbalances the calamities of Life.

To Hannah Smith, Philadelphia, January 17, 1800

May you never want either pleasure or amusement. We were made for active Life and idleness and happiness are incompatible.

To Caroline Smith, Quincy, November 17, 1808

— *Peace*

Yet we are told that all the Misfortunes of Sparta were occasiond by their too great Sollicitude for present tranquility, and by an excessive love of peace they neglected the means of making it sure and lasting. They ought to have reflected says Polibius* that as there is nothing more desirable, or advantageous than peace, when founded in justice and honour, so there is nothing more shameful and at the same time more pernicious when attained by bad measures, and purchased at the price of liberty.

To John Adams, Braintree, August 19, 1774

*Polybius, *Histories.*

Peace, Peace my beloved object is farther and farther from my Embraces I fear.

To John Adams, October 8, 1780

The Great Author of our Religion frequently inculcates universal Benevolence and taught us both by precept and example when he promulgated peace and good will to Man, a doctrine very different from that which actuates the Hostile invaders, and the cruel ravagers of mighty kingdoms and Nations.

To Charles Adams, May 26, 1781

I now most sincerely rejoice in the great and important event which sheaths the Hostile Sword and, gives a pleasing presage that our spears may become pruning hooks;* that the Lust of Man is restrained, or the powers and revenues of kingdoms become inadequate to the purposes of distruction.

To John Adams, April 7, 1783

*Micah 4:3.

When a people have not ability to go to War, why they must be at Peace if they can.

To Charles Storer, London, May 22, 1786

The more we cultivate peace and good will to Man, the happier we shall be.

To Elizabeth Shaw, London, July 19, 1786

The still voice of Reason and the firm and steady hand of patriotism have conducted us thus far safely, shelterd from the Storms and tempests which harrow up all the contending Nations of Europe and make it one Golgotha.

Thanks to an over ruling and mercifull providence, may we long continue to enjoy the blessings and have Hearts to know their value and rightly appreciate them.

To John Quincy Adams, Quincy, June 10, 1796

If peace depend upon our Government, it will be preserved. There is but *one wish*. It is, to avoid war if it can be done without prostrating our National honour, or sacrificing our independence.

To Thomas Boylston Adams, Philadelphia, June 20, 1797

Peace . . . always ought to be the object aimed at.

To Mercy Otis Warren, Quincy, June 20, 1813

We pant for peace, because we lament the horrors of war and the ravages and calamities which are inseperable to it. The brave fellows who fall in the contest wring my Heart with anguish.

To John Quincy Adams, Quincy, October 22, 1813

I can most Sincerely join in that petition, "Give us peace in our day O Lord"* but whether I live or not to see it, I hope our children may.

To Julia Rush, Quincy, December 21, 1813

*The Evening Prayer in *The Book of Common Prayer.*

I rejoice as a Lover of peace, harmony and humanity, that a termination is put to the War.

To John Quincy Adams, Quincy, February 28 and March 4, 1815

The temple of Janus is once more closed and long may it remain so.

To Thomas B. Johnson, Quincy, March 3, 1815

By your Letter I learn that Mars and Belona have quitted the Stage to give place to Venus and Cupid, and the loud Clangor of Arms is lulled into a soft Hymenial Sympathy and concord of uniting Hands and consenting Hearts.

To Louisa Catherine Adams, Quincy, September 30, 1816

— People

We know little of vileness in our state when compared to those cities who have Such Numbers of Foreigners as N. York and Philadelphia—

Aliens

To Mary Cranch, Philadelphia, January 9, 1791

Most of our troubles in this Country arise from imported foreigners, Men who have neither an affection for our Laws, Government or people, who many of them, escape from the just vengeance of their own Country and flee to this which afford them protection and shelter. Here they are still wrestless and turbulent, and prove that the Leopard cannot change his Spots.*

To Catherine Johnson, Philadelphia, July 8, 1798

*Jeremiah 13:23.

Foreign influence tho wounded and limping and hobling, Halts, and Rallies, and finds in every State some votaries. Tho their Numbers are few their Mischief is extensive.

To John Quincy Adams, Philadelphia, July 20, 1798

Assassins   Against an open and avowed Enemy we may find some guard, but the Secret Murderer and the dark assassin none but that Being without whose Notice not a Sparrow falls to the ground, can protect or secure us.*

To Hannah Storer, Braintree, March 1, 1778

*Paraphrase of Matthew 10:29.

Assistants   Good and confidential assistants are very essential.

To John Quincy Adams, Quincy, October 15, 1817

Bachelors   The Stoickism which every Batchelor discovers ought to be attributed to him as a fault.

To James Lovell, Braintree, December 15, 1777

I saw the Gloom which spread over the countenances of some of his Female acquaintances here when he [Charles Storer] bid them adieu [for Europe], the other day, and as it was a circle of sensible, virtuous Girls, it was a proof of his merit, considering there was no partiality of a particular kind amongst them.

To John Thaxter, May 23, 1781

I advise him to get married, for a Man makes but a poor figure solo.

> To Cotton Tufts, Auteuil, January 3, 1785

Most old Batchelors . . . become nearly useless.

> To Abigail Adams Smith, Braintree, August 6, 1788

The Man who voluntarily lives a Bachelor deprives himself of one great end of his Being, Social happiness.

> To Thomas Boylston Adams, East Chester, N.Y., November 7, 1797

Dr. Franklin says a Batchelor is not a complete Human being. He is like the odd half of a pr [of] Scissors, which has not yet found its fellow, and therefore is not half so useful as they might be together.*

Now I think a single Lady not to say an old——** is a very usefull Being, much more so, than a single man. Yet you know I have ever been a warm advocate for matrimony—and with Allen Ramsay in the gentle Shepard—I [feel?] that men were made for us—and we for men."†

> To Harriet Welsh, Quincy, May 5, 1817

*Benjamin Franklin, *Advice on the Choice of a Mistress*, June 25, 1745.
**An old maid.   †Allan Ramsay, "The Gentle Shepherd," Act 1, scene 2.

Batchelors poor solemn Beings, contract anti-social Habits. Become frequently Singular in their manners, in short they are like Dr. Franklin's half p[ai]r of Scissors—He who formed Man & best knows his Nature pronounced it not good for him to be alone*—

> To Abigail Adams Shaw Felt, Quincy, February 10, 1818

*Genesis 2:18.

Such is the company in which he is seen that he cannot fail to bear a part of the reproach even if he is innocent.   *Bad Company*

> To John Quincy Adams, Braintree, May 30, 1789

There is no touching pitch without being defiled.

> To John Adams, Quincy, January 12, 1794

Evil communications corrupt the Morals and deprave the understanding.

> To Elizabeth Peabody, Quincy, July 10, 1811

Can one touch pitch, and not be poluted?

> To George Washington Adams, Quincy, May 23, 1816

Boys [Of her grandson George Washington Adams:] He is a good Boy, save now and then, a little mischief which all Boys are by nature prone to.

> To John Quincy Adams, Quincy, February 1809

I have not any ambition to have them Men, while they are but boys.* I have seen the fatal consequence of premature acquirements. Altho calculated to dazzel the beholders, their duration is short lived.

> *"A Blaize betokens Brevity of Life."***

> To John Quincy Adams, Quincy, March 16, 1814

*Her grandsons, John Adams 2nd and George Washington Adams.
**Edward Young, *Night Thoughts* (1742–1745).

You must not look for old heads upon young shoulders. A Grave Sedate Boy will make a mopish dull old Man.

> To John Quincy Adams, Quincy, August 15, 1815

I have the Authority of Dr. Priestly to Say "that it is well known that if we expect that Boys should ever make valuable Men, they must continue some time in the State of Boys or they will never make Men worth forming."

> To Louisa Catherine Adams, Quincy, April 24, 1816

You think you have arrived at an Age when a Boy ought to behave as a Man, but Nature made you a Boy first, and while you are a Child, you will think as a Child, and act as a Child. I do not wish you to be prematurely a Man—but a discrete Boy, of manly sentiments, honourable principles, and hold yourself accountable to your Maker for your conduct, and you will then learn to bear the troubles of Life, where they assail you, with firmness.

To John Adams 2nd, Quincy, May 21, 1816

My Love to your Brother. Be kind and affectionate to each other. *Brothers* Do not dispute, yeald, give up something to each and be assured the more friendly you are to each other, the more you will promote your own happiness and the pleasure and comfort of all around you.

To George Washington Adams, Quincy, May 25, 1812

Love each other, cultivate harmony, and remember how good and how pleasant a thing it is for Brethren to dwell together in unity.

To George Washington Adams and John Adams 2nd, Quincy, July 12,

1815

I rejoice in a preacher who has some warmth, some energy, some *Clergy* feeling. Deliver me from your cold phlegmatick Preachers, Politicians, Friends, Lovers and Husbands. I thank Heaven I am not so constituted myself and so connected.

To John Adams, August 5, 1776

Since I have been here and the pulpit has been supplied as they could procure *Labourers*—by Gentlemen who preach without Notes, all of whom are predestinarians and whose Noise & vehemince is to compensate for every other difficency.

To Mary Cranch, Richmond Hill, October 4, 1789

They are certainly a most respectable *order* of Men with us, Men of Learning of Religion, and in general of Liberality. From my own personal knowledge and acquaintance with a large Number of those

Gentleman, I do not believe that in either of the 12 other states can be selected an equal Number of So respectable for their ingenuity and abilities, their Gentlemanly deportment and manners as our State furnishes. Yet very few of those Gentlemen think themselves qualified to open the Bible and give you a discourse of half an hour or more, without having previously studied their discourse, & committed it to writing. If the Clergymen here study, it is too deeply for me. I cannot comprehend or believe all their doctrines. They are worthy Good Men, but deciples of good old Calvin, and will Scarcly allow Man to be a free Agent.

To Hannah Lincoln Storer, Richmond Hill, January 29, 1790

As to an orater, the oratary of a Clergyman here consists in foaming loud speaking Working themselves up in such an enthusiam as to cry, but which has no other effect upon me than to raise my pitty. O when when shall I hear the Candour & liberal good sense of a [Richard] Price again, animated with true piety without enthusiasm, Devotion without grimace and Religion upon a Rational System.

To Mary Cranch, New York, July 4, 1790

The poor Sallery of a Minister can barely give him a living.

To Thomas Boylston Adams, Quincy, November 30, 1794

Clods I never could endure a clod, yet it has been my lot, to have met *with them.*

To Mary Cranch, Philadelphia, April 26, 1800

Deserters No one can tell the secret designs of such fellows whom no oath binds—he may be sent with assassinating designs.

To John Adams, Braintree, July 31, 1775

Discontents There are and always will be wristless discontened Spirits, who live to fish in troubled waters and always have an apple of Discord at hand.

To John Quincy Adams, Quincy, May 1, 1814

We have had fine Spring rains which makes the Husbandry promise   *Farmers*
fair. . . . I shall be quite a Farmeriss another year.

> To John Adams, Braintree, May 14, 1776

The voice of the landed interest is not for war and I dare Say it will
be found a Sound maxim that the possessers of the Soil are the best
Judges of what is for the advantage of the country. If an Enemy in-
vades our country, every Man will rise for its defence, but when only
the Mercantile property is Struck at, tho it ultimately affects the
landholder Yet the Body of the people had rather Suffer than wage
war.

> To John Adams, Quincy, April 25, 1794

A Farmer can not be content with the profits he once made.

> To John Adams, Quincy, March 13, 1797

To derive a proper improvement from company it ought to be select,   *Good Company*
and to consist of persons respectable both for their Morals, and their
understandings.

> To Mary Cranch, London, January 20, 1787

With mischievous men, no honest man would hold communion:
but with Men who have been misled, and who possess integrity of
Heart, every good Man would be desirous of standing fair.

> To John Adams, Quincy, March 12, 1797

Good folks are scarce.   *Good People*

> To John Adams, Weymouth, April 12, 1764

Uneasy wrestless spirits are to be found in all quarters of the world.   *Gossipers*

> To Mary Cranch, Richmond Hill, August 9, 1789

We have lived in perilous times, and tho we reap not the full Harvest   *The Great*
we have earned—I trust future generations will feel the benefit of   *Generation*

the sacrifices we have made: and do justice to the memory of those, who have sufferd much, and endured much for their benefit.

> To Sarah Adams, Quincy, January 20, 1808

Grumblers   If I may judge by the Newspapers, there is no state in the union where there are so many grumblers as in our own.

> To Mary Cranch, Richmond Hill, October 4, 1789

Grumblers there always was & always will be—

> To Mary Cranch, New York, July 4, 1790

Some grumbling we must always expect.

> To Mary Cranch, Bush Hill, March 12, 1791

The Grumblers will growl.

> To Mary Cranch, New York, June 25, 1795

They will grumble at all events, and under all circumstances, and so let them.

> To Mary Cranch, Philadelphia, December 4, 1799

A few Grumblers there will be, who are never satisfied and who envyd the present Rulers the Glory they have acquired. I am ready to ask in the Language of the poet

> *"Shall man alone when rational, we call*
> *Be pleased with nothing, if not blesst with all?"*＊

> To John Quincy Adams, Quincy, April 1, 1815

＊Alexander Pope, *An Essay on Man.*

Heroes   The Hero is not like to acquire more fame, from his pen than from his Sword.

> To John Adams, Quincy, January 20, 1799

Shall I not See you become an honour to your profession in the exercise of a generous candour, an inflexible integrity; strict punctuality, and exact decision, virtues which are by no means incompatable with your profession, notwithstanding the Sarcastick reflexions it is daily liable to.

To Royall Tyler, June 14, 1783

Annihilate the profession of the Law, and the Liberties of the Country would soon share the same fate. If they wish to suppress the influence of the Bar, Let them practise justice. and consider the Maxim, "that can never be politically right, which is morally wrong."*

To John Quincy Adams, London, July 21, 1786

*Lord Shaftesbury (Anthony Ashley Cooper).

We have children rising into Life educated to the Law, without a competant knowledge of which no Man is fit for a Legislator or a statesman. Let us look into our National Legislature, Scarcly a man there makes any figure in debate, who has not been Bred to the Law.

To Mary Cranch, Richmond Hill, February 20, 1790

The first and principal thing is to form a Grand Idea of your profession. It is a profession which qualifies a Man best for the chief employments of the State. What esteem does it not gain those who distinguish Themselves in it, either in pleading or giving counsel. Is there any finer sight, than to see a numerous auditory attentive, immoveable, and as it were hanging upon the Lips of a pleader, who manages speech common to all with so much art that he charms and ravishes the minds of his hearers, and makes himself absolute master over them. But beside this Glory which would be Trifling enough were there no other motive, what solid joy is it for a virtuous man to think he has received a talent from God, which makes him the Sanctuary of the unfortunate, the protector of Justice: and enables him to defend the lives, fortunes, and honours of his Brethren? I am convinced that a Genius is the first and most necessary quality for a pleader but I am also certain that study is of the utmost importance. Tis like a second nature, and if it does not impart a Genius to him who had none before, it rectifies, polishes, improves and invigorates it.

To John Adams Smith, Quincy, 1808

Middle Class But if we are not the favorites of fortune, let us be; what is of much more importance to us, the Votaries of Virtue, and consider that being denied the former we are secured from many temptations that always attend upon that fickle Dame. The Prayer of Augur, was that of a wise Man, who was aware that Poverty might expose him to acts of injustice towards his fellow creatures, and riches, to ingratitude towards his Maker. He therefore desird that middle state which would secure him from the temptations of the first, and Guard him from the impiety of the latter.* And in that middle State, I believe the largest portion of Humane happiness is to be found.

To John Quincy Adams, London, March 20, 1786

*Paraphrase of Proverbs 30:8–9.

Mobs An unprincipled mob is the worst of all Tyrannies.

To Elizabeth Shaw, London, May 2, 1787

The raging of the Sea, and the Tumult of the people have been aptly compared; who can say to either, thus far shalt thou go, and no further,* and here shall thy proud waves be stayed; or peace be still.

To John Quincy Adams, Philadelphia, November 23, 1797

*Job 38:11.

The Next As to conjecturing what is to be the Lot, and portion of the next
Generation generation, my only anxiety is that they may have good and virtuous Educations, and if they are left to struggle for themselves they will

be quite as like to rise up virtuous and distinguished Characters as
tho they had been born to great expectations.

> To John Adams, Quincy, January 12, 1799

Strip Royalty of its pomp and power, and what are its votaries more
than their fellow worms?

Nobility

> To John Adams, Braintree, December 15, 1783

Dukes and Duchesses, Lords and Ladies, bedizened with pomp, and
stuck over with titles, are but mere flesh and Blood, like their fellow
worms, and sometimes rather frailer.

> To Charles Storer, Auteuil, January 3, 1785

I found the Court like the rest of Mankind, mere Men and Women,
and not of the most personable kind neither.

> To John Quincy Adams, London, June 26, 1785

Blessed are the peacemakers said a great Authority,* for they restore
harmony in which all nature delights.

Peacemakers

> To Elizabeth Shaw, London, March 10, 1787

*Matthew 5:9.

I have not a doubt but all the discords may be tuned to harmony, by
the Hand of a skilfull Artist.

> To John Adams, Quincy, January 15, 1797

Each Servant [in France] has a certain Etiquet, and one will by no
means intrude upon the department of another. . . . Your cook will
dress your victuals, but she will not wash a dish, or perform any
other kind of business.

Servants

> To Cotton Tufts, Auteuil, September 8, 1784

She has two qualities which you value—silence & modesty.

> To John Adams, Braintree, May 26, 1789

The help I find here is so very indifferent to what I had in England, the weather so warm that we can give only one dinner a week. I cannot find a cook in the whole city but what will get drunk, and as to the Negroes, I am most sincerely sick of them, and I can no more do without Mr. Brisler,* than a coach could go without wheels or Horse to draw it. I can get Hands, but what are hands without a Head, and their chief object is to be as expensive as possible.

> To Mary Cranch, Richmond Hill, August 9, 1789

*John Brisler, the Adamses' majordomo.

I know not where to find Honour, Honesty, integrity & attachment.

> To Mary Cranch, Richmond Hill, October 4, 1789

Of all things I hate to hear people forever complaining of servants but I never had so much occasion as since I came here. One good servant attached to you is invaluable.

> To Mary Cranch, Richmond Hill, October 11, 1789

I have a pretty good Housekeeper, a tolerable footman, a midling cook, an indifferent steward and a vixen of a House maid.

> To Mary Cranch, Richmond Hill, November 3, 1789

The chief of the Servants here who are good for any thing are Negroes who are slaves, the white ones are all Foreigners & chiefly vagabonds—

> To Mary Cranch, New York, April 28, 1790

It is next to impossible here to get a servant from the highest to the lowest grade that does not drink, male or Female.

> To Mary Cranch, Richmond Hill, April 28, 1790

You wrote me in your Letter of Janry. 25th of a Negro Man and woman whom you thought would answer for me this summer. If she is cleanly and only a tolerable cook I wish you would engage her for me. I had rather have black than white help, as they will be more like to agree with those I bring. I have a very clever black Boy of 15 who has lived with me a year and is bound to me till he is 21.

> To Mary Cranch, Bush Hill, March 12, 1791

I am going to send you an excellent Servant as represented to me by my Sister Peabody. Sober, honest and industerous, he lived Eleven Years with Genll. Peabody, is a Native American, and will carry with him what Tom Jones calld a good Letter of Recommendation. I mean a good countanance.* He may be confided in and will be a great acquisition to Mr. Brisler if he answers the Character given him. He has been used to waiting [i.e., being a waiter], tho not altogether in the manner he may be calld to now.

> To John Adams, Quincy, December 2–3, 1798

*Henry Fielding, *The History of Tom Jones.*

Faithfull and good domesticks I consider as amongst my most valuable Friends.

> To William Smith Shaw, Quincy, January 3, 1799

A Cook I shall want, and she must be a woman. I will have no more men cooks.

> To Mary Cranch, Philadelphia, April 17, 1800

Much of a well ordered home depends upon our domesticks: and it is so difficult to get in this Land of ease and freedom such as will serve with honesty and integrity that the task of entertaining company is a toil, a vexation and a Trouble. Servitude is disdained by all who can acquire a Living in any other mode of Life.

> To Louisa Catherine Adams, Quincy, February 1, 1818

A single woman whether maiden, or widow, wants some Friend of the other Sex to protect her, and her property or she becomes the prey of every Sharper.

Single Women

> To Abigail Adams Smith, Quincy, November 3, 1808

Sisters   Never was there a stronger affection than that which binds in a
           threefold cord your Mamma and her dear sisters. Heaven preserve
           us to each other for many Years to come.
                           To John Quincy Adams, London, February 16, 1786

Slave Owners   I have sometimes been ready to think that the passion for Liberty
                cannot be Equally Strong in the Breasts of those who have been ac-
                customed to deprive their fellow Creatures of theirs. Of this I am
                certain that it is not founded upon that generous and christian prin-
                cipal of doing to others as we would that others should do unto us.*
                                    To John Adams, Braintree, March 31, 1776

           *Matthew 7:120.

Slaves   There has been in Town a conspiracy of the Negroes. At present it is
           kept pretty private and was discoverd by one who endeavourd to dis-
           waid them from it—he being threatned with his life, applied to Jus-
           tice [Edmund] Quincy for protection. They conducted in this way—
           got an Irishman to draw up a petition to the Governor telling him
           they would fight for him provided he would arm them and engage
           to liberate them if he conquerd, and it is said that he attended so
           much to it as to consult Pircy* upon it, and one [Lieut.?] Small has
           been very buisy and active. There is but little said, and what Steps
           they will take in consequence of it I know not. I wish most sincerely
           there was not a Slave in the province. It allways appeard a most in-
           iquitious Scheme to me—fight ourselfs for what we are daily rob-
           bing and plundering from those who have as good a right to free-
           dom as we have. You know my mind upon this Subject.
                                    To John Adams, Boston, September 22, 1774

           *Hugh, Earl of Percy, the commander of British forces in Boston.

           Poor Falmouth has shared the fate of Charlestown; are we become a
           Sodom? . . . The Sin of Slavery as well as many others is not washed
           away.
                                    To John Adams, Braintree, October 25, 1775

If any person wishes to see the banefull effects of Slavery, as it creates a torpor and an indolence and a spirit of domination, let them come and take a view of the cultivation of this part of the United States.

> To Mary Cranch, Washington, December 21, 1800

In our New England States, rank is less thought of and practised than in any other part of the Union. No Native white American will permit himself to be called a servant or acknowledge a master. Being the Yeomanry of the Country, they consider their rulers as the work of their own hands and as they really are dependent upon them for the power they possess. From hence arises that familiarity in society between the rich and the poor, which levels distinction. Not so in Europe.

Social Classes

> To John Quincy Adams, Quincy, May 20, 1815

I have never yet seen the southern man—Washington excepted—who could bear close application for any length of Time.

Southerners

> To Cotton Tufts, Philadelphia, December 6, 1797

The enlargement of knowledge should be the constant view and design of every student.

Students

> To Charles Adams, London, c. February 16, 1786

Like most successors, [he] finds fault with his predecessor.

Successors

> To Caroline Smith, Quincy, August 6, 1812

You must be conscious of how great importance it is to youth, that they should respect their teachers. Therefore whatever tends to lessen them, is an injury to the whole Society.

Teachers

> To John Quincy Adams, London, July 21, 1786

When shall we cease to have Judases?

Traitors

> To Mary Cranch, Philadelphia, July 6, 1797

Visitors   You must not stay so long as to not make your Friends twice glad.

To Susanna B. Adams, Quincy, October 19, 1810

Youth   Every virtuous example has powerfull impressions in early youth.
Many years of vice and vicious examples do not erase from the mind
seeds sown in early life. They take a deep root, and tho often crop'd
will spring again.

To John Adams, Braintree, October 25, 1775

Youth youth is the time, they have no pains but bodily, no anxiety of
mind, no fears for themselves or others, and then the Disease is
much lighter.

To John Adams, July 30, 1776

If you indulge yourself in the practise of any foible or vice in youth,
it will gain strength with your years and become your conquerer.

To John Quincy Adams, January 19, 1780

Youth is the proper season for observation and attention—a mind
unincumberd with cares may seek instruction and draw improvement from all the objects which surround it. The earlier in life you
accustome yourself to consider objects with attention, the easier
will your progress be, and more sure and successfull your enter-
prizes. What a Harvest of true knowledge and learning may you
gather from the numberless varied Scenes through which you pass
if you are not wanting in your own assiduity and endeavours.

To John Quincy Adams, Braintree, January 21, 1781

Unstable as water, thou shalt not excell said the good old patriarch to
his son*—it is an observation as true as it is ancient; and founded
upon a knowledge of humane Nature. Youth are peculiarly liable to
this frailty, and if it is not early curbed and restrained both by example and precept, it takes root and saps the fountation, it shoots out
into unprofitable branches, if the Tree blossoms, they wither and

are blown by every change of the wind so that no fruit arrives to maturity.

The Character which a youth acquires in the early part of his Life is of great importance towards his future prosperity—one false step may prove irretrievable to his future usefulness. The World fix their attention upon the behaviour of a person just setting out, more particularly so if they stand in a conspicuous light with Regard to family or estate, and according to their discretion, prudence or want of judgment, pronounce too precipately perhaps, upon the whole of their future conduct. Of how great importance is it, that good principals be early, inculcated and steadily persued in the Education of youth?

To Charles Storer, Braintree, April 28, 1783

*Jacob's dying words to his firstborn son, Reuben. Genesis 49:4.

Youth is the season for Innocent Gayety and mirth.

To John Quincy Adams, c. March 15, 1784

I would not, that a son of mine, should form any sentiments with respect to any female, but those of due decorum, and a general complaisance, which every Youth acquainted with good manners, and civility will practise towards them, untill years have matured their judgment, and learning has made them wise. I would; that they should have no passion but for Science, and no mistress but Literature.

To Elizabeth Shaw, Auteuil, January 11, 1785

The longer I live in the world, and the more I see of mankind, the more deeply I am impressed with the importance and necessity of good principles and virtuous examples being placed before youth, in the most amiable and engaging manner, whilst the mind is uncontaminated, and open to impressions.

To Elizabeth Shaw, London, March 4, 1786

The Youth of our Country must turn their minds to Agriculture, to Manufactories, and endeavour to benifit their Country in that way. There is vast scope for them.

> To Charles Storer, London, March 23, 1786

Young people are fond of Boasting sometimes not considering how great they make the merrit of the conquerer.

> To Elizabeth Shaw, London, July 19, 1786

Youth are seldom wise, but by experience, and unhappily few are so attentive in the first portion of Life as to remark with accuracy the causes of indisposition occasiond by excesses, either of food, animal or Mental. A great Student ought to be particularly carefull in the regulation of his diet, and avoid that bane of Health late suppers.

> To John Quincy Adams, London, January 17, 1787

No youth is secure whilst temptations surround him, and no age of Life but is influenced by habits & example, even when they think their Character's formed.

> To John Quincy Adams, Braintree, May 30, 1789

Time and example will prevail over youthfull folly I trust.

> To Mary Cranch, Richmond Hill, July 12, 1789

Youth is so imitative, that it catches at every thing.

> To Abigail Adams Smith, Philadelphia, February 21, 1791

Whilst our presence is easy to youth, it will tend to guide and direct them.

> *"Be to their faults a little blind,*
> *Be to their virtues ever kind,*
> *And fix the padlock on the mind."**

> To Abigail Adams Smith, Quincy, February 3, 1794

*Matthew Prior, *An English Padlock*, lines 79–81.

Young people Love Society; and it is natural they should. We old Folks who have Families find our enjoyment in them; and look not abroad for our principle happiness. I Love the company of Young People.

> To Elizabeth Peabody, Quincy, February 12, 1796

As you tell me that the enthusiasm of Youth has subsided, I will presume that reason and judgment have taken its place.

> To John Quincy Adams, Quincy, May 20, 1796

We cannot expect the judgment of Age, upon the shoulders of youth. Experience is the best school.

> To Elizabeth Peabody, Quincy, February 10, 1797

Rejoice O young Man in thy youth and let thy Heart Cheer thee. This is the language of Soloman.* Youth is therefore the Season of rejoicing; nor can there be anything more suitable provided that joy is temperate, moderate and Rational.

> To William Smith Shaw, Quincy, January 3, 1799

*Ecclesiastes 11:9.

A cold youth, would be a frozen Age.

> To Mary Cranch, Philadelphia, March 18, 1800

The kind and friendly admonitions of parental experience, should check the enthusiasm of youth, and teach them to view the world as it really is, and humane nature as it will be found, full of imperfections, much to forgive and much to be forgiven. Youth is the season for joy, for hope, for pleasure and for improvement; it is excess alone which renders these blessings hurtfull.

> To Mary Cranch, Philadelphia, April 16, 1800

The innocent playfullness of youth is a sweet solace.

> To Caroline Smith, Quincy, November 17, 1808

I am glad to see your mind so much engaged in the pursuit of knowledge. It is a young Man's best security against temptation and dissipation.

To John Adams Smith, Quincy, 1808

Waste not the Season of Youth, it is a treasure you can possess but once. I often think no price would be too great to give if I could at this Age possess the retentive powers of Youth; the true value of which I never rightly estimated but by their loss.

To George Washington Adams, Quincy, May 25, 1812

Caution, advice, even precept and example, are but weak barriers against the ardour of youth, the warmth of passion, and the allurements of pleasure.

To John Quincy Adams, Quincy, May 20, 1815

The positiveness of youth Age and experience will correct.

To George Washington Adams and John Adams 2nd, Quincy, July 12, 1815

Few youths have acquired firmness sufficient to resist the allurements of vice or can pronounce that all important monisyllable NO.

To Louisa Catherine Adams, Quincy, October 20, 1815

How hard is it to restrain the ardour of Youth—they see not the thousand thousand troubles which "Man is Heir to."*

To John Adams Smith, Quincy, March 12, 1817

*Shakespeare, *Hamlet,* III:1.

Zealots   Send no man [to Congress] who can not stand fire and fight too if necessary. No half way people in such times as these. We want Martyrs.

To William Smith, Philadelphia, June 19, 1798

— *Politics*

You know my mind is much occupied with the affairs of our Country. If as a Female I may be calld an Idle, I never can be an uninter-
ested Spectator of what is transacting upon the great Theater, when
the welfare and happiness of my Children and the rising generation
is involved in the present counsels and conduct of the Principal Actors who are now exhibiting upon the stage.

To John Adams, Quincy, December 31, 1793

You will see by a Letter received from me before this time, how
nearly we agree in sentiment upon this Subject, and I may adopt the
words of Mr. Blount in a Letter to Pope, "that I have a good opinion
of my politics, since they agree with a man who always thinks so
justly."*

To John Adams, Quincy, April 18, 1794

*Letters to and from Edward Blount, Esq., from 1714 to 1725. Letter 2.

Be assured I am remarkably cautious upon the Subject of Politicks. I
am satisfied mine would essentially clash with any one, who could
call the Peace System, a milk and water system.

To John Adams, Quincy, June 15, 1795

I know you are attentive to what is passing in the political World. Indeed who can be an indifferent Spectator in Times so critical, so allarming and so big with Consequence as the present?

To William S. Shaw, Philadelphia, March 20, 1798

I cannot wean myself from the subjects of politicks.

To Catherine Johnson, Philadelphia, May 9, 1800

Faction . . . may turn every Innocent action to evil.   *Faction*

To Mary Cranch, Richmond Hill, July 27, 1790

Partisan Politics I firmly believe if I live Ten Years longer, I shall see a devision of the Southern & Northern States, unless more candour & less intrigue, of which I have no hopes, should prevail.

> To Mary Cranch, Philadelphia, April 20, 1792

I pitty those who are blinded by party.

> To John Adams, Quincy, December 29, 1792

Partizans may Rail, but sound reason will enlighten and prevail.

> To John Quincy Adams, Quincy, December 30, 1793

Partizans are so high, respecting English and French politicks, and argue so falsly and Reason so stupidly that one would suppose they could do no injury, but there are so many who read and hear without reflecting and judging for themselves and there is such a propensity in humane Nature to believe the worst, especially when their interest is like to be affected, that if we are preserved from the Calamities of War it will be more oweing to the superintending Providence of God than the virtue and wisdom of Man.

> To John Adams, Quincy, December 31, 1793

Heaven avert the dangers which threaten us, and as we reside in a glass House, may our politicians beware of throwing stones.

> To George Cabot, [January 1794]

All the Social feelings which bind man to man and humanize Society, are wearing away; and bitter party Spirit, Calumny and falsehood are linked together to lay prostrate all those kind affections without which Life is a curse instead of a blessing.

> To Benjamin Rush, August 1794

Party will spew itself, and be bitter.

> To Mary Cranch, New York, June 25, 1795

To an honest heart and an upright mind what must be the feelings to behold faction, Intrigue and the worst of foreign politicks with the violence of a whirlwind threatning to lay waste with the pestilence of its breath our Laws, government and Religion, and to involve in all the horrors of war and in calamities which neither we or our children will ever see an end of, and for the sake of gratifying the most malicious and basest of passions, Revenge, Stirring up hatred and animosities. Family against Family, Parents against Children, and Children against Parents. Destroying the Character of the most honest, Fair and independent of men, attributing to them views and motives of which their souls were incapable.

To Abigail Adams Smith, Quincy, August 14, 1795

In times like the present, all Neutral Ground should be abandoned, and those who are not for us, be considerd as against us.

To Hannah Cushing, Philadelphia, March 9, 1798

Party spirit is fomenting bitterness, wrath and every evil work.

To John Quincy Adams, Philadelphia, February 28, 1800

The Zeal pot of politicks is boiling over, and much of the Scum rising.

To Thomas Boylston Adams, Quincy, August 15, 1800

The Spirit of party has overpowerd the Spirit of Patriotism.

To John Quincy Adams, Washington, January 29, 1801

Party hatred by its deadly poison blinds the Eyes and envenoms the heart. It is fatal to the integrity of the moral Character.

To Thomas Jefferson, Quincy, August 18, 1804

The great object of the honest men of both parties should be to unite for the common good, and to cultivate a spirit of candour, liberality and harmony. Untill that can be effected our country will be torn alternately by contending factions.

To Abigail Adams Smith, Quincy, May 20, 1808

The vile spirit of Party, has sacrificed at their shrine, honour, integrity and talents.

> To Abigail Adams Smith, Quincy, August 29, 1808

Virgil, in one of his odysseys, describes Æolus as confining the winds in a bag, and relates the terrible havoc they made when unskillfully let loose. We may compare the spirit of party to these winds, which blew the embers of discontent in flames, and threatened destruction to every obstacle which opposes their progress.

> To Abigail Adams Smith, Quincy, May 23, 1809

The spirit of party so warps the judgment and blinds the understanding as to lead good and honest men blindfold. . . . When party spirit yealds to reason and sober sense, this will be the equitable decision.

> To Abigail Adams Smith, Quincy, June 19, 1809

How shall violence of party Spirit be quelld and the Spirit of animosity to which it gives rise be softned down into a sacred regard for the honour, interest & Liberty of our dear and beloved Country now threatned to become a scene of discord, hatred and revenge. Let the civil Wisdom of Age check the fiery ardour of Youth and let not that Religion which proclaims peace on earth and good will to man be prostituted to kindle and spread abroad false political doctrines and incendiary Newspaper publications & pamphlets instead of subordination to Rulers and Submission to Government. I am sorry to say such discourses I have heard from the pulpit. What can we expect from the flock when the pastor there misleads them?

> To Mercy Otis Warren, Quincy, August 9, 1812

Much of the Spirit of party still subsists in N. England, but it does not leven the Whole Loaf.

> To John Quincy Adams, Quincy, June 29, 1815

Spirit of party, so ambitious of conquest, is driven forward by passion, which judgment has little controul.

To John Quincy Adams, Quincy, April 1, 1816

When we see the intrigues the Ambition the Envy the malice and ingratitude of the world, who would not rather, retire and live unnoticed in a country village, than stand the Broad mark for all those arrows to be shot at placed upon a pinicle.   *Political Attacks*

To John Adams, Quincy, January 21, 1796

I have no disposition to seclude myself from society, because I have met with unkind or ungratefull returns from some; I would strive to act my part well and Retire with that dignity which is unconscious of doing or wishing ill to any, with a temper disposed to forgive injuries, as I would myself hope to be forgiven, if any I have committed.   *Political Grudges*

To Mary Cranch, Washington, January 15, 1801

Like Moles, much work has been done in this state underground.   *Political Intrigue*

To Thomas Welsh, Quincy, November 15, 1792

— Religion

Come then Religion thy force can alone support the Mind under the severest trials and hardest conflicts humane Nature is subject to.

> *"Religion Noble comfort brings*
> *Disarms our Griefs or Blunts their Stings."* *

To John Thaxter, Braintree, February 15, 1778

*Oliver Goldsmith, *History of the Earth and Animated Nature.*

The only sure and permanent foundation of virtue is religion. Let this important truth be engraved upon your heart. And also, that the foundation of religion is the belief of the one only God, and a just sense of his attributes, as a being infinitely wise, just, and good, to whom you owe the highest reverence, gratitude, and adoration; who superintends and governs all nature, even to clothing the lilies of the field, and hearing the young ravens when they cry; but more particularly regards man, whom he created after his own image, and breathed into him an immortal spirit, capable of a happiness beyond the grave; for the attainment of which he is bound to the performance of certain duties, which all tend to the happiness and welfare of society, and are comprised in one short sentence, expressive of universal benevolence, "Thou shalt love thy neighbor as thyself."* This is elegantly defined by Mr. Pope, in the "Essay on Man."

> "Remember, man, the universal cause
> Acts not by partial, but by general laws,
> And makes what happiness we justly call,
> Subsist not in the good of one, but all.
> There's not a blessing individuals find,
> But some ways leans and hearkens to the kind."

Thus has the Supreme Being made the good will of man towards his fellow-creatures an evidence of his regard to Him, and for this purpose has constituted him a dependent being and made his happiness to consist in society. Man early discovered this propensity of his nature, and found

"Eden was tasteless till an Eve was there."

To John Quincy Adams, March 20, 1780

*Matthew 19:19.

However the Belief of a particular Providence may be exploded by the Modern Wits, and the Infidelity of too many of the rising generation deride the Idea, yet the virtuous Mind will look up and acknowledge the great first cause, without whose notice not even a sparrow falls to the ground.*

. . . but there is one consolation to which I must ever resort, in all my anxietyes. I thank Heaven who has given me to believe in a su- perintending providence Guiding and Governing all things in infinite wisdom and "to look through and Trust the Ruler of the Skye."**

To John Adams, October 15, 1780, and October 21, 1781

*Paraphrase of Matthew 10:29.   **Alexander Pope, *Imitations of Horace,* Book I, Epistle VI.

The great Author of our religion frequently inculcated universal be- nevolence and taught us both by precept and example when he pro- mulgated peace and good will to man, a doctrine very different from that which actuates the hostile invaders and the cruel ravagers of mighty kingdoms and nations.

To John Quincy Adams, Braintree, May 20, 1781

Religion . . . is the only fountain to which we can repair when bowed down with distress.

To Isaac Smith, Sr., London, July 31, 1786

The Universal Parent has dispensed his blessings throughout all cre- ation, and, though to some he hath given a more goodly heritage than to others, we have reason to believe that a general order and harmony are maintained by apportioning to each his proper station. Though seas, mountains, and rivers are geographical boundaries, they contract not the benevolence and good will of the liberal mind, which can extend itself beyond the limits of country and kindred, and claim fellowship with Christian, Jew, or Turk. What a lesson, did the great Author of our religion give to mankind by the parable of the Jew and the Samaritan; but how little has it been regarded! To the glory of the present age, they are shaking off that narrow, con- tracted spirit of priestcraft and usurpation, which has for so many ages tyrannized over the minds of mankind, and deluged the world in blood. They consider religion not as a state stalking-horse, to raise men to temporal power and dignity; but as a wise and benevolent system, calculated to still the boisterous passions, to restrain the malevolent ones, to curb the ambitious, and to harmonize mankind to the temper of its great Author, who came to make peace and not to destroy.

To Elizabeth Shaw, London, November 21, 1786

Bred a desenter and approveing that mode of worship, I feel a reluctance at changing tho I would always go to church, if I resided where there was no other mode of worship.

To Mary Cranch, Richmond Hill, October 4, 1789

You complain that there is, in the rising generation, a want of principle. This is a melancholy truth. I am no friend of bigotry; yet I think the freedom of inquiry, and the general toleration of religious sentiments, have been, like all other good things, perverted, and, under that shelter, deism, and even atheism, have found refuge. Let us for one moment reflect, as rational creatures, upon our "being, end, and aim," and we shall feel our dependence, we shall be convinced of our frailty, and satisfied that we must look beyond this transitory scene for a happiness large as our wishes, and boundless as our desires. True, genuine religion is calm in its inquiries, deliberate in its resolves, and steady in its conduct; is open to light and conviction, and labors for improvement. It studies to promote love and union in civil and in religious society. It approves virtue, and the truths which promote it, and, as the Scripture expresses it, "is peaceable, gentle, easy to be entreated."* It is the anchor of our hope, the ornament of youth, the comfort of age; our support in affliction and adversity, and the solace of that solemn hour, which we must all experience. Train up, my dear daughter, your children, to a sober and serious sense of the duty which they owe to the Supreme Being. Impress their infant minds with a respect for the Sabbath. This is too much neglected by the rising generation. Accustom them to a constant attendance upon public worship, and enforce it by your own example and precept, as often as you can with any convenience attend. It is a duty, for which we are accountable to the Supreme Being.

To Abigail Adams Smith, Quincy, March 10, 1794

*James 3:17.

Half the year I must sit under as strong Calvinism as I can possibly swallow.

> To Mary Cranch, Philadelphia, December 12, 1797

As we descend the Hill of Life, our gay and visionary prospect vanish, and what gilded our Meridian days, our Zenith of Life, as the Shadows lengthen, we see through a different medium and may justly estimate many of our persuits, as vanity and vexation of spirit.

"But there's a Brighter world on high" which opens to us prospects more permanent, and pleasures more durable. To that let us aspire in the sure and certain hope, that by a patient Continuence in the path of Religion and Virtue, we shall assuredly reap, if we faint not, the happy fruits of a glorious immortality.

> To Mary Cranch, Philadelphia, March 27, 1798

I do not believe that a people are ever made better by always hearing of the terrors of the Lord. Gloom is no part of my Religion. To maintain a conscience void of offence, as far as is consistant with the imperfect State we are in, both towards God and Man, is one article of my Faith, and to do good as I have opportunity, and according to my means I would wish to make the Rule of my practise to do justly, walk Humbly and to Love mercy—are duties enjoind upon every Christian, and if we can attain to those graces, we may cheerfully look for our recompence and reward, where it is promised to us.

> To Mary Cranch, Philadelphia, November 26, 1799

I do not believe, with some divines, that all our good works are but as filthy rags; the example which our great Master has set before us, of purity, benevolence, obedience, submission and humility, are virtues which, if faithfully practiced, will find their reward; or why has he pronounced so many benedictions upon them in his sermon on the mount?*

> To Caroline Smith, Quincy, November 19, 1812

*Matthew 5:8.

Altho I sometimes feel my own insignificance in the creation, especially when contemplating the first Good, first perfect and first fair, I derive pleasure and assurance from the word of inspiration—that not a swallow falleth without notice.*

> To John Quincy Adams, July 1, 1813

*Paraphrase of Matthew 10:29.

Abbe* is much improved in her person and may be said to be beautifull, altho she has not yet settled into woman. She is like the half bloom Rose, and there is an interesting pensiveness in her countenance, which the Religious Sentiments, which have been instilled into her mind gives to hers. The Rejection of every amusement, however innocent in itself and congenial to youth. It is no part of my Religion for I read in the Scriptures that there is a time to dance & to Sing.**

> To Elizabeth Peabody, Quincy, November 20, 1814

*Abbe Louisa Adams, AA's sixteen-year-old granddaughter. **Ecclesiastes 3:4.

When the Lawyer consulted our Saviour asking what he should do to inherit Eternal Life?* He said unto him what is written in the Law? how readest thou? and he answering said Thou Love the Lord thy God with all thy Heart, with all thy Soul and with all thy Strength & with all thy mind, and thy Neighbour as thy Self. And he said unto him, thou hast answerd right. This do and thou Shalt Live. Then follows that beautifull explanation of who is thy Neighbour.** This I call true Religion the Love of God, and our Neighbour, in the enlarged Sense of our Saviour—not confined to Country, Nation or party. Altho as Pope expressed it "Friend, Country first, and then all humane Race."†

> To Harriet Welsh, Quincy, February 8, 1815

*Luke 10:26–27. **The story of the good Samaritan (Luke 10:30–34).
†Alexander Pope, *An Essay on Man*, Epistle IV, lines 267–68.

Life and immortality are brought to light only by the gospel. Good people cannot think alike, even upon important Subjects. Fear God and keep his commandments, is the whole duty of Man, and his faith cannot be essentially wrong, whose Life is in the Right.*

> To John Quincy Adams, Quincy, February 10, 1816

*Alexander Pope, *An Essay on Man,* Epistle III, lines 205–6.

When I look in my Glass I see that I am not what I was. I scarcely know a feature of my face. But I believe that this Mortal Body shall one day put on immortality and be renovated in the World of Spirits. Having enjoyed a large portion of the good things of this life and few of its miseries, I ought to rise satisfied from the feast, and be gratefull to the Giver.

> To John Quincy Adams, Quincy, May 10, 1817

When will Mankind be convinced true religion is from the Heart, between Man and his Creator and not the Imposition of Man or creeds and tests.

> To Louisa Catherine Adams, Quincy, January 3, 1818

I do not profess to be a theologian. I never would puzzle my head with their disputes; but I have endeavoured to exercise my own understanding:

*What can we reason, but from what we know?**

And from the Scriptures I learn that there is but one God to whom worship is due. That he is the Creator, preserver and governor of universal Nature—Thou shalt have no other Gods before me, is the first command after that of Loving God.** There is no other object of Religious worship but the one Supreme Deity. There is no other Being of whom we have sufficient reason to think that he is constantly present with us, and a witness of all our thoughts, words and actions. And there is no other Being to whom our Supplications ought to be addressed. The language of Jesus Christ, is "thou shalt worship the Lord thy God, and him only Shalt thou Serve.†

If the doctrine of the Trinity is not here, what must that worship be which is grounded upon It? Now if three persons acting different parts, sustaining different Characters are each of them equally God, there can be but one God. Or if this is possible, and three persons make but one Nature, how is it possible that two Natures should make but one person in Jesus Christ? My Reason tells me there cannot be two Supremes and my arithmetic cannot make one two & two one.

In one thing we are agreed that he who feareth God, and Worketh Righteousness‡ shall be accepted of him and his Faith "cannot be wrong whose Life is in the Right."§

> To Louisa Catherine Adams, Quincy, April 15, 1818

*Alexander Pope, *An Essay on Man,* Epistle I.   **Exodus 20:3.
†Matthew 4:10.   ‡Acts 10:35.   §Alexander Pope, *An Essay on Man,* Epistle III.

Faith   I have Faith that will remove mountains.*

> To Mercy Otis Warren, London, May 14, 1787

*I Corinthians 13:2.

God   God is like a refuge for us.

> To John Adams, Braintree, June 8, 1775

I will not distrust the providential Care of the supreem disposer of events, from whose Hand I have so frequently received distinguished favours.

> To John Adams, April 10, 1782

Dr. Blair gave us an excellent discourse a Sunday or two ago. "Trust in the Lord, for in the Lord Jehovah is everlasting Strength."* If it was not for that trust and confidence, our Hearts would often fail us.

> To Mary Cranch, Philadelphia, July 6, 1797

*Isaiah 26:4.

May we be ever led to trust in that goodness which is over all the works of his hands.

To Catherine Johnson, Philadelphia, May 1800

Providence for wise purposes has oftentimes since the commence-   *God's Direction*
ment of this war brought about our deliverence by ways and means
which have appeard to us the most improbable and unlikely—has
given into our hands those things which we were destitute of, and in
the greatest necessity for. So true it is acknowledge him in all thy
ways, and he shall direct thy paths.*

To John Adams, October 20, 1777

*Proverbs 3:6.

Providence over rules all things for the best, and will work out our
Salvation for us in the wisest and best manner—provided we perform our Duty.

To John Adams, November 18, 1777

We trust that the supreem Ruler of the universe knows what is best
for his creatures.

To Elizabeth Peabody, Quincy, July 18, 1800

I feel perfectly tranquil . . . hoping and trusting that, the Being in
whose Hands are the Hearts of all Men, will guide and direct our national counsels for the peace and prosperity of this great people.

To Mary Cranch, Columbia City of Washington, November 21, 1800

Tho the Clouds are impenetrable, and the ways of providence dark
and intricate, he who permits not a sparrow to fall, unnoticed,* assuredly overrules the more important interests and concerns of
kingdoms and nations.

To Cotton Tufts, Washington, January 15, 1801

*Paraphrase of Matthew 10:29.

All events are under the Controul of a supreem being who will order and direct them, I trust for our best good: and may it please him to avert from us the horrors of war.

To Abigail Adams Smith, Quincy, March 18, 1808

The Hereafter   [On the death of her father:] I do not wonder that the unhappy House looks desolate and mourns. Desolate indeed will it ever look to us. But the House not made with hands, is the mansion I trust where our dear parents are, and there may all their children meet them, is the prayer of your ever affectionate AA.

To Elizabeth Shaw, after September 17, 1783

Placed as we are in a transitory scene of probation, drawing nigher and still nigher day after day to that important crisis which must introduce us into a new system of things, it ought certainly to be our principal concern to become qualified for our expected dignity.

To John Quincy Adams, Braintree, November 20, 1783

Why may we not suppose, that, the higher our attainments in knowledge and virtue are here on earth, the more nearly we assimilate ourselves to that order of beings who now rank above us in the world of spirits? We are told in scripture, that there are different kinds of glory, and that one star differeth from another.* Why should not those who have distinguished themselves by superior excellence over their fellow-mortals continue to preserve their rank when admitted to the kingdom of the just? Though the estimation of worth may be very different in the view of the righteous Judge of the world from that which vain man esteems such on earth, yet we may rest assured that justice will be strictly administered to us.

To Lucy Cranch, London, August 27, 1785

*I Corinthians 15:41.

Thanks to our Benificent Creator who tho he has constituted us subject to mortality has given us the broad Basis of a future happy existance to build our hopes upon, and the best grounded assurance, that we shall obtain it; by pursuing the dictates of our consciences, in the exercise of Love to God and good will to man.

> To Mary Cranch, London, January 10, 1786

Our own duration is but a Span, then shall we meet those dear Friends and relatives who have gone before us and be engaged together in more elevated views, and purer pleasures and enjoyments than Mortality is capable of. Let this Idea Sooth the afflicted mind, and administer Balm to the wounded Heart; all things are under the Government of a supreeme all wise director, to him commit, the hour the day the year.

> To Mary Cranch, London, February 25, 1787

If it was not for the sure and certain hope of a superiour State of existance beyond this transitory Scene of Noise, Bustle, pain & anxiety—we should be of all Beings the most miserable.*

> To Mary Cranch, Philadelphia, May 7, 1798

*I Corinthians 15:19.

What is to be our future Lot, and Destiny, remains to be unfolded. I hope we may still Continue to be "that happy people saved of the Lord."*

> To Mary Cranch, Philadelphia, May 7, 1798

*Psalms 144:15.

Mrs. Field is relieved from the infirmities under which she sufferd, and having acted well, very well, her part in Life, will, I doubt not, have her reward.

> To Mary Cranch, Philadelphia, June 4, 1798

[On the death of Jeremy Belknap:] With his near and more particular connections I tenderly sympathize, and pray that they may receive comfort from the reflection, that he is called to a higher, and more dignified Station than that which he sustained upon Earth, and is receiving the reward promised to Good and faithfull Servants.*

To John Belknap, Philadelphia, July 9, 1798

*Matthew 15:21.

I must say to you as you do to me, pray keep up your Spirits and Buffet the Waves. We shall find a safe post I trust at last, If not in this world, I trust awaits us. This is a consolation that our firm belief in the Christian Religion holds out to us, and of this, the world cannot deprive us.

To John Adams, Quincy, December 21, 1798

I am frequently reminded, that here I have no abiding place.

To Mercy Otis Warren, Quincy, October 5, 1799

If in this Life only you have hope, say the scriptures, ye are of all men the most miserable.* It is looking beyond this transitory scene where all is fleeting, transitory and delusive to the well grounded of a blessed immortality, which mitigates the pains of sickness, the crosses, vexations and trials to which "flesh is Heir to,"** and silence the Christian to that patient submission which teaches to endure all things.

To Thomas Boylston Adams, Washington, January 2, 1801

*I Corinthians 15:19.   **Shakespeare, *Hamlet*, III:1.

We must live all the days of our appointed time, and when our change commeth, may it be happy to us.

To Mary Cranch, Washington, January 15, 1801

Your Friends tho not exempt from the infirmities of age, are in the enjoyment of many blessings, amongst which is a comfortable portion of Health, and rural felicity. We enjoy the present with gratitude, and look forward to brighter prospects and more durable happiness in a future state of existance, where we hope to meet and rejoice with those whom we have loved, and revered upon Earth.

To Mercy Otis Warren, Quincy, January 16, 1803

Your Letter, my dear Madam, written so much in the stile of Mrs. Warren's ancient Friendship, renewed all those Sensations which formerly gave me pleasure, and from which I have derived sincere and durable gratification, and I anticipate a still closer and more cordial union in the World of Spirits to which we are hastning, when these earthly tabernacles shall be moulderd into dust.

To Mercy Otis Warren, Quincy, March 9, 1807

Every moment should be devoted to some useful purpose, that we might ask the moments as they passed, what report they bore to Heaven—that the more we cultivated and improved our intellectual powers, the more capable we should be of enjoyment in a higher and more perfect state of existence; the nearer we should be allied to angels, and the spirits of just men made perfect; and that in order to cultivate our faculties to advantage, we must have order and method in all our affairs.

To Caroline Smith, Quincy, January 24, 1808

How is the bitter cup sweetened by a mercifull providence that we may be enabled to support the calamities which "the flesh is heir to"*—and how unsatisfactory would every connexion we can form in Life be without the belief of that Religion which teaches us to look beyond the Grave, with the hope of Shareing together a happiness durable and uninterupted.

To John Quincy Adams, Quincy, February 15, 1811

*Shakespeare, *Hamlet,* III:1.

My hope and consolation is that her* last change introduced her to a world where the weary are at rest and to the Society of the just made perfect.

To Julia Rush, Quincy, September 24, 1813

*AA's daughter, Abigail Adams Smith.

We both of us [John and Abigail] know that our time is short. I hope that when we get beyond this "congeragated Ball, self centered Sun and Stars that rise and fall,"* we shall be introduced into a higher class of Beings and improve in knowledge and virtue to an endless duration.

To François Adriaan Vanderkemp, Quincy, February 23, 1814

*Horace's Epistle VI.

May all those dear Friends who have gone before us and we who are soon to follow rise to a happy Life of immortality in the day of final retribution.

To François Adriaan Vanderkemp, Quincy, May 26, 1815

A little while, and I also shall join the great congregation. . . . I hope to meet him and my dear daughter* in the world to which we are hastening.

To Caroline deWindt, Boston, June 5, 1816

*William Stephens Smith and Abigail Adams Smith.

Our decayed Linements must soon Crumble to dust, but I hope we have another and a better Country to repair to, whose builder and Maker is the most high, and when I trust we shall meet those dear to us, who have gone before us.

To John Quincy Adams, Quincy, June 29, 1816

Her Babe has joind its kindred Spirits in the Regions of Bliss—

To Louisa Catherine Adams, Quincy, September 30, 1817

My Ideas are confined pretty much to my own fire side, sometimes pleasant, sometimes anxious, sometimes painfull. Who is without their share of all this. Who that thinks and reflects can avoid it. This State is a state of trial; whether we glide on under a full sail of prosperity, or are driven by adverse winds upon a tempestuous coast, adversity calls forth more graces and virtues, than prosperity usually exhibits. The prayer discovered a mind fully sensible of this truth.

To Ann Harrod Adams, Quincy, February 16, 1806

This world we are told is our school may we all of us improve aright, the usefull Lessons we are taught.

To Elizabeth Peabody, Quincy, June 10, 1807

I am permitted a longer sojourn to fullfill some duty, to repent of some omission or commission, to relieve some wants, to correct some errors, [or] to Sooth some anguish.

To François Adriaan Vanderkemp, Quincy, May 26, 1815

If you have a due sense of your preservation, your next consider- ation will be, for what purpose you are continued in life. It is not to rove from clime to clime, to gratify an idle curiosity; but every new mercy you receive is a new debt upon you, a new obligation to a diligent discharge of the various relations in which you stand connected; in the first place, to your great Preserver; in the next, to society in general; in particular, to your country, to your parents, and to yourself.

To John Quincy Adams, March 20, 1780

That we may not neglect the main object of Life, a preparation for death.

To Cotton Tufts, London, August 1, 1786

What is the chief end of man? is a subject well worth the investigation of every rational being. What, indeed, is life, or its enjoyments, without settled principle, laudable purposes, mental exertions, and internal comfort, that sunshine of the soul; and how are these to be acquired in the hurry and tumult of the world?

To Mary Cranch, London, January 20, 1787

It is surely an unsatisfactory Idea to live and die without persueing any other purpose, than mere personal gratification. If we have received pleasures & advantages from the efforts of others, it is also incumbent upon us to do Something for the benefit of those who are to follow us.

To Cotton Tufts, London, April 29, 1787

Always remember that you are accountable to that being who brought you into existence, for your time and talents; that you were not born for yourself, but to fill every hour with some useful employment.

To Caroline Smith, Quincy, February 2, 1809

Wherever you are, you are doing good, and this is the true end of Life.

To Harriet Welsh, Quincy, April 13, 1815

Prayer The effectual fervent prayer of the Righteous, availeth much.*

To Elizabeth Peabody, Quincy, February 10, 1797

*James 5:16.

Instead of praises, let me have your prayers for the discharge of my duties.

To Harriet Welsh, Quincy, October 1, 1817

Quakers I thank you for your amusing account of the Quaker[s].* Their great stress with regard to coulours in their dress &c. is not the only ridiculous part of their Sentiments with regard to Religious Matters.

To John Adams, Braintree, October 21, 1775

*JA's letter of September 27, 1775, with his account has not been found.

No free Government can stand, which is not supported by Religion and virtue.

To Jeremy Belknap, Philadelphia, May 24, 1798

Religion and Government

I wish with you that I could see as great a Change for the better in Morals as in politicks, but it is a part of Religion as well morality, to do justly and to love mercy and a man can not be an honest and zeal-ous promoter of the principles of a Free Government, without pos-sessing that Good will towards man which leads to the Love of God and respect for the Deity, so that a proper appreciation of our Rights and duties as citizens is a prelude to a respect for Religion, and its in-stitutions. To destroy and undermine Religion has been the chief en-gine in the accomplishment of this mighty Revolution throughout Europe. We have felt no small share of the banefull influence, of the Age of Reason.*

To Mary Cranch, Philadelphia, May 26, 1798

*Thomas Paine's *Age of Reason*, 1793–1794.

You observe . . . that you are not fond of mixing Religion with poli-ticks. That is the Idea. I know not (as the paper is lent) whether I have the exact words. I think however when Religion has been equally attackd with the Liberty and Government of the Country, it is proper to manifest a due Respect for that upon which both the other Rest. I have been assured from respectable Authority that the opportunity which the Chief Majestrate has embraced of bearing publick testimony to Religion, in his replies to many of the addresses presented him, and his pointed dissapprobation of infidelity, has done more to stop the progress of it, and to bring into disrepute

French principles than all the Sermons preachd by the Clergy of our Country.

> To John Adams, Quincy, January 20, 1799

Such times are approaching for our country, as require the skill, knowledge, experience, and industry of all who regard peace and harmony, order, and regular government as blessings worth preserving, to be upon their guard, and to defend themselves, and their country against the machinations which are formed to destroy its tranquility and prosperity.

> To Abigail Adams Smith, Philadelphia, May 11, 1800

Religious Liberty The late act of toleration pass'd by Virginia* is Esteemed here as an example to the World.

> To Elizabeth Shaw, London, November 21, 1786

*In January 1786 Virginia enacted an Act for Religious Freedom, drafted by Thomas Jefferson in 1777 and shepherded through the legislature by James Madison.

Submission to the Will of God My poor father like a firm Believer and a Good christian sets before his children the best of Examples of patience and submission.

> To John Adams, Weymouth, October 1, 1775

So short sighted and so little a way can we look into futurity that we ought patiently to submit to the dispensation of Heaven.

> To John Adams, Braintree, July 16, 1777

An all wise Providence has seen fit to curtail our wishes and to limit our enjoyments, that we may not be unmindfull of our dependance or forget the Hand from whence they flow.

> To Mary Cranch, Richmond Hill, July 12, 1789

The equanimity of your disposition will lead you to a patient submission to the allotments of Providence.

> To Abigail Adams Smith, Philadelphia, February 21, 1791

May that being who doth not afflict willingly, support, sustain and comfort you, and that holy Religion which we profess and believe "justify the Ways of God to Man."*

To Susanna Warner Tufts, Philadelphia, May 8, 1798

*John Milton, *Paradise Lost.*

What ever Scenes you may be call'd to pass through, may you be sustaind and supported by that Being in whom we trust, satisfied that however grevious his dispensations, they are wise and just, and we will strive to adore the Hand that "strikes our comforts dead."*

To Elizabeth Peabody, Philadelphia, June 22, 1798

*Isaac Watts, *Submission to Afflictive Providences, Job 1:21.*

I hope the variety of cares which call for your daily attention will serve to dispell the Weight of Grief which in spight of all your exertions was visible at your Heart, and that the bitterness of Sorrow will be healed by the lenient hand of time and the more powerfull aid of Religion, which teaches us whilst we explore the Counsels of the most high. Certain of the paternal care of our Creator, our part is submission to his will.

To Elizabeth Peabody, Quincy, December 30, 1798

[On the death of Charles Adams:] The Scripture expresses it as a mitigation of sorrow when we do not sorrow as those who have no hope. The Mercy of the almighty is not limited; to his sovereign will I desire humbly to submit.

To Mary Cranch, Washington, December 8, 1800

[Writing to the widow of Charles Adams:] May I be enabled in silence to bow myself in submission to my maker whose attributes are Mercy, as well as judgments.

To Sarah Smith Adams, Washington, December 8, 1800

I repine not, at any of the allotments, or dispensations of providence.

> To John Quincy Adams, Washington, January 29, 1801

To the Sovereign Disposer of all events, I would strive cheerfully to submit.

> To Caroline Smith, Quincy, August 12, 1809

I believe there is much in the natural constitution and habits, but more in that Religion which teaches us Submission to the allotments of divine providence & patience and resignation to the will of our heavenly Father. This makes the Rich Man happy, in the plenty given "and the poor content him, with the care of heaven."*

> To Elizabeth Peabody, Quincy, November 24, 1810

*Alexander Pope, *An Essay on Man.*

Patient submission and resignation to the dispensations of providence is a duty at all times incumbent upon us and what we ought to strive for & cultivate upon us and yet the example of our blessed Redeemer taught us not only to feel, but to weep over the graves of our departed Friends.

> To Unknown, Quincy, January 7, 1811

Religion my Friend does not forbid us to weep and to mourn for our departed Friends, but it teaches us to cast our sorrows upon that Being in whose hands and at whose disposal we are, and who can heal the wounded Bosom and bind up the broken heart.

> To Catherine Johnson, Quincy, January 19, 1811

You have had great calls upon your fortitude, and the trial of your virtues since your separation from your Friends—
We know upon what Terms we hold our existence here. The Christian looks beyond this State of trial for the reward promised to those who endure unto the end. Altho when in trouble the dark

shade of the picture only is seen, we find the Light is the more powerfull, for it dispels the Darkness. Few of us but have greater cause to
sing of mercies than of Judgment. When we can bring our minds to
think that

"partial Evil is universal good"*

And that whatever troubles assail us in this Life are but parts of
the great plan, in which everything will in time appear to have been
orderd and conducted in the best manner. We are in the hand of a
mercifull Being who does not willingly afflict, and who will heal the
wounded heart which trusts in him.

Despond not my dear Daughter, be cheerfull, submissive and
resignd. God loves a Cheerfull Christian, and he will not call us to
harder trials than he will give us Strength to endure.

To Louisa Catherine Adams, Quincy, July 24, 1813

*Alexander Pope, *An Essay on Man,* Epistle I.

To his will we must Submit.

To John Quincy Adams, Quincy, December 24, 1813

Nature must pay its tribute. Religion forbids it not. Nor is it inconsistant with that Submission & Resignation which is required of us as
christians; provided we do not sorrow to excess, but Bless the hand
which afflicts and can heal our sorrows.

To Mary Otis, Quincy, May 13, 1814

We have daily mercies to be thankfull for, tho no state is exempt
from trouble and vexation.

Thanksgiving

To Mary Cranch, Richmond Hill, June 9, 1790

We have as a people the greatest cause for Gratitude and thankfullness to the Supreme Ruler of the Universe for our present happy and
prosperous circumstances as a Nation.

To Mary Cranch, Bush Hill, March 12, 1791

Thanks to that all gracious Providence whose kindness has been so frequently displayd towards us.

To Mary Cranch, Philadelphia, December 18, 1791

Your Mother was well this day. She spent it with me. She and your Brother and family all dinned with me on thanksgiving day as well as our Son. Tis the first thanksgiving day that I have been at Home to commemorate for Nine years. Scattered and dispersed as our Family is, God only knows whether we shall ever all meet together again. Much of the pleasure and happiness resulting from these N England Annual festivals is the family circles and connections which are brought together at these times, but whether seperate or together I am Sensible that every year has been productive of many Blessings, and that I have great cause of thankfulness for preserving mercies both to myself and Family.

To John Adams, Quincy, December 4, 1792

This is our Thanksgiving day. When I look Back upon the Year past, I perceive many, very many causes for thanksgiving, both of a publick and private nature. I hope my Heart is not ungratefull, tho sad; it is usually a day of festivity when the Social Family circle meet together tho seperated the rest of the year. No Husband *dignifies my Board,* no Children add gladness to it, no Smiling Grandchildren Eyes to sparkle for the plumb pudding, or feast upon the mind Eye. Solitary and alone I behold the day after a sleepless night, without a joyous feeling. Am I ungratefull? I hope not.

To John Adams, Quincy, November 29, 1798

On Thursday next four of our N England States keep thanksgiving. I would not suffer the day to pass without noticeing it here by the Symbols of the festival as commemorated by us. I have invited a chosen set to dine upon that day, and whilst we share in & are plentifully supplied with the good things of this world, I hope we shall not be unmindfull of the many blessings of the past year, which we have abundant cause to be thankfull for.

To Mary Cranch, Philadelphia, November 26, 1799

At dinner I looked round, I hope with a thankful heart, but alas! how many of my dear children were absent, not one of them to give pleasure to the festive table; the young shoots and branches remained; I had two from each family; these promising successors of their parents rejoiced over their plum puddings without knowing what were the reflections and anxious solicitude of their grandmother, respecting some of their absent parents.

For health, food, and raiment, for peace, and for society, and unnumbered other favours, may my heart pour forth its grateful effusions.

To Caroline Smith, Quincy, December 9, 1809

Yesterday was our Thanksgiving day. In our own way, and with tempers suited to the occasion, we gave thanks for those blessings which we felt had been granted to us in the year past, for the restoration and recovery from dangerous sickness of members of our own family; and, although in one instance we had been called to weep, in many others we had cause of rejoicing. We were in health; we had good news from a far country; we had food and raiment, and we still enjoyed liberty, and our rulers were men of our own election, and removable by the people.

To Caroline Smith, Quincy, November 27, 1812

When we contrast our own Situation with other nations, we have abundant cause for gratitude and thankfulness.

To John Quincy Adams, Quincy, January 8, 1817

And unto him who mounts the Whirlwind and directs the Storm I will chearfully leave the ordering of my Lot, and whether adverse or prosperous Days should be my future portion I will trust in his right

Trust in God

Hand to lead me safely thro, and after a short rotation of Events fix me in a state immutable and happy.

To John Adams, Braintree, September 17, 1775

Unitarianism The only fire at present like to burst forth is of a religious kind upon the Subject of unitarianism—the Soil of N. England will not cultivate nor cherish Clerical biggotary or intolerance altho, there is a Struggle to introduce it.

To John Quincy Adams, Quincy, May 20, 1815

[The religious conflict taking place] may be sumed up in that couplet of Pope's

> *"For modes of Faith, let graceless Zealots fight*
> *His can't be wrong whose Life is in the Right."*★

I acknowledge myself a unitarian in Dr. Clark's Sense. Believing that the Father alone is the Supreme God, and that Jesus Christ derived his Being, and all his powers and honours from the Father. I regret to see a narrow selfish exclusive System gaining ground, instead of that liberal Spirit of christianity recommended by St. Paul.

To John Quincy Adams, Quincy, October 12, 1815

★Alexander Pope, *An Essay on Man*, Epistle III, lines 205–6.

There is not any reasoning which can convince me, contrary to my senses, that three, is one and one three. Is it possible for the humane mind to form an idea of the Supreme Being, without some visible qualities such as wisdom, power, and goodness. The creator, preserver and governor of the world. The first commandment forbids the worship of but one God.★ That Jesus Christ was sent into the world by the Father to take upon him humane nature, to exalt redeem and purify the world, to set an example to all his followers of sinless obedience and holiness of life and conversation, and to bring life and immortality to light, the scriptures fully testify, and that a conformity to his precepts and example, as far as humane nature is capable of it, will be rewarded by future happiness in the world to come, is my firm belief.

Is there not a subordination to the Father manifested in the whole life and character of Jesus Christ? Why said he call ye me good. There is none good but one that is God. Again, I do nothing of my-self, but the Father in me.** . . . From these and many other passages of scripture, I am led to believe in the unity of the Supreme Being.

To John Quincy Adams, Quincy, May 4, 1816

*Exodus 20:3.   **Matthew 19:17; John 8:28.

Blessed be God, his Ear is not heavy that he cannot hear, but he has bid us call upon him in time of Trouble. *The Will of God*

To John Adams, Weymouth, October 1, 1775

The Ways of Heaven were dark and intricate.

To Nathaniel Willis, Braintree, after January 4, 1781

Shall not the judge of all the earth do right and have I not experi-enced signal favours—shall I distrust his providentiall care?

To Elizabeth Shaw, Braintree, February–March 1782

Let us ask the rising year, now open to our view yet wrapped in darkness, whither dost thou lead? Let cheerful hope receive the wel-come guest, gratefully recollecting the many blessings of the past year, and committing ourselves to the wise and overruling Provi-dence, who suffers not a sparrow to fall to the ground without his notice.*

To Caroline Smith, Quincy, February 2, 1809

*Paraphrase of Matthew 10:29.

I have some troubles in the loss of friends by death, and no small solicitude for the motherless offspring, but my trust and confidence are in that being who "hears the young ravens when they cry."*

To Caroline Smith, Quincy, February 26, 1811

*Psalms 146:9.

To a mind elevated and endowed like your own, full of confidence and hope, you can look through nature to Nature's God and trust the Ruler of the skies,* sure that all events are permitted and contrould, by infinite wisdom, justice, and Benevolence.

To Mercy Otis Warren, Quincy, May 5, 1814

*Alexander Pope, *Imitations of Horace*, Book I, Epistle VI.

— Travel and Transportation

Carriages

More Carriages . . . are quite a useless expence which I neither wish or desire.

To John Adams, Quincy, January 5, 1794

Cosmopolitanism

A Gentleman of understanding . . . who has travelld merly to remark Men and Manners, will never be indiscriminate either in Praising or Blaming Countries or people collectively. There is something I dare say esteemable in all, and the liberal mind regards not what Nation or climate it spring up in, nor what *color* or *complexion* the Man is of.

To William Stephens Smith, London, September 18, 1785

However I might hanker after the good things of America, I have been sufficiently taught to value and esteem other countries besides my own.

To Thomas Brand-Hollis, New York, September 6, 1790

It is only by visiting the World and marking the manners as they rise, that the mind can be enlarged and local prejudices subdued.

> To John Quincy Adams, Quincy, August 26, 1815

Sightseeing

Leyden, Utrect, Haerlem, all have monuments of art, worthy a stranger's notice; and the painted glass in the windows in a church at Gorcum are a great curiosity. All these and many others which I visited I can traverse again with you; and it renews the pleasure to recite it to one who is going to enjoy the same gratifications.

> To Thomas Boylston Adams, Quincy, February 11, 1795

They . . . brought with them the best Sause for travellers—a good appetite.

> To Harriet Welsh, Quincy, October 1, 1817

Traveling

Some Author that I have met with compare a judicious traveller, to a river that increases its stream the farther it flows from its source, or to certain springs which running through rich veins of minerals improve their qualities as they pass along.

> To John Quincy Adams, January 19, 1780

I grow more and more apprehensive of the dangers of the sea, tho I have really no Right to Quarrel with old Neptune, since he has 3 times safely transported my Friend. Tho he has grumbled and growld, he has not shewn the extent of his power.

> To John Adams, March 1, 1780

You have seen how inadequate the aid of Man would have been, if the winds and the seas had not been under the particular government of that Being who streached out the Heavens as a span, who holdeth the ocean in the hollow of his hand, and rideth upon the wings of the wind.*

> To John Quincy Adams, March 20, 1780

*Psalms 104:3.

You cannot reside amongst a people, without learning Something of their Laws, customs and Manners. Nor can you if you are capable of the Reflection which I think you are, omit comparing them with those of your own Country, and others which you have travelled through.

> To John Quincy Adams, November 13, 1782

The true use of travel is to enlarge the understanding, to rectify the judgment and to correct and rub off most of those local attachments which every man is apt to acquire by a prejudice in favour of his own Country and Laws and manners and Government, by comparing his own with other Nations, he will be led to believe there is something to praise and something to amend in each.

> To Chandler Robbins, Jr., c. January 10, 1783

You invite me to you, you call me to follow you, the most earnest wish of my Soul is to be with you—but you can scarcely form an Idea of the conflict of my mind. It appears to me such an enterprize, the Ocean so formidable, the quitting my habitation and my Country, leaving my Children, my Friends, with the Idea that perhaps I may never see them again, without my Husband to console and comfort me when I feel unequal to the trial. But on the other hand I console myself with the Idea of being joyfully and tenderly received by the best of Husbands and Friends, and of meeting a dear and long absent Son. But the difference is, my fears, and anxieties are present; my hopes, and expectations, distant.

But avaunt ye idle Specters, the desires and requests of my Friend are a Law to me. I will Sacrifice my present feelings and hope for a blessing in persuit of my duty.

> To John Adams, Braintree, February 11, 1784

[Onboard ship traveling to England:] If I did not write every day, I should lose the days of the month and of the week; confined all day on account of the weather, which is foggy, misty, and wet. You can hardly judge how irksome this confinement is. When the whole ship is at our service, it is little better than a prison.

Sea Journal, July 7, 1784

Those only, who have crossed the ocean, can realize the pleasure which is felt at the sight of land. The inexperienced traveller is more sensible of this, than those who frequently traverse the ocean. I could scarcely realize that thirty days had removed me so far distant from my native shore.

To Hannah Lincoln Storer, Auteuil, January 20, 1785

Travelling sick is a very dissagreeable business.

To John Quincy Adams, Fairfield, Conn., May 12, 1791

As you are a New Traveller I expect from your pen; many judicious observations.

To Thomas Boylston Adams, Quincy, November 30, 1794

My Journey was as pleasant as my thoughts upon what was past, and my anticipations of what was to come would permit it to be.

To Mary Cranch, Philadelphia, May 16, 1797

I had rather prepare to come Home than to go from it.

To Mary Cranch, Philadelphia, March 5, 1798

There is something always melancholy, in the idea of leaving a place for the last time. It is like burying a Friend.

To Mary Cranch, Philadelphia, February 27, 1800

My journey is a mountain before me, but I must climb it.

To John Adams, Quincy, October 27, 1800

— Vices

You have entered early in life upon the great theatre of the world, which is full of temptation and vice of every kind. You are not wholly unacquainted with history, in which you have read of crimes which your inexperienced mind could scarcely believe credible. You have been taught to think of them with horror, and to view vice as

> "a monster of so frightful mien,
> That, to be hated, needs but to be seen."*

Yet you must keep a strict guard upon yourself, or the odious monster will soon loose its terror, by becoming familiar to you.

To John Quincy Adams, June 10?, 1778

*Alexander Pope, *An Essay on Man,* Epistle II, lines 217–18.

My anxieties have been and still are great, lest the numerous temptations and snares of vice should viciate your early habits of virtue, and destroy those principles, which you are now capable of reasoning upon, and discerning the beauty and utility of, as the only rational source of happiness here, or foundation of felicity hereafter.

To John Quincy Adams, Braintree, November 20, 1783

. . . vice, that great disturber of human happiness.

To Abigail Adams Smith, Philadelphia, January 25, 1791

The Poison is not less destructive for the gilding.

To George Washington Adams, Quincy, May 23, 1816

Anger The passion of anger . . . is generally the most predominant passion at your age, the soonest excited, and the least pains are taken to subdue it.

To John Quincy Adams, March 20, 1780

When a spirit of private animosity is permitted to influence the mind, it always produces an illiberal conduct.

Animosity

> To Mary Cranch, Philadelphia, December 23, 1799

Indolence Created first an apathy, and apathy Crept on untill all that was estimable and praise worthy in Man, was sunk into torpor, like waters that stagnate when they cease to flow. It ought to be a warning to every man not to contract habits of sloth, and inaction, to consider that no Man liveth for himself.*

Apathy

> To Mary Cranch, Philadelphia, May 3, 1800

*Romans 14:7.

Age, a knowledge of the world, and experience will correct it, and modify it into firmness and inflexibility.

Arrogance

> To Louisa Catherine Adams, Quincy, May 15, 1810

I am disgusted when I see low artifice substituted, for candor, falshood for truth, and the same arts resorted to support a good cause, which were used to accomplish a bad one.

Artifice

> To Abigail Adams Smith, Quincy, August 29, 1808

How is it possible that the love of Gain and the Lust of domination should render the Humane mind so callous to every principal of honour, Generosity and Benevolence.

Avarice

> To John Adams, Braintree, July 25, 1775

Ambition and avarice reign every where and where they predominate there will be bickerings after places of Honour and profit. There is an old adage kissing goes by favour that is daily verified.

> To John Adams, November 5, 1775

Most men grow either Avaricious or ambitious as they advance in Life.

> To John Adams, Quincy, January 12, 1794

I have not yet attaind to the Years of Avarice, nor would I wish my Children to sacrifice to it.

> To Thomas Boylston Adams, Quincy, March 10, 1796

There has been too prevalent, and a eager grasping after property, an unbounded thirst for speculation, and a sacrifice of principle, of Honour, of Conscience at the shrine of Mammon.

> To William Cranch, Philadelphia, December 3, 1797

Bigotry   I am no friend of bigotry.

> To Abigail Adams Smith, Quincy, March 10, 1794

Bitterness   Every soul knows its own bitterness.

> To Mary Cranch, Norfolk, Conn., May 26, 1800

Bluster   Bluster will scarcely produce a mouse.

> To Abigail Adams Smith, Philadelphia, January 8, 1791

Bribery   It would be very difficult to find the thing in this country which money will not purchase, provided you can bribe high enough.

> To Elizabeth Shaw, London, March 4, 1786

Cheating   Both in England and here I find such a disposition to Cheat, that I dare not take a step alone. Almost every person with whom you have to deal, is fully determined to make a prey of you.

> To Cotton Tufts, Auteuil, September 9, 1784

Corruption   Corruption is corruption from whatever source it originates.

> To Mary Cranch, Philadelphia, July 6, 1797

Cowardice   If Men turn their backs and run from an Enemy they cannot surely expect to conquer them.

> To John Adams, Boston, October 25, 1777

There must be some essential defect in the Government and Morals *Crimes*
of a people when punishments lose their efficacy and crimes
abound.

> To Elizabeth Cranch, London, September 2, 1785

We ought never to dispair of what has been once accomplished.* *Despair*

> To John Thaxter, August 26, 1778

*The Duc de Sully's *Mémoires*.

It was a maxim of an able warior never to dispair of what had been
once accomplished.

> To Jonathan Mason?, Braintree, August 1778

Unaccustomed to tread the stage of dissipation, I cannot shake off *Dissipation*
my anxiety for my Country and my dearest connextions.

> To John Adams, April 23, 1781

Is there a Trait of Frivolity and dissipation left? Examine your own
Heart with candour, let it not deceive you. These are the Rocks and
quick Sands. Dissipation enervates the Man, dissolves every good
purpose and resolution, it excuses a thousand ways his deviations
from the path of Rectitude, and in the end becomes his destroyer. It
puts on like a mere Proteus* a thousand different forms, and too frequently calls itself Relaxation. The one is necessary the other ruinous. To draw the line requires both skill and judgment; perhaps
there is no more certain cure for dissipation, than method, and order, and were I to advise any one liable to this infirmity, it would be
to portion out the Day, and appropriate a certain Number of Hours
to Study, or to Business. With a determined Resolution to be inflexible against every temptation which might allure them from their
purpose; untill fixed habits were formed which could not be easily
shaken.

> To Royall Tyler, June 14, 1783

*In Greek mythology, Proteus was a minor sea god who had the ability to
assume different shapes in order to escape answering questions.

Luxery, dissipation and vice, have a natural tendency to extirpate every generous principle, and leave the Heart susceptable of the most malignant vices, to the total absence of principle.

To Mercy Otis Warren, London, May 14, 1787

[Of her son Charles Adams:] He was no man's Enemy but his own— He was beloved, in spight of his Errors, and all spoke with grief and sorrow for his habits.

To Mary Cranch, Washington, December 8, 1800

Dueling Major [William] Jackson has been fighting a duel with [Alexander] Gillion and was wounded in the thigh, not dangerously I believe. This detestable practise I abhor and hold it inconsistant with the principals of Religion, in no sense better than Murder or Suiside. Can the fault of another contaminate the Honour of a Man who is noway accesary to it? And is there any species of honour repugnant to virtue? The Man whose life is uniformly virtuous will be in no danger of the imputation of cowardice for abstaining from Murder, but on the other hand he who is not invariably restrained by the fear of evil will hardly be thought to refuse a challenge from moral restraints, since his virtue is more than suspicious whose conscientious Scruples accompany only those Sins which are attended with danger. But he who has a due sense of religion will not willingly bid defiance to his Creator by ungratefully disowning a Blessing in mercy bestowed, or robbing it from another. I have hopes my worthy Friend that however custom may have sanctified this Breach of the Laws of God and Man, your virtue and good Sense will deter you at all times, and upon all occasions, from so immoral and absurd a custom. It is a philosophick observation, that he who deserves an affront has no right to resent it, and he who is base enough to affront another without cause is unworthy of any thing but contempt.

To John Thaxter, July 18, 1782

When will the unruly passions of man yeald to reason, and that Member which we are told is set on fire of hell, cease to Stir up wrath, which leads to Blood and is allayed only by Sword and pistol. Our Country is disgraced. Religion outraged by the frequent Duells which Stain our annals. Are we a civilized people? and give countenance to so Savage a custom?

To Catherine Johnson, Quincy, December 19, 1809

I despise a Janus. *Duplicity*

To John Adams, Quincy, January 28, 1797

On the Isle of Wight . . . all my patience was exhausted by a three *Ennui* weeks' detention [in waiting to sail back to America], without Work, without Books. I never knew before the force of that expression, Ennui, for which I believe we have not any English word, but the thing itself I felt in all its force.

To John Quincy Adams, Quincy, February 29, 1796

There is envy and jealousy sufficient in the world to seek to lessen a *Envy* character however benificial to the Country or useful to the State.

To Elbridge Gerry, March 13, 1780

You must expect to contend with envy, Jealousy and other malignant passions, because they exist in Humane Nature.* As the poet observes "envy will merrit as its shade persue"** but a steady adherence to principals of Honour and integrity, will Baffel even those foes.

To John Quincy Adams, New York, July 11, 1790

*The draft continues "and because they frequently serve as Agents against distinguished abilities." **Alexander Pope, *An Essay on Criticism,* line 468.

The whole Country through which we past was in full Bloom, and every spot wore the face of Peace & contentment. The people instead of murmers & complaints, expresst themselves happy and satisfied under the administration of their Government. There are however two inhabitants envy and Jealousy who are not perfectly content, but as they are characters for whom I have an utter aversion I can only pitty their folly and avoid them.

> To Martha Washington, Braintree, June 25, 1791

It is with Kingdoms and States as with individuals. Their prosperity and happiness is the subject of Envy and Jealousy.

> To William Smith, Philadelphia, July 1, 1797

Envy is not banished from our Land.

> To John Quincy Adams, Quincy, January 8, 1817

Those baneful passions of envy and jealousy, are wide awake, and will follow you in every direction.

> To Louisa Catherine Adams, Quincy, January 3, 1818

Envy and jealousy would gladly pluck the Laurels. We see it every day—get fame honestly if you can, but at any rate, get fame, is the language of some.

> To Louisa Catherine Adams, Quincy, May 20, 1818

Falsehoods   A false weight and a false ballance are an abomination.

> To John Adams, January 28, 1781

Falsehood is so current a coin on such occasions that I am slow of belief.

> To John Adams, Quincy, February 1, 1793

Falsehood is propagated to answer political purposes.

> To Cotton Tufts, Quincy, November 22, 1799

I have heard of so many lies and falsehoods propagated to answer electioneering purposes since I left Philadelphia and for the last three weeks that I was there, that I am disgusted with the world and the chief of its inhabitants do not appear worth the trouble and pains they cost to save them from destruction. You see I am in an ill humour.

> To Mary Cranch, Norfolk, Conn., May 26, 1800

No falsehoods . . . have been thought too grose to palm upon the public.

> To Benjamin Rush, Quincy, October 18, 1800

I would fain hope that those faults which you discover, proceed more, from a wrong Head, than a bad Heart. *Faults*

> To John Adams, Weymouth, April 12, 1764

I am no Friend to Favoritism. *Favoritism*

> To George Cabot, [January 1794]

An officer who enters, as the sailors say, at the Cabin window, is never equally respected, as one who rises by regular gradations.

> To John Quincy Adams, Quincy, May 10, 1817

Gameing that Bane of civil Society, that antidote to good Humour *Gambling* and Beauty, that destroyer of female delicacy and honour, is not yet; and I pray Heaven, it never may become fashionable amongst the Females of the Northern States.

> To John Thaxter, Braintree, October 20, 1783

I hope you will guard your Brother against that pernicious vice of gameing, too much practised at the university.

> To John Quincy Adams, London, April 24, 1786

How can a Nation of Gamblers be a respected Nation? I mean by the Nation, the Nobility and Gentry who are the leading Members of it, and direct its counsels.

> To Mary Cranch, London, May 24, 1786

Idleness   Idleness is the parent of contention and disobedience.

> To Cotton Tufts, London, October 19, 1786

We were made for active Life and idleness and happiness are incompatible.

> To Caroline Smith, Quincy, November 17, 1808

Ill Humor   A man's humor contributes much to the making him agreeable or otherwise. Dark and sour humors, especially those which have a spice of malevolence in them, are vastly disagreeable. Such men have no music in their souls.

> Sea Journal, July 16, 1784

Ill humours break out in some people, and finds their way into the common sink of Newspaper publication.

> To Thomas Boylston Adams, June 12, 1800

Ingratitude   That ingratitude was considerd by the Athenians as a sin, we are told.

> To John Quincy Adams, Washington, January 29, 1801

Intemperance   How difficult to recover the right path when the feet have once wandered from it. How much resolution is necessary to overcome evil propensities? More particularly a habit of intemperance.

> To Mary Cranch, London, September 11, 1785

Any calamity inflicted by the hand of providence, it would become me in silence to submit to but when I behold misiry and distress, disgrace and poverty, brought upon a Family, by intemperance my heart bleads at every pore.

> To Mary Cranch, Quincy, October 31, 1799

Jealousy   Upon this Occasion I am like Some other persons perhaps jealous without cause.

> To John Adams, Quincy, December 29, 1792

Liberty ought not to become licentiousness.   *Licentiousness*
> To Thomas Welsh, London, July 22, 1786

Malevolence is unbounded.   *Malevolence*
> To Mary Cranch, Philadelphia, June 3, 1797

Pride commeth before Humility and a haughty Spirit before a fall.   *Pride*
> To John Adams, June 17, 1782

It is natural to the humane Heart to swell with presumption when conscious of superiour power, yet all humane excellence is comparative, and he who thinks he knows much today, will find much more still unattained, provided he is still eager in persuit of knowledge.
> To John Quincy Adams, London, October 12, 1787

Pride you know was not made for Man, nor Woman neither.
> To Caroline Smith, Quincy, November 17, 1808

With all our boasted Simplicity, there is not upon the Globe, a prouder people; or one more tenacious of Rank and titles, from the Subaltern, to the president of the united States, without the honesty to acknowledge it.

The obnoxious word "Well Born" which has rung as many changes in America as Burke's Swinish multitude* has in England is founded in the principles of Human Nature.

> *"In pride, in Reasoning Pride the Error lies"*
> *"All quit their Sphere, and rush into the Skies."***

> To Louisa Catherine Adams, Quincy, February 27, 1818

*Edmund Burke, *Reflections on the French Revolution*.   **Alexander Pope, *An Essay on Man*, Epistle II.

There can be no time more proper than the present.   *Procrastination*
> To John Adams, Weymouth, April 16, 1764

Prostitution   What Idea my dear Madam can you form of the Manners of a Nation one city [Paris] of which furnishes (Blush o, my sex when I name it) 52,000 unmarried females so lost to a Sense of Honour, and shame as publickly to enrole their Names in a Notary Office for the most abandoned purposes and to commit iniquity with impunity; thousands of these miserable wretches perish, annually with Disease and Poverty. . . . Which of the two Countries can you form the most favourable opinion of, and which is the least pernicious to the morals? That where vice is Licensed: or where it is suffered to walk at large soliciting the unwary, and unguarded as it is to a most astonishing height in the Streets of London and where virtuous females are frequently subject to insult. In Paris, no such thing happens, but the greatest Decency and Respect is shown by all orders to the female Character. The Stage [i.e., the theater] is in London made use of as a vehicle to corrupt the Morals. In Paris no such thing is permitted, they are too Polite to wound the Ear.

To Mercy Otis Warren, Auteuil, September 5, 1784

Of these [crimes] which excite my greatest Regret, is the prostitution of the Female character, and the frequent infidelity of those who hold in their hands, the honour and dignity of the Nation, and posterity. All conjugal principles appear to have lost their weight, and the seduced and seducer compromise their iniquity by a fine, by a payment of a fine for damages.

To John Quincy Adams, Quincy, May 9, 1816

— *Virtues*

Pure and disinterested Virtue must ever be its own reward. Mankind are too selfish and too depraved to discover the pure Gold from the baser mettle.

To John Adams, Boston, August 29, 1776

Pride, vanity, Envy, Ambition and malice, are the ungratefull foes that combat merit and Integrity. Tho for a while they may triumph to the injury of the just and good, the steady, unwearied perseverance of Virtue and Honour will finally prevail over them.

> To John Adams, February 26, 1780

"Virtue alone is happiness below,"* and consists in cultivating and improveing every good inclination and in checking and subduing every propensity to Evil.

> To John Quincy Adams, March 20, 1780

*Alexander Pope, *An Essay on Man,* Epistle IV.

The only sure and permanent foundation of virtue is religion. Let this important truth be engraved upon your heart.

> To John Quincy Adams, March 20, 1780

It is easier to admire virtue than to practise it, especially the great virtue of self denial.

> To John Adams, July 16, 1780

Give to every virtue its due weight.

> To James Lovell, March 17, 1781

May your mind be thoroughly impressed with the absolute necessity of universal virtue and goodness, as the only sure road to happiness, and may you walk therein with undeviating steps.

> To John Quincy Adams, Braintree, December 26, 1783

Virtue is the dignity of Humane nature.

> To Charles Adams, London, c. February 16, 1786

If our prospects are built upon a virtuous foundation, it is all we can do towards ensuring their success.

> To Mary Cranch, London, February 26, 1786

The "soul's calm sunshine"* can result only from the practice of virtue, which is congenial to our natures. If happiness is not the immediate consequence of virtue, as some devotees to pleasure affirm, yet they will find that virtue is the indispensable condition of happiness.

To Elizabeth Shaw, London, March 4, 1786

*Alexander Pope, *An Essay on Man*, Epistle IV.

To derive a proper improvement from company, it ought to be select, and to consist of persons respectable both for their morals and their understanding; but such is the prevailing taste, that provided you can be in a crowd, with here and there a glittering star, it is considered of little importance what the character of the person is who wears it. Few consider that the foundation stone, and the pillar on which they erect the fabric of their felicity, must be in their own hearts, otherwise the winds of dissipation will shake it, and the floods of pleasure overwhelm it in ruins.

To Mary Cranch, London, January 20, 1787

Virtue like the stone of Sysiphus* has a continual tendency to roll down Hill & requires to be forced up again by the never ceasing Efforts of succeeding moralists.

To Thomas Boylston Adams, London, March 15, 1787

*The mythological king Sisyphus kept pushing a large boulder up a hill, but it kept rolling back.

The most virtuous and unblemished Characters are liable to the Malice and venom of unprincipald Wretches.

To John Adams, Quincy, February 26, 1794

Who shall say that, virtue is not its own reward?

To John Quincy Adams, Quincy, March 3, 1797

Virtue, virtue, how little consideration is paid to it these days.

To William Smith, Philadelphia, July 7, 1798

Is there virtue in the woman who artfully seeks to display the rich luxuriance of nature's Charms, at the hazard and expence of sporting with all claim to chaste appearance?

> To Mary Cranch, Philadelphia, March 15, 1800

Conscious innocence, virtue and integrity are prime ingredients to tender every succeeding year of your Life pleasant to you.

> To Thomas Boylston Adams, Washington, January 2, 1801

Assiduities

Life takes its complexion from inferiour things, it is little attentions and assiduities that sweeten the Bitter draught and smooth the Rugged Road.

> To John Adams, October 25, 1782

Candor

Whilst I ask candour for myself, I am willing to extend it to others.

> To March Cranch, London, June 24, 1785

Charm

I have now to thank you for your charming letter of December. Cultivate, my dear, those lively spirits, and that sweet innocence and contentment, which will rob the desert of its gloom, and cause the wilderness to bloom around you. Destitute of these qualifications, a palace would not yield satisfaction, or the most affluent circumstances bestow peace of mind, or tranquillity of heart.

> To Caroline Smith, Quincy, February 2, 1809

Cheerfulness

I hope you will be in good spirits all the Time I am gone, remembring Soloman's advice that a merry Heart does good like a medicine.*

> To John Adams, Hartford, November 16, 1788

*Proverbs 17:22.

It grieved me to see you so dull, you used to keep up your Spirits better. Do not let them flagg. A merry Heart does good like a medicine.

> To Mary Cranch, Providence, R.I., June 19, 1789

Pray let me hear from you. The season is plentifull. Let us rejoice &
be glad. Cheer up my good sister, a merry Heart does good like a
medicine.

> To Mary Cranch, Richmond Hill, August 9, 1789

A Cheerful Heart doth good like a medicine.

> To John Adams, Quincy, December 26, 1794

I endeavour to feel cheerfull.

> To John Adams, Quincy, April 30, 1797

Soloman tells us that a cheerfull heart doth good like a Medicine.

> To Elizabeth Peabody, Quincy, November 24, 1810

I must exhort you to cultivate a cheerfullness of mind, which doeth
Good like a medicine.

> To François Adriaan Vanderkemp, Quincy, May 26, 1815

Circumspection The society of a few friends is that from which most pleasure and
satisfaction are to be derived. Under the wing of parents, no notice
would be taken of your going into public, or mixing in any amusement; but the eyes of the world are always placed upon those whose
situation may possibly subject them to censure, and even the friendly
attentions of one's acquaintance are liable to be misconstrued, so
that a lady cannot possibly be too circumspect. I do not mention this
to you through apprehension of your erring, but only as approving
your determination.

> To Abigail Adams Smith, Philadelphia, January 8, 1791

You will say I must hold my Tongue. That I shall assuredly do, nor to
any Being but you . . . a word upon the subject.

> To John Adams, Quincy, November 15, 1798

My Love to William. Tell him to mind my injunction of an *open Ear, but a close[d] Mouth.*

> To John Adams, Quincy, November 25, 1798

How often when the Heart is sorrowfull are we called upon to assume the smile of cheerfulnes, and the aspect of content?

> To Elizabeth Peabody, Quincy, April 9, 1799

Courage is a laudable, a Glorious Virtue in your Sex, why not in mine? (For my part, I think you ought to applaud me for mine.)

> To John Adams, Weymouth, April 16, 1764

Courage

Courage I know we have in abundance, conduct I hope we shall not want, but powder—where shall we get a sufficient supply?

> To John Adams, Braintree, June 16, 1775

Danger sometimes makes timid men bold.

> To John Adams, June 22, 1775

Danger they say makes people valient.

> To John Adams, Braintree, July 5, 1775

True courage is always humane.

> To Isaac Smith, Jr., October 30, 1777

Courage is always humane.

> To John Quincy Adams, London, February 16, 1786

There is more good to be done in Life, says a judicious observer of Humane Nature, by obstinate diligence and perseverence, than most people seem aware of. The Ant and Bee are but little and weak animals; and yet, by constant application they do wonders.

> To John Thaxter, April 29, 1783

Diligence

There is not any thing to be obtaind without application and attention.

> To George Washington Adams, Quincy, January 9, 1813

I hope he* is properly imprest with the necessity of arduous application.

> To John Quincy Adams, Quincy, October 15, 1817

*George Washington Adams, AA's grandson.

Discretion Poets and painters wisely draw a veil over those Scenes which surpass the pen of the one and the pencil of the other.

> To Mary Cranch, Auteuil, December 12, 1784

You need not be apprehensive least I should shew your Letters or divulge What is committed to me. All rests within my own Breast. Not the least lisp has escaped me to any one for tho I love Sociabil[it]y, I never did or will betray a trust.

> To John Adams, Quincy, February 20, 1796

Your letters delight me very much. I must enjoin confidence and secrecy. But I shall soon be free and then I will write you with less reserve. In private life I will speak and write when I please.

> To Thomas Boylston Adams, Washington, January 24, 1801

Elegance Caroline without being Handsome, is all in manners, disposition, habits and principles that a lovely Woman ought to be, united with personal ease and elegance of manners. It is something than Beauty dearer.

> To John Quincy Adams, Quincy, July 12, 1812

Even Temper I am not suddenly elated or depressed.

> To John Adams, July 16, 1780

Excellencies is never granted to man but as the Reward of Labour, *Excellence*
but those who persevere in habits of industry however slow their
advances will meet a sure recompence in the end.

To Thomas Welsh, London, August 25, 1785

Whatever you undertake aim to make yourself perect in it, for if it is *Excelling*
worth doing at all, it is worth doing well.

To John Quincy Adams, March 2, 1780

In Striving to excell, there is no sin provided you are modest and
unassuming.

To John Adams 2nd, Quincy, November 28, 1815

Those certainly get through the World best who trouble themselves *Foresight*
least, but a foresight prevents many evils and vexations.

To John Adams, Quincy, March 28, 1796

We all have much to be forgiven, and as we hope for mercy, so may *Forgiveness*
we extend it to others.

To Mary Cranch, Philadelphia, May 3, 1800

I bear no malice, I cherish no enmity. I would not retaliate if I could
—nay more in the true spirit of christian Charity, I would forgive, as
I hope to be forgiven.

To Thomas Jefferson, Quincy, July 1, 1804

When I look back upon my past days, I can see many faults, many
errors, both of omission and commission, for which I have need of
pardon and forgiveness.

To Abigail Adams Smith, Quincy, April 10, 1809

You must as Christians forgive, tho you are not enjoind to forget.

To Louisa Catherine Adams, Quincy, May 9, 1815

Good Deeds To be Good, and do Good, is the whole Duty of Man, comprized in a few words; but what a capacious Field does it open to our view? And how many Characters may grow from this root, whose usefull branches may shade the oppressd; May comfort the dejected: may heal the wounded: may cure the sick, may defend the invaded; may enrich the poor. In short those who possess the disposition will never want employment.

To Elizabeth Shaw, Auteuil, January 11, 1785

As one of the principle pleasures of my Life has been to do good according to my ability with the means indulged me; my sole regreet [about the outcome of the 1800 election], as it personally respects myself is, that those means will in future be so greatly curtailed, and limited; the wish and the will will not forsake me I trust.

To Elizabeth Peabody, Quincy, c. February 1801

Good Intentions All that is well intended is not well received.

To Mercy Otis Warren, London, May 24, 1786

Goodness True goodness is uniform and consistant.

To John Adams, October 19, 1783

If the Heart is good, all will go well.

To John Adams, Braintree, November 11, 1783

Honesty I . . . am obliged to be as good as my word.

To John Adams, Braintree, July 16, 1775

Honesty is the best policy for a Nation, as well as an individual.

To Elizabeth Shaw, London, October 15, 1786

. . . that great ornament of society, Honesty, without which all the Graces and Embelishments of Life are but varnish and unsubstantial qualities which the artfull assume for purposes of deceit.

To Elizabeth Shaw, London, January 20, 1787

[On JQA's new personal secretary:] Honesty of Heart must compensate to you for whatever is deficient in the Graces.

> To John Quincy Adams, Philadelphia, July 20, 1798

It is impossible to make all Men honest or disinterested, and there is no preventing many such getting into places of trust and employment.

> To Elizabeth Peabody, Quincy, November 20, 1814

[On news of the treason of Benedict Arnold:] How ineffectual is the *Honor* tye of Honour to bind the Humane Mind, unless accompanied by more permanent and Efficacious principles? Will he who laughs at a future state of Retribution, and holds himself accountable only to his fellow Mortals disdain the venal Bribe, or spurn the Ignoble hand that proffers it.

> To John Adams, October 8, 1780

True conscious Honour is to know no Sin—

> To John Adams, Braintree, August 1, 1781

Honour and virtue, are they not inmates and companions?

> To Royall Tyler, June 14, 1783

May your honour, your integrity and virtue always prove your safe guard.

> To John Quincy Adams, London, February 16, 1786

Hope [is] the anchor of the Soul. *Hope*

> To John Adams, June 8, 1777

Deferred hope . . . maketh the Heart sick.

> To James Lovell, July 28, 1779

I hope and hope till hope is swallowed up in the victory of Dispaire.

> To John Adams, August 1, 1781

Hope is my best Friend and kindest comforter.

To John Adams, April 10, 1782

The airy delusive phantom Hope, how has she eluded my prospects.

To John Adams, February 11, 1784

Let hope dictate what Revelation does not confute.

To Ann Quincy Packard, Quincy, March 11, 1805

Hope deferred maketh the Heart Sick.

To Harriet Welsh, Quincy, August 1, 1816

Hospitality   I shall be very glad to see my Friend Next week, any week or any time she may be assurd of a hearty welcome from her affectionate, Portia.

To Mercy Otis Warren, Braintree, August 27, 1775

My Country cannot Boast that extensive cultivation or that refinement in arts and Manners which old and more luxurious kingdoms and empires have arrived at, but you will find amongst the people of America a sincerity, hospitality and benevolence of disposition which are rarely exceeded abroad.

To Anna Quincy, Paris, September 4, 1784

Mrs. [John] Brown met me at the door & with the most obliging Smile accosted me with, "Friend I am glad to see thee here." The simplicity of her manners & dress with the openness of her countenance & the friendlyness of her behaviour charmed me beyond all the studied politeness of European manners—

To Mary Cranch, Richmond Hill, June 28, 1789

Your kind invitation to visit you in the only stile which can ever be agreable to me, that of Hospitality and freedom, would have given both Mr. Adams and myself great pleasure.

To Mercy Otis Warren, Quincy, October 1, 1797

I might . . . request you to consider this House as your Home when you visit this city.

> To Catherine Johnson, Philadelphia, March 13, 1800

To be attentive to our guests is not only true kindness, but true politeness: for if there is a virtue which is its own reward, hospitality is that virtue. We remember slight attentions, after we have forgotten great benefits.

> To Caroline Smith, Quincy, August 30, 1808

True kindness which is true politeness attends to the little wishes and wants of those we entertain, and we often remember slight attentions, after we have forgotten great benefits. Thus a cup of cold water with a pleasant cheerfull countenance is more gratefull to your Guests, than a feast of fat things, or a profusion of farfetched Luxury, if good humour and affability are wanting. A desire to please seldom fails of success.

> To Susanna B. Adams, Quincy, September 12, 1808

It is the Nature of our Country not only to be hospitable to Strangers, but fond of them.

> To Louisa Catherine Adams, Quincy, March 27, 1816

A cordial welcome and a cup of cold water with it is more gratifying than a Royal Feast, into which the Host does not enter.

> To Louisa Catherine Adams, Quincy, February 27, 1818

There are still imperfections enough in every Humane Being to excite Humility, rather than pride.

Humility

> To Charles Adams, May 26, 1781

Pride commeth before Humility and a haughty Spirit before a fall.

> To John Adams, June 17, 1782

I have a favour to request of all my near and intimate Friends. It is to desire them to watch over my conduct and if at any time they perceive any alteration in me with respect to them, arising as they may suppose from my situation in Life, I beg they would with the utmost freedom acquaint me with it. I do not feel within myself the least disposition of the kind, but I know mankind are prone to deceive themselves, and some are disposed to misconstrue the conduct of those whom they conceive placed above them.

To Mary Cranch, Richmond Hill, July 12, 1789

Too long a habit of humiliation, does not seem a very good preparative to manly and vigorous sentiments.

To Mercy Otis Warren, Quincy, April 25, 1798

I heard a sermon yesterday upon the Subject of Humility. I believe I do not yet possess enough of that negative quality to make me believe that I deserve all that can be inflicted upon me by the tongues of falsehood.

To Mary Cranch, Norfolk, Conn., May 26, 1800

Industriousness   Every moment should be devoted to some useful purpose, that we might ask the moments as they passed, what report they bore to Heaven.

To Caroline Smith, Quincy, January 24, 1808

My Imagination frequently visits you, and always finds you occupied. To be Idol would be novel altogether to you. We cannot be sufficiently thankfull to our early instructors for teaching us habits of industery, training us up in the way we should go, that in age we may not depart from it. It is a true saying, that the devil will find work for those who have not any employment. The mind is naturally active and the body requires it also.

To Abigail Adams Smith, Quincy, May 8, 1808

Industry & steady application will do much towards acquiring reputation—these qualities . . . will ensure you future Success in Life.

> To John Adams Smith, Quincy, March 12, 1817

May justice and Liberty finally prevail.   *Justice*

> To Mercy Otis Warren, Braintree, February 3?, 1775

See what an influence justice, honour, integrity and Reverence for
the deity had upon the Nations and kingdoms when ever they pre-
dominated either in the Rulers or the people. Behold the Havock
and devastation of Rapine, cruelty, Luxery, avarice and ambition.

> To Charles Adams, London, c. February 16, 1786

May justice and judgment be the stability of our Government, and
Mercy temper justice where it can, may our laws be a terror to evil
doers, whilst they encourage those who do well.

> To Abigail Adams Smith, Philadelphia, April 27, 1800

My most fervent petition is that Justice may flow down as a River,
and Righteousness as a mighty Stream; and that for the honour and
happiness of our common Country, "no foes may ravish her, and no
false friend betray her, while professing to defend."*

> To Louisa Catherine Adams, Quincy, February 24, 1805

*William Cowper, *Table Talk.*

May we . . . be as ready to do justice as to receive it.

> To Abigail Adams Smith, Quincy, May 13, 1809

Remember truth and Justice have two Ears.

> To Elizabeth Peabody, Quincy, January 13, 1814

Can there be a greater pleasure in Life than rendering kindness to   *Kindness*
those we love and esteem and who we know are every way worthy
of our regard.

> To Mary Cranch, New York, October 17, 1791

The Law of Kindness was written upon her Heart.

To William Smith, Quincy, November 1, 1798

Knowing Oneself Suffer me to recommend to you one of the most useful lessons of life, the knowledge and study of yourself. There you run the greatest hazard of being deceived. Self-love and partiality cast a mist before the eyes, and there is no knowledge so hard to be acquired, nor of more benefit when once thoroughly understood.

To John Quincy Adams, March 20, 1780

Modesty General [John] Thomas has the character of an Excelent officer. His Merit has certainly been overlook'd, as modest merit generally is.

To John Adams, Braintree, July 16, 1775

Be modest, be diffident, be circumspect, kind and obliging. These are Qualities which render youth engaging, and will flourish like a natural plant; in every clime.

To Charles Adams, May 26, 1781

Modest Merrit must be its own Reward.

To John Adams, September 5, 1782

Where the Semblance of modesty is wanting, there is strong ground to presume the absence of the virtue itself.

To Mary Cranch, Philadelphia, March 15, 1800

Modesty may sometimes depress and weaken a great and well-formed genius, but seldom fails of attaching to it the Benevolent & virtuous minds, noble sentiments and unworthy actions can never reside in the same bosom.

To John Adams Smith, Quincy, after February 11, 1810

Patience Tomorrow will be 3 weeks since you left home in all which time I have not heard one word from you. Patience is a Lesson I have not to learn so can wait your own time, but hope it will not be long er'e my anxious heart is releaved.

> To John Adams, Braintree, September 17, 1775

Great difficulties may be surmounted, by patience and perseverance.

> To John Adams, Braintree, November 27, 1775

I have summond patience and endeavourd to submit to my destiny.

> To John Adams, November 18, 1777

Patience, patience, patience, is the first, second, and third virtue of a seaman, or, rather, as necessary to him as to a statesman.

> Sea Journal, July 15, 1784

Whoever has anything to do with Courts [i.e., of monarchs], must have Patience, for the first, Second, and third requisites. I wish I was well out of the Way of all of them.

> To Mary Cranch, London, May 21, 1786

Patience, perseverance, industry, and frugality will accomplish great things.

> To Mary Cranch, London, April 28, 1787

All young men must have patience, especially in his profession.

> To Mary Cranch, Philadelphia, January 9, 1791

A world of patience is necessary, and moderation too, to bear all that we see and hear.

> To Cotton Tufts, March 6, 1800

Patience and fortitude will make a smooth road where the pick-axe has never levelled the inequalities as it will soften the mattress, and make a pillow of down to the contented mind.

> To Sarah Adams, Quincy, January 20, 1808

Prudence   Prudence dictates silence in me, take a draught of Lethe.*

> To William Stephens Smith, London, September 18, 1785

*In Greek mythology, when the dead drank of the River Lethe in Hades, they forgot their past lives.

Prudence is a gift from heaven—a duplicity of character will be discover'd sooner or later wherever it is—

> To Mary Cranch, Braintree, December 1790

Without a liberal prudence, virtue is continually harrassed by Necessity; pleasure has but an interrupted enjoyment and Life becomes a Chequered Scene of agitation and distress.

> To Thomas Boylston Adams, Quincy, May 16, 1801

Righteousness   The Scriptures tell us righteousness exalteth a Nation.

> To Mercy Otis Warren, Braintree, c. November 5, 1775

It is Righteousness, not Iniquity, that exalteth a Nation.

> To John Adams, October 8, 1780

I trust and hope we may as a people be of that happy Number, whose God is the Lord, and never forget that it is Righteousness which exalteth a Nation, whilst Sin is their Reproach.

> To Mary Cranch, Philadelphia, March 31, 1798

⇀ War

The Maxim in time of peace prepare for war (if this may be call'd a time of peace) resounds throughout the Country.

> To John Adams, Boston, September 22, 1774

It is come to that pass now that the longest sword must decide the contest.

> To John Adams, Braintree, March 17, 1776

I feel in a most painfull situation between hope and fear, there must be fighting and very Bloody Battles too I apprehend. O! how my Heart recoils at the Idea. Why is Man calld Humane when he delights so much in Blood, Slaughter and devastation; even those who are stiled civilizd Nations think this little Spot worth contending for, even to Blood.

To John Adams, September 24, 1777

War, Tyranny and Desolation are the Scourges of the Almighty, and ought no doubt to be deprecated.

To John Quincy Adams, January 12, 1780

If we cannot make peace, at least make War.

To John Thaxter, July 18, 1782

I most sincerely wish the contending Nations at peace, for after all the great and mighty victories of conquering Nations, this war upon our own species is a savage Business, unworthy a Rational and immortal Being whose study ought to be the happiness and not the destruction of Mankind.

To John Quincy Adams, November 13, 1782

War cannot be ranked amongst the liberal arts, and must ever be considerd as a scourge & a calamity, & should Humiliate the pride of man that he is thus capable of destroying his fellow creatures.

To Thomas Boylston Adams, London, March 15, 1787

Your Letter of April 5th and 7th reached me last Evening, and they fill me with more apprehension of a War than any thing I have before heard. The Body of the people are decidely against war, and if a War is madly or foolishly precipitated upon us, without the union of the people, we shall neither find men or money to prosecute it, and the Government will be Cursed and abused for all the consequences which must follow. . . . The people without are willing to wait the result of Negotiation as far as I can learn, and in the mean time we ought to prepare for the worst.

To John Adams, Quincy, April 18, 1794

Men War-like and innured to Arms and conquest, are not very apt to become the most quiet Submissive Subjects.

To John Adams, Quincy, December 6, 1794

Happy indeed if we may be permitted to escape the calamities of War.

To John Quincy Adams, Philadelphia, November 23, 1797

But in self defence we may be involved in war; and for that we ought to be prepared.

To Mary Cranch, Philadelphia, March 27, 1798

War is a dreadfull Scourge to any Country, most devoutly to be deprecated, but Subjugation is worse.

To Catherine Johnson, Philadelphia, May 4, 1798

Every day is producing such astonishing Events, such Scenes of carnage, havock and devastation of the Humane Species, upon the Theatre of the World, that we stand agast at the desolation, and think our "blindness to the future kindly given."* May the thunders which roll around us, and the lightnings which flash, still continue to pass over this part of the Globe, without kindling it into a Blaze; and whilst with a pittying Eye we behold at a distance, the horror which it spreads. May we with gratefull hearts ascribe praise unto that Being who maketh us to differ from other Nations who still permitteth us to enjoy in peace the fruits of our Labour.

To John Quincy Adams, Philadelphia, December 30, 1799

*Alexander Pope, *An Essay on Man,* Epistle I.

Yet is it a measure that I am convinced was the best calculated to avert the horrors of war, of any which prest on all sides as our Government were, could have been resorted to, cruelly oppressive as it appears, and hard as it is to be borne. We had better suffer temporary privations, than the calamities of War, which when once commenced, no one can calculate or estimate.

To Abigail Adams Smith, Quincy, March 18, 1808

What havock and destruction of the Human Species! Can Man be born then, only to be destroyed by his fellow Man. Yet plagues and Earthquakes break not heaven's designs. Are we rational Creatures?

To John Quincy Adams, Quincy, December 30, 1812

Such is the warlike state of Nations and their various destinies, that we cannot calculate what is to be the end of these things, who are to be the conquerors, or why they thus destroy each other, but thus it has been from Age to Age, and will continue so, as long as time endures.

To Mercy Otis Warren, Quincy, June 20, 1813

Neither religion or Morality prohibit our rejoycing, or giving thanks to the God of Armies for delivering our Enemies into our hands.

To John Quincy Adams, Quincy, November 8, 1813

When will wars cease? When I Sit and cooly reflect upon the carnage of the humane Species, I cry out What is Man? Rational Man?

To Harriet Welsh, Quincy, January 27, 1815

I hope in this Country we shall never be tempted to commence an offensive War, or incroach upon the Right and Liberties of other Nations.

To Louisa Catherine Adams, Quincy, October 20, 1815

Altho the mind is shocked at the Thought of sheding Humane Blood, more Especially the Blood of our Countrymen, and a Civil War is of all Wars, the most dreadfull Such is the present Spirit that prevails, that if once they are made desperate Many, very Many of our Heroes will spend their lives in the cause, With the Speach of

Civil War

Cato in their Mouths, "What a pitty it is, that we can dye but once to save our Country."*

To Mercy Otis Warren, Boston, December 5, 1773

*Joseph Addison, *Cato,* Act IV, scene iv.

Defense   To defend ourselves is our duty.

To Mary Cranch, Philadelphia, March 5, 1798

Revolutions   All revolutions are alike in many features.

To Thomas Boylston Adams, Washington, January 24, 1801

Shays's Rebellion   The Riots and dissentions in our state have been matter of very serious concern to me. No one will suppose that our situation here is renderd more Eligible in consequence of it, but I hope it will lead the wise and sensible part of the community in our state as well as the whole union to reflect seriously upon their Situation, and having wise Laws execute them with vigor, justice and punctuality.

To Mary Cranch, London, January 20, 1787

May the triumph of the wicked be short, and the fair fabrick of Liberty still be protected by Minerva,* whilst Discord and faction those vile deamons are banishd to their Native Regions of Darkness.

To Elizabeth Shaw, London, January 20, 1787

*Roman goddess of wisdom and patroness of the arts and trades.

With regard to the Tumults in my Native state which you inquire about, I wish I could say that report had exaggerated them. It is too true Sir that they have been carried to so allarming a Height as to stop the Courts of Justice in several Counties. Ignorant, wrestless desperadoes, without conscience or principals, have led a deluded multitude to follow their standard, under pretence of grievances which have no existance but in their immaginations. Some of them were crying out for a paper currency, some for an equal distribution of property, some were for annihilating all debts. . . . By this list you will see, the materials which compose this Rebellion, and the necessity there is of the wisest and most vigorous measures to quell and suppress it.

To Thomas Jefferson, London, January 29, 1787

For what have we been contending against the tyranny of Britain, if we are to become the sacrifice of a lawless banditti? Must our glory be thus shorn and our laurels thus blasted? Is it a trifling matter to destroy a government? Will my country-men justify the maxim of tyrants, that mankind are not made for freedom? I will, however, still hope that the majority of our fellow-citizens are too wise, virtuous, and enlightened, to permit these outrages to gain ground and triumph.

To Mary Cranch, London, February 25, 1787

By the latest accounts from America (the 10 of Febry) general [Benjamin] Lincoln had marched against the insurgents dispersed and quelld them; so that I hope they will no longer impede the course of Justice, or disturb the good order of society. Ebullitions of this kind will break out in all free governments, like humours in a Healthy Body; but I presume they cannot proceed to any dangerous height—

To John Cranch, London, March 7, 1787

I dread the ocean and yet more the turbulent spirit of my Country-men. It is a damp to all the pleasureable ideas of a return to it—God save the people is a prayer in which I can most sincerely join—

To Cotton Tufts, London, July 1, 1787

The disagreeable Situation of the Massachusetts for some months past is changed I presume for the better, and I would hope the Rebellion quite Suppressed. The discontents of the people cannot be grounded in reason, for there is no Country in the world where the liberties and properties of the subject are more sacredly preserved, nor are there any subjects who pay less for the ease and security which they enjoy, but the Idea of these insurgents is that they ought to pay nothing nor be at any trouble for preserving to themselves the Blessings of Peace & security. To please Such persons is impossible, and the disagreeable alternative of reduceing them to obedience by force was the only recource. This has Stained our annals with a civil war, and gratified the benevolence of our Good Friends on this Side of the water.

To Mary Rutledge Smith, London, July 14, 1787

War of 1812   We have passed through one revolution and have happily arrived at the goal, but the ambition, injustice and plunder of foreign powers have again involved us in war, the termination of which is not given us to see.

If we have not "the gorgeous palaces or the cloud-capp'd towers" of Moscow to be levelled with the dust, nor a million of victims to sacrifice upon the altar of ambition, we have our firesides, our comfortable habitations, our cities, our churches and our country to defend, our rights, privileges and independence to preserve. And for these are we not justly contending? Thus it appears to me; yet I hear from our pulpits and read from our presses that it is an unjust, a wicked, a ruinous and unnecessary war. If I give an opinion with respect to the conduct of our native State, I cannot do it with approbation. She has had much to complain of as it respected a refusal of naval protection, yet that cannot justify her in paralyzing the arm of government when raised for her defence and that of the nation. A house divided against itself*——and upon that foundation do our enemies build their hopes of subduing us. May it prove a sandy one to them.

To Mercy Otis Warren, Quincy, December 30, 1812

*Luke 11:17.

I do not view this war, as waged for conquest, or ambition, but for our injured Rights, for our freedom, and the security of our Independence, and therefore shall rejoice when any Naval victory, or military success attend upon our Arms, which may give us any hope or prospect of Peace, which always ought to be the object aimed at,

and I sincerely believe is so by our Government. Most sincerely do I
wish that war could have been avoided.

> To Mercy Otis Warren, Quincy, June 20, 1813

Some ask the Question what have we obtained by the war? I answer
we have proved to G. B. and the world, that She is not all powerfull
upon the ocean—and that we will not in future be insulted with impunity. We have proved that we can with our government, free and
republican as it is, both make war and peace. If we have occasion to
make war again, experience will instruct us to be more provident
and better prepared. The war has created us fine officers, brave soldiers, and invincible sailors. It has built us a Small Navy. It has fortified many of our Seaports. It has given us Rank and respect with
foreign Nations, and I hope the Back woods men have taught the
Atlantic States no more to reproach them, or to be so vain as to
think that they only can fight Battles.

> To Harriet Welsh, Quincy, March 3, 1815

The war has given us many usefull lessons. It has taught us to feel
our own strength and to use it. It has convinced us that we can and
we will share the waves—that we can combat, and conquer both by
land and Sea.

> To John Quincy Adams, Quincy, March 10, 1815

Peace in America was received with unfeigned and universal joy,
altho she was at that time, triumphing with victory, conquering both
by Sea and Land, exhalting our National Character and Inambling
her Enemy. The War is happily terminated, leaving to us Commanders both by Land and Sea, whose Bravery, Courage, intrepidity &
Skill have been only exceeded by their Benevolence and Humanity
to the conquered. They have coverd themselves with Glory, effaced
former stains and crowned their Country with honours, quietly returnd to their Homes and reassumed the impliments of Husbandry,
for the Weapons of War.

> To Louisa Catherine Adams, Quincy, May 9, 1815

— *Women*

[Responding to John Adams's complaint that Abigail crossed her legs:] A gentleman has no business to concern himself about the Leggs of a Lady.

To John Adams, Weymouth, May 9, 1764

From my Infancy I have always felt a great inclination to visit the Mother Country as tis call'd and had nature formed me of the other Sex, I should certainly have been a rover. . . . Women you know Sir are considered as Domestick Beings, and altho they inherit an Eaquel Share of curiosity with the other Sex, yet but few are hardy eno' to venture abroad, and explore the amaizing variety of distant Lands. The Natural tenderness and Delicacy of our Constitutions, added to the many Dangers we are subject to from your Sex, renders it almost impossible for a Single Lady to travel without injury to her character. And those who have a protecter in an Husband, have generally speaking obstacles sufficient to prevent their Roving, and instead of visiting other Countries; are obliged to content themselves with seeing but a very small part of their own. To your Sex we are most of us indebted for all the knowledge we acquire of Distant lands.

To Isaac Smith, Jr., Braintree, April 20, 1771

The Natural timidity of our sex always seeks for a relief in the encouragement and protection of the other.

To Mercy Otis Warren, Braintree, February 3?, 1775

I long to hear that you have declared an Independancy—and by the way in the new Code of Laws which I suppose it will be necessary for you to make I desire you would Remember the Ladies, and be more generous and favourable to them than your ancestors. Do not put such unlimited power into the hands of the Husbands. Remember all Men would be tyrants if they could. If particular care and attention is not paid to the Ladies we are determined to foment a Rebellion, and will not hold ourselves bound by any Laws in which we have no voice, or Representation.

That your Sex are Naturally Tyrannical is a Truth so thoroughly established as to admit of no dispute, but such of you as wish to be happy willingly give up the harsh title of Master for the more tender and endearing one of Friend. Why then, not put it out of the power of the vicious and the Lawless to use us with cruelty and indignity with impunity. Men of Sense in all Ages abhor those customs which treat us only as the vassals of your Sex. Regard us then as Beings placed by providence under your protection and in immitation of the Supreem Being make use of that power only for our happiness.

To John Adams, Braintree, March 31, 1776

He [i.e., John Adams] is very saucy to me in return for a List of Female Grievances which I transmitted to him. I think I will get you to join me in a petition to Congress. I thought it was very probable our wise Statesmen would erect a New Government and form a New Code of Laws. I ventured to speak a Word in behalf of our Sex who are rather hardly Dealt with by the Laws of England, which gives such unlimited power to the Husband to use his Wife Ill. I requested that our Legislators would consider our case, and as all Men of Delicacy and Sentiment are averse to exercising the power they possess, yet as there is a Natural propensity in Humane Nature to domination, I thought the most Generous plan was to put it out of the power of the Arbitrary and tyrannick to injure us with impunity by establishing some Laws in our favour upon just and Liberal principals.

I believe I even threatened fomenting a Rebellion in case we were not considered, and assured him we would not hold ourselves bound by any Laws in which we had neither a voice nor representation.

In return he tells me he cannot but Laugh at my Extraordinary Code of Laws; that he had heard their Struggle had loosened the bonds of Government; that children and apprentices were disobedient; that Schools and Colledges were grown turbulent; that Indians slighted their Guardians, and Negroes grew insolent to their Masters. But my Letter was the first intimation that another Tribe more Numerous and powerfull than all the rest were grown discontent. This is rather too coarse a compliment, he adds, but that I am so saucy he won't blot it out.

So I have helpd the Sex abundantly; but I will tell him I have only been making trial of the disinterestedness of his Virtue and when weighd in the balance have found it wanting.

It would be bad policy to grant us greater power, say they, since under all the disadvantages we labour we have the assendancy over their Hearts.

To Mercy Otis Warren, Braintree, April 27, 1776

I can not say that I think you very generous to the Ladies, for whilst you are proclaiming peace and good will to Men, Emancipating all Nations, you insist upon retaining an absolute power over Wives. But you must remember that Arbitrary power is like most other things which are very hard, very liable to be broken—and notwithstanding all your wise Laws and Maxims we have it in our power not only to free ourselves but to subdue our Masters, and without violence throw both your natural and legal authority at our feet—

> Charmed by accepting, by submitting sway
> Yet have our Humour most when we obey.*

To John Adams, Braintree, May 7, 1776

*Alexander Pope, *Moral Essays,* Epistle II.

We are no ways dispirited here, we possess a spirit that will not be conquered. If our Men are all drawn off and we should be attacked, you would find a Race of Amazons in America.

To John Adams, Braintree, September 20, 1776

America will not wear chains while her daughters are virtuous, but corrupt their morals by a general depravity, and believe me sir a state or nation is undone. Was not Adam safe whilst Eve was Innocent? If you render us wicked you inevitably bring ruin upon yourselves.

To John Thaxter, July 21, 1780

"Man active resolute and bold"
"is fashioned in a different mould."

More independent by Nature, he can scarcely realize all those ties which bind our sex to his. Is it not natural to suppose that as our dependance is greater, our attachment is stronger? —I find in my own breast a sympathetic power always operating upon the near approach of Letters from my dear absent Friend. I cannot determine the exact distance when this secret charm begins to operate. The time is some times longer and sometimes shorter, the Busy Sylphs are ever at my ear, no sooner does Morpheus close my Eyes,* than "my whole Soul, unbounded flies to thee."

To John Adams, December 25, 1780

* Morpheus, son of the Greek god of sleep, was the god of dreams.

What female mind—young beautifull rich—must she not be more than woman if vanity was not the predominate passion?

To John Quincy Adams, London, February 16, 1786

A lady cannot possibly be too circumspect.

To Abigail Adams Smith, Philadelphia, January 8, 1791

Our Legislatures never having considerd our Sex sufficiently dangerous to erect a Salique Law* or perhaps entertaining too good an opinion of us to suppose we would encroach upon their *establishd* perogatives have left us to the free exercise of our Judgments and opinions upon political subjects fixing however a sutle Stigmata upon the character of a Female politician to deter us from entering too far into the character. At such an Aeon as the present who can be an unconcern'd Spectator? of the mighty Revolutions which are revolving round us, in which kingdoms, Principalities and powers are shaken to their center, when the shocks of the old world extend their agitations even to our peacefull shoars and could envelope us in the general Crush if the materials of which we are composed were alike combustible.

> To George Cabot, [January 1794]

*The Salic Law excluded females from succeeding to the throne in France and Spain.

The Female Character, consisted not in the Tincture of the skin, or a fine set of Features, in the lilly's white, or the Rose's red, but in something still beyond the exterior form.

> To Elizabeth Peabody, Quincy, February 12, 1796

However brilliant a woman's tallents may be, she ought never to shine at the expence of her Husband. Government of States and Kingdoms, tho God knows badly enough managed, I am willing should be solely administered by the Lords of the Creation, nor would I object, that a Salique Law should universally prevail. I shall only contend for Domestick Government, and think that best administerd by the Female.

> To John Quincy Adams, Quincy, May 20, 1796

I will never consent to have our sex considered in an inferiour point of light. As each planet shines in their own orbit, God and nature designd it so. If man is Lord, woman is *Lordess*. That is what I [. . .] for, and if a woman does not hold the Reigns of Government, I see no reason for her not judging how they are conducted.

> To Elizabeth Peabody, Quincy, July 19, 1799

Many of the female characters in Scripture, both of the Old and New Testament, do great honour to the sex. It is a pleasing and grateful circumstance, to read in the life and character of our Saviour, the affection and tenderness which he manifests to women— to Mary, to Martha, to the widow of Samaria, and many others.

> To Caroline deWindt, Quincy, March 22, 1818

Dangerous thing for a Female to be distinguished for any quallifica-
tion beyond the rest of her sex. Whatever may be her Deportment,
she is sure to draw upon herself the jealousy of the men and the
envy of the women, nor do I see any way to remedy this evil but by
increasing the number of accomplished women. A monopoly of any
kind is always envidious.

*Accomplished
Women*

To Mary Cranch, London, April 28, 1787

It irks very certain, that a well-informed woman, conscious of her
nature and dignity, is more capable of performing the relative duties
of life, and of engaging and retaining the affections of a man of understanding, than one whose intellectual endowments rise not above
the common level.

There are so few women who may be really called learned, that I
do not wonder they are considered as black swans. It requires such
talents and such devotion of time and study, as to exclude the performance of most of the domestic cares and duties which exclusively
fall to the lot of most females in this country. I believe nature has assigned to each sex its particular duties and sphere of action, and to
act well your part, "there all the honor lies."*

To François Adriaan Vanderkemp, Quincy, February 3, 1814

*Alexander Pope, *An Essay on Man*, Epistle IV.

I believe in the expression of your Sentiments you have united those
of most Gentlemen, who Seek rather for a companion than a Rival.
From the Life of Madam de Steal* I learn that it was her Superiour
learning and tallents not prudently Conceald which caused the coldness, estrangement and unhappiness of her Life with the Baron.

To François Adriaan Vanderkemp, Quincy, 1817

*Germaine de Staël (1766–1817), French writer.

If you complain of neglect of Education in sons, What shall I say
with regard to daughters, who every day experience the want of it.
With regard to the Education of my own children, I find myself
soon out of my depth, and destitute and deficient in every part of

Female Education

Education. . . . If we mean to have Heroes, Statesmen and philosophers, we should have learned women.

To John Adams, Boston, August 14, 1776

It is really mortifying Sir, when a woman possessd of a common share of understanding considers the difference of Education between the male and female Sex, even in those families where Education is attended to. Every assistance and advantage which can be procured is afforded to the sons, whilst the daughters are totally neglected in point of Literature. Writing and Arithmetick comprise all their Learning. Why should children of the same parents be thus distinguished? Why should the Females who have a part to act upon the great Theater, and a part not less important to Society (as the care of a family and the first instruction of Children falls to their share, and if as we are told that first impressions are most durable) is it not of great importance that those who are to instill the first principals should be suiteably qualified for the Trust, Especially when we consider that families compose communities, and individuals make up the sum total. Nay why should your sex wish for such a disparity in those whom they one day intend for companions and associates. Pardon me Sir if I cannot help sometimes suspecting that this Neglect arises in some measure from an ungenerous jealousy of rivals near the Throne—but I quit the Subject or it will run away with my pen.

To John Thaxter, Braintree, February 15, 1778

I can hear of the Brilliant accomplishments of any of my Sex with pleasure and rejoice in that Liberality of Sentiment which acknowledges them. At the same time I regret the trifling narrow contracted Education of the Females of my own country. I have entertained a superiour opinion of the accomplishments of the French Ladies ever since I read the Letters of Dr. Sherbear,* who professes that he had rather take the opinion of an accomplished Lady in matters of polite writing than the first wits of Italy and should think himself safer with her approbation than of a long List of Literari, and he gives this reason for it that Women have in general more delicate Sensations than Men what touches them is for the most part true in Nature, whereas men warpt by Education, judge amiss from previous prejudice and referring all things to the model of the antients, condemn that by comparison where no true Similitud ought to be expected.

But in this country you need not be told how much female Education is neglected, nor how fashionable it has been to ridicule Female learning, tho I acknowledge it my happiness to be connected with a person of a more generous mind and liberal Sentiments.

To John Adams, Braintree, June 30, 1778

*John Shebbeare's *Letters on the English Nation,* 2 vols. (London, 1755), I, 177–78.

We have sent your cousins some books, amongst which is Rousseau upon Botany; if you borrow it of them, it will entertain you; and the world of flowers, of which you are now so fond, will appear to you a world of pleasing knowledge. There is also Dr. Priestley upon Air, and Bishop Watson upon Chemistry, all of which are well worth the perusal of minds eager for knowledge and science, like my Eliza's and Lucy's. If they are not the amusements which females in general are fond of, it is because trifles are held up to them in a more rational amusements. Your papa, who is blest with a most happy talent of communicating knowledge, will find a pleasure in assisting you to comprehend whatever you may wish explained; a course of experiments would do more, but from these our sex are almost wholly excluded.

To Elizabeth Cranch, London, July 18, 1786

[Illness has prevented me from attending] Seven Lectures out of 12 to which I Subscribed, and which I fear I shall never have the opportunity of attending. They would have afforded me much matter for future recollection & amusement from a retrospect of the Beauties of Nature, and her various opperations manifested in the Works of creation, an assemblage of Ideas entirely new, is presented to the mind. The five Lectures which I attended were experiments in Electricity, Magnetism, Hydrostatics, opticks, [and] pemematicks, all of which are connected with, and are subservient to the accommodation of common Life. It was like going into a Beautifull Country, which I never saw before, a Country which our American Females are not permitted to visit or inspect, untill Dr. Moyes visited America,* all experimental Phylosophy was confined within the walls of our Colledges. The Study of Household Good, as Milton terms it,** is no doubt the peculiar province of the Female Character. Yet surely as rational Beings, our reason might with propriety receive the highest possible cultivation. Knowledge would teach our Sex candour, and those who aim at the attainment of it, in order to render themselves more amiable & usefull in the world would derive a double advantage from it, for in proportion as the mind is informed, the countenance would be improved & the face ennobled as the Heart is elevated, for wisdom says Soloman maketh the face to shine.† Even the Luxurious Eastern Sage thought not of rouge or the milk of roses—but that the virtuous wife should open her mouth with wisdom & the law of kindness dwell upon her Tongue,‡ nor did he think this inconsistant with looking well to the ways of her household, or suppose that she would be less inclined to superintend the domestick oeconomy of her family, for having gone beyond the limits of her dressing room & her kitchen. I quote Soloman on this occasion, as we may naturally suppose the picture drawn of a virtuous wife to be the result of his experience & his wisdom, after ranging at large amongst the Eastern Beauties: he pronounces the price of a virtous woman to be far above rubies & the only character on which the Heart of a Husband may safely rest§—the present mode of fashionable education is not calculated to form the rising generation upon the system of Soloman. Futile accomplishments are substituted instead of rational improvements, settled principals of Truth, integrity & Honour are little attended to. Laudible motives of action & incentives to virtue, give place to the form of the Body, the Grace of motion, and a conscious air of superiority which knows neither the Blush of modesty, or diffidence. A Boarding school miss, that should discover either would be thought quite a novice—

To Lucy Cranch, London, April 26, 1787

*Dr. Henry Moyes, a blind philosopher of natural history from Britain, lectured in Boston in the fall of 1785.   **Milton, *Paradise Lost*, Book IX, line 233.   †Psalms 104:15 and Ecclesiastes 8:1.   ‡Proverbs 31:26. §Proverbs 31:10–11.

Patriotism in the female Sex is the most disinterested of all virtues. Excluded from honours and from offices, we cannot attach ourselves to the State or Government from having held a place of Eminence. Even in the freest countrys our property is subject to the controul and disposal of our partners, to whom the Laws have given a sovereign Authority. Deprived of a voice in Legislation, obliged to submit to those Laws which are imposed upon us, is it not sufficient to make us indifferent to the publick Welfare? Yet all History and every age exhibit Instances of patriotick virtue in the female Sex; which considering our situation equals the most Heroick of yours.

To John Adams, June 17, 1782

Patriotic Women

The most Forlorn and Dismal of all States is that of widowhood, how often does my Heart bleed at thinking how nearly my own Situation is allied to that, nor can I sometimes refrain from wishing that the wisdom of the continent had made choise of some person whose separation from his partner would have been little or no pain, or mortification—many such might have been found I dare say. Heaven can witness for me that I judge not by my own feelings, but from the conduct of too many of my sex.

To Mercy Otis Warren, Braintree, December 10, 1778

Widows

There scarce was ever any such thing under the Sun as an inconsolable widow.

To Elizabeth Shaw, Braintree, February–March 1782

Your Aunt [Elizabeth Shaw] is left as Clergymen's widows usually are in low circumstances.

To John Quincy Adams, Quincy, April 22, 1795

Mrs. C[harles] Adams has been writing in my chamber to Norfolk—from whence she had a Letter yesterday—a correspondence is kept up, but whether more than mere Friendship is meant, or rather whether any connection will ever take place is very uncertain: I wish she was well settled in Life, but without good prospects, she is better as she is.

To Abigail Adams Smith, Quincy, December 28, 1808

It is much to be regretted that those who undertake the settlement of estates are frequently so dilatory in the adjustment of them to the detriment frequently of the widow and the orphan.

To Mrs. Black, Quincy, January 24, 1813

To us, who in the course of nature expect, and hope to join the Spirits of the just; are consolations, which to the bereved Widow; and Children, are more distant and remote; for they may Survive, to feel all the anguish, of a long seperation; and to lament the loss, of a tender, affectionate, attentive, Husband, and doating Father.

To Mercy Otis Warren, Quincy, May 5, 1814

Wives   A wife should never suffer a rival in kindness or attention.

To John Adams, Quincy, October 26, 1799

I have always wished to impress upon the minds of my children that no man ever prospered in the world without the consent and cooperation of his wife. How few of our sons and daughters take this prudent caution into consideration.

To Elizabeth Peabody, Quincy, June 5, 1809

Woman's Man   I always despised the appelation woman's Man. To be a Gallant a man must have a little of the Fop.

To William Smith Shaw, Quincy, February 1, 1799

The American ladies are much admired here [i.e., in London] by the gentlemen, I am told, and in truth I wonder not at it. O, my country, my country! preserve, preserve the little purity and simplicity of manners you yet possess. Believe me, they are jewels of inestimable value; the softness, peculiarly characteristic of our sex, and which is so pleasing to the gentlemen, is wholly laid aside here for the masculine attire and manners of Amazonians.

Women in America

Travel Journal, July 24, 1784

I think our ladies ought to be cautious of foreigners.

To Abigail Adams Smith, Quincy, March 10, 1794

A real well bred French Lady has the most ease in her manners that you can possibly conceive of, it is studied by them as an Art, and they render it Nature.

Women in France

To Mary Cranch, Auteuil, December 9, 1784

The dress of the French ladies is, like their manners, light, airy, and genteel. They are easy in their deportment, eloquent in their speech, their voices soft and musical, and their attitude pleasing. Habituated to frequent the theatre from their earliest age, they become perfect mistresses of the art of insinuation and the powers of persuasion. Intelligence is communicated to every feature of the face, and to every limb of the body; so that it may with truth be said, every man of this nation is an actor, and every woman an actress. . . . The fashionable shape of the ladies here is, to be very small at the bottom of the waist, and very large round the shoulders—a wasp's—pardon me, ladies, that I should make such a comparison, it is only in shape that I mean to resemble you to them. You and I, Madam, must despair of being in the mode.

To Hannah Lincoln Storer, Auteuil, January 20, 1785

Dr. Clark visits us every day; says he cannot feel at home anywhere else; declares he has not seen a handsome woman since he came into the city; that every old woman looks like Mrs. H———, and every young one like ——— like the D———l. They paint here nearly as much

Women in London

as in France, but with more art. The head-dress disfigures them in the eye of an American. I have seen many ladies, but not one elegant one since I came; there is not to me that neatness in their appearance, which you see in our ladies.

Travel Journal, July 24, 1784

As to the ladies of this country, their manners appear to be totally depraved. It is in the middle ranks of society, that virtue and morality are yet to be found. Nothing does more injury to the female character than frequenting public places; and the rage which prevails now for the watering-places, and the increased number of them, are become a national evil, as they promote and encourage dissipation, mix all characters promiscuously, and are the resort of the most unprincipled female characters, who are not ashamed to show their faces wherever men dare to go. Modesty and diffidence are called illbreeding and ignorance of the world; an imprudent stare is substituted in lieu of that modest deportment, and that retiring grace, which awes whilst it enchants.

To Mary Cranch, London, September 15, 1787

Women in the Netherlands

The ladies of this country have finer complexions than the English, and have not spoilt them by cosmeticks. Rouge is confined to the stage here. There is the greatest distinction in point of dress, between the peasantry of the Country and people of distinction, that I have seen in any Country, yet they dress rich and fine in their own way.

To Abigail Adams Smith, Amsterdam, August 23, 1786

Women in Philadelphia

The ladies here are well-educated, well-bred, and well-dressed. There is much more society than in New York, and I am much better pleased and satisfied than I expected to be when I was destined to remove here.

To Elizabeth Shaw, Bush Hill, March 20, 1791

If our State constitution had been equally liberal with that of New Jersey* and admitted the females to a vote, I should certainly have exercised it.

> To Mary Cranch, Philadelphia, November 15, 1797

*Because the New Jersey constitution of 1776 gave the suffrage to "inhabitants," women could vote. Their franchise was revoked in 1844.

Desire and Sorrow were denounced upon our Sex; as a punishment for the transgression of Eve. I have sometimes thought that we are formed to experience more exquisite Sensations than is the Lot of your Sex. More tender and suscetable by Nature of those impressions which create happiness or misiry, we Suffer and enjoy in a higher degree. I never wonderd at the philosopher who thanked the Gods that he was created a Man rather than a Woman.

> To John Adams, April 10, 1782

Pupil of Woolstoncraft* confesses the Truth, and own that when you are sick of the Ambition, the intrigues, the duplicity and the Treachery of the aspiring part of your own sex, it is a comfort and consolation to retire to the simplicity, the Gentleness and tenderness of the Female character. Those qualities, says a candid writer are more beneficial to the human race than the prudence of all its individuals, and when conducted with good sense, approach to perfection.

> To John Adams, Quincy, February 2, 1794

*Mary Wollstonecraft, author of *A Vindication of the Rights of Women* (1792).

Appendix

Chronology

Bibliography

Acknowledgments

Index

Appendix: Alternate Spellings Commonly Used by Abigail Adams

abiss = abyss
addrest = addressed
advise = advice
agast = aghast
agreable = agreeable
allarms = alarms
an other = another
arround = around
asscribe = ascribe
breathren = brethren
buisness = business
buisy = busy
chearfullness = cheerfulness
choise = choice
chuse = choose
colledge = college
compleat = complete
compaired = compared
concequence = consequence
connexion = connection
diety = deity
desert = dessert
dyed = died
feild = field
Fryday = Friday
genious = genius
havock = havoc
heitherto = hitherto
humane = human
immitation = imitation
industery = industry

lawrels = laurels
merrit = merit
misiry = misery
mixt = mixed
of = off
off = of
ospring = offspring
persueing = pursuing
pitty = pity
possesst = possessed
practise = practice
prest = pressed
principal = principle
principle = principal
publick = public
quallifications = qualifications
reflexion = reflection
sallery = salary
scarcly = scarcely
seperation = separation
shoar = shore
softned = softened
spair = spare
speach = speech
spight = spite
staid = stayed
stile = style
strikt = strict
suiside = suicide
supreem = supreme
suscetable = susceptible

sutle = subtle
tallents = talents
through = throw
untill = until
usefull = useful

visitudes = vicissitudes
voilence = violence
waist = waste
wholy = wholly
yealds = yields

— Chronology

1744
November 22   AA born in Weymouth, Mass. (Nov. 11 o.s.)

1759
Spring   AA meets JA

1762
October   Correspondence with JA begins

1764
April–May   JA quarantined while getting inoculated for small-
               pox
October 25   Marriage to JA. Live in Braintree

1765
July 14   Birth of Abigail Adams 2nd (Nabby)

1767
July 11   Birth of John Quincy Adams (JQA)

1768
April   The Adamses move from Braintree to Boston
December 28   Birth of Susanna Adams (dies February 4, 1770)

1770
May 29   Birth of Charles Adams

1771
April   Adamses move back to Braintree

1772

September 15	Birth of Thomas Boylston Adams
November	Adamses return to Boston

1774

June	Adamses return to Braintree
August	JA travels to First Continental Congress in Philadelphia

1775

April 19	Battles of Lexington and Concord
April	JA travels to Second Continental Congress in Philadelphia
Summer–Fall	Outbreak of dysentery, kills AA's mother on October 1
December	JA returns home to serve in Massachusetts Council

1776

January	JA travels to Congress in Philadelphia
March 17	British evacuate Boston
July 2	Congress votes for independence
July	AA and children inoculated for smallpox
October	JA returns from Congress

1777

January	JA travels to Congress in Baltimore (and then Philadelphia)
July 11	Elizabeth Adams is stillborn
November	JA returns from Congress

1778

February 15	JA and JQA sail for France

1779

August	JA and JQA return to Braintree

Aug.–Nov.	JA writes Massachusetts Constitution
November	JA, JQA, and Charles Adams sail to Europe

1782
January	Charles Adams returns home to Braintree

1784
June–July	AA and AA 2nd sail for Europe
August	Adamses settle in Auteuil, France

1785
May	JQA returns to America; JA, AA, and AA 2nd move to London

1786
	Marriage of Abigail Adams 2nd to William Stephens Smith

1787
April 2	William Steuben Smith born, AA's first grandchild

1788
April	JA and AA leave England and return to America in June
November	AA travels to New York for birth of second grandson

1789
April	JA elected Vice President; travels to New York City
June	AA joins JA in Richmond Hill, New York City
Oct.–Dec.	JA returns home during congressional recess, AA stays in New York

1790
November	Adamses move to Philadelphia, the new capital

1792

February 22   Northern precinct of Braintree becomes Quincy

November   JA returns to Philadelphia; AA stays in Quincy

1793

February 13   JA reelected Vice President

March   JA returns to Quincy

November   JA leaves for Philadelphia; AA stays in Quincy

1794

June–November JA in Quincy, then returns to Philadelphia alone

1795

February–June JA in Quincy, then returns to Philadelphia; AA
              travels to New York

July–December JA in Quincy, then returns to Philadelphia alone

1796

May–December JA in Quincy, then returns to Philadelphia alone

1797

February 8   JA elected President

April   JA travels to Philadelphia

May   AA joins JA in Philadelphia

1798

July   JA and AA return to Quincy

November   JA returns to Philadelphia; AA seriously ill, stays in
              Quincy

1799

March–October JA in Quincy

October   AA travels to Philadelphia to join JA

1800

May	AA goes to Quincy
June 2-14	JA visits Washington, D.C., before returning to Quincy
Oct.–Nov.	JA and AA return to Washington and occupy president's house
November 20	Charles Adams dies in New York City

1801

February 11	JA defeated for reelection as U.S. President
February	AA returns to Quincy
March 4	JA leaves Washington for Quincy

1811

October 16	Death of Richard Cranch, AA's brother-in-law
October 17	Death of Mary Cranch, AA's older sister
	AAS has mastectomy

1813

August 14	Death of AAS

1815

April 19	Death of Elizabeth Peabody, AA's younger sister
December 8	Death of Cotton Tufts, AA's uncle

1816

June 10	Death of William Stephens Smith, AA's son-in-law

1818

October 28	Death of AA in Quincy

1826

July 4	Death of JA in Quincy

~ Bibliography

The biographies listed in this bibliography are all excellent. No biography, how-ever, can match the in-depth personal experience of reading the sixty years of letters written by and to Abigail Adams. The modern edition of the *Adams Papers*, started under the editorship of Lyman H. Butterfield and now continued under the direction of C. James Taylor, is a literary and historical masterpiece that grows in significance with each new volume published. The microfilm published fifty years ago broke new ground as does today's Web site for the Adams Papers at the Massachusetts Historical Society. Through these voluminous manuscripts, the lives of Abigail and John Adams are more open to scrutiny than those of any other married couple in American history.

Adams Family Papers: An Electronic Archive. Massachusetts Historical Society. http://www.masshist.org/ff/.

Adams Papers, Massachusetts Historical Society.

Adams, Charles Francis, ed. *Letters of Mrs. Adams, Wife of John Adams.* 2 vols. Boston, 2nd ed., 1840.

Akers, Charles W. *Abigail Adams: A Revolutionary American Woman.* New York, 3rd ed., 2007.

Bobber, Natalie S. *Abigail Adams: Witness to a Revolution.* New York, 1995.

Butterfield, L. H., Marc Friedlander, and Mary-Jo Kline, eds. *The Book of Abigail and John: Selected Letters of the Adams Family, 1762–1784.* Cambridge, Mass., 1975.

Butterfield, L. H., et al., eds. *Adams Family Correspondence.* 9 volumes to date. Cambridge, 1963–.

——. *Papers of John Adams.* 10 vols. to date. Cambridge, 1977–.

Crane, Elaine Forman. "Political Dialogue and the Spring of Abigail's Discontent." *William and Mary Quarterly,* 3rd series, LVI, No. 4 (October 1999), 745–74.

Gelles, Edith B. *Portia: The World of Abigail Adams.* Bloomington, Ind., 1992.

Hogan, Margaret A., and C. James Taylor, eds. *My Dearest Friend: Letters of Abigail and John Adams.* Cambridge, 2007.

Kaminski, John P. *Abigail Adams: An American Heroine.* Madison, Wis., 2007.

Levin, Phyllis Lee. *Abigail Adams: A Biography.* New York, 1987.

Withey, Lynne. *Dearest Friend: A Life of Abigail Adams.* New York, 1981.

— *Acknowledgments*

A tremendous debt of gratitude is owed to the Adams family and the Massachusetts Historical Society for saving and preserving the family's voluminous correspondence and diaries. Starting with Lyman H. Butterfield in the 1950s, and continuing today with C. James Taylor, the staff of the Adams Family Papers have been expertly editing these papers, which have been invaluable to the research community. The National Historical Publications and Records Commission and the National Endowment for the Humanities have provided much of the funding for this magisterial literary and historical accomplishment. The Belknap Press of Harvard University Press has been publishing these magnificent volumes for the last half century. The Massachusetts Historical Society also placed its entire holdings of Adams Family Papers on microfilm in the mid-1950s and has continued in the forefront of technology by placing all of the correspondence between Abigail and John (images and transcriptions) on its Web site, as well as all of the published volumes of the Adams Papers. I have benefited from all of these efforts and from several published volumes containing Abigail's letters. (See the bibliography for these citations.)

I have received unfailing assistance and hospitality from the entire staff of the Adams Family Papers, especially on my two site visits. Jim Taylor and Maggie Hogan regularly gave me their assistance, and Sara B. Sikes was gracious in fulfilling my photocopying requests. I also appreciate the assistance of MHS Librarian Peter Drummey and the reading room staff at the MHS for their help.

I am particularly grateful to Yvonne Greenwood and Jeanne Wray, who each read about sixty letters from Abigail to John from the MHS online correspondence and submitted their compilations to me.

This volume is dedicated to Jan L. Miller and Linda DeLeon and to the staff, consultants, and scholars of the Texas Bar Association's Law

Related Education program. Their dedication, expertise, and camaraderie have produced a superb program of civics education for elementary, middle, and high school teachers. They have made a phenomenal contribution to law-related education in Texas. Anyone who attends these programs as a participant or speaker (as I have been privileged to do on numerous occasions) can readily see the important work being accomplished. Abigail Adams would certainly have been proud of the educational opportunities provided by Jan Miller and her gifted associates.

⁓ Index

abodes, xx, xxii, xxix–xxx, xxxiv, 20, 22, 42, 86, 320. *See also* home

absence, xv, 153–154, 224, 226, 227. *See also* separation

accommodation, 154

accomplishments, 154–155, 325

actions, 154, 221

activity, 155, 267, 330, 344. *See also* motion, graceful

Adams, Abigail (AA): birth, xix; daily routine, xiii, 40, 41; death, xxxvi; educating children, xv; education, xi, xix; illnesses, xix; in London, xxviii; marriage, xx; mercantile activities, xxvii; penmanship shortcomings, xi; religious beliefs, xix–xx; travels to Europe, xxviii; wants her correspondence burned, xi, 38, 40, 147, 191; writing skills, xi

Adams, Abigail L. S. (granddaughter; daughter of CA), 47–48, 104, 298

Adams, Ann Harrod (daughter-in-law; wife of TBA), 51, 167, 307. *See also* Harrod, Ann

Adams, Charles (CA; middle son), xiii, xxii, xxv, xxx, xxxiv, 29, 36, 85, 145, 146, 151, 171, 174, 185–186, 211, 249, 267, 283, 311, 326, 333, 343, 345, 346

Adams, Charles Francis (grandson; son of JQA), xxxv, 215, 225

Adams, Elihu (JA's brother), xxiv

Adams, George Washington (grandson; son of JQA), xxxiv, xxxv, 84, 89, 96, 181, 195, 211, 258–259, 272, 273, 288, 322, 338

Adams, John (JA; husband), passim; advice from, 1; birth of, xx; in Congress, xxiv; described as "an old oak," 133; diplomatic service, xxvi–xxix; elected vice president, 167; health, 77; land holdings, xx–xxi, xxii; as president, xxxi; and presidential election of 1796,

xxxi; and presidential election of 1800, xxxiii–xxxiv, 340; reads AA's mail, 39; as vice president, xxix

Adams, John 2nd (grandson; son of JQA), xxxv, 5, 24, 84, 89, 96, 97, 195, 233, 234, 252, 255, 273, 288, 339

Adams, John Quincy (JQA; eldest son), passim; xiii, xxi–xxii, xxv, xxvi, xxviii–xxix, xxxii; diplomatic service, xxxiv–xxxv; meets mother and sister in London, xxviii

Adams, Louisa Catherine (LCA; daughter-in-law, married to JQA), xiii, xxxiv, 4, 8, 13, 41, 42, 43, 48, 51, 53, 55, 56, 61, 64, 70–71, 73, 78, 85, 88, 90, 93, 106, 125, 138, 140, 159, 161, 164, 167, 174, 177, 181, 184, 199, 204, 219, 230, 232–233, 236, 245, 256, 265, 266, 269, 272, 281, 288, 299, 300, 306, 312–313, 323, 328, 331, 339, 343, 345, 351, 355

Adams, Samuel (Mass. politician), xxii, xxiii, xxvi

Adams, Sarah Smith (daughter-in-law, married to CA), 40, 142, 231, 276, 311, 347, 366

Adams, Susanna (Suky; daughter), xxii

Adams, Susanna (niece, daughter of Elihu Adams), xxiv

Adams, Susanna B. (granddaughter; daughter of CA), xxxiv, 3, 73, 138, 157, 252, 284, 343. *See also* Clark, Susanna B. Adams

Adams, Thomas Boylston (TBA; youngest son), xiii, xxii, xxv, xxxiv, 3, 13, 17, 23, 24, 30, 38, 39, 44, 56, 67, 68, 72, 73, 75, 77, 80, 88, 90, 91, 92, 94, 102, 103, 104, 107, 112, 136, 138, 141, 147, 150, 156, 175, 192, 203, 209, 211, 212, 226, 227, 239, 240, 252, 254, 268, 271, 274, 291, 304, 319, 321, 324, 330, 334, 335, 338, 349, 352

Adams Papers, 147; AA wants her letters burned, xi, 38, 40, 147, 191

Addison, Joseph, 127, 352
address, 155
adjusting to circumstances, 155
adversity, 61, 215, 307, 315. *See also* afflictions; troubles
advice, xxxi, 1–4, 84, 88, 107, 108, 164, 173, 288; from enemies, 4–5; for government officials, 4; to students, 5. *See also* recommendations
Aesop's *Fables*, 219, 220
affability, 343
affection, xv, 160, 242, 360
afflictions, 49, 51, 54, 172, 216, 219, 220, 222, 224, 230, 241, 243, 303, 313. *See also* adversity; troubles
African Americans, 123–124, 280–282, 358; James, 123–124, 280–281; Judah, xxi. *See also* slaves
age, 4, 163, 288, 323
aging, 217
agitation, 217, 348. *See also* anxiety
agriculture, xxi, xxii, 25, 261–262, 275, 286. *See also* farmers
aiming at perfection, 156. *See also* excel
alcohol, 108
alertness, 156
Algerines, 245
Alien and Sedition Laws, xxxii
aliens, 193, 269–270
ambassadorships, 113–114
ambition, 67, 68, 119, 134, 146, 149, 150, 150–152, 174, 180, 214, 293, 296, 323, 333, 345, 369
America, 5–13; compared with Europe, 8; endangered, 8–10; as land of freedom, 136, 353; nature in, 259; and the new Constitution, 7–8
American education, 10
American Revolution, xxii–xxvii, 10–13, 20, 144, 148, 213, 282, 301, 348, 351, 358
America's enemies, 13
anarchy, 68, 121
anger, 322
animosity, 291, 323
anticipation, 156, 220, 321. *See also* expectations
antiquity, references to, 60; Adonis, 16; Æolus, 292; Alexander the Great, 145, 150; Amazons, 359, 367; Mark Anthony, 60, 215; Apollo, xi, 16; Assyria, 145; Athenians, 330; Bellona, 269; Caesar, xxxi, 150; Caesar's wife, 130; Cataline, 60, 215; Cato, 352; Ceres, 80; Cicero, 60, 215; Cupid, 269; Cyrus, 145; Diana, 33; Graces, 201; Greeks, 363; Hamilcar, 22; Hannibal, 22, 158; Hercules, 27, 133; Homer, 92; Horace, 306, 318; Janus, 269, 327; Lethe River, 348; Mars, 269; Millo, 60, 215; Minerva, 16, 352; Morpheus, 359; Muses, xi, 16, 201; Neptune, 319; Parnassus, xi, 16; Penelope, 125; Persia, 145; Plato, 173; Pliny, 162; Plutarch, 104, 130; Polybius, 9, 267; Pomona, 80; Portia, 35, 197, 243, 342; Proteus, 325; Pythagoras, 189; Romans, 146; Seneca, 52; Sisyphus, 334; Sparta, 9, 267; Sylphs, 354; Syrens, 145; Themistocles, 104; Venus, 16, 269; Verres, 60, 215; Virgil, 292; Zeuxis, 228, 229
anxiety, xv, 44, 57, 68, 96, 97, 108, 196, 203, 205, 217, 219, 238, 243, 251, 278, 284, 295, 303, 307, 315, 320, 322, 325, 347. *See also* agitation
apathy, 213, 229, 323
appearances, 59, 71, 113–114, 133, 156, 165, 166, 168–170, 210, 335, 342. *See also* fashion; first impressions
application, 249, 283, 337, 338, 345. *See also* industriousness
appointments to office, 121–122, 323. *See also* officeholders
appreciation, 156. *See also* gratefulness; gratitude; thankfulness
apprehension, 153, 157, 266. *See also* anxiety; fear
appropriateness, 156
ardor, 152, 288, 338
aristocracy, 69, 122. *See also* monarchy; titles
arms, bearing, 156
army, standing, 247. *See also* military; military service; soldiers
Arnold, Benedict (Revolutionary War general and traitor), 341
arrogance, 323
arson, 123
arts, the, 14–18, 29, 319, 342

assassins, xxvi, 100, 270, 274
assiduity, 284
assistants, 270
atheism, 296. *See also* God; religion
Atlantic Ocean, 112, 154
attachment, 280
attention, 5, 284, 335, 338, 343, 366
avarice, 62, 65, 102, 119, 146, 149, 185, 323, 345

Bache, Benjamin Franklin (Philadelphia newspaper printer), 192
bachelors, 103, 104, 270–271
bad company, 3, 271–272
bad news, 33, 44
balanced government, 122
balloons, 17
Baltimore, Md., 29
banishment, 122
banks, 65, 72
Barbary States, 6. *See also* Algerines
beauty, 156, 210, 224, 242, 248, 259, 261, 266, 338
behavior, 177
being a burden, 218. *See also* old age
believing the worst, 290. *See also* pessimism
Belknap, Jeremy (Boston clergyman, historian), 303, 309
Belknap, John (son of Jeremy Belknap), 303–304
benevolence, 22, 51, 63, 90, 170, 173, 176, 185, 190, 202, 253, 267, 294, 295, 297, 318, 323, 342, 346, 355. *See also* charity; kindness
Biblical references, xix, xx; Acts, 300; Aaron's rod, 65; Adam, 150, 359; angels, xv, 47, 48, 146; Augur, 278; Cain, 193; Corinthians, 300, 302, 303, 304; the Devil, 221, 223, 344, 367; Ecclesiastes, xiv, 14, 264, 287, 298; Eden, 158, 261, 294; Eve, 83, 158, 175, 294, 359, 369; Exodus, 65, 299, 300, 317; First Commandment, 36; Genesis, 91, 99, 100, 101, 157, 193, 198, 221, 271, 285; Golgotha, 268; Hebrews, 46, 54, 223; Isaiah, 10, 300; Jacob, 284, 285; James, 296, 308; Jeremiah, 270; Jesus, xiv, xix,

46, 171, 267, 296, 297, 298, 299, 300, 312, 316, 317, 360; Job, 54, 224, 236, 278; John, 198, 317; Jonah, 245; Joseph and his brothers, 221; Judas, 283; Lazarus, xiv, 46, 54, 171; Luke, 33, 91, 298, 354; Martha, 360; Mary Magdalene, 360; Matthew, xiv, 3, 47, 60, 120, 124, 178, 183, 198, 208, 235, 270, 279, 282, 294, 295, 297; Micah, 268; Noah's dove, 51, 57, 99, 100; Paul, 316; Proverbs, xiv, 3, 4, 16, 21, 46, 54, 81, 104, 138, 182, 223, 253, 278, 301, 335–336, 365; Psalms, xiv, 50, 57, 84, 94, 216, 219, 228, 229, 233, 239, 246, 259, 260, 303, 318, 319, 365; Reuben, 284, 285; Romans (book of), 60, 203, 232, 323; Samaritan, 295, 298; Satan, 150; scriptures, 29, 302, 304, 311, 316, 348, 360; Sermon on the Mount, 297; Sodom, 282; Solomon, 3, 61, 130, 264, 287, 335, 336, 364; Ten Commandments, 252, 299, 316; Trinity, 300, 315–316; vestals, 167; widow of Samaria, 360. *See also* God; religion
bigotry, 145, 296, 316, 324
birds, 184, 213, 255–256, 257, 259, 260, 261, 265
bitterness, 236, 291, 324
Black, Esther (Mrs. Moses), 194, 366
Blair, Rev. Dr. Samuel, Jr. (Germantown Presbyterian minister; chaplain of Congress), 10, 300
blame, 162
bleeding, 137–138, 140
blessings, 211, 219, 228, 230, 243, 247, 314, 315, 317, 320
Blount, Edward, 289
bluster, 324
boastful, 286
Bonaparte, Napoleon, 62, 167
Book of Common Prayer, The, 194, 269
books, xxi, 14, 234
Boston, 18, 27
boys, 272–273. *See also* children; grandchildren
Brand-Hollis, Thomas (English political philosopher), 23, 116, 255–256, 318
bravery, 238, 355. *See also* courage
bread, 109
bribery, 324, 341

Brisler, John (Adams's major domo), 280, 281

brothers, 273

Brown, Sarah (Mrs. John; wealthy Providence socialite), 342

Bunker Hill, battle of, xxiv, 11

Burgh, James, 63

Burgoyne, John (British general), 12

Burke, Edmund (British politician), 127, 331

Burr, Aaron (New York lawyer/politician), xxxiii

Burton, Robert, 244

Butler, Samuel, 86

Cabot, George (merchant), 290, 329, 359–360

calmness, 60, 62, 111, 154, 155, 215, 248, 296, 334

calumny, 66, 193, 290

Calvin, John, xix, 274

candlelight, 156

candor, 147, 163, 274, 276, 279, 290, 291, 323, 325, 335, 364. *See also* honesty

capital punishment, 122–123

carriages, 28, 318

cats, 183, 184

cause and effect, 156

caution, xv, 85, 288. *See also* circumspection

cayenne pepper, 171

certainty, 56, 238

chance, 241. *See also* fortune; luck; opportunity

character, 255, 285, 291, 348. *See also* integrity

charity, 250–251, 339. *See also* benevolence; helping hand; kindness

Charlestown, Mass., 282

charm, 335, 342, 358

chastity, 202. *See also* purity

cheating, 324

checks and balances, 135. *See also* balanced government

cheerful demeanor, 236, 337–343

cheerfulness, 313, 317, 335–336. *See also* happiness

childbirth, xxv, 86–88

child rearing, xxii, 88. *See also* parenting

children, 51, 90–93, 196; allowances given to, 93; boys, 272–273; of celebrities, 93, 285; sick, 92, 108

Christianity, 22, 51, 84, 90, 110, 124, 223, 304, 312, 313, 316, 339. *See also* clergy; religion

circumspection, xv, 336–337, 346, 359. *See also* caution

circumstances, 157, 173, 214, 253

cities, 17

civic virtue, 251

civil dissension, 123

civility, 22, 285

civil rights, 123–124

civil war, 9, 137, 351–352, 354

Clark, Dr. John (Unitarian minister), 316, 367

Clark, Susanna B. Adams (granddaughter), 105, 163. *See also* Adams, Susanna B.

clergy, 72, 234, 273–274, 292, 366

climate, 255. *See also* springtime; weather

clods, 274

clothing, 315. *See also* appearances; fashion

Cobbett, William (English newspaper printer), 147

coffee, 171. *See also* tea

college dangers, 84

comfort, 44, 103, 157, 224, 311, 342, 369. *See also* ease

comfort and perplexity, 157

commerce, 65, 80, 110, 112

common sense, 174

communicating pleasure, 33

communications, 33–44

companions, xv, 157, 361

companionship, 157–158

comparativeness, 158

comparisons, 158, 331

competence, 82, 228

complaints, 158–159, 218

composure, 154

condolences, 48–51

confinement, 321

Congress, 6, 110, 124–125

conjugal faith, 202. *See also* marriage

conjugal infidelity, 100, 332

connections, 215

conscience, xx, 251–252, 297, 303, 324, 326, 352. *See also* morality

consistency, 159, 340

consolation, 159, 216, 229, 304, 369

Constitutional Convention (1787), 125–126

contempt, 159–160, 168, 326

contention, 330

contentment, 160, 171, 237, 312, 327, 335, 337, 347. *See also* cheerfulness; happiness

Continental Congress, xxiv

conversation, 33, 34, 176

correspondence, xi–xvi, 33–42, 197, 203, 210, 234, 338, 359

corruption, 18, 31, 78, 324

cosmopolitanism, 318–319

courage, 337, 355. *See also* bravery; intrepidity

cowardice, 244, 324, 326

Cowper, William, 158, 226, 345

Cranch, Elizabeth (niece; daughter of Mary Cranch), 5, 14–15, 17, 22, 37, 86, 87, 94, 146, 165–166, 183–184, 189, 209–210, 214, 256–257, 259, 325

Cranch, John (nephew of Richard Cranch), 26, 131, 353

Cranch, Lucy (niece; daughter of Mary Cranch), 18, 37, 78, 97, 131, 148–149, 153, 165, 176, 202, 211, 216, 302, 364–365

Cranch, Mary (elder sister), xiii, xix, xx, xxi, xxxv, passim

Cranch, Richard (brother-in-law), xix, xx, xxxv, 47, 209–210, 363

Cranch, William (nephew; son of Mary Cranch), 14, 95, 139, 173, 204, 224, 241

Creation, the, 363

credit, 72

creed of life, 252

crimes, 325

criticism, 160

cruelty, 345

curiosity, 152

Cushing, Hannah (friend; widow of William Cushing), 46, 47, 82, 130, 207, 229, 246, 261, 291

Cushing, William (friend; Mass. chief justice; U.S. associate justice), 229, 324

customs, 19, 160–161, 171, 320, 326. *See also* habit

Dalton, Ruth (friend; wife of Mass. senator Tristram Dalton), 240

dance, 19, 155, 167, 298

dangers, 62, 218, 240, 337

Darwin, Erasmus, 258, 259

daughters, 93

daydreaming, 56. *See also* dreams; imagination

death, xiv, xx, xxxv–xxxvi, 44–55, 122, 201, 228, 229, 235, 316; in childbirth, xxv, 88; of a daughter, 51, 216, 306; of friends, xiv, 51–54, 118–119, 161, 228, 229–230, 312; preparation for, 307

debauchery, 60, 145

debt, 72–73, 76

deceitfulness, 244, 340, 344

decency, 202

decision, 277

Declaration of Independence, xxiv, xxv

decorum, 161

defense, 352

deism, xix, 296

deliberate, 296

delicacies, 161

democracy, 126, 252

departures, 161

dependence, 108, 161–162, 227, 310, 359

deportment, 83, 244, 249

depravity, 31

depression, 138–139

descriptions, 162

deserters, 274

desolation, 349

despair, 154, 156, 203, 325, 341

despondency, 139, 221, 223

destiny, 231, 240, 347

deWindt, Caroline (granddaughter; daughter of AAS), 42, 147, 190, 255, 307, 360. *See also* Smith, Caroline

Dickinson, John (Del. and Pa. politician), 11

diets, 109, 286

differing opinions, 162

difficulties in life, 1, 76, 218, 249, 347

diffidence, 1, 61, 107, 152, 346, 364, 368. *See also* humility; modesty
dignity, 293
diligence, 5, 83, 84, 221, 249, 307, 337–338
disappointment, 219–220
discontents, 274
discord, 274, 292
discretion, 44, 67, 81, 86, 90, 179, 285, 338
disease, xxx, 139, 229, 284. *See also* illness
disgrace, 61
disinterestedness, 341, 358
disobedience, 330
disorder, 68
disposition, 266, 338
dissimulation, 66
dissipation, 78, 81, 82, 85, 108, 142, 250, 288, 325–326, 334, 368
distress, 221, 295, 348
diversity, 197. *See also* variety
dogs, 184, 220, 256–257. *See also* cats; pets
doing what is right, 252, 308. *See also* conscience; morality
domination, 126–127, 283, 323, 357. *See also* power
doubt, 266. *See also* uncertainty
dread, 73, 266. *See also* anxiety; fear
dreams, 56, 96, 197. *See also* imagination
duels, 193, 326–327
duplicity, 327, 348, 369
duty, 47–48, 51, 55, 57, 59–60, 63, 65, 69, 71, 75, 76, 100, 105, 157, 170, 173, 202, 214, 232, 243, 251, 252, 253, 296, 299, 301, 307, 308, 309, 312, 320, 340. *See also* public service

ease, 338
easier said than done, 221
East Indies Company, xxiii
economize, 76
economy, 72–82, 86, 103, 114, 126, 166
education, 18, 82–85, 88, 98, 107, 211, 278, 285; female, xix, 83, 211, 361–365. *See also* knowledge
effeminacy, 81
elegance, 338
empires, 127. *See also* monarchy
empty nest, 93
encouragement, 162

end results, 162
endurance, 157, 203, 220, 304, 310. *See also* perseverance
enemies, xxvii, 110, 117, 156, 208, 215, 324, 351, 354. *See also* party spirit; war
English Channel, 23, 27
enmity, 339. *See also* hatred
ennui, 327. *See also* idleness; indolence
enterprise, 152
envy, 66, 67, 73, 115, 133, 150, 180, 253, 276, 293, 327–328, 323, 333, 361. *See also* jealousy
equality of human beings, 115–116
equity, 111
error, 162, 339
esteem, 228, 249, 318
eternity, 220. *See also* hereafter
Europe, 6, 17–18; AA goes to, xiii
European education, 18
European travel, 18
European wars, 110–111
even temper, 338
eventful times, 60
evil, xx, 149, 221
evil into good, 221, 313
evil propensities, 330
exaggeration, 162–163
example, 83, 84, 107, 163, 171, 254, 267, 284, 285, 286, 288, 295, 296, 310, 316
excel, 151, 339. *See also* aiming at perfection
excellence, 252, 331, 339
excuses, 163
execrations, 244
exercise, 139–140, 143
expectations, 56–57, 155, 174, 205, 217, 240, 279, 320. *See also* anticipation
expecting good news, 56
expedience, 154
expenditures, 73
experience, 4, 107, 163–164, 194, 197, 208, 209, 215, 220, 249, 251, 252, 254, 286, 287, 288, 310, 317, 323, 355, 364
extravagance, 73, 80
eyes, 140, 175

factions, 62, 146, 179, 192, 290, 291, 352. *See also* party spirit

faith, 300. *See also* trust in God
faithfulness, 253, 281, 323
Falmouth, Maine, 282
false brethren, 240
false glory, 23
falsehoods, 43, 44, 192, 290, 323, 328–329
false notions, 220
fame, xxxi, 61, 68, 146, 253, 276, 328
family, 94–95, 213
famine, 109
farmers, 74, 265, 275, 283. *See also* agriculture
fashion, 19, 68, 161, 164–167, 169, 171, 254, 255, 367. *See also* appearances; style
fate, 237
fathers, 90, 107
fatigue, 244
faults, 329, 339
favoritism, 329. *See also* preferment
favors, 167
Faxon, Azariah (neighbor), 123
fear, xxiv, 87, 217, 266, 320. *See also* anxiety; dread
fear of death, 44. *See also* death
feelings, 167
felicity, 212, 304
Felt, Abigail Adams Shaw (niece), 271
fickleness, 167
Fielding, Henry, 168, 281
financial embarrassments, 73
financial well-being, 73
firmness, 136, 249, 254, 268, 273, 288, 323. *See also* fortitude; perseverance; steadiness
first impressions, 168, 362. *See also* appearances
First Lady, 127
first principles, 89
fixed habits, 325
flattery, 168
flowers, xxvii, 20, 213, 222, 224, 248, 256–257, 258, 259, 260, 261, 263, 363. *See also* gardens
follies of men, 168–169, 236
folly, 219
food and drink, xxi, 108–110, 286, 315
forbearance, 4, 13
foreign affairs, 110–115, 120
foreign language, 208–209

foresight, 339
forgetfulness, 231
forgiveness, 22, 287, 293, 339
fortitude, 146, 159, 195, 312, 347. *See also* firmness; perseverance; steadiness
fortune, 75, 76, 82, 237–238, 278
Foster, Mrs., 103
France, 25, 101, 112, 113, 165–166; agriculture of, 25; dancing in, 19; and Great Britain, 24–27, 332; opera in, 15–16; press in, 192; undeclared war with U.S., 112, 113; women in, 20, 176, 362–367, 368. *See also* Paris
Franklin, Benjamin, xxvi, xxvii, xxviii, 137, 195, 271
freedom, 115–116. *See also* liberty
French language, 209–210
French Revolution, 21, 62, 127–128, 309–310
frequent elections, 128–129, 134
friendliness, 342
friends, 42, 50, 86, 98, 99, 100, 117–118, 161, 162, 213, 228, 253, 303, 306, 320, 336, 344; advice from, 1, 2; confer with, 3; death of, 51–54, 118–119, 161, 228, 229–230, 312, 318; dependence upon, 117; parents as, 107; servants as, 281
friendship, 98, 103, 118–119, 160, 171, 172, 158, 201, 204, 241, 242; with spouse, 102
frivolity, 325. *See also* laughter
frugality, 5, 6, 73, 73–74, 75, 78, 113, 126, 214, 347. *See also* parsimony
furniture, 95
future, 238–239, 310

gambling, xiv, 329
gardens, 22, 86, 261–262, 356–358. *See also* flowers
Gates, Horatio (friend; army general), 245
genealogy, 147
generosity, 152, 173, 185, 323. *See also* benevolence; charity; helping hand
Genêt, Edmond (ambassador from France), 115, 116
genius, 153, 248, 278, 346. *See also* knowledge
George III, 12

Gerry, Elbridge (merchant; Mass. politician), 128, 162, 327
gifts, 169
Gillion, Alexander (duelist), 326
gloominess, 169–170, 297
glory, 169, 246, 276, 277, 302, 337, 353, 355
God, 4, 44, 46, 47, 100, 126, 211, 214, 221, 231, 238, 239, 247, 249, 262–263, 293, 294, 299, 303, 316, 357; direction of, 69, 301–302; smiles on America, 7, 8; submission to, xiv, 47–48, 159, 170, 219, 247, 297, 304, 310–313, 330; trust in, 194, 315–316; will of, 170, 219, 317–318. *See also* hereafter; religion
Goldsmith, Oliver, 70, 71, 194, 202, 293
good and bad times, 221
good and evil, 228
good appearances, 169. *See also* appearances
good-byes, 42
good company, 157, 275, 334, 376
good deeds, xix, 297, 340
good intentions, 340
goodness, 215, 219, 222, 275, 301, 308, 314, 333, 340
good news, 43, 91; expecting, 56
good people, 275
good sense, 274, 326
goods of fortune, 240
good spirits, 141, 158, 162, 169, 180, 213, 233, 304, 335, 343
good temper, 213
good will, 24, 253, 267, 268, 292, 294, 295, 303
Gordon, William (historian), 146
gossipers, 275. *See also* rumors
government, 119–137; balanced, 122
graces, 200, 340, 341, 364
grammar, 210
grandchildren, 95–96
grandparents, 96–98
gratefulness, 170, 212, 219, 314, 315, 317, 343, 350. *See also* gratitude; thankfulness
gratitude, 65, 174, 212, 304–305, 313, 315. *See also* gratefulness; thankfulness
Gray, William (Mass. lt. governor), 128
Great Britain, xxvii, 6, 21–27, 110, 112, 113, 147, 165, 200, 355; AA wants to visit, 356; compared with France, 24–27, 332; navy of, xii, xxvi, 246
great generation, the, 275–276
great thoughts, 170
Green, Hannah (friend; wife of Boston merchant), 53
Greenleaf, Lucy Cranch (great-niece; granddaughter of Mary Cranch), 236
grief, xiv, 50, 170–171, 311, 326. *See also* joy and grief; mourning
grievances, 223–224
grievous words, 171
grumblers, 276, 319
grumbling, 13
guilt, 244, 352

habit, xxviii, 1, 19, 88, 161, 171–172, 176, 207, 255, 286, 312, 325, 338, 344. *See also* customs
halfway invitations, 172
Hall, Susanna Boylston Adams (JA's mother), xx, xxi, 45, 49, 52, 226, 314
Hamilton, Alexander (N.Y. lawyer, politician), xxxi, xxxiii
Handel, George Frederick (composer), xiv, 15; *Messiah*, 15
happiness, xxvii, 1, 8, 11, 13, 17, 33, 57, 59, 60, 61, 67, 68, 75, 81, 82, 86, 93, 94, 98, 102, 103, 104, 105, 106, 107, 116, 120, 145, 171, 179, 197, 213–214, 219, 223, 227, 235, 241, 243, 248, 250, 254, 267, 268, 271, 273, 278, 287, 293, 294, 296, 304, 305, 312, 313, 314, 316, 317, 322, 328, 329, 330, 333, 334, 345, 349, 363. *See also* cheerfulness; contentment
harmony, 212, 213, 214, 215, 264, 269, 273, 279, 291, 295, 296, 310
Harrod, Ann, 213. *See also* Adams, Ann Harrod
harsh words, 172
hatred, 244, 291, 292. *See also* enmity
haughtiness, 24, 331, 343
health, xiv, xxxi, 94, 109, 140–141, 143, 153, 169, 192, 206, 213, 228, 233, 304, 315; bleeding, 137–138; coughs, 138; depressions, 138–139; disease, 139; eyes, 140, 175, 231, 233, 234

hearing, 231, 232, 233, 234
Heath, Master (teacher), 123
helping hand, 253–254. *See also* benevolence; charity
hereafter, the, xx, 48, 51, 83, 83–84, 146, 175, 201, 212, 227, 229, 235, 252, 293, 294, 296, 297, 299, 302–306, 312, 315–316, 317, 322, 341, 366. *See also* religion
heroes, 276, 362
hindsight, 172
history, 12, 62, 69, 70, 127, 135, 144–147, 215, 249, 253, 322, 365
Holcroft, Thomas, 170
home, 98. *See also* abodes
homesickness, 98–100
honesty, 151, 280, 281, 340–341. *See also* candor; truth
honor, 9, 12, 59, 61, 67, 185, 242, 244, 247, 267, 280, 292, 317, 323, 324, 327, 329, 333, 345, 364. *See also* character; integrity
hope, 174, 196, 203, 217, 240, 244, 320, 341–342
hope and fear, 172, 224, 349
hospitality, 22, 29, 117, 284, 342–343. *See also* benevolence; kindness
House of Representatives, U.S., 129–130
housewives, 100, 101. *See also* wives
Howe, William (British general), 12
Hudibras, 86
Hudson River, 27
humanity, 22, 63, 146, 172, 202, 241, 269, 355
human nature, 145, 147–150, 195, 216, 251, 252, 284, 287, 290, 333, 357
human relations, 153–208
Hume, David, 84
humility, 84, 297, 331, 343–344. *See also* diffidence; modesty
husbands, xxv, 100, 108, 356, 357. *See also* bachelors

idleness, 8, 76, 81, 108, 155, 267, 330, 344. *See also* inactivity; indolence
ill humor, 328, 330. *See also* sour disposition
illness, xiii, xv, xx, xxiv, 92, 142, 158, 175, 213, 226, 230, 244, 315. *See also* disease
imagination, xv, xxvi, 43, 57–58, 86, 167, 196, 206, 219, 234, 259, 344, 352. *See also* daydreaming; dreams
imitative, 286
immortality. *See* hereafter
impossibilities, 172–173
improvement, 173
inactivity, 65, 323. *See also* idleness; indolence
inbred, 153
inclination, 173
inconsistency, 151
indentured servants, 123–124, 280–281
independent character, 67, 71, 75, 76, 77, 78, 136, 237, 254, 268
indifference, 213
indignation, 168, 173
indiscretion, 179, 236
indisposition, 286
indolence, 31, 78, 81, 139, 209, 283, 323. *See also* inactivity; idleness
industriousness, 5, 6, 8, 74, 78, 103, 126, 173, 221, 250, 281, 310, 339, 344–345, 347. *See also* application
infamy, 61, 244
infidelity, 60, 84, 309, 332
inflation, xxv–xxvi, 74
inflexibility, 323, 325
ingratitude, 67, 293, 330
innocence, 335
insolence, 24, 81
integrity, 17, 64, 67, 136, 176, 244, 247, 276, 277, 280, 281, 291, 292, 327, 333, 335, 341, 345, 364. *See also* character; honor
intellect, 153. *See also* genius
intemperance, 330
interest, 150, 173
interest on debt, 74
internal improvements, 72
intimacy, 242
intimidation, 174
intrepidity, 62, 63, 249, 355. *See also* bravery; courage
intrigue, xxxi, 67, 134, 174, 290, 293, 369
investments, 75. *See also* financial embarrassments
ironing, 100
irritability, 89
Izard, Ralph (S.C. friend, planter, diplomat), 198

Jackson, William (duelist), 326
James (indentured servant), 123–124, 269, 280–281
jealousy, 133, 253, 327–328, 330, 361, 362. *See also* envy
Jefferson, Maria (Polly; Jefferson's daughter), 105
Jefferson, Thomas (Va. planter, politician), xxv, xxviii, xxxiii, 20, 23, 25, 27–28, 51, 69, 105, 117, 121, 133, 134, 135, 155, 162, 167, 171, 193, 194, 200, 233, 234, 238, 253, 310, 339, 352–353
Johnson, Abigail L. S. (Abbe; granddaughter, daughter of CA), 88, 104
Johnson, Catherine (friend; mother of Louisa Catherine Adams), 13, 27, 29, 31, 42, 43, 62, 69, 74, 88, 106, 114, 115, 122, 133–134, 141, 150, 156, 162, 174, 190, 204, 222, 223, 226, 235, 237, 241, 257–258, 269–270, 289, 301, 312, 343
Johnson, Dr. Samuel (England), 130
Johnson, Thomas B. (brother-in-law of JQA), 136, 147, 178, 246, 269
joy and grief, 174, 287. *See also* grief
Judah (servant), xxi
judges, removal by address, 130
judgment, 1, 62, 111, 174, 177, 179, 223, 285, 287, 292, 293, 311, 313, 319, 326–327, 345, 350
judiciary, independent, 130
Juno (AA's dog), 256
just, 174, 297, 333
justice, 6, 7, 9, 21, 63, 112, 120, 147, 148, 159, 174, 177, 202, 251, 267, 277, 302, 318, 345, 352
just pursuits, 174
just rewards, 174–175

kindness, 170, 251, 254, 294, 314, 343, 345, 346, 364, 366. *See also* benevolence; charity; helping hand
knowing oneself, 157, 346. *See also* self-analysis
knowledge, xx, 82–85, 214, 247, 283, 284, 288, 302, 306, 310, 331, 364. *See also* education
knowledge of the world, 323

laborers, 20, 72
language, 208–209
large and small issues, 175
late hours, 142
late suppers, 286
laughter, 175. *See also* frivolity
Lavater, Johann Caspar, 168
law and justice, 131
law of nature, 194
laws, 345, 352
lawyers, 277–278
leadership, 60–61
learning by observation, 85
leaving a place, 321
leaving loved ones, 243. *See also* separation
Lee, Arthur (Va. politician), xxvi
legislation, repealing of, 135
lenity, 131
leveling principles, 149
liberality in governing, 131, 291
liberty, 9, 10, 11, 13, 24, 116, 119, 315, 345, 353. *See also* freedom
licentiousness, 101, 331
life's blessings, 211–215
life's difficulties, 215–237
life's journey, 219, 302, 307
life's purpose, 307–308
life's uncertainties, 237–241
Lincoln, Benjamin (friend; Rev. general), 353
Lincoln, Hannah, 81, 106, 156, 173, 219–220. *See also* Storer, Hannah Lincoln
literary figures: Joseph Addison, 127, 352; Aesop, 219, 220; Edward Blount, 289; James Burgh, 63; Edmund Burke, 127, 331; Robert Burton, 244; William Cowper, 158, 226, 395; Erasmus Darwin, 258, 259; John Dickinson, 11; Henry Fielding, 168, 281; Oliver Goldsmith, 70, 71, 194, 202, 293; Thomas Holcroft, 170; David Hume, 84; Dr. Samuel Johnson, 130; Johann Caspar Lavater, 168; Longinus, 14; George Lyttleton, 138; Machiavelli, 61; Bernard Mandeville, 84; John Milton, 103, 104, 150, 151, 261, 262, 311, 364, 365; Molière, 16, 164–165; Michel de Mon-

taigne, 153; Henry Moyes, 364, 365; Ossian, 228, 229; Thomas Otway, 102; Thomas Paine, xiv, 5, 187, 309; Pennsylvania Farmer (John Dickinson), 11; Alexander Pope, xiv, 16, 49, 52, 53, 66, 69, 92, 115, 116, 120, 151, 181, 190, 191, 206, 207, 216, 232, 276, 294, 295, 298, 299, 300, 312, 313, 316, 318, 322, 327, 331, 333, 334, 350, 358, 361; Matthew Prior, 2, 219, 223, 244, 286, 289; Allan Ramsay, 271; Samuel Richardson, xiv, 244; François de la Rochefoucauld, 2, 201; Jean-Jacques Rousseau, 153; Lord Shaftesbury (Antony Ashley Cooper), 279; William Shakespeare, xiv, 14, 31, 46, 52, 71, 79, 128, 178, 187–188, 288, 304, 306; John Shebbeare, 362, 363; Laurence Sterne, 146, 158, 222, 227, 236; Jonathan Swift, 173, 178; James Thomson, 231; Voltaire, 84; Isaac Watts, 81, 89, 195, 311; John Wesley, 259, 260; Mary Wollstonecraft, 369; Edward Young, 9, 49, 55, 132, 229, 272; Johann Georg Zimmerman, 158
literature, 14, 18, 285
living within one's means, 75–78. *See also* independent character
London, 18, 22, 27–28, 31, 143, 332. *See also* Great Britain
loneliness, xxx, 224–225. *See also* separation; solitude
Longinus, 14
long suffering, 13. *See also* forbearance
loquacity, 40, 175, 225
losses, 175
lost opportunities, 175
Louis XIV (France), 121
love, 24, 94, 159, 160, 170, 241–242, 273, 297; expressions of, 242–243; on the rebound, 243
loved ones, 243; reuniting with, 244
Lovell, James (Mass. politician), 12, 35, 57, 156, 182, 191, 197, 200, 204, 207, 270, 333, 341
lovers, 243; reconciling, 243
lover's duty, 243
luck, 154, 173. *See also* chance; fortune; opportunity

lust, 268
luxuries, 8, 17, 20, 78, 81, 82, 145, 225, 326, 343
Lyde, Nathaniel (ship captain), xxviii
Lyttleton, George, 138
Lyttleton, Thomas, 138

Macaulay, Catherine Sawbridge (English historian), 10
Machiavelli, 61
Madison, James (Va. politician), xxxv, 69, 134, 310
maladies, 225
Malcolm, Samuel B. (private secretary to President JA), 133, 174
malevolence, 192, 293, 295–296, 331
maliciousness, 67, 180, 333, 334, 339
Mandeville, Bernard, 84
manly sentiments, 273
manners, 22, 26, 30, 49, 78, 82, 94, 161, 172, 176–177, 249, 285, 318, 319, 320, 332, 338, 342, 367, 368. *See also* politeness
manufactures, 78, 286
marital infidelity, 100, 332
marriage, xix, 4, 100–105, 198, 271; of a daughter, 105; wish, 105, 106. *See also* conjugal faith
Mason, Jonathan, Jr. (JA's law clerk), 152, 325
Massachusetts: constitution (1780), xxvi; clergy in, 273–274; criticized for opposition to War of 1812, 354; as New England's parent, 29
material things, 78
meanness, 21, 177
means and ends, 177
medications and treatments, 142
melancholy, 138, 321
memories, 14, 59, 225, 233, 234; painful, 59
memory, 288
menopause, 225
merchants, xxiii, 74, 275
mercy, 177–178, 219, 223, 297, 305, 309, 311, 313, 314, 339, 345
merit, 178–179, 333; modest, 178, 346
method, 325
middle class, 278. *See also* social classes

military, 31, 244–247. *See also* navy; soldiers
military leadership, 244–245
military service, 64, 68, 156, 245
Miller, Edward, 241
Milton, John, 103, 104, 150, 151, 261, 262, 311, 364, 365
mischievousness, 272, 275
misconstruction, 344
misrepresentation, 179
mobs, xxii, 278
moderation, 84, 179, 347
modesty, 8, 146, 166, 167, 168, 202, 249, 279, 339, 346, 364, 368. *See also* diffidence; humility
Molière, 16, 164–165
monarchy, 6, 110, 131, 347. *See also* empires
monopoly, xxiii, 78, 361
Monroe, James (Va. politician), 60
Montaigne, Michel de, 153
morality, xiv, xx, 18, 73, 89, 90, 94, 221, 247–255, 272, 275, 277, 291, 302, 309, 325, 332, 351, 368. *See also* conscience
Moreau, General Jean Victor Marie (French officer exiled by Napoleon), 113
moroseness, 94
mothers, xxiv, 1, 55, 90, 102, 106, 170, 224, 226, 248; prayer of, 106
mother wit, xvi
motion, graceful, 155, 364
Mount Vernon, 28
mourning, xiv, 54–55, 157, 170, 302, 312. *See also* grief
moving residences, 106
Moyes, Henry (British philosopher), 364, 365
music, 14–16. *See also* opera

national character, 131
national embarrassments, 131
national honor, 268
national respect, 132
natural ease, 323
natural world, 255–266
nature, xxiv, 53, 207, 213, 258–259, 299, 313, 363; in America, 259. *See also* order

navy, 24, 112, 245, 355. *See also* military
near-death experience, 142, 232
neatness, 166
necessity, 225–226, 249, 250, 348
neglect, 179, 217
negotiations, xxvii, xxxv, 110, 132, 350
Netherlands, The, xxvii, 28–29, 144, 319, 368
neutrality, 132
Newburyport, Mass., 245
New England, 2, 29, 30, 283, 292, 314, 316; education, 84; and female education, xix
New Jersey, constitution of, 369
New Orleans, battle of, 147
news, 43, 147
newspapers, xxi, xxxii, 4, 43–44, 276, 292, 330; British, 200
New York City, 29, 245, 269; clergy in, 234, 273–274
next generation, 278–279
"no" (the word), 288
nobility, 26, 279
noble sentiments, 346
noisiness, 160, 179, 303
North and South, 29–30, 290
Norton, Elizabeth Cranch (niece; daughter of Elizabeth Cranch), 87

obedience, 238, 297, 358
obliging, 346
observance, 180
observation, 174, 284
obstacles, 226. *See also* adversity; afflictions; difficulties in life; troubles
obstinacy, 182
occupation, 67, 79, 347
ocean, 258, 259–260, 278, 319, 320, 321, 353
offenses, 180
officeholders, 315. *See also* appointments to office
old age, xxxvi, 45, 47, 53, 102, 117, 118, 183, 205, 225, 226–234, 255, 297, 299, 304, 306–307
old values, 255
openness, 342
opera, xiv, 15–16, 19

opinion, 180
opportunity, 154, 162, 173. *See also* chance; fortune; luck
optimism, 180. *See also* cheerful demeanor; cheerfulness; contentment; happiness
oratory, 277
order, 68, 98, 120, 148, 180–181, 212, 213, 231, 281, 295, 302, 305, 310, 313, 325, 353
orphans, 72, 250, 318, 366
Ossian, 228, 229
Otis, James, Jr. (Mass. politician), xxiii
Otis, Mary Smith Gray (cousin), 50, 175
Otway, Thomas, 102
outsiders' opinions, 181
overcommitments, 181
overpriced goods, 181. *See also* value
overworked, 181

Packard, Ann Quincy (relative through Quincy line), 50, 228, 342
pain, 266–267, 303, 307
Paine, Eunice (friend; sister of Robert Treat Paine), 43
Paine, Thomas (pamphleteer), 5, 187, 309
painful memories, 59
painters (artists), 14, 244, 338
Paradise, Lucy Ludwell (wealthy Va. socialite), 8, 23
parenting, 106–107, 196–197, 287, 288. *See also* child rearing; children
parents, 51, 107–108, 227, 247. *See also* fathers; grandparents; mothers
Paris, xxviii, 18, 19, 20, 25, 28, 165, 332. *See also* France
parsimony, 69, 70, 73, 79, 93. *See also* frugality
partialities, 182, 346
parting, 182. *See also* separation
partisan politics, xiv, xxxi–xxxii, 111
party spirit, 111, 128–129, 290–293
passions, xx, 23, 63, 182–183, 242, 288, 293, 295
past, the, 183. *See also* history
patience, 4, 13, 67, 79, 84, 146, 163, 171, 216, 220, 310, 312, 346–348. *See also* endurance; perseverance; steadiness

patriotism, 31, 62–65, 268, 291, 365
Paxton Case (1761), xxiii
Peabody, Elizabeth (younger sister), 30, 44, 47, 48, 53, 58, 69, 82, 84, 96, 100, 102–103, 108, 121, 122, 141, 156, 164, 175, 179, 188, 199, 222, 224, 229, 230, 231, 235–236, 237–238, 239, 265, 272, 281, 287, 298, 301, 307, 308, 311, 312, 336, 337, 345, 360, 366. *See also* Shaw, Elizabeth
peace, 12, 68, 120, 215, 228, 267–269, 275, 292, 295, 310, 315, 327, 348, 349. *See also* negotiations; treaties; war
peacemakers, 279
peevishness, 182
penmanship, xi, 210–211
Pennsylvania Farmer (John Dickinson), 11
people, will of, 137
perplexities, 234
Perry, Oliver Hazard (naval commander), 246
perseverance, 79, 146, 175, 195, 249, 333, 337, 339, 347. *See also* endurance; patience; steadiness
perspective, 183
pessimism, 154, 183, 290
petition, 120
pets, 183–184. *See also* cats; dogs
Philadelphia, xxxiii, 30–32, 86, 245, 269, 368
physiognomy, 168
Pinckney, Charles Cotesworth (S.C. politician), xxxiii
Pinckney, Thomas (S.C. politician), xxxi
pleasantness, 184, 307, 335
pleasure, 33, 214, 233, 235, 266–269, 288, 314, 334, 336, 340, 341, 345, 348
poetry, xi, 16, 48, 54, 55, 65, 70, 86, 104, 126, 132, 158, 159, 190, 191, 207, 226, 244, 258, 259, 276, 286, 293, 294, 313, 316, 322, 331, 358–359
poets, 244, 338
politeness, 31, 177, 345. *See also* manners
polite society, 184
political attacks, 293. *See also* party spirit
political grudges, 293
political intrigue, 293

politics, 289–293, 309

Pope, Alexander, 16, 49, 52, 53, 66, 69, 92, 115, 116, 120, 151, 181, 190, 191, 206, 207, 216, 232, 276, 289, 294, 295, 298, 299, 300, 312, 313, 316, 318, 322, 327, 331, 333, 334, 350, 358, 361

positiveness, 288

power, 119, 126–127, 145, 148, 185, 214, 268, 319, 358. *See also* domination

practice, versus theory, 218, 235

praise, 162, 168, 185–186

prating, 186

prayer, 308

precepts, 247–248, 267, 284, 288, 295, 296, 317. *See also* principles

precipitate slips, 179

preeminence, 178, 186

preferment, 186. *See also* favoritism

preparedness, 186, 350, 355

presidency, the, 132–134; Adams's compared with Jefferson's, 134; election of 1796, xxxi, 135; election of 1800, xxxiii–xxxiv, 340

press, liberty of, 192, 193

Price, Richard (English clergyman, reformer), 274

pride, 81, 146, 150, 174, 186, 218, 331, 333, 343, 349

Priestly, Joseph, 272, 363

principles, 30, 255, 322, 324, 338; first, 89. *See also* precepts

Prior, Matthew, 2, 219, 223, 244, 286

probity, 8, 12, 106, 255

Proclamation Line (1763), xxiii

procrastination, 331

property, xxv, 11, 13, 20, 24, 324, 353

propriety, 177

prosperity, 80, 214, 216, 220, 285, 307, 310, 313, 315, 328

prostitution, 20, 332

provincialism, 18, 186–187, 320

prudence, 1, 39, 44, 61, 62, 67, 76, 90, 93, 154, 179, 199, 285, 348, 366, 369

public approbation, 71, 187

public confidence, 187

public credit, 187

public happiness, 61

public opinion, 187

public service, 4, 65–71, 77

punctuality, 276, 277, 352

purity, xv, 297, 367. *See also* chastity

Quakers, 31, 308–309

quick changes, 187

Quincy, Anna (English relative through Quincy line), 342

Quincy, Edmund (judge), 282

Quincy, Eliza Susan (relative through Quincy line), 62, 191, 225

quotations, xiv, 187

racial prejudice, 187–188

rain, 262, 263, 264, 275. *See also* weather

Ramsay, Allan, 271

rashness, 85

reading, xxi

reality, 188

reason, 1, 254, 268, 287, 290, 292, 299, 322, 326, 331

reasoning, 188

rebellion, 120, 357. *See also* sedition

recollection, 188

recommendations, 188. *See also* advice

recrimination, 188

rectitude, 91, 191, 251, 253, 325

reflection, 174, 189, 205, 303, 325

rejections, 235

relatives, 86, 108, 303. *See also* children; family; fathers; grandchildren; grandparents; housewives; husbands; mothers; parents; wives

relaxation, 325

religion, 50, 62, 101, 103, 145, 170, 242, 250, 292, 293–317, 333, 351; and the French Revolution, 309–310; and government, 309–310; opposes dueling, 326. *See also* clergy; God

religious liberty, 310

religious toleration, 131

repealing legislation, 135

repentance, 189

repine, 189, 235

repose, 217, 235, 248

reproach, 133, 244

reputation, 72, 255, 345

reserve, 338

resignation, 216, 219, 312, 313
resolution, 189, 254, 329, 330
restless spirits, 275
retaliation, 189, 339
retirement, 75, 77, 215, 235, 249
reuniting with loved ones, 244
revelation, 342
revenge, 146, 291, 292
reverence, 345
revolution, 352
rheumatism, xiii, xxxvi, 142
Rhode Island, 8
Richardson, Samuel, xix, 244
ridicule, 189–190
righteousness, 120, 148, 216, 239, 300, 308, 345, 348
Robbins, Chandler, Jr. (tutor of AA's boys), 320
Rochefoucauld, François de la, 2, 201
Rogers, Abigail Bromfield (London friend), 64
Rousseau, Jean-Jacques, 153, 363
rumors, xxvi, 189. *See also* gossipers
Rush, Benjamin (friend; Philadelphia physician), 109, 128, 206, 290, 329
Rush, Julia (friend; widow of Benjamin Rush), 7, 42, 174, 230, 269, 306
Rush, Richard (diplomat; son of Benjamin Rush), 70, 104, 116, 152
Russia, 256

sacrifice, 69, 71, 196, 243, 253, 275–276
Salic Law, 359, 360
sarcasm, 190
satire, 190–191
satisfaction, 160, 191, 336
Schuykill River, 27
seasickness, 142–143, 321
secrecy, 191
secrets, 191, 338
sectionalism. *See* North and South
sedentariness, 192
sedition, 192–194. *See also* rebellion
self-analysis, 194. *See also* knowing oneself
self-condemnation, 194
self-deception, 194, 346
self-defense, 194

self-denial, 333
self-importance, 195
selfishness, 149, 173, 180, 332
self-love, 61, 195, 346
self-regulation, 195
self-reliance, 195
self-respect, 252
Senate, U.S., 135
sensibility, 195, 213, 224, 251, 292
separation, xiv–xv, xxi, xxiv, xxv, xxix, xxx, xxxv, 42, 43, 63, 67–68, 196–198, 312, 314, 320, 365. *See also* absence; loneliness; solitude
Septennial Act (1716), 129
servants, xiv, xx, xxi, xxxi, 114, 279–281, 283; cooks, 279, 280, 281
Shaftesbury, Lord (Antony Ashley Cooper), 277
Shakespeare, William, 14, 31, 46, 52, 71, 79, 128, 178, 187–188, 288, 304, 306
shame, 244
sharing bad news, 44
Shaw, Elizabeth (younger sister), xiii, xix, xxi, xxxvi, 6, 19, 20, 25–26, 27, 28, 37, 58, 72, 78, 82, 83, 87, 94, 95, 96–97, 99, 105, 108, 122, 131, 132, 143, 146, 155, 163, 164–165, 166, 168, 170, 179, 180–181, 184, 187–188, 195, 202, 212, 221, 222, 225, 228–229, 249, 252, 258, 259, 260, 268, 278, 279, 285, 286, 295–296, 302, 310, 317, 324. *See also* Peabody, Elizabeth
Shaw, William Smith (nephew; son of Elizabeth Shaw), 32, 58, 61, 103, 140, 142, 168, 281, 287, 289, 366
Shays's Rebellion, 7, 57, 352–354
Shebbeare, John, 362, 363
shortcomings, 198
sick children, 92, 108
sickness. *See* disease; illness
Siddons, Sarah (English actress), 187–188
sightseeing, 319. *See also* travel
silence, 67, 110, 125, 135, 175, 199, 212, 279, 304, 311, 330, 336, 337, 338
simplicity, 199, 210, 331, 342, 367, 369
sincerity, 199, 342
single women, 281
slander, 199–200
slave owners, 282

slaves, 280, 282–283
sleep, 200
sleeplessness, 143
sloth, 323. *See also* idleness; indolence
small beginnings, 200
small means, 200
smallpox, xxv
small problems, 200
Smith, Abigail Adams (AAS; daughter),
xiii, xxi, xxv, xxviii, xxix, xxx, xxxv, 21,
24, 27, 28–29, 41, 43, 51, 52, 53, 58, 78,
83, 87, 89, 93, 94, 96, 98, 100, 107–108,
112–113, 117, 120, 133, 136, 143, 149, 150,
152, 160, 164, 172, 176, 177, 180, 191, 194,
198, 202, 205, 206, 207, 212, 214, 219,
229, 235, 237, 239, 241, 252, 254, 255,
261–262, 263, 266, 271, 281, 286, 290–
291, 292, 296, 302, 306, 310, 322, 323, 324,
336, 339, 344, 345, 351, 359, 366, 367, 368
Smith, Caroline (granddaughter; daughter of AAS), 3, 41, 46, 47, 83–84, 97,
109, 118, 147, 163, 168, 181, 184, 189, 195,
200, 203, 205, 212, 216, 229, 231, 246,
256, 265, 267, 283, 287, 297, 305, 308,
312, 315, 317, 318, 330, 331, 335, 343, 344
Smith, Elizabeth Quincy (mother), xix,
xxiv
Smith, Elizabeth Storer (aunt), 18, 22, 79
Smith, Hannah (cousin), 45–46, 215, 267
Smith, Isaac, Jr. (cousin), 12–13, 49, 208,
209, 337, 356
Smith, Isaac, Sr. (uncle), 114, 207, 295
Smith, John Adams (grandson; son of
AAS), 14, 41, 85, 95, 96, 203, 277–278,
288, 345, 346
Smith, Mary Rutledge (S.C. friend), 125–
126, 353–354
Smith, William (brother), xix, 45, 52, 62,
69, 125, 137, 150, 152, 182, 206, 239, 250,
288, 328, 334, 346
Smith, William (father), xix, xx, 45, 302,
310
Smith, William Stephens (son-in-law;
married to AAS), xiii, xxix–xxx, xxxv,
xxxvi, 4, 95, 105, 127, 180, 215, 252, 306,
318, 348
Smith, William Steuben (grandson; son
of AAS), 115

smuggling, xxiii
sober sense, 292
sobriety, 103, 280, 281
sociability, 175, 201–202, 338
social classes, 26, 283. *See also* middle
class
social graces, 30, 200, 340, 341, 364
society, 202, 287, 294, 315
soldiers, 101, 247, 269. *See also* military
solicitude, 68, 315, 318
solitude, 158, 202–203. *See also* loneliness;
separation
sour disposition, 203. *See also* ill humor
Southerners, 283. *See also* North and
South
speculation, 80, 324
spite, 149
sprained ankles, 143
springtime, 260–262
Staël, Germaine de (French writer),
361
Stamp Act (1765), xxiii
standing army, 247. *See also* military; military service; soldiers
steadiness, 93, 111, 203, 249, 268, 296, 333,
345. *See also* firmness; perseverance
Sterne, Laurence, 146, 158, 222, 227, 236
stocks, 80
Stoicism, 49, 203, 213, 270
Storer, Charles (distant relative but close
friend of AA and JA), 6, 19, 43, 99, 101,
110, 114, 163, 183, 225, 247, 268, 270, 279,
284–285, 286
Storer, Hannah Lincoln (Boston friend),
86, 165, 186–187, 221, 270, 273–274, 321,
367. *See also* Lincoln, Hannah
students, 283
studied politeness, 99, 199, 342
style, 203. *See also* fashion
subjugation, 350
submission to the will of God, xiv, 47–
48, 159, 170, 219, 247, 297, 304, 310–313,
329, 330
success, 204
successors, 283
suffering, 204
sufficiency, 204
Sugar Act (1764), xxiii

suicide, 27, 204
Sully, Duc de, 325
sunshine, 40, 43, 256, 262, 263
superiority, 204
superstition, 204
suspicion, 266
Swift, Jonathan, 173, 178
Switzerland, 32
sympathy, 50, 51, 53, 204, 303

talents, 60, 62, 82, 83, 91, 175, 200, 205, 277, 292, 308
taxes, xxiii; on houses, 135
tea, xxiii, 109–110; Boston Tea Party, xxiii; Tea Act (1773), xxiii
teachers, 5, 283, 344
temperance, 159
temptations, 44, 85, 89, 278, 286, 288, 322, 325
tenderness, xv, 146, 205, 213, 242, 243, 360, 369
terrors, 205, 297, 322, 345
thankfulness, 212, 235, 344
thanksgiving, 11, 253, 313–315
Thaxter, John (friend; JA's law student and secretary), 8, 56, 73, 74, 76, 100, 101, 110, 120, 155, 161, 162, 169, 172–173, 174, 183, 197, 199, 201, 207, 210, 242, 243, 270, 293, 326, 329, 337, 349, 358–359, 362
theater, xiv, 16–17, 332, 367
theory vs. practice, xxvii, 218, 235
thinking, 3, 205
Thomas, John (Am. Rev. general), 346
Thomson, James, 119, 231
time, 85, 170, 173, 175, 205–206, 226, 227, 232, 234, 239, 241, 242, 250, 286, 288, 308, 311, 325
timidity, 337. *See also* diffidence; humility; modesty
titles, 17, 26, 178, 213, 249, 279, 331
torpid, 31, 283, 323
traitors, 283
tranquility, 69, 77, 117, 120, 160, 179, 206, 234, 235, 267, 301, 310, 335
transportation, 318–321
travel, 318–321

travel journal, xxviii, 27, 122, 142–143, 178, 207, 242, 320–321, 330, 347, 367–368
treachery, 66, 369
treason, 341
treaties, xxvi, xxvii, xxviii, 6, 112, 246
trees, 54, 258, 260–261, 265
Trinity, 300, 315–316
troubles, xx, 81, 219, 223–224, 228, 235–236, 273, 312, 313, 317. *See also* adversity; afflictions; life's difficulties
Trumbull, John (Conn. painter), 146
Trumbull, William, 189
trust in God, 315–316
truth, 120, 147, 149, 174, 190, 206, 220, 247, 296, 323, 345, 364. *See also* candor; honesty
Tufts, Cotton (uncle and business manager), xiii, xxxvi, 20, 27, 32, 37, 51, 58, 64, 74, 75, 76, 99, 100, 108, 110, 111, 112, 114, 117, 121, 122, 125, 149, 156, 157, 161, 165, 171, 175, 176, 235, 239, 240, 251, 271, 279, 283, 301, 307, 308, 324, 328, 330, 347, 353
Tufts, Lucy Quincy (Cotton Tufts' first wife), 20, 26, 127
Tufts, Susanna Warner (Cotton Tufts' second wife), 55, 311
Tyler, Royall (friend, lawyer; courted Abigail Adams 2nd), 2, 17, 101, 151, 161, 176, 249, 258, 277, 325, 341
tyranny, 278, 349. *See also* domination; power
tyrants, xxv, 135, 216, 356. *See also* husbands

unassuming, 339
uncertainty, 58, 240–241
uncharitableness, 180
unforeseen events, 241
uniformity, 206, 249. *See also* diversity; variety
Union, 6, 8, 30, 105, 112, 136, 218
Unitarianism, xx, 300, 315–316
unreserve, xii, 37
usefulness, 45, 47, 160, 170, 206, 229, 232, 251, 271, 285, 305, 308
uselessness, 155, 271

valiance, 218

valor, 22, 147. *See also* bravery; courage; intrepidity; valiance

value, xi, 68, 100, 146, 169, 206, 318

value judgment, 207

Vanderkemp, François Adriaan (Dutch patriot; exiled to U.S.; agriculturist), 54, 204, 241, 306, 307, 336, 361

vanity, 45, 227, 297, 333, 359

variety, 207, 356. *See also* diversity

veneers in society, 207

venom, 334. *See also* enmity; hatred

Vice President, U.S., 136–137

vices, 23, 78, 88, 219, 284, 288, 322–332

viciousness, 207

vicissitudes of life, 237

Virginia, 32; Act for Religious Freedom, 310

virtue, xx, 5, 6, 8, 64, 89, 90, 91, 103, 106, 149, 151, 154, 173, 195, 214, 216, 225, 244, 247, 249, 250, 277, 293, 296, 302, 306, 322, 326, 332–348, 368

visitors, 256, 284

Voltaire, 84

walking, 143–144. *See also* exercise

war, 23, 110–111, 269, 275, 291, 348–355; civil war, xxxii, 9, 137, 351–352, 354; with France, xxxii–xxxiii; offensive, 351

War of 1812, xxxv, 246, 354

Warren, James (Mass. politician), xxii

Warren, Mercy Otis (friend; playwright and historian), xi, 8, 10, 11, 12, 16, 21, 24, 25, 34, 37, 40, 46, 51, 56, 59, 62–63, 64, 65–66, 68, 71, 78, 84, 91, 97, 98, 99, 109, 112, 117, 118, 131, 132, 136, 141, 144, 147–148, 150–151, 152, 154, 166, 180, 183, 185, 189, 191, 192, 201, 213, 221, 227, 230, 231, 236, 237, 240, 244, 262, 263, 266, 268, 292, 300, 304–305, 318, 326, 332, 340, 342, 344, 345, 348, 351–352, 354–355, 356, 357–358, 365, 366

Warren, Winslow (son of Mercy Otis Warren), 157, 176

Washington, George, xxix, xxx, 28, 50, 67, 77, 92, 133, 283

Washington, Martha, xxx, xxxi, 50, 67, 68, 327–328

Watson, Richard (English clergyman; professor of chemistry), 363

Watts, Isaac, 81, 89, 195, 311

ways and means, 221

wealth, 81–82, 214, 237

weather, 261, 262–266, 321; harsh, xiv; rain, 262, 263, 264, 265, 275; snow, 198, 262, 263, 264, 265, 266; sunshine, 262, 263. *See also* climate; springtime

Welsh, Harriet (friend), 14, 77, 79, 93, 135, 147, 162, 177, 186, 187, 194, 195, 206, 220, 231, 232, 234, 238, 265, 266, 271, 298, 308, 319, 342, 351, 355

Welsh, Thomas (Boston physician), 72, 78, 128, 215, 293, 331, 339

Wesley, John, 259, 260

White House, The, 32, 133

wickedness, 223, 236

widows, 50, 72, 250, 365–366

willingness to fight, 208. *See also* bravery; courage; intrepidity; military; soldiers

Willis, Nathaniel (Boston publisher and newspaper printer), 317

will of God, 170, 219, 317–318, 330

will of the people, 137

wisdom, 5, 6, 7, 8, 22, 61, 163, 164, 174, 194, 208, 215, 289, 318, 364

wishful thinking, 208

wives, xxiv, xxvii, 104, 170, 225, 364, 366. *See also* housewives

Wollstonecraft, Mary, 369

woman's man, 366

women, 115, 152, 166, 179, 210, 247, 281, 285, 329, 332, 335, 356–369, 378; accomplished, 361; in America, 367; decorum toward, 285; education of, xix, 83, 211, 361–365; in France, 20, 176, 362, 367, 368; in London, 143, 357–368; more sensitive than men, xxiv, 363, 369; need to be circumspect, 93, 336, 359; patriotic, 365; in Philadelphia, 368; "Remember the Ladies" letter, xxiv, 356; single, 281; sisters, 282; suffrage for, xxiv, 369. *See also* fashion; grandparents; housewives; mothers; prostitution; wives

worry, 208. *See also* anxiety
writs of assistance, xxiii

Young, Edward, 9, 49, 55, 132, 191, 201,
    229, 272
youth, xiv, 18, 64, 74, 83, 89, 107, 119, 147,
    164, 165, 179, 184, 205, 227, 248, 249,
283, 284–288, 346, 347; education of,
    18, 82, 83, 84. *See also* boys; children;
    grandchildren; parenting

zealots, 145, 288, 316
Zimmerman, Johann Georg, 158